Religion Today
An Integral Approach

Brennan R. Hill, Ph.D.

lec†io

Lectio Publishing, LLC
Cincinnati, OH

www.lectiopublishing.com

Cover design by ActiveCanvas

Edited by Leah Wolf

Most Scripture texts in this work are taken from the *Revised Standard Version* (RSV); others are taken from the Catholic Study Bible, which uses the *New American Bible* (NAB) translation.

Lectio Publishing, LLC
Cincinnati, Ohio 45140
www.lectiopublishing.com

ISBN 978-0-9898397-0-9
Library of Congress Control Number: 2013948169
Printed in the United States of America

DEDICATION

To all my families:
The Hills, Englishes, Martens, Armbrusters and Nickels.

Contents

ACKNOWLEDGEMENTS

Much gratitude to my wife, Marie Hill, Sue Goldberg and Leah Wolf for their help with this book. Thanks also to the librarians at Xavier University and OhioLink for all their assistance.

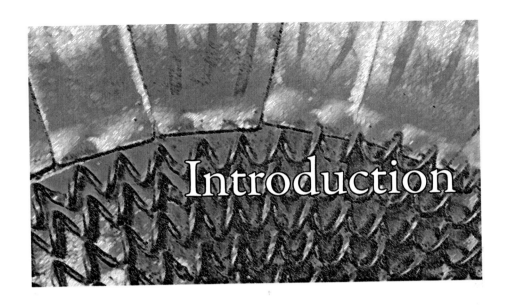

Introduction

"*For we know that our patchwork heritage is a strength, not a weakness. We are a nation of Christians and Muslims, Jews and Hindus—and non-believers... We cannot help but believe that the old hatreds shall someday pass; that the lines of tribes shall soon dissolve; that as the world grows smaller, our common humanity shall reveal itself; and that America must play its role in ushering in a new era of peace.*"
— President Barack Obama, 2nd Inaugural Address, 2013

Religion is one of the most powerful forces in human culture. Distorted religion can stimulate hatred and drag martyrs to the coliseum, burn "heretics" at the stake, light the crosses of the KKK, build concentration camps and steer planes into the World Trade Center. Conversely, healthy religion can unite people with a Higher Power and build magnificent cathedrals, mosques and temples where the devout can gather for fellowship and worship. Healthy religion is inclusive in that it breaks down prejudice and barriers among people. Healthy religion moves one to service of others: the grieving, the poor and the homeless. It moves many people to assist the victims of monster earthquakes and storms and care for disabled children.

Scholars have never been able to discover the historical beginnings of religion. The evidence is lost in the sands of time. In addition, religion defies definition. It is practiced too diversely, is too divided both within each religion and among religions, and has such different cultural histories to ever be limited to one meaning. Religion is an extremely complicated phenomenon and must be described from many vantage points.

In this book, I will in part use the integral method devised by Ken Wilber to examine religion today from different perspectives. I will look at religion from the point of view of history, psychology, anthropology, sociology, science, literature and other disciplines. In four chapters I use Wilber's four-quadrant model and examine religion from the point of view of the "I," the "Thou," the "We," and the "It."

The Origins of Religion

Religion is uniquely human and does not arise from other species, no matter how intelligent or gifted they might be. Religion seems to arise from the unique human capacities to be open to the sacred. They often begin with some type of enlightenment or revelation to some human individual. Religions seem to be derived from the human capacity to question and search for meaning. Religions originate in the human awareness of the dignity of the self and others, out of a love and concern for the Ultimate Other that is the source of everything. They come forth from the human drive to have a meaningful life and to serve others. Religions also have their origins in the human capacity to feel deep emotions, "reasons of the heart," that move us to faith and love. Humans seemed to be uniquely "wired" for religion so that they can experience and warmly relate to an Ultimate. Love and compassion are the centerpieces of most religions. Humans can stand in awe before the mystery of the divine.

Humans are also uniquely social and thus religion has its origins in the need for community. Healthy religion brings people together to celebrate, mourn, ask for forgiveness and give thanksgiving. It offers a sense of belonging.

And finally, religion finds its source in the human drive to act, to transform the self and to serve the needs of others. It provides "ways of life" that as Abraham Lincoln put it, appeal to "the better angels of our nature."

The great originators of religions, the outstanding seers and prophets were human beings like all of us. Their human capacities disposed them to be the receptors of unique revelations that could be shared by other human beings; revelations that in part showed some aspect of limitless divine truth as well as ways to live out these truths in a community.

The Components of Religion

Religions are usually made of a number of components: revelations, founders, sacred texts, beliefs and interpretations, moral codes and rituals. Religions are usually based on unique revelations of divine or ultimate truths that are given to unique human individuals like the Buddha, Jesus or Muhammad, or to unknown seers and prophets. These receivers of revelations share these truths with others and thus become founders of religions.

After these revelations are shared, the truths the founders revealed were usually gathered into sacred text or scriptures after their death. Examples of such texts are the Hebrew Scriptures, the New Testament, the Qur'an or the Vedas. For many followers of religions these are the living Word of God, the laws that shape their lives.

Often out of these sacred revelations, beliefs, doctrines and moral codes are developed and these in turn are interpreted by commentators, thinkers or theologians. These interpretations open the door concerning the meaning of the teachings and mandates of the moral codes. Finally, religions develop their own rituals through which they may revisit their revelations, worship their Higher Powers, and share in the celebration of events past and present.

The "I" as Receptor and Participator of Religion

The first quadrant in Wilber's integral approach to religion is the "I." The ancient Greek adage was "know thyself." The "I" is such a central player in religion because it is the "I" that responds and relates to the Ultimate, accepts and believes the revelation of the religion, lives out the life that is advocated in the revelation and celebrates the rituals of a given religion. A genuine response is given by "the true self," the self created by the divine, the self that is destined for the religion's ultimate goal.

The more one knows about the self, the more one is able to participate in religion genuinely, inclusively and with the love and compassion which most religions advocate.

Today we have many resources to help us understand the stages of development of the "I." Erikson's brilliant work on the stages of human development, Fowler's classic work on the stages of faith development, and Kohlberg's useful insights into the stages of moral development, as well as the more recent studies of "the emerging adult" have important lessons to teach about how and why each of us either relates to or rejects religion. These studies are also valuable in helping us better understand why individuals respond to religion differently as they mature.

Recent studies of gender are also discussed and reveal how women and men relate differently to religion. The irony is not missed that often religions are predominantly led by men and yet often followed more intensely by women.

Finally, studies of "Personality Types" can shed light on why people relate to religion so differently. Understanding the Enneagram can explain how each of the nine personality types relates differently to religion, and insights from the Myers-Briggs Personality Profile can explain how different types respond to religions with their varying beliefs, practices and rituals.

The "Thou" or the "Other" in Religion

The second quadrant deals with the "Thou" or the "Other." Religion is a reaching out of the "true self" for the other, ultimately The Other. Many religions ascribe to some form of the adage of loving others as one loves the self. The more inclusive this notion of other is, the more genuine the religious response.

The United States, as well as many countries in Europe are encountering a growing diversity of peoples in their midst. Americans have long been trying to cope with a "melting pot" of Native Americans, Blacks, and immigrants from Asia and Europe. Now an explosion of Latinos is presenting a challenge to many Americans. Some react quite negatively to all this diversity, still imaging the United States as a "white Christian" country and reacting negatively to the growing diversity. They often ignore their own proximity to an Islamic mosque or a Hindu Temple as well as the large communities of Muslims or Hindus in their midst. The issues surrounding gays, lesbians, the transgendered or bisexual are also challenging to many religious people. An acceptance of homosexuals in the military, Boy Scouts, professional sports, the clergy, as well as approval of homosexual marriages is difficult for many religions to accept.

Religions are struggling with old prejudices and biases. It is becoming clearer that authentic religion needs to be inclusive. This includes seriously routing out prejudice against others for their race, ethnic background, religion, gender, sexual preference or disabilities. One ray of hope here is that many young adults are more open to various lifestyles, cultures and religions. Better integration of the mentally or physically challenged into schools and sports has helped many of the younger generation be more inclusive.

The "We" and Religion

The "We" quadrant focuses on society's creation of culture, politics, globalization and social media and how all these dimensions of human social realities relate to religion. Culture is a broad notion, referring sometimes to family, neighborhood, city, nation or even the world. We derive so much of who we are as a people from all these realities. In the "We" chapter, we discuss the various shifts that have occurred in the culture of the United States, affecting each generation and their relation to religion differently.

Many cultural shifts have affected the religions in the United States and, conversely, religions have themselves played a role in these cultural changes. There are varying views about these interactions. We consider Paul Tillich's approach where culture looks to religion for certain answers, and examine David Tracy's perspective, wherein both culture and religion exchange both questions and answers and deeply affect each other.

The growing secularization of American culture has profoundly affected the separation of religion from life. Secularization has brought some serious opposition to religion and has seriously reduced religious practice in society. So-called "civil religion," whereby a nation attempts to describe itself in religious terms, has also affected religious practice in this country.

In spite of all these difficulties, religion has enjoyed remarkable staying power in the American culture. Those who have predicted its demise have always been far off the mark. Even the unique separation of Church and State in this country, which some have used to attempt to exclude religion, has actually worked in religion's favor. It has forestalled government interference with religion and has given religions the freedom to develop according their own lights. It has also provided strong laws against religious discrimination.

Neither has this separation of Church and the State prevented people of religion from having their say against injustice. Some outstanding examples include Cesar Chavez, who marshaled his Christian beliefs to gain justice for migrant farm workers, and Martin Luther King Jr., whose religious commitment galvanized efforts to gain civil rights for Blacks in the United States. Obviously, religion has also played an important role in the most recent political campaigns.

Globalization, which has been intensified by the international linking of trade and economics, connections through the internet and social media, easy access to travel and other factors have accorded the social "We" a new global consciousness.

This new global awareness has enabled many to become more familiar with religions other than their own and has increased opportunities for interfaith dialogue as well as interfaith service of others. Churches and religions have begun to change their mission from one of conversion to one of service in partnership. Global consciousness has also focused a spotlight on the brutal abuses of the poor, women, children, refugees and the environment throughout the world and has moved religions to take action.

The "It" - The Objective World and Religion

The fourth and the final quadrant refers to the "It," or the objective realities that are studied by scientists, evolutionists and environmentalists. Today the "It" is surrounded by many academic and religious questions.

Science and religion take different paths in their search for truth. Modern science deals with evidence, proof and demonstration and each of the individual sciences has its own methodology. Religion deals with ultimates that are veiled in mystery and therefore is based on faith in revelation, the power of symbols and rituals, and religious experience. Science offers proofs from its experts; religion appeals to the authority of God or a representative. Science is interested in progress and new discoveries while religion is often more interested in preserving and proclaiming.

Obviously, there will always be contentions between such disparate approaches to reality. Modern science and Christianity have clashed over such scientific discoveries as Galileo's proof that the earth was not the center of the universe, as well as Darwin's teaching on evolution. Recent scientific discoveries of contraceptive and reproductive methods have especially been challenging to Catholicism. On the other hand, there have been many contemporary efforts to initiate dialogue between scientists and religious thinkers. Pope John Paul II and the Dalai Lama are two outstanding examples of religious leaders who were open to modern science.

Science has made great strides in studying the universe. These studies have greatly interested many religious thinkers and have moved them to rethink their theories about creation. Modern perspectives on evolution have also intrigued many religious thinkers. The Jesuit Teilhard de Chardin was a pioneer in integrating cosmology and evolution with Christian beliefs. Teilhard's vision still stands as a milestone for those wanting to integrate religion and science. At the same time, many religious fundamentalists still accept the biblical versions of creation and reject modern scientific views on the cosmos and evolution.

Recently, many churches and religions have also turned to scientific findings on ecology. Religions have become duly concerned about issues such as climate change, air and water pollution, waste, endangered species, the destruction of the rainforests. Religions have turned their values and beliefs about action against environmental destruction and have even banded together to resist such devastation.

Spirituality

Spirituality should be at the heart of religion in that it involves the practices and prayers that nourish the life of the spirit and creates openness to the experience of the divine. Unfortunately, spirituality has often become separated from religion, even to the point where many people today claim to be "spiritual but not religious." Many have made that choice because they claim that their religion actually became an obstacle to their spiritual freedom and growth.

Today, there is a great interest in spirituality; in the experience of the divine within; in searching for the "true self"; in various forms of contemplation, yoga, meditation, simple living, and transformation; and in serving others as a means of spiritual transformation.

Many Christians have reclaimed their religion as a spiritual way of life modeled after the gospels. They look to their religious leaders, often with frustration, for modeling and guidance in leading such a life. Some find their own religion lacking in this regard and have integrated teachings from other religions such as Buddhism and Hinduism.

Faith

"Faith" evokes various meanings. It can refer to "the faith" or the contents of a religion's tradition. It can refer to the trust one puts in another person or in one's God or religion. Faith can also be a process of believing that can deepen or be lost. Faith is also relational—a commitment to someone, or to one's God or religious community.

Humans have a unique capacity for faith, in that they can make decisions such as to establish a friendship, join a community or join a movement. Human faith is all about trust in the self and others and the commitment and action that arises from that trust. Faith comes from the mind, the heart, the will. It is distinguished from beliefs, which are more formulations in which one places trust.

Religious faith is unique in that it puts one's trust in a Higher Power, the divine, a God. Christians view religious faith as a gift since it is inconceivable that humans could make such a leap toward Mystery on their own. Biblical faith is often seen as trust in God's revelation, saving power, call toward union, and fidelity to divine law, good living and open-hearted service of others. Many Christian writers over the ages have offered treasured insights into the meaning of faith. Ultimately, Christian faith is trust in Jesus Christ as the "way, the truth and the life." (John 14:6) Other religions have their own perspectives on the nature of faith and these will be explored in this text.

Dealing with Diversity

It becomes more and more difficult today to live in a "religious ghetto" cut off from other religious traditions. Even the most traditional religions such as Orthodox Jews and the Amish Christians are finding it challenging to keep to themselves and not be influenced by the other religions and cultures around them.

Just the normal acts of shopping or going to sports events or school puts one in touch with atheists, agnostics or followers of most of the world religions. We encounter varied beliefs in Gods and Goddesses, different views on the afterlife, and a wide variety of celebrations and rituals.

Since authentic religion is to be inclusive, there exists a new challenge to become informed about other religions, open to their truths, willing to celebrate with their followers, and eager to dialogue with them in a spirit of openness and respect. All religions are being called to break out of their traditional declarations of possessing the exclusive truth and way to salvation. This is not an easy transition to be sure, but one that requires consideration in the interest of world unity and peace.

Religion and Social Issues

Religions often do not have a good track record when it comes to social issues. Religions have often tended to be insular and world denying, identified with "the haves" rather than "the have-nots." Religions have often been patriarchal and discriminatory toward women. Religions too often have supported and even initiated wars. Until recently, religions have not been concerned about social justice, gay rights or protecting the earth and its many species and resources.

All of this is beginning to change. Religions have come to realize the desperation of the poor throughout the world and have begun to take serious steps to assist the poor throughout the world. One only has to watch the CNN Heroes program each year around Thanksgiving to discover heroes from many of the world religions that are dedicated to the poor and social issues.

Women's rights have become paramount in many of the world religions. Male dominance is being challenged as the norm and women's voices are being heard from White feminists, Black Womanists and Latina Mujeristas. Religions are being confronted with gender equality and women's rightful place in religious administration and ministry.

As mentioned earlier, religions have often been instigators of violence, among their own members as well against each other. In present times there is still strong animosity and violence between Sunni and Shia in Islam, between Muslims and Jews in Israel, between Christians and Muslims in Egypt, to name only some of the conflicts. Catholics and Protestants still struggle in Northern Ireland,

Muslim Taliban members kill moderate Muslims in Afghanistan and Muslim Janjaweed slaughter Black Africans in Darfur.

At the same time, hope shines through the work of so many religious peacemakers in modern times: Gandhi, Thomas Merton, Dorothy Day, Dan and Philip Berrigan, Cesar Chavez, Archbishop Romero, Martin Luther King, Jr., Archbishop Tutu, Thich Nhat Hanh, Aung San Suu Kyi, Eboo Patel and the Dalai Lama, to mention only a few.

Peacemakers have risen up in all religions, reminding their members that their traditions call for love and compassion, non-violence and a respect for the sacredness of all life. Religions are coming to realize that they have the numbers, resources and cherished traditions to make a difference in a world plagued with violence.

Religion today seems to be heading into a new era of soul searching. Religions are called to accommodate and serve a rapidly changing world. Religions are challenged to absorb all that has been discovered about the self, the other, the "we" of society and culture and the findings of modern science about the "it." Religions are challenged to reexamine their texts and traditions and discover new ways to strengthen a healthy sense of community, and create deeper faith and a stronger spirituality. They are faced with calling their faithful from passivity to action for justice and peace.

The Origins of Religion

God has no religion.
— Mahatma Gandhi

This is my simple religion. No need for temples. No need for complicated philosophy. Your own mind, your own heart is the temple. Your philosophy is simple kindness.
— Dalai Lama XIV

Religion seems to exist to link humans with ultimacy, whether that ultimacy be called nirvana, the divine, the ultimate mystery or God. This reality is referred to as "ultimate" because it is beyond comparison and outstanding to any other reality. Religions trace their origins to a time when human individuals received some kind of revelation or enlightenment from this ultimate source or Creator. Often, as in the case of the Buddha, Mahavira, Moses, Jesus, Muhammad and Nanak, we know who originally received the revelations. In the case of other religions, such as Hinduism and the indigenous religions of the Americas or Africa, the original founders remain anonymous, but we assume they were ancient sages, gurus or shamans. In this chapter, we will examine the basic human traits that facilitate the reception of such religious revelations, as well as some of the traditions that were received. In the human capacity to receive revelation from the ultimate reality, we find the very origins of religion.

The crux of any study of the origin of religion is whether or not the spiritual, transcendent, or ultimate reality actually exists. Is the holy or sacred real or is it illusionary as Freud proposed, a mere projection as Feuerbach posited, or some kind of narcotic for the masses as the Marxists indicated? "Theology" starts with the approach that the Ultimate does exist and then proceeds to teach and interpret a particular religious tradition where that belief is a given. "Religions studies" takes a more scientific view of religion and whether the approach is psychological, anthropological, biological or neurological, commonly no position is taken as to whether any one religion offers "the one truth."

Here we have chosen a middle way. We will explore religion as a human response to revelation, and rather than take the side of any one religion, we will examine the traditions of established religions objectively. In these religions, the acceptance of the ultimate reality is a given and is deemed acceptable to human needs and aspirations. Each of the world religions grows out of a specific revelation and develops a tradition trusting the truth of that revelation or enlightenment. Communities are formed, beliefs established, sacred texts assembled and rituals are devised. A religion then becomes a dynamic movement attracting numerous followers.

A Brief History of the Search for Religion's Origin

The search for the origins of religion began in earnest in the 19th century and was stimulated by the discovery of evolution. In the following section, there is an overview of some of the main scholars who contributed to this search.

Charles Darwin (1809-82) shook up Western religious thinkers in the 19th century. First of all, his theory of evolution through natural selection and species adaptation, as presented in *On the Origin of Species* (1859), seemed to eliminate any need for a Creator. Then, in his book *The Descent of Man* (1871), Darwin dropped another bombshell when he proposed that humans descended from ape-like pre-human figures. Darwin's positions, as well as the 19th century's new emphasis on the widespread application of the scientific approach, shook the very foundations of religion and prompted many attempts to discover the origins of religion and many challenges to the authenticity of religion itself. Let's take a look at a sampling of these theories.

Herbert Spencer (1820-1903) accepted the theory that the human species evolved to the point where it could not only dream but could reflect on dreams and be affected by them. He proposed that religion arose from the human ability to leave the body in dreams. He thought that this awareness led to the belief that ancestors could be experienced in dreams and worshipped alongside other prominent figures who were viewed as gods. Edward Tylor (1832-1917) accepted Spencer's view, then focused on a belief in the continued existence of "souls" and proposed that religion began with "animism:" the primitive assignment of souls both to animate and inanimate objects. James Frazer (1854-1941) offered the view that religion began with magic, and when magic failed, primitive humans turned to a belief in spirits as a basis for religion. He maintained that in the modern era, science now replaces magic and religion as a means of understanding reality.

Bronislaw Malinowski (1884-1942) theorized that religion began as a function of human survival and served the purpose of calming anxieties in the face of life's uncertainties and dangers. Emile Durkheim (1858-1917), one of the most influential scholars of religion, emphasized the social function of religion. Durkheim focused on religious symbols and how they reflect the social values of society. And finally, Claude Levi-Strauss (1908-2009) was a student of the design of the mind and was interested in how the human mind builds social structures. He studied religion as a cultural construct arising out of human biology.

Each of these theories deeply affected how people viewed religion in the past and indeed, still affect the way many view religion today. At the same time, many contemporary scholars agree that most of these theories about the origins of religions are mere theories, with insufficient evidence to render them conclusive. We now must admit that we know little about human origins and even less about the historical origins of religion. As Robert Bellah, one of the most significant contemporary scholars on religion, points out: "Early history [of religion] is almost as obscure as the history of our earlier lineages, with only a glance over the shoulder, so to speak, at earlier members of our genus."[1]

More recent studies of religion have moved away from a concern over historical origins and have begun to examine religion as a phenomenon with specific characteristics, elements or functions. **Gerardus van der Leeuw** (1890-1950) sought to describe the essence of religion and studied religion as it was experienced and understood in various cultures. In his classic book, *The Idea of the Holy* (1917), **Rudolf Otto** (1869-1937) maintained that religion was an encounter with the "wholly other," the "holy." Mircea Eliade (1907-1986), a major contributor to the study of the origins of religion, took the position that religion is best understood in terms of how people of the past related to the universe as "sacred" and stood in awe and wonder before it. He wrote extensively on how religious people express their sacred history and interaction with gods in myths.[2] Ninian Smart (1927-2001), a leading contemporary commentator on religion, highlighted the functionality of the phenomenon of religion and proposed that religion has many dimensions: ritual, doctrinal, mythic, experiential, ethical, social, artistic, and political.[3]

Many contemporary studies of religion examine the human person, and look at evolution, human biology, neurology, genetics, gender, and personality development. From this point of view, religion emerges out of human capabilities and needs for understanding the ultimate source and goal of all things. Following this approach, let's examine the human species and its unique capacity for receiving religious revelation and organizing religions, and discuss the traits that facilitate the reception of these revelations.

The Unique Capacities of Human Nature

Human nature has evolved to the point where it has gone far beyond animal capacities in the areas of: **1. Cognition, 2. Emotion, 3. Socialization** and **4. Conscious Action.** The human person has an extraordinary capacity for cognition, which includes imagination and intuition. In addition to that, humans experience a wide array of emotion and can both reflect and move on their emotions in ways beyond the instinctual drives of animals. Humans are also social beings and can make commitments that allow them to form intimate relationships, social groups, and complex cultures. Finally, humans can act based on a guiding conscience judgment of what is right and wrong. These four unique traits allowed humans to receive the revelations that sparked religion. It is these same capacities that continue to allow religions to be received today.

1. Cognition — *Religion tries to explain life issues*

The human species is distinctive for its powers of cognition. Many other species go far beyond humans in strength, endurance, sense of smell, vision and hearing, even in bonding, but the cognitive brain gives humans a decided edge over all other species.[4] Human brains have developed to the point where we not only can know as other animals can, but we "know that we know." Humans have a deep consciousness and access to an influential subconscious. The human species can reflect, deeply understand and intentionally love.

The development of cognitive powers within the human species is astounding. There is no other creature in the universe (that we know of) with such powers to analyze, synthesize, develop a worldview, learn languages, problem solve, invent new things, design, and create. Humans are great "figurers." The early hunters and gathers had to figure out many things, such as how to start fires, make tools, hunt dangerous animals, make clothes and build shelter.

In the last few centuries, breathtaking advances have been made in science, medicine, transportation, technology and space travel. Astronomers are attempting to observe what seem to be the infinities of the universe with new and powerful telescopes. Scientists have unlocked the mysteries of the atom and the genome. They have made astonishing advances in the medical field. There is no end to such discovery, for humans are constantly driven to further understand, question, and push back the curtains of the unknown.

Humans as Questioners and Searchers

Karl Rahner, the renowned Catholic theologian, states that the humans are questioners and that as human "beings," we want to know all about the reality that surrounds us. From the time we are small children, we are curious about what things are and why things happen. That searching and questioning continues throughout life, and the mature person is ever open to new perspectives and understandings. Human questioning usually includes ultimate queries like "where does all this come from?" and "who am I?" Rahner points out that questions like these can link us with the "truth of being" and help us understand everything that surrounds us. He maintains that each human person is a "spirit in the world" with a foot in both spiritual and material reality. Our "worldly existence" can indeed mediate an understanding of spiritual things.[5] Rahner describes the human person as "an openness to being," an openness to all truth, and ultimately an openness to Truth itself: God.

The human person is by nature a searcher for meaning, indeed a maker of meaning. There is a story of three men carrying stones to build a cathedral. The first man is a slave and to him, carrying the stone means drudgery and pain. The second man is a stonemason and in carrying the stone takes pride in his work and in making a living for his family. The third man is a pilgrim and carrying the stone means contributing to the building of a great house of God. For all three workers, carrying the stone has meaning, but only two of them find the kind of meaning that brings satisfaction and happiness.[6]

Meaning can be defined in terms of a number of areas: a. **personal meaning and human dignity** b. **meaning of "the other"** and c. **the meaning of life.** In the following section, we discuss each of these domains and how religion relates to them.

Personal Meaning and Human Dignity

Human beings need to have personal meaning because without it, we can be subject to depression, psychosis and even suicidal desires. We need to maintain a certain personal dignity, a sense of being worthwhile, in order to be happy and secure.

When people are stripped of human dignity, they become de-humanized. The organizers of the Nazi concentration camps understood this well. They pulled prisoners from their homes, families, professions, jobs and possessions - all the things that gave their lives meaning.

In his classic book, *Man's Search for Meaning*, Viktor Frankl writes of his experience as a prisoner at the infamous Nazi camp, Auschwitz. He explains that even in such horrendous circumstances, some people were able to hold on to their dignity and sustain meaning in their lives. For Frankl, the secret to maintaining human dignity was the ability to freely choose how one dealt with the circumstances, face the present as a test of inner strength, and set future goals in which to hope. One of Frankl's key insights is that "it did not really matter what we expected from life, but what life expected from us."[7] It was his conviction that humans must shape their own fate, no matter what the circumstances. He quotes the classic statement by Nietzsche: "He who has a why to live for can bear with almost any how."[8]

Religion and Personal Meaning

Frankl points out that religion was often a factor in maintaining human dignity in Auschwitz. He wrote: "The religious interest of the prisoners... was the most sincere imaginable. The depth and vigor of religious belief often surprised and moved a new arrival. Most impressive in this connection were improvised prayers and services in the corner of the hut, or in the darkness of the locked cattle truck, in which we were brought back from a distant work site, tired, hungry and frozen in our ragged clothing."[9]

Elie Wiesel, who lost most of his family in the same concentration camp, pointed out that some Jewish prisoners lost faith in God for not keeping his covenant to protect them. The Jewish beliefs that had given purpose and meaning to their lives often collapsed and left many in a quandary of doubt and darkness. Other prisoners "put God on trial" all through the night, arguing for God's innocence or guilt in this horror. In the end, God was pronounced "guilty." But then, with typical Jewish faith, all recited the morning prayer.[10]

Additionally, religious traditions have a great deal to contribute to personal meaning. Many of the religious texts and major religious figures tell believers what they should strive for and what they should value in their lives.

Judaism

The Hebrew Scriptures depict humans as being made in the divine image: "Let us make humankind in our own image. So God created humankind in his own image." (Gen. 1:26-27) (There is a similar teaching in the Winnebago Indian religion, where it says that "Earthmaker" "took a piece of earth and made it like himself.")[11] Strikingly, the Hebrew texts also depict God in feminine images, as nursing and carrying her children "as a mother comforts her child..." (Is. 66:12-13)

Hinduism

In the Hindu tradition, God is "present within every living being."[12] This presence, which serves to make our existence more dignified, is called "the soul" and it is "through finding the soul that we become immortal."[13] Coming to knowledge of the soul "is to dwell in perfect light" because "the soul is God."[14] The Hindus scriptures also speak of the love that God has for all human beings, which gives dignity to each one of them: "I look upon all living things equally; I do not love one being more and another being less. But those who love me live in me, and I come to life in them."[15]

Gandhi is perhaps the best-known Hindu of the modern era. He was a saintly man who worked diligently for the freedom of his Indian people from British domination. When he served them in South Africa and India, Gandhi constantly reminded his people of his belief that each person is a child of God so he could give them back the dignity that societal oppression tried to take away. Gandhi was a strong believer in human equality and dignity. He dressed like the poorest of the poor, lived simply, and took the cheapest seats on the train. Everywhere he went, Gandhi reminded people, including the rich and famous, of their human dignity and rights. In this way, he won over both the oppressors and the oppressed.

Buddhism

The Buddha offered a unique perspective on human dignity. Where traditional religions often base human dignity on the belief that God created humanity and sustains them with divine power, the Buddha held that human dignity was based on independence and self-sufficiency. According to the Buddha, humans have within themselves all the resources they need to attain ultimate happiness. He taught that "You are a light for yourselves. You are to be a refuge for yourselves. Do not seek any external refuge. Hold firmly to the Way as your lamp. Hold firmly to the Way as your refuge. Do not look to anyone besides yourselves as a refuge."[16] For the Buddha, all people have the power to be the architects of their own consciousness. "By ourselves is evil done. By ourselves we pain endure. By ourselves we cease from wrong. By ourselves become we pure. No one saves us but ourselves, no one can and no one may. We ourselves must tread the Path; Buddhas only show the way."[17]

Buddha resisted the Indian caste system and insisted that people were equal and that all living things were precious. "Do no harm!" was Buddha's commandment and was the basis for his strong commitment to non-violence (*ahimsa*). Loving kindness and compassion were the virtues he most wanted his disciple to acquire.

Islam

Islam is similar to Judaism and Christianity in the belief that human dignity is partly based on the fact that humans have been created by God. The Qur'an offers a unique account of this: "We created them from an extract of clay; then we placed him as a drop of semen in a secure resting-place. Then we turned the semen into a clot; next we turned the clot into tissue; and then we turned the tissue into bones and clothed the bones with flesh. Then we reproduced him as a fresh creation."

Another strong affirmation of human dignity (*karamah*) is found in the Qur'an, "We have bestowed dignity on the children of Adam...and conferred upon them special favors above the greater part of our creation."[18] Given this

God-given human dignity, Islam takes a strong stand against discrimination for reason of race or religion. Islam also opposes oppression and injustice.

The Meaning of the Other

Religions can provide not only insights into the meaning and dignity of the self, but also perspectives on the profound meaning of others. **Martin Buber** (1878-1965), in his classic book I and Thou, pointed out that people often reduce others to "It" rather than rightly seeing them as "Thou" (another fully formed human), and in so doing the human dignity and the meaning of the other are discounted. Once the lives of others are deprived of meaning, those others can be avoided, driven from their homelands or even killed without remorse. Once people become de-personalized, reduced to inferiority or the perception of being sub-human, they are deemed to be disposable. Human history is filled with examples of such de-personalizing. Once individuals are declared to be "enemies" or "inferior" or even "vermin," they can be killed summarily.

In World War II, over 40 million people, including many women and children, were annihilated for no other reason that they were Jews, Slavs, Germans, Russians or Japanese. Since the end of this war there have been many more genocides in Cambodia, Iraq, Bosnia, and Africa.

Religion and Assisting the Other

The so-called Golden Rule in the Christian gospels — "Whatever you want people to do to you, do also to them" (Mt 7: 12) is taught in similar words in the sacred texts of at least eight other religions, going as far back as Confucianism. In ancient Chinese Taoism, the Tao, or the eternal energy in the world, the very offspring of heaven, is to be emulated for the way in which it benefits everyone by sharing with others. "The sage does not accumulate; the more he does for people the more he saves, the more he gives to people the more he has. The Tao of heaven benefits and does not harm."

The Hindu religion has a strong tradition to "do no harm to others." In the Bhagavad Gita, a key Hindu scripture, we read: "I shall describe the people whom I love. They have good will toward all living beings and are incapable of ill will. They are friendly and compassionate. They love friends and enemies equally."[19]

Both the Jains and Buddhists follow "ahimsa," which forbids doing violence to any living beings. The Buddha teaches: "I wish to remove the

suffering of every living being, enabling all to move towards enlightenment...
my concern for the welfare of others gains me greater merit than any act of
worship."[20] The Buddhist mission is encapsulated in the following teaching:
"Through my love and compassion, may all those who are currently suffering
in body and mind, plunge into an ocean of happiness and joy."[21]

A Meaningful Life

While humans perennially search for meaning in their lives, there are
different periods of history when this search became more intense, even
frantic. An example of this is the calamitous period of the Black Death, where
possibly 40% of the population of Europe was wiped out by disease. This was
a period of anguish and questioning. Why all this suffering and death? Is this
the end of the world? Can there be any purpose to life other than to die and
be hauled off in a cart with other corpses? Where is God in all this?

The horror of the Black Death shook the Catholic Church to its
foundations, challenged the faith of the masses, and moved many to such
an obsessive fear of death and the punishments of hell that these fears still
exist in some Catholics today.[22] These fears drew many toward superstitions
and turned followers to the practice of buying indulgences that promised to
lessen the punishment for sin after death, (a practice later opposed by Martin
Luther, who ignited the Protestant Reformation).

In the aftermath of World War II, where more than 40 million people
were killed including 12 million of whom were murdered in concentration
camps, the faith of many was shaken. Great cities were leveled, Germany
was bombed into oblivion, and atomic bombs devastated two Japanese cities
along with their civilian populations.

Thinkers like Jean Paul Sartre, in works like *Nausea* and *No Exit*, declared
that we must face the fact that life is without meaning (absurd) and that
all worldviews, including religion, had failed to explain the meaning of life.
During the same period, Albert Camus in his novels, *The Stranger* and *The
Plague*, also explored the absurdity of life, but Camus urged people to rebel
against life's absurdity with courage and persistence.

In our time, some post-modern thinkers maintain that there are no
absolutes in life. They take a new contemporary look at language and culture
and conclude that most of the classifications and "facts" that have been
assumed to be true are no longer so. Post-modernists often challenge the
traditional narratives about religion, history and even science, and subject
these narratives to vigorous "de-construction." Many post-modern thinkers

focus on the role of language and culture and conclude that much of what we think of reality is socially conditioned, relative and subjective. Concepts like unity, identity, factuality and tradition tend to be replaced by diversity, plurality, doubt and challenge.

On a practical level, this trend toward relativity might contribute to the present wide spectrum of views on morality. Absolutes have commonly been relativized in most moral areas including sexuality, war and the practice of prolonging life.

Religion and the Meaningful Life

Many religions set out through their beliefs systems and theological reflection to help people find what every human being wants in life — happiness. Happiness is interpreted differently among the religions.

For the Buddhist, happiness is freedom from suffering and from attachments to things that cause suffering. Happiness is freedom from the toxic desires and thoughts that poison one's life. Happiness is living life the right way through good thoughts, words and actions, and in death being free from endless rebirths.

In Christianity, happiness is the blessedness that comes from exchanging love with God and serving others. The hope is that this happiness will continue through eternal life after death.

For the Muslim, happiness comes from being subject to Allah and faithful to the teachings that came through his prophet, Muhammad. The Muslim finds happiness and fulfillment in worship of Allah, prayer, and in the struggle (jihad) for justice. The hope is to be rewarded with everlasting happiness after death.

So far, we have explored the cognitive capacities of human beings and examined how religion attempts to provide answers to ultimate questions as a well meaning to personal, social and life issues. Now we turn our attention to a second human capacity, emotion, to see how religion is linked to this trait.

2. Emotion

Emotions are a powerful driving force in human life. Emerging in the pre-human period, and still in some manner present in other mammals, emotions are key factors in human decision-making. Love can move us to commit to another person for life, or drive us to sacrifice our life for another. Fear can warn us of danger and save our life. Anger can move us to harm another or even take another's life. Grief from the loss of a loved one can lay hold of us and paralyze us. Separated from cognition, emotions can move individuals to horrendous actions. As we shall see, emotions also play an important role in religion by moving devotees to worship, forge deep bonds in community and serve others.

Approaches to Emotion

Emotions have been examined since the time of the ancient Greek philosophers. **Socrates** (469-399 BCE) linked emotions with the heart, blood and brain and emphasized their connection with morality. **Plato** (429-347 BCE) associated emotions with the immortal soul, which in turn affected the body. **Aristotle** (384-322 BCE) classified the emotions and linked them with both the body and cognition. **Augustine** (354-430 CE) linked emotions with the will and was wary of their guidance, since they can lead to good or evil.[23] In the 19th century, many psychologists starting with Freud, confined their attention to the negative emotions of fear, anger, guilt, lust and anxiety. Charles Darwin stimulated much study of the emotions from the perspective of evolution. He focused on basic emotions such as fear, anger and rage from the point of view of survival and adaptation, and accented the physical and facial reactions of emotions.

In the 20th century, emotions have been widely studied by academics who often look at emotion from the point of view of animal behavior and cultural movements, as well as from the perspective of various disciplines like psychology or sociology. More recently, neuroscience has done extensive examination of emotions and been able to demonstrate that emotions arise in the limbic area of the brain. Science has also discovered the path of emotions, beginning with the senses giving signals through the spinal cord, then the response of emotions in the limbic system, and then (hopefully) proceeding to the frontal lobe to be considered by cognition.[24]

Contemporary scholars have moved away from the Freudian view that emotions are infantile parts of the "id" as well as from the emphasis on negative emotions like anger, fear and hatred. Recently, much more attention has been given to positive emotions such as joy, faith, love, compassion, hope and forgiveness. Neurology especially has made major contributions with regard to the study of positive emotions. Studies have revealed that the human brain has not necessarily been constructed for heartless progress "red in tooth and claw," as Darwin would have it. This shift has provided religion with an approach to emotion that seems much more positive and healthy.[25] These studies also have contributed to the possibility of a new kind of religious leadership – one that leads by inspiration rather than by fear.

The Study of Religion and Emotions

Blaise Pascal (1623-62), an important 17th century contributor to both the areas of science and religion, made this classic statement about feelings: "The heart has reasons, reason knows not of."[26] By this, he seems to have meant that while reason can tell us a great deal about the world, it is the heart (a common metaphor for the seat of feelings) that is the source of faith and love, which are the emotions that can lead us to the presence of God.[27] **Jean Vanier** (1928-), who has provided homes that care for many mentally challenged people throughout the world, opens real discussions with "What is in your heart?" He has learned that the people he serves are much more in touch with their feelings than they are with their thoughts.

The scientific study of the relationship between religion and emotion accelerated in the 20th century. Many previous studies looked at localized religious practices in very specific cultural areas and cannot often be applied to the role of emotion in the world religions. Today, there are many valuable studies of religion and emotion, but they tend to focus on morality, cognition and language. We are only beginning to uncover the integral and vital role emotion can play in religious practice.[28] Some scientists have brought questions about religion and emotion to the laboratory, such as with tests that have shown how areas of the brain are altered by the emotions generated during meditation.

Scholars of religion and emotion vary in their views about the existence of the Ultimate Reality. Some scientists conclude that humans are wired to gain some advantage from religion, but maintain that this fact neither proves nor disproves the existence of an Ultimate Reality.[29] Others view the relationship of religion and emotion as a "closed circuit" that excludes any belief in a transcendent reality. And, of course, there are still many who follow the lead of Freud and maintain that religion is an illusion, aimed at satisfying the childish emotions of helplessness and vulnerability. Finally, there are some scholars who maintain that the human emotional structures support the authenticity of religion.[30] There are also those who are unimpressed with scientists meddling with the mysteries of life at all. As e. e. cummings put it:

> *"while you and i have lips and voices*
> *which are for kissing and to sing with,*
> *who cares if some one eyed son of a bitch*
> *invents an instrument to measure Spring with?*[31]

Emotions in World Religions

Religion has always had some connection with the emotions that has sometimes benefitted devotees, sometimes not. At times, emotions get separated from cognition and the result is religious frenzy or even self-destruction. Those who followed the infamous Jim Jones were controlled by fear of persecution from the outside world and were persuaded by the twisted Jones to drink poison cool aid to save themselves.

Historically, religions based on fear and domination tend to disappear.[32] The religions that used such emotions have had to reform themselves in order be sustained. The prophets of Judaism often warned their people that unjust domination and fear-mongering would bring destruction to Israel.

Judaism

Recently, Jewish scholars have turned their attention to the role that positive emotions play in Judaism. It now seems clear that Judaism has always valued happiness, but not as a subjective feeling that lasts a short time. The happiness treasured by Judaism is the happiness of flourishing, thriving and experiencing well-being as a human person. It is a happiness that links virtue to living.[33] The love and joy experienced in Judaism is more a satisfaction of being in covenant with God and in being faithful to Torah. Here, emotions are linked to the virtues needed to be faithful to the covenant: fidelity, patience and courage.[34]

Buddhism

Dealing with emotions is a crucial part of the Buddhist tradition. Buddhism rejects the negative emotions of anger and hatred as toxic. Such emotions can lead to doing harm to others, which is inimical to the Buddhist commandment "to do no harm." Buddhist meditation aims to eliminate these emotions from the consciousness. In addition, any other emotions that cause suffering, such as fear, anxiety, greed or other selfish desires are seen to be obstacles to happiness and are to be "let go" from the consciousness.

The emotions most valued among Buddhists are love and compassion. The goal of the way of Buddha is to free individuals from all that causes suffering and achieve loving kindness toward all persons and things through a righteous life. The Buddha proclaims: "Let us live joyfully. Let us form a community of love in a world full of hatred. Let us live without any kind of hatred. Let us live joyfully. Let us form a community of peace in world full of rivalry... Let us live on spiritual bliss, radiating spiritual light."[35]

Christianity

The Christian tradition has often been ambiguous toward the emotions. While Christian art and architecture has strongly appealed to the emotions (think of the magnificent cathedrals and the art of the renaissance), the Church has simultaneously been wary of emotions. Aquinas, who had enormous impact on Christian thinking, relegated emotions to the lower senses of the body, while seeing reason and will as the higher and more spiritual faculties. This emphasis often valued the importance of rational belief over emotional experience. The emotions were often left to the mystical or the devotions, which were not considered part of mainstream Christian tradition. Both the rational and emotional dimensions of Christianity were criticized by Martin Luther, who at one point declared that "reason is the devil's whore," and by some other original Protestant reformers, who along with Luther put stress on the centrality of "faith."

Feelings of hatred and prideful superiority over others drove Christians during the Crusades as well as during Colonialism, and even moved many Christians to support slavery. All of these movements were inimical to Christianity's beginnings, which were founded on love, humility and the service of others.

Among Christians there have been serious divisions that were often generated by fear, hatred and revenge. Such emotions separated Eastern Christianity from the West and Protestant Christians from Catholic. Negative emotions have brought long period of wars among Christians, as well as the tortures and executions of the Inquisition; all of which were in direct contradiction to the original teaching of Jesus concerning love of enemies as well as friends, and non-violent response.

Cardinal Suenens, who supported the introduction of Pentecostalism into modern Catholicism, described Catholics as "God's frozen people."[36] Roman Catholic theology has also tended to be overly cerebral, as opposed to the theology of the Orthodox churches which is more inclined to be mystical and appealing to the emotions.

In recent times, the Catholic reforms from Vatican II shifted many members from a morality based on fear of punishment to a faith in reconciliation, and from a God of fear to a God of love. **Bernard Haring** (1912-1998), the most renowned moral theologian of the time, shifted Christian morality from the legalism of church law to the "Law of Christ," which is the gospel "law" of love. The Council advocated that Jesus be restored to the center of Christianity and be the role model of a loving life. Catholics were encouraged to see love as the centerpiece of gospel living and to respond to the suffering of the world with compassion. The Church was called to be in solidarity with people in need throughout the world: "The joys and the hopes, the griefs and the anxieties of the men of this age, especially those who are poor or in any way afflicted, these are the joys and hopes, the griefs and anxieties of the followers of Christ."[37]

In Protestantism, the traditional emphasis has been on faith, beginning with Luther's insistence on "faith alone." The mainline Protestant churches generally have been resistant to emotional expression, whereas Pentecostal churches, as well as evangelical churches and Black churches, have been much more comfortable with emotional expression.

Friedrich Schleiermacher (1768-1834), often called "the father of modern Protestant theology," strongly linked emotion with religion in modern times. Schleiermacher placed the origin of religion in the consciousness, which he maintained had a sense of the Infinite and an understanding of the finite through the Infinite.[38] He described religion as "the feeling of absolute dependence." Schleiermacher's association of religion and feelings had a great deal of influence on the subsequent Protestant experience.

Rudolph Otto (1869-1937) also held that the origin of religion was linked to emotion. In *The Idea of the Holy*, Otto wrote specifically of the unique experience of the "numinous," the mysterious presence of the Holy within the deepest realms of the soul. Such an experience inspires feelings of both awe and dread. He wrote movingly about such feeling: "The feeling of it may at times come sweeping like a gentle tide pervading the mind with a tranquil mood of deepest worship. It may pass over into a more set and lasting attitude of the soul, continuing, as it were, thrilling, vibrant and resonant until at last it dies away and the soul resumes its non-religious mood of everyday experience." Otto further describes this experience as hushed, trembling, even at times wild and shuddering.[39]

Shintoism

In Japan's religion, Shintoism, there have always been deep feelings toward the "*kami*" (spirits), as well toward sacred land and leadership. In the 20th century this propensity was used to emotionally move the Japanese people toward imperial conquest. Shintoism was used to generate feelings of religious patriotism and devotion to a "divine Emperor," and his advisors, who wished to build an Empire in the Orient.

There are several emotions that are central to healthy religion. We will focus on two: awe (wonder) and compassion. Love is a key emotion for many religions and will be addressed later under "socializing."

Awe

Traditionally, it has been the feeling of awe that has driven the religious experience. The experience of awe is fundamental to human experience. Here, we do not refer to the "shock and awe" of invading another country and terrifying and killing its people. Rather, awe is the wonder registered at the immensity of the Grand Canyon, the breath-taking beauty of Michelangelo's Pietà, or the moving experience of a symphony by Mozart. We see this reverence for the sublime so clearly evidenced in the medieval gothic cathedrals. Awe, or wonder, is a kind of seeing, an "eye-opener," an emotion that excites and transforms. We also see this emotion in children who are so easily moved by wonder to believe, to explore, and to dream. For adults who sustain their sense of awe, wonder can move them to understand their world more deeply, as well as to contemplate more deeply whatever person, place or thing that generates such wonder.[40]

Awesome Nature

For many, awe is experienced in nature. For John Muir, the great American naturalist, the wonder of nature moved him to be closer to the "godful beauty" of the world around him. It revealed the mystery of harmony in nature and brought him closer to the intelligent planner of all things, the origin of the harmony of it all. For years, the wilderness was Muir's "university," and the longer he marveled at nature's wonders, the closer he came to their source. He wrote: "How interesting to trace the history of a single raindrop! Since the first raindrop fell on the newborn leafless Sierra, each drop is God's messenger, angel of love sent on its way with majesty and pomp and display of power that makes man's greatest shows ridiculous."[41]

Ralph Waldo Emerson was another "natural mystic" who believed that he was transformed and given a new vision of life. He commented that when alone in nature "all mean egotism vanishes. I become a transparent eyeball; I am nothing. I see all; the currents of the Universal Being circulate through me. I am part and parcel of God."[42] Emerson believed that every person has the potential for such experience and needs but to be open to the awe before nature. For him, such experience serves to open us to the infinities of the universe, the depths of nature and enables our souls to "mingle with the Universal Soul."[43]

Thin Places

In ancient Celtic spirituality, there is reference to "thin places." They believed that there exists a veil between the natural and the supernatural, the human and divine, the material and the spiritual. It was believed that in some places, that veil is so thin that one can be put in touch with "the divine presence," the spiritual dimension of reality. Pilgrims still travel to places like Brandon's Mountain, Dingle Bay, the Hill of Mara, the Knock Shrine and St. Bridget's Well seeking an experience of the Holy in nature.

Awe in World Religions

In most of the world religions, awe is seen as "the opportunity to witness the divine."[44]

Hinduism

The Hindu tradition goes back five thousand years to when "the eternal law" (*Sanatana dharma*) was revealed in the Indus Valley of the Himalayas. In the sacred texts that resulted from these original revelations, we read the songs that were chanted during the sacred rituals of these people as they stood in awe before their divine gods and goddesses, seeking to be one with the absolute reality, Brahman. Here is a passage from one of these songs:

> "God is one. He rules all living beings from within their hearts. The world came from him at the beginning of time... There is nothing higher than God, and there is nothing separate from God. He is infinitely small, and infinitely large. He is the roots of the world, the trunk of the world, and its branches. God fills the world, and yet he transcends it. Those who know God, transcend sorrow and death. Those who do not know him, remain trapped by suffering. God wants us to know him. He prompts our hearts to seek him. His flame shines within us, showing us the way to him. By stilling the mind we can find him."[45]

Buddhism

The Theravada Buddhist tradition began about 2500 years ago with the enlightened revelation of Siddhartha Gautama, the Buddha. Here, the disciple does not stand in awe of the divine, nor does he or she ask for divine help. Instead, the disciple strives to achieve the awe or wonder experienced in enlightenment, the liberation from self and from all that causes suffering to the self or to others.

In deep meditations, the Buddhist acts as the architect of his or her own consciousness and makes constant efforts to purify the consciousness of all toxic feelings and thoughts. Living a life of righteousness in all things, the disciple lets go of all attachments and strives to be a loving, kind and compassionate person that does no harm. The disciple stands in awe and wonder before the ultimate goal, liberation (*moksha*). In the writings of the Buddha, we read about the awesomeness of this goal: "The traveler has reached the end of the journey! In the freedom of the Infinite, He is free from all sorrows, the fetters that bound him are thrown away, and the burning fever of life is no more. Those who have high thoughts are ever striving: they are not happy to remain in the same place... Who can trace the path of those who know the right of life and, rejecting over-abundance, soar in the sky of liberation, the infinite Void without beginning... Who can trace the invisible part of the man who soars in the sky of liberation?"[46]

Islam

In the religion of Islam, the Muslim prostrates him or herself in awe and humility toward Allah, who is ascribed a number of beautiful and superlatives names: Totally Aware, All-Compelling, Evident, Subtle, Strong, Eternal, Merciful. This wonder moves the Muslim to deep gratitude toward God, deep desire for union, and fear of possible separation."[47] At the same time, Allah is beyond all imagining or symbols.

Compassion

Many religions value the feeling of compassion for others. Religion reaches out to the other and thus enables people to be unselfish. The word compassion is derived from the Latin verb *patior* with the prefix *con*, and literally means "to suffer with." Compassion draws us into the pain and brokenness of others; it moves us to cry with those in misery, grief or pain.

Hinduism

Hinduism recognizes the divine within the self and within others, as well as the interconnection of all things. This gives Hinduism a commitment to the sacred within all and moves its followers to compassion for all living things. A contemporary example of such courageous compassion is Anuradha Koirala, who won the 2010 CNN Hero Award. Anuradha is a Hindu woman who stands at the borders of Nepal and India waiting for the young women to get off busses who think they are getting jobs, when in fact they are being sold into the sex trade. She takes these naïve young women to her shelter, where she gives them food, clothing, education and safety. On other days, she actually goes into the brothels to extricate young women from the slave trade.

Buddhism

Compassion is a central emotion in Buddhism. Buddhist wisdom accepts the interconnectedness of all beings and is committed to bringing happiness to the self and others. The path of the Buddha is the path of understanding the suffering of others and moving toward them with compassion, which Buddhists see as energy for the heart. As we have seen, Buddhists are committed to "do no harm" (*ahimsa*) and to nurture and protect all living things. This combination of compassion for the oppressed and resolve to resist non-violently moved the great Hindu leader, Mahatma Gandhi to liberate India from the British. It was this same drive that moved Martin Luther King, Jr. to struggle for civil rights for Blacks in the United States.

Christianity

Compassion is also an important emotion in Christianity. Jesus told his followers: "Be compassionate as your heavenly Father is compassionate." (Lk 6:36) Here, God is the source of compassion, and human compassion is a participation in that divine feeling toward others. Jesus is presented as the epitome of such compassion, a person deeply moved by the blind, the deaf, and the diseased. The climax of his life is his compassion on all of humanity and his decision to offer his life for them. In his preaching, Jesus proclaimed his beatitudes, the solemn directives to his disciples to have compassion for those who suffer and to serve them. He also tells a story of the final judgment where people are rewarded or punished according to how they have shown compassion for the poor and oppressed.

Sister Ita Ford is a good example of the compassionate Christian. She is one of the four women missionaries who were raped and murdered by members of the Salvadoran military for siding with the poor refugees fleeing the civil war in 1980. When Sister Ita wrote home, she said that there was little she could do to change the horrible situation these people endured. She explained that all she able to do was walk with these poor people and share their lives and their pain. Ita was willing to risk her life for that, and eventually she paid the ultimate price for her compassion.

Judaism

Compassion is also important to Judaism. Jews believe that they have been called to a covenant with their compassionate God who walks with them and cares for them. Psalm 23 proclaims:

"The Lord is my shepherd; I shall not want....
Surely goodness and mercy shall follow me all the days of my life:
And I will dwell in the house of the Lord forever" (Ps. 23:1, 6)

In the Hebrew Scriptures, God is portrayed as a role model for compassion and is sometimes compared to a mother caring for her child: "You shall nurse and be carried on her arm and dandled on her knees. As a mother comforts her child, so I will comfort you...." (Is 66:12-13) "Can a woman forget her nursing child, or show no compassion for the child of her womb? Even these may forget, yet I will not forget you. See, I have inscribed you on the palm of my hands." (Is 49:15-16)

Abraham Joshua Heschel (1907 – 1972) was a Polish-born American rabbi and one of the leading Jewish theologians of the 20th century. It was his conviction that "the greatest passion is compassion" and he wrote and spoke movingly against the horrors of the Holocaust, racism, and the senseless killings in Vietnam.

Islam

Each day, Muslims are required to stand before Allah five times and recite the opening of the Qur'an: "All praise belongs to God, Lord of all worlds, the Compassionate, the Merciful, Ruler of Judgment Day." This compassionate God is a model for the Muslim's life as he carries out his or her day acknowledging and reaching out to the needs of others.

In 2011 the Nobel Peace prize was awarded to Tawakkul Karman, a 32-year-old Muslim woman and mother from Yemen who heads the human rights group, Women Journalists without Chains. Karman was been a leading figure in the protests against Yemeni President Ali Abdullah Saleh and his oppression of her people. When she heard of her award, she said: "I am very happy about this prize. This prize is not for Tawakkul, it is for the whole Yemeni people, for the martyrs, for the cause of standing up to (Saleh) and his gangs."[48]

The Red Crescent, a Muslim assistance program, has worked for many years with the Red Cross internationally to promote humanitarian principles and assist people who face emergency situations such as natural disasters. They provide food, water, clothing and medical care to disaster victims worldwide.

Native American Religions

The Native American tradition also values the emotion of compassion, as is evidenced in this Winnebago creation story where the Great Spirit is portrayed as the compassionate Creator, a role model for how humans should reverence the earth and other human beings:

> *"He began to think of what he should do and finally he began to cry and tears began to flow from his eyes and fall down below him. After a while he looked down below him and saw something bright. The bright objects were his tears that had flowed below and formed the present waters... Earthmaker began to think again... He wished for light, and it became light... Then he again thought and wished for earth and this earth came into existence.... He took a piece of earth and made it like himself. Then he talked to what he had created but it did not answer... So he made it a mind..... He made it a soul... Earthmaker breathed into its mouth and talked to it and it answered."*[49]

We have looked at emotions and given some examples of the role they play in religion. Now we turn to the human capability to relate, and examine the role this social capacity plays in religion.

3. Socialization

Humans are social beings and therefore can become psychologically impoverished and incomplete without relationships with others. In the ancient Hebrew book of Genesis, the Creator says: "It is not good that man should be alone." (Gen 2:18) Even Aristotle described the human species as "social animals."

Throughout evolution, humans carried on the social tendencies of their fellow animals and uniquely developed these social characteristics. Scientists point out that originally, survival was the main concern so the "selfish genes" developed for protection. Self-interest trumped the service of others. But, over the last 50,000 years, human strength and cunning developed and humans began to establish kinships and share in communities.[50] Strong bonds with others developed for protection, effective hunting and gathering and for the care of the young. Gradually, the human social structures were shaped into families, tribes and then nations.

Belonging, attachment, loving and being loved in return are important priorities throughout our entire lives. Rejection, divorce, break-ups, and the death of loved ones usually cause humans great distress and anxiety. In the United States, we see some young people being tragically driven to suicide as a result of ridicule from their classmates. In China, some young workers in factories are taking their lives as a result of isolation, extended hours and pressure to produce.

It is widely accepted that supportive family members, marriage partners, friends, and even pets help people live long, happier lives and cope with stress. It is interesting to note that the so-called "millennial" generation that is now entering the workforce has come to appreciate this reality and often characterize themselves as people who place friends and relationships over their jobs, which is an attitude that distresses some employers.

Religion's Social Dimension

Religions originate in human life and cultures and are linked with the social capacities of the human species as well as with their social structures. Religions have always integrated with the social structures that were in place at the time of their beginnings. At times, this was a tribal structure, as in the case of early Judaism (c. 1500 BCE), or Islam (700 CE). Other religions sprung up within already developed civilizations. Hinduism emerged from the ancient Vedic civilization in ancient northern India (c. 4000 BCE); Buddhism was initiated within the Indian civilization (c. 500 BCE); and Christianity emerged from the Judaic national civilization that was under the domination of the Roman Empire. (1-33 CE). Christianity seems to have emerged out of an effort to reform the people of Judaism, while Islam purported to reform both the people of Judaism and Christianity. By way of example, let's examine the social dimensions of some of the important world religions: Judaism, Christianity, Islam and Buddhism.

Judaism

Judaism began in the tribal areas of present day Iraq. The biblical narrative tells of a divine call to a tribal leader, Abram, to a covenant with God which included the promise of his descendants becoming a future nation of people who would inhabit a "promised land." The narrative continues to tell the establishment of the family of Abraham (his new name), their eventual enslavement in Egypt and their escape to freedom led by Moses, a central figure in Judaism. The "people of God" struggled through a long period in the desert and then settled in the land of Canaan, where they emerged as the dominant people. Gradually this people developed into a nation around 1000 BCE, a nation which was then divided into the Northern and Southern kingdoms. The people then experienced conquest, exile, periods of rebuilding, and then devastation and dispersal by the Romans. While many other religions of the period disappeared, "God's people" stubbornly maintained their identity and religion. At times, they flourished as strong communities, faithful to Torah and gathered in their synagogues. At other times, they were forced into ghettos, persecuted in pogroms and driven into new exiles. In the 20th century, the Jews were threatened with extinction as 6 million of their women, men, and children were shipped off to death camps and murdered by their Nazi captors. The Jews now flourish in the State of Israel, which was established in 1948, as well as live in strong communities in the United States and in parts of Europe. Today, Judaism stands strong - still "the people of God" called to teach the world the fidelity of God's promises.

Like all religions, the Jewish people have had their divisions. In modern times, Judaism has been divided into the Orthodox who strictly follow Torah, the Conservative who do some accommodation to change and culture, and the Reform who are open to modern customs and liberal interpretations of the Torah. In spite of their diversity, there is a foundational unity among Jews. As one scholar puts it, "what unites the most diverse groups within Judaism is first, an acceptance of largely hereditary membership of a specific social community, and secondly, an acceptance that this community originated because of belief in a divine vocation."[51] The strongest bond in Jewish religion is that of love: love of the One God and love of neighbor. The Psalms proclaim: "Behold, how good it is, and how pleasant, where brothers and sisters dwell as one." (Ps. 133)The history of Judaism is the history of Yahweh' s enduring love for the people he holds in covenant, as well as the return of that love by his people.

Jews have strong social bonds among themselves and have been especially wary of criticism or opposition since the Holocaust. "Never Again" has become their international motto, and Jews world-wide keep a watchful eye out for signs of anti-Semitism. Practicing Jews devoutly celebrate Sabbath at home with their families, as well as with the communities in synagogue. Tradition says that to form a "synagogue" there must be at least ten males gathered, and in solemn community the faithful celebrate the High Holy Days of Rosh Hashanah and Yom Kippur, as well as Passover and other feasts.

Today, Jews are also recognized as an ethnic community, some of whom are "secular" non-practicing Jews, even atheists. Jews now have their own nation of Israel where there are over 5 million Jews. An equal number live in the United States and there are significant Jewish communities in Europe, Russia and South America. There are small communities of Jews in African and Asia.

Christianity

The fledgling Jesus movement in Jerusalem attempted to follow their Jewish faith and the discipleship of Jesus, but eventually they were thrown out of the Temple and persecuted by local Jews for their "heretical" beliefs that Jesus was the anointed one of God, the Messiah. Emboldened by a Pentecost experience of the Spirit, these disciples grew from frightened and confused followers to become inspired missionaries. Small communities of both Jews and Gentiles began to spring up in Antioch, Derbe, Lystra, Colossae, Ephesus (in present day Turkey), Corinth, Philippi, Thessalonica, Athens, and in Rome.

These communities met mostly in secret in house churches and shared meals and Eucharist together. They were known for their sharing, their love for each other, as well as their devotion to Jesus Christ. Led by both women and men, these communities, in spite of persecution, continued to thrive and spread throughout the Middle East and North Africa. Paul the Apostle wrote to the community in Rome that Jesus had told his disciples to "love one another as I have loved you" and he urged them to strive to be loving and caring communities. *Acts,* a biblical narrative of the early church, describes the early Christians as "the multitude of those who believed were of one heart and one soul; neither did anyone say that any of the things he possessed was his own, but they had all things in common (Acts 4:32). In his letter to the Philippians, Paul appeals to a strong sense of community: "If therefore there is any encouragement in Christ, if there is any consolation of love, if there is any fellowship of the Spirit, if nay affection or compassion, make my joy complete by being of the same mind, maintaining the same love, united in spirit, intent on one purpose."(Phil. 2:1-2) **Tertullian** (160-220 CE), an early Christian writer, pointed out that in his day people would say "see these Christians, how they love one another."

In 313 CE, the Roman Emperor Constantine converted to Christianity and soon the movement became the official religion of the Empire. Through the work of early missionaries, Christianity spread and eventually became a global religion. It suffered serious divisions, first East from West in 1054, then with the Protestant Reformation in the 16th century. The Protestant movement rejected the centralized institutional model of church centered in Rome and emphasized the local congregational model, with a strong emphasis on local community identity and autonomy, especially in the Baptist and Congregational churches. The Catholic Church divided into dioceses and local parishes, but did not allow much local autonomy. A strong sense of community was sustained in monasteries and convents.

At the Vatican Council II (1962-65), the Catholic Church described Christians as "the people of God." This more populist description of church changed the self-identity of many Catholics. Previously, the word "church" tended to refer to the official church and its hierarchy of pope, bishops and clergy. Now the meaning of "church" could range from the global community to the local parish congregation and also refer to the family, the very real "domestic church." The Catechism of the Catholic Church explains that the church began in households and that today it resides in "the priesthood of the baptized" as exercised by all family members.[52]

With Vatican II's stress on ecumenism, there has been much dialogue among the churches and congregations and a stronger feeling of community among Protestants and Catholics. Intermarriage has also further bonded members of different faiths. Many Catholics today have a stronger identity with their parish community and experience more participation in Catholic liturgy.

Taizé is good example of a Christian community that has had significant effect on the world, especially among young people. Founded in 1940 by Brother Roger, a Protestant, it is an ecumenical community with its center in Taizé, France. Today it is a monastic community of 100 monks from different faith traditions, dedicated to prayer and meditation as well as peace and social justice. Each year, over 100,000 young people make pilgrimages to Taizé to catch the inspiration of the monks, as well as to study, pray and learn how they can make a difference in the world.

Today there are 2.5 billion Christians throughout the world, living in every country. The strongest revitalization of Christian communities is now in countries that were once dominated by strongly anti-religious Communist regimes in Vietnam, China, and the former Soviet Union.

Islam

Muhammad (570-632), the prophet of Islam, began to have his revelations from Allah in Mecca. Neither he nor his teachings were well received in Mecca, so Muhammad and his early followers had to flee (the *hijira*) to Medina, where he formed the first Muslim community or nation (*ummah*).

Muhammad's vision of community was unique. There would be equality, even gender equality, and women could now inherit from their husbands and could maintain their own dowries throughout the marriage.[53] The community would pray together in the mosque and members were bound to give alms that would be distributed to the poor and needy. After Muhammad's death, the Ummah expanded explosively and grew to be the largest empire in the world.

The Islamic community, like most religions, has been subject to divisions. The most serious breach occurred early on over a dispute over who should succeed the Prophet. The Shia maintained that the leadership should be passed to blood relatives, while the Sunni held that the leadership should be selected from competing individuals. To this day, this heated and often violent dispute goes on within countries (the Sunnis and Shia of Iraq) and between nations. (the Sunnis of Iraq and the Shia in Iran).

Buddhism

The central chant in Buddhism is: "I take refuge in the Buddha; I take refuge in the Dharma (teaching); I take refuge in the Sangha (community)." Early on, the Buddha surrounded himself with a community of monk followers. They lived an ascetic life of celibacy, fasting, abstinence from alcohol, simplicity, and prayer. The monks generally ate only once a day and they only ate food offered to them while doing the rounds begging. They were to avoid any kind of violence, were in fact not to harm any living being, and were to avoid any harmful speech. They did not sleep in comfortable beds. They studied the teachings of the Buddha and instructed the laity through example and teaching. Later, the Buddha was persuaded to also ordain nuns, who would also follow the ascetic life. The commitment to monastery or convent living, however, need not be permanent.

The Buddhist laity were to see the monks as role models and when the monks came begging for food, they would put food in their begging bowls and thus gain merit. At festivals, the laity would bring the monks cloth for new robes, as well as food and the other necessities of life.

The first major division among the Buddhists came early on, and it was over the role of the monastics over and against the role of the laity. The Theravada tradition held that the monks and nuns lived the life of perfection and the laity was to be seen as outsiders existing to serve the monks as a way of gaining merit. Eventually, there was a strong reaction to such exclusivity and the reactionary movement called itself "Mahayana" (greater raft). In this more inclusive model, both the laity and monastics were able to seek perfection. Here, Sangha included monks, nuns and laity, and all were called to be examples to each other and to reflect to each other the peace, joy, kindness and compassion of the Buddha.

Thich Nhat Hanh (1926-), a renowned Mahayana monk from Vietnam, offers his version of that tradition. He shows that the Buddha taught that there is a very safe place within everyone that is an island of the true self. Everyone, monk or lay, can go within that place during the storms of life. All people, (monks, nuns and laity) can take refuge in that place. It is there that one can find his or her true home, ancestors, and the three "Jewels" of Buddhism: the Buddha, the Dharma and the Sangha (community). Here, all have access to Buddhahood and the search of nirvana or liberation.[54]

Thich Nhat Hanh states that it would be a distortion to see Buddhist community life as escapist. The monks and nuns live simply and in seclusion and deprive themselves so as to avoid distractions such as pleasure, greed, hatred or delusion. Their ascetical life and their meditations serve to purify them of toxic thoughts, emotions and actions and move them to live lives of loving kindness and compassion. Hahn insists that Buddhism should be an engaged Buddhism, very much involved in world issues.

In the Mahayana tradition, the layperson can pursue the Buddhist values at home as well as on visits to monasteries or convents, where they learn from spiritual guides. This way, the sangha as a whole "benefits the world with the opportunity for generating abundant, auspicious, purifying 'merit.'"[55] As the Buddha teaches: "Let us live joyfully. Let us form a community of peace, in a world full of rivalry... Let us form a community that possesses nothing. Let us live on spiritual bliss, radiating spiritual light."[56]

With the collapse of the Soviet Union and the improved freedom of religion in Communist countries, the number of Buddhist monks and nuns has increased in China and Vietnam. There has also been a marked increase in the ordination of Buddhist nuns throughout the world.

The Dalai Lama stands as an excellent example of Buddhist social ideals. Though loyal to his community in Dharamsala in India, where he has lived in exile from his beloved Tibet since 1959, the Dalai Lama has been a citizen of the world. He is well-known for his gentle compassion to people of all nations and religions. He has tirelessly circled the globe and has diligently shared the Buddhist message of non-violence, peace and kindness to countless numbers.

4. Conscious Action

Humans are distinguished from other living beings by their power to reflect before they act. While our cognitive faculties are drawn toward the truth, our faculties of desiring and willing are drawn toward the good. The powers of cognition, imagination and volition move humans to accomplish the seemingly impossible. Humans are actors and doers; they have created great art, music, literature and architecture.

Religions and Action

Religions are commonly driven to vigorous action by their beliefs and values. Most religions have one form or another of the "Golden Rule." Long before Christians said "Do to others what you would have them do to you," Confucius said "What you do not want for yourself, do not do unto others."[57] According to this universal wisdom, if you want respect, care and love, then respect, care and love others. If you want help when you are in need, help others in need. If you want compassionate care when you are suffering, disabled or sick, then do the same for others.

Religions as Ways of Life

Religions often teach a way of life that will transform the followers and move them toward the religion's ultimate goal, whether it be union with the divine or some state of ultimate freedom.

Judaism

Judaism calls upon its followers to be faithful to God's law (Torah), to honor their covenant with God, and to live lives of love and justice. At the heart of Torah is love of God and neighbor. The commandments call for having no gods before the one God, showing mercy toward those who love God and keeping his commandments, honoring parents, and avoiding adultery, theft, false witness and coveting one's neighbor's house or wife. (Ex. 20:1-17).

The Hebrew prophets vehemently provided a corrective to Jewish actions. Isaiah proclaimed that the Lord God stands in judgment of those who oppress: "What do you mean by crushing my people, and grinding down the poor, when they look to you? Says the Lord, The God of Hosts."(Is. 3:15) Isaiah also confronted those who were unjust to the defenseless: "Woe to those who enact unjust statutes and who write oppressive decrees, depriving the needy of judgment and robbing my people of their rights, making widows their plunder, and orphans their prey."(Is. 10:1-2) The prophet Jeremiah praised the person who defended the vulnerable: "Because he dispensed justice to the weak and the poor, it went well with him. Is this not true knowledge of me? says the Lord."(Jer 22:16)

Christianity

Jesus uniquely identified himself as the "way" to salvation when he said "I am the way, the truth and the life."(Jn. 14:6) He asked his followers to love others in the same fashion as he had loved them. He called them to "learn from me, for I am gentle and humble in heart."(Mt. 11:29) In the famous Sermon on the Mount, Jesus taught the beatitudes, a description of the good life that has moved countless people, including Dorothy Day and Gandhi, to courageous action. In this sermon, Jesus declared the blessedness of the poor in spirit, as well as of those who mourn, the meek, those who hungered and thirst for righteousness, the merciful, the pure of heart, the peacemakers, those who are persecuted for righteousness and those who are persecuted, reviled and falsely accused." (Mt 5:3-11)

Sikhism

The Sikh religion is a latecomer as religions go. It was established in the 15th century in the Punjab area of northern India. Sikhism is based on an amazing revelation to Guru Nanak. Its message is simple: meditate on the Holy Word of the One God, recognize human equality and serve others. The central temple in Punjab is the Golden Temple, where over a hundred thousand pilgrims go daily to listen to the chanting from the scriptures, honor God's name, and serve others. Attached to the Temple is a large area where volunteers serve meals to all of those who come. It is estimated that free meals are served there to 50,000 people each day. At all the Sikh Temples around the world, the same events take place: people listen to the Word of God, the sacred texts of Nanak and other gurus, and then meals are served to all who show up. It is simple way of connecting the importance of the Word with serving others.

Buddhism

There are many other examples of how religions point the way to fulfillment, goodness and happiness. There is the Buddhist way, which seeks liberation from suffering of the self and others by letting go of attachments to those things that cause suffering. Buddha taught that the goal was loving kindness and compassion and that the way was living a life of righteousness in all areas of human life, from understanding, speech, action to livelihood, effort, mindfulness and concentration in meditation. A Buddhist poet described this passionate way of service in a touching fashion: "May I be a balm to the sick, their healer and server until sickness come never again; May I quench with rains of food and drink the anguish of hunger and thirst; May I be in the famine of the ages their drink and meat; May I become an unfailing store for the poor, and serve them with manifold things for their need."[58]

Other "ways"

There is the way of Islam, with its five pillars of belief: creed, prayer, fasting, alms, and pilgrimage to Mecca. Muslims are required to prayer five times a day, fast during Ramada, regularly give donations to the poor and at least once in their lifetimes make their way to the sacred city of Mecca.

There is the way of Taoism, which puts the individual in touch with the Tao, the universal energy or dynamic being in the universe, and calls disciples to live their lives in harmony with this Force. There is the way of Confucius, which is dedicated to human excellence and the human virtues of generosity, sincerity and kindness, duties to family and friends and commitment to the community; all guided by "the heavens." It is a selfless and humane way dedicated to the dignity of the self and others.

International Religious Service organizations

The call of religions for action has led to the development of many religious organizations committed to service of others. There are a number of international religious organizations. **The Parliament of World Religions** is an international organization that was founded in 1993. The Parliament gathers leaders of world religions every four years to engage in vigorous interfaith dialogue and to make resolutions for service throughout the world. The last meeting was held in Melbourne, Australia in 2010. Resolutions were made to address action in the areas of ecology, the assistance of indigenous peoples, the availability of water and food to the poor of the world, and the promotion of projects involving peace and justice.

Another impressive international interfaith organization is the **Alliance of Religions and Conservation**. Prince Philip of England founded this group when he invited religious leaders from around the world to discuss ecology at Windsor Castle in 1995. ARC now works with 11 faiths worldwide. These faiths and their networks embrace 85% of the world's population - some 5 billion human beings. Each faith has pledged to draw a 7-year plan to deal with environmental problems in their areas. ARC has now been working on ecology for 16 years and has made a major contribution to improving the global environment.

The **World Council of Churches** was founded in 1948 and describes itself as "A worldwide fellowship of 349 churches seeking unity, a common witness and Christian service." In the area of service, the WCC participated in the struggle against apartheid in South Africa and supported efforts to bring about an end to the two decades-long civil conflict in Sudan. It also was involved in moves toward the reunification of North and South Korea, and the defense of human rights in Latin America during the decades of brutal military dictatorships in that region. Currently, it is working on the protection of religious minorities in Pakistan and advocating for the rights of refugees.

Catholic Relief Services is an organization in the United States that has been extremely active in helping the needy worldwide. Founded in 1943 by the U.S. bishops, the agency provides assistance to 130 million people in more than 90 countries and territories in Eastern Europe, Africa, Asia, Latin America and the Middle East. The CRS has focused on emergency relief in the wake of disasters and civil conflict as well as long-term development programming in the areas of agriculture, community health, education, health, HIV/AIDS, micro finance and peace building. CRS embraced a vision of global solidarity and incorporated a justice-centered focus into all of its programming, using Catholic social teaching.

The **Charter for Compassion** is an impressive movement among world religions. Karen Armstrong, an expert in world religions, launched this effort in 2009. The movement and its charter aim to draw world religions to restore compassionate thinking and action in today's world. It takes a position against hatred and contempt and calls religions to walk in the shoes of the oppressed with empathy and resolve to act creatively to meet the needs of our time.

Summary

Efforts to find the historical origins of religion have not been successful, so scholars have turned to examine religions as phenomena. It is possible to look at the origins of religious phenomena, especially the so-called world religions. Generally, these religions originate when a human being receives a revelation or enlightenment. Following this approach, it is useful to look at human capacities that are receptive to religious phenomena and provide examples of how this is manifested in various religions.

The human species has four unique capacities that can connect with religious phenomena: cognition, emotion, socialization, and conscious action.

1. **Cognition** enables humans to question, search, and find meaning in the areas of the personal, the other and life. Religious traditions can provide meaning in all three areas.
2. **Emotion** is a driving force in human nature and has recently gained more scholarly attention, especially the positive emotions. Emotions are integral to healthy religious experience, especially the emotions of awe and compassion that are the foundation of many religions.
3. **Socialization** is an essential human capability in that humans have social needs. Religions meet social needs of humans. They began with small groups of disciples, usually experience divisions, and, if they are to survive, spread and multiply in numbers. Religions often develop strong bonds within their communities.
4. **Conscious Action** is a normal outcome of cognition and feeling. Humans are willful doers. Religion normally moves followers toward action, especially since religions characteristically provide models for a particular way of life. Today, religious individuals and organizations are providing vital service both locally and globally.

Religion seems to be the most authentic and effective when it offers support and nourishment for every aspect of the human person, with all our capacities and potential.

▭◧ VIDEOS ONLINE

Viktor Frankl: *Why to believe in others*
        http://www.ted.com/talks/viktor_frankl_youth_in_search_of_meaning.html

Mahatma Gandhi. *Talks- First Indian Talking Movie*
        http://www.youtube.com/watch?v=2GgK_Nq9NLw

Anuradha Koirala.
        https://www.youtube.com/watch?v=EpMX1eSVWpY

Rabbi Abraham Joshua Heschel. *Interview Clips*
        https://www.youtube.com/watch?v=4xTAh2txiLc

Thich Nhat Hanh. *Daffodil Festival Dharma Talk* — 10 Mar 2013
        https://www.youtube.com/watch?v=yzCWBpS67jg

Dalai Lama, *Inner Peace and Non-Violence*
        https://www.youtube.com/watch?v=-psluirNDJc

Karen Armstrong, *2008 TED Prize wish: Charter for Compassion*
https://www.youtube.com/watch?v=SJMm4RAwVLo

NOTES

1. Robert N. Bellah, *Religion in Human Evolution*. (London: Harvard University Press, 2011), 84.

2. Leonard Swidler and Paul Mojzes, *The Study of Religion in an Age of Global Dialogue*. (Philadelphia: Temple University Press, 2000), pp. 140-143.

3. Ninian Smart, *Dimensions of the Sacred*. (Berkeley: University of Calif. Press, 1996), pp. 10-11.

4. Andrew Newberg and others, *Why God Won't Go Away* (New York: Ballantine Books, 2001), pp. 9ff.

5. Karl Rahner, *Hearers of The Word*. (New York: Herder and Herder, 1969), 3

6. Dennis Ford, *The Search for Meaning*. (Berkeley, California: University of California Press, 2007), 18.

7. Viktor E. Frankl, *Man's Search for Meaning: An Introduction to Logotherapy*. (New York: Washington Square Press, 1968), 85.

8. Ibid., 84.

9. Ibid., 46.

10. Elie Wiesel, *Night*. (New York: Bantam Books, 1982), 29ff.

11. Mircea Eliade, *Essential Sacred Writings from Around the World*. (San Francisco: Harper, 1967), 84.

12. Robert Van de Weyer, ed., *366 Readings from Hinduism*, (Cleveland: The Pilgrim Press, 2000), 9/21.

13. Van de Weyer, *Brih Upanishad* 4:4. 12-15, 17-19 2/29.

14. Van de Weyer, 4/14 *Kena Upan* 2.1-5 and *Katha Upan* 5.2-8 4/19)

15. Van de Weyer, 6/7 *Gita* 9.26-34)

16. Roberts Van de Weyer, ed., *366 Readings from Buddhism*. (Delhi: Jaico Publishing House, 2003), 4/11.

17. Lee Smith and Wes Bodin, eds., *The Buddhist Tradition*. (Allen, Texas: Argus Communications, 1978), 42.

18. Ibid., 17:70.

19. Van de Weyer, 6/13 *Gita* 12, 13-19.

20. Van de Weyer, *366 Readings from Buddhism*, 8/12.

21. Van de Weyer, *366 Readings from Buddhism*, 8/30.

22. Stuart Walton, A Natural History of Human Emotions. (New York: Grove Press, 2004), 17.

23. John Corrigan, ed., *Oxford Handbook of Religion and Emotion*. (New York: Oxford University Press, 2007), 3ff.

24. Andrew Newberg, *Why We Believe What We Believe*. (New York: Free Press, 2006), 28ff.

25. George Vaillant, *Spiritual Evolution: A Scientific Defense of Faith*. (New York: Broadway Books, 2008), 20ff; Jay R. Feierman, *The Biology of Religious Behavior*, Ninth ed. (Denver: Praeger, 2009), 81ff.

26. Blaise Pascal, *Pensees*. (London: Penguin, 1995), 127.

27. Bellah, 108-109.

28. Corrigan, 170.

29. Loyal Rue, *Religion is Not About God*. (London: Rutgers University Press, 2005), 78ff.

30. Newberg, 108 ff

31. Vaillant, 183.

32. Vaillant, 47.

33. Hava Tirosh-Samuelson, *Happiness in Pre-Modern Judaism*. (Cincinnati, Ohio: Hebrew Union Press, 2003), 2-3.

34. Corrigan, 99ff.

35. Van de Weyer, *366 Readings from Buddhism*, 6/3.

36. Church Herald, UK. April 29, 2011: 8.

37. Paul VI, *Gaudium et Spes, Pastoral Constitution on the Church in the Modern World.* December 7, 1965.

38. Corrigan, 457.

39. Ibid., 460.

40. Robert C. Fuller, *Wonder: From Emotion to Spirituality*. (Chapel Hill: University of North Carolina Press, 2006), 14ff.

41. Fuller, 49.

42. Ibid., 50.

43. Ibid., 51.

44. Ibid., 10.

45. Van de Weyer, *366 Readings from Hinduism*. Svetasvatara Upan 3.1-4, 7, 9-10, 12, 4/27.

46. Juan Mascaró, trans., *The Dhammapada*. (New York: Penguin, 1973), 48-49.

47. Rue, 231.

48. Ahmed Al Haj and Sarah El Deeb, "Nobel Peace Prize Winner Tawakkul Karman Profile: 'The Mother of Yemen's Revolution,'" *The Huffington Post*, http://www.huffingtonpost.com/2011/10/07/nobel-peace-prize-winner-karman-profile_n_999774.html.

49. Mircea Eliade, *Essential Sacred Writings from Around the World*. (San Francisco: HarperSanFrancisco, 1992), p. 84.

50. Vaillant, 45.

51. Keith Ward, *Religion and Community*. (Oxford: Clarendon Press, 2000), 20-21.

52. *Catechism of the Catholic Church: Revised in Accordance with the Official Latin Text Promulgated by Pope John Paul II*, 2nd ed. (Vatican City: Libreria Editrice Vaticana,

1997), Section 3: 1655-1657.

53.   Reza Aslan, *No god But God: The Origins and Evolution of Islam*. (New York: Random House, 2011), 61

54.   Thich Nhat Hanh, *Peace is Every Breath: A Practice for Our Busy Lives*. (New York: HarperOne, 2011), 35.

55.   Peter Harvey, *Introduction to Buddhism: Teachings, History and Practices*. (New York: Cambridge University Press, 2007), 178.

56.   Van de Weyer, *366 Readings from Buddhism*.The Dhammapada, 197-201 6/2.

57.   Bellah, 418.

58.   World Religions Curriculum Development Center, *The Buddhist Tradition*, Filmstrip. (Niles, Illinois: Argus Communications, 1978).

The Components of Religion

2

Religion has been exiled to Sunday morning, to a place into which one gladly withdraws for a couple of hours, but only to get back to one's place of work immediately afterward.
— Dietrich Bonhoeffer

The whole purpose of religion is to facilitate love and compassion, patience, tolerance, humility, and forgiveness.
— Dalai Lama XIV

We have seen that religion's purpose involves putting human beings in touch with the Holy, the Sacred. Religions have a number of components whereby this connection between the human and the divine can be generated. It is generally agreed that the seven main components are: **revelation**, treasured **founders**, **sacred texts** that are organized and cherished, **beliefs** formed by followers, and **theology**, **moral codes**, and **rituals** developed around the beliefs. In this chapter, we will discuss these seven components.

Revelation

The word revelation comes from the Latin word "revelare," which means "to unveil." Applied to religious revelation, the meaning seems to refer to the unveiling or disclosure of the Ultimate Mystery. We might say that revelation is a self-disclosure of the holy, the sacred, or the divine. If indeed these revelations are authentic, then it would seem that the divine has an all-consuming drive for disclosure. This persistence of divine self-disclosure faces serious limitations on the part of the human receivers. These mysteries "so excel the created intellect that even after they have been given in revelation and accepted in faith, they still remain covered by the veil of faith and wrapped in a kind of darkness."[1]

In most religions, the Ultimate Mystery is transcendent, beyond reality, beyond human understanding, and at the same time immanent or within all reality. This immanence and intimacy, which is the basis for revelation, is captured in the wonderful Hindu greeting in which, with hands folded, one bows to another and says "Namaste" (the divinity in me honors the divinity in you).

Often, this self-disclosure of the sacred is given through insights that come from individual human experience of nature, personal encounters, conscience, events and actions. Revelation can come through sounds, singing, words, myths, metaphors and symbols constructed by the "hearers of the Word," to use a term by Karl Rahner.

As we have seen earlier, humans seem to be "wired" to receive such revelation. They seem to have within their human capacities a receptivity to truth about the transcendent. As we saw in Chapter one, humans have powers of cognition, emotion, intuition, sociability and action, which can all be potentially open to revelation.

Some revelations are very personal and private. For example, during the Hutu genocide in Rwanda in 1994, a young woman named Immaculee Ilibagiza survived the slaughter by being locked in a tiny bathroom with seven other starving women and children for 91 days. In her book, *Left to Tell*, Immaculee reveals the powerful personal revelations she had about the forces of evil, the darkness of despair and hatred, God's protective power, and the need to forgive. She now tours the world sharing her revelations. She believes that through her ordeal she was graced with the understanding she needed to survive indescribable horrors, and she now feels called to share them with others. Immaculee chose to give her revelations more global exposure.

Other revelations are more "public," and come through all religions. Vatican II pointed out that all religions "often reflect a ray of that Truth which enlightens all human beings."[2] It is widely accepted among Christian theologians that "God reveals self in many or all religions, which complement each other by manifesting different aspects of the divine mystery."[3] It is also widely accepted that divine revelation is on-going process, dynamic and constantly addressing the needs of each age.[4]

Religions usually originate with some profound and lasting public revelation. In the Hindu tradition, the ancient Vedas, consisting of over 1000 songs, contain the "Eternal Law" (*Sanatana Dharma*). This eternal law or teaching is experienced through chanting and listening to the sounds of these songs, through which the mysteries of God or Brahman are revealed. Divine truth is also believed to be revealed in later texts like the Upanishads and Bhagavid Gita, where additional ultimate questions are addressed.

Buddhism

The Buddhist tradition has unique notions of revelation. The original awakening to the Truth was reportedly experienced by Siddhartha Guatama, the Buddha or the Enlightened One. In his historic enlightenment, the way to liberation from suffering was revealed. The Buddha spent the rest of his life teaching his enlightenment, which formed the Four Noble Truths that concern the universality of suffering and describe how to liberate oneself from it by following the Eightfold Path of righteous living.

The unique insight into revelation in Buddhism is that all persons have within themselves the power to seek the truth. Here, there is no need for a divine outside communicator, no need for "supernatural help" or "grace" to receive the truth. Buddha encourages each person "to be a light unto yourself." In Mahayana Buddhism, each person has her or his own "buddhahood," whereby enlightenment and liberation can be achieved.[5]

Judaism

In the ancient Jewish tradition, revelation comes from God through the great patriarchs and prophets. The Hebrew revelation is contained in Torah, or the Law, which is the account of a God revealing himself and his law throughout history. There are many opinions on how the revelation of Torah has changed over the millennia. The great 12th century Jewish philosopher, Moses Maimonides taught that Torah came from heaven and was handed down to Moses. This revelation was not given so much in "speaking," but in a manner of communication known to Moses alone.

In the modern period, there have been proposals that Moses' revelation came from a number of diverse sources, even pagan influences. Today, Jewish views on the source of Torah vary widely. At a recent conference, a noted Rabbi explained that "There is a wide range of views. Many Orthodox Jews believe that Torah comes directly comes from God, while many Conservative Jews hold that Torah evolved from human authors inspired by God. Many Reform Jews hold that Torah comes from human sources." Whatever their views, most Jews allow for broad interpretations of Torah and some form of adaptation to modern times.[6]

Christianity

Christians generally believe that "God has acted in a special way in the history of ancient Israel and in Jesus Christ to reveal who God is and what God wills for the entire human community and all of creation."[7] For Christians, revelation comes through Jesus Christ, the incarnation of God. In the Gospel of John, Jesus declares that "No one has seen God at any time. The only begotten Son, who is in the bosom of the Father, He has explained him" and "As my Father taught me, I speak these things... I speak what I have seen with my Father" (Jn 8:28, 38; Jn 1:18). For many Christians, the ultimate revelation is Jesus Christ himself in his person, life, death and resurrection.

For Christians, revelation is viewed as a free gift from God and an intimate self-disclosure from God, who offers individuals special "graces" to accept divine revelation in faith. The Christian tradition always cautions that this revelation remains obscure, or as the apostle Paul puts it: "seeing in a glass darkly" (1 Cor. 13:12). The Church readily admits to its limitations in receiving divine revelation. Christians follow the Semitic tradition that divine revelation comes through nature as well as through scripture. In the Catholic tradition, revelation is found not only in scripture, but also in the traditions of the Church.

Islam

By way of contrast, revelation in Islam exists in the actual words given to Muhammad in Arabic over a period of twenty-some years. Through "divine words," Allah communicated to people the duties given by their Creator and to others to seek peace and justice and to ask forgiveness of sin.[8]

For Muslims, revelation comes from the Arabic word "waha," which means "to put in the mind." In the case of divine revelation, this refers to informing someone of something that has been hidden from others.[9] For Islam, revelation is only given to select prophets and messengers. It is believed that "Divine Words" came to Muhammad through the Angel Gabriel and that the Prophet was commanded to "recite" these revelations to others. Muhammad is considered to be the last and final prophet who has been given revelation. Others in Islam who have received messages from God have received "inspirations."

Founders

Most of the world religions have founders whose original revelations have made enormous impacts on the world.

The great founder of Buddhism was Siddhartha Gautama. As we have seen, the Buddha was enlightened to the truth about how to be liberated from the desires that cause suffering. He spent the rest of his long life sharing this enlightenment with the communities that developed around his teachings. The communities he founded have spawned countless others for 2500 years throughout the Orient and other parts of the world.

Judaism looks to Abraham as the one called to the Covenant with God, and to Moses as the source of Torah, which is the heart of Jewish revelation. Abraham began a nation and Moses led this nation out of Egypt to the Promised Land and gave them the Law. From these two patriarchs, a new religious movement was founded, which for over 4000 years has survived conquests, persecution and a concerted effort to annihilate this chosen people in recent history.

Jesus is recognized as the founder of Christianity, although during his life he seems to have been a Jewish reformer and never mentioned beginning a new religion. During his brief ministry, Jesus founded a small movement, which after his resurrection, developed into a "church" that would ultimately become global.

The founder of Islam is Muhammad, who was born in 570 in Mecca in the Quraysh tribe and established a religious movement which became an empire after his death. It now stands at over one billion followers, one-sixth of the world's population, and continues to spread throughout the world.

Sacred Texts

Most religions have some collection of sacred texts. In some instances, in pre-literate societies like the Native American and African religions, the sacred stories are preserved orally. Others, as in the case of Hinduism, Buddhism, Judaism, Christianity and Islam, the texts were originally in oral form and were only later recorded in writing.

Hinduism

The Hindu religion has no definitive set of scriptures; rather it has a collection of sacred texts that emerged over many centuries. The earliest collection, the Sruti ("what is heard" and considered to be infallible), includes the Vedas, a collection of thousands of ancient hymns that are believed to be the revelation of "the eternal law." The most famous of these is the Rig Veda, which was completed c. 1000 BCE and is where many of the notions of the gods and goddesses emerge. The last of the Sruti, the Upanishads, appeared in the so-called Axial period (800-200 BCE) and is where we find Hinduism addressing the sophisticated ultimate questions about life, death, karma, rebirth and liberation.

The Smriti ("what is remembered," not considered to be infallible) are vast and include the epics Ramayana and Mahabharata. The Bhagavad Gita is a part of the latter. In the Gita, Krishna, the magnificent avatar of Vishnu, expounds on the protective friendship of God and how devout love, offerings, and the help of divine grace can lead to eternal happiness. Gandhi considered the Gita and Jesus' Sermon on the Mount to be the two greatest spiritual writings in history.[10] Finally, there is a collection of devotional literature called Puranas and the Codes of Conduct (Laws of Manu).

Buddhism

The Buddhist texts are vast and there is no one definitive canon in the way we understand canons. The tradition, of course, begins with the Buddha, Gautama, who spent many years transmitting his teachings orally to his disciples. When the Buddha died, he did not appoint a successor, intending that the Dharma (Teaching) and the Sangha (community) would transmit his teaching. Following his death, a council was held in Rajagaha in 483 BCE, where his disciples spent seven months collecting Buddha's authentic sayings and committing the collection to memory. These teachings were later written down on palm leaves and separated into three baskets, one for monastic rules, another for teachings and the last one for discussion of further issues. The authority of the texts does not come from God, as it does in other religions, but from the teachings' effectiveness in bringing about enlightenment.

When Mahayana Buddhism arose in the 1st century CE, a new canon was developed that is known as the Chinese Canon. Its many volumes represent further development of the tradition. In his monumental synthesis *Old Path White Clouds*, Thich Nhat Hanh has shown that there is clear continuity between the two traditions and that the original teaching of the Buddha is at the core of both.[11] In the 7th century CE, Buddhism came to Tibet and subsequently Tibetan scholars added hundreds more volumes to the canonical Buddhist texts. The entire Buddhist collection of texts is 50 times larger than the Bible. Even though the tradition has so many written volumes, the oral tradition from the great Buddhist teachers remains paramount.

There are two levels of authority in the Buddhist texts: the primary level is considered to be the word of Buddha and the other level consists of commentaries by later Buddhist masters. "Revelation" does not only come from the Buddha, it is also derived from others who have achieved enlightenment. The truth factor in Buddhism is not doctrinal but is measured on its effectiveness in bringing one to enlightenment- an on-going historical process.[12] Uniquely, there is no single primary text around which the Buddhist canon is centered.

Judaism

For Judaism, the *Torah* (or first five books of the Hebrew Bible: Genesis, Exodus, Leviticus, Numbers and Deuteronomy), is the heart of the tradition. Overall, the Jewish scriptures are called the *Tanakh* and consist of Torah, the Prophets (Joshua, Judges, Samuel, Kings, Isaiah, Jeremiah, Ezekiel, Hosea, Joel, Amos, Obadiah, Jonah, Micah, Nahum, Habakkuk, Zephaniah, Haggai, Zechariah and Malachi) and the Writings (Chronicles, Psalms, Job, Proverbs, Ruth, Song of Songs, Ecclesiastes, Lamentations, Esther, Daniel, Ezra and Nehemiah).

Christianity

In contrast to the millennium over which the Hebrew Scriptures were written, the Christian scriptures were composed in less than fifty years, beginning only about a generation after the death of Jesus. The first texts of the New Testament include some of the letters of the Apostle Paul, who began writing letters to small Christian communities around 50 CE.

The first gospel written was the Gospel of Mark (c. 80 CE). The author is unknown and the community from which the gospel emerged was possibly in Rome or Syria, a non-Jewish community that was undergoing persecution. A decade or so later, the Gospel of Matthew emerged from the small Christian community in Antioch. This is a strongly Jewish gospel and seems to have been written as a kind of teaching manual for missionaries. The Gospel of Luke also appears to have been written in the 80s, possibly in Syria or Greece. Both the gospels of Matthew and Luke seem to be modeled after the Gospel of Mark and use an additional source named the *The Sayings of Jesus* that is usually labeled as "Q." Finally, there is the Gospel of John, which is thought to have originated in Ephesus around 90 CE and been completed around 100 CE after a number of revisions.

Islam

The Qur'an for Muslims is the revelation of Allah's words to Muhammad revealed by the angel Gabriel over a period of 22 years. These revelations were partially recorded in Muhammad's lifetime and collected into a book after his death. It is composed of 114 chapters, called Surahs, and is organized from the longest chapter to the shortest, which often presents a problem of intelligibility for the non-Muslim reader. Most Muslims are quite literal in their reception of the Qur'an as coming directly from Allah. A secondary text for Muslims is the Hadith, which is a record of the sayings and practices of Muhammad and his early followers. There is much dispute among Muslims over which versions of the Hadith are authentic.

Experiencing Sacred Texts

There are diverse ways that sacred texts can be experienced. They can be sung as they are in Hindu temples, Jewish synagogues and some Christian churches. They can be chanted as they are in Trappist monasteries where the monks gather seven times a day for prayer, or they can be chanted in the low lugubrious tones of the Buddhist monks. Sacred texts can also be read aloud as they are in so many churches, synagogues, and mosques. Many followers like to read the texts of their religion privately, allowing the inspiration to wash over them and sink into their psyches. One thinks of the countless faithful who ponder their texts privately in their room or perhaps at their home altars early in the morning or late at night.

Reading religious texts from a "spiritual" perspective is often quite beneficial to the religious reader. Some collections, such as many Buddhist sutras, the Hebrew psalms, some of the Qur'an, and portions of the Christian gospels are straightforward and offer their meanings readily. In his last statements to his disciples, Buddha said: "During the last forty-five years of my life, I have withheld nothing from my teachings. There is no secret teaching, no hidden meaning; everything has been taught openly and clearly."[13] Jesus at one point said: "O Father, Lord of heaven and earth, thank you for hiding these things from those who think themselves wise and clever, and for revealing them to the childlike" (Lk 10:21).

Reading sacred texts from a scholarly or academic perspective is quite different from reading them through the spiritual lens. Such reading requires background in archeology, languages, literary form, sources and cultural studies. This kind of study can help the reader discover the original context of the texts as well as the original meanings. Done properly, such reading can often reveal depth and relevancy in the texts.

Sacred texts are often used in the rituals of religion. The Hindu texts are sung and danced to in community celebrations and are believed to convey their revelation and power of transformation in the "hearing." Hindus often believe that in tapping into the sounds of the Vedas, one gets in touch with the eternal sounds reverberating throughout the universe. By sounding the OM, (the ultimate sound) and other mantras, practitioners become one with the ultimate power, Brahman.[14] Celebrating the many stories about the gods, goddesses and avatars, Hindus learn how to live virtuous lives and enjoy good rebirths.

Literal or Contextual

Many Christians approach their scripture literally. From this perspective, the Genesis accounts of creation and life in the Garden of Eden are stories of what really happened. The Creation Museum near Petersburg, Kentucky is a good example of this approach. There, scenes from the Bible have been constructed as they are supposed to have happened, including a life-size Noah's ark. People of this literal mindset often do not accept the scientific discoveries such as the Big Bang Theory or Evolution. Similarly, literal readers (sometimes referred to as fundamentalists) read the stories of Jonah being swallowed by a whale or Joshua causing the sun to stand still as historical events.[15]

Since the time of the 18th century Enlightenment, there has been movement to view scripture not so much as divinely given, but as humanly authored. Scholars have discovered the sources used by the authors, different styles of writing, the use of varied literary forms, evidence of editing, and the cultural backgrounds from which texts emerged. Some of these findings occurred as early as the 16ᵗʰ century when a Catholic priest, Fr. Richard Simon (1638-1712), studied the differing styles in the Jewish Torah and concluded that Moses was not the author. Subsequently, scholars began to detect the hand of not one author but two to four authors in the Torah. To this day, the debate goes on about the authorship and inspiration of the Torah among various Christians and among Orthodox, Conservative and Reform Jews.

Within the Jewish traditions, there is disagreement over the literal/ mythical meanings of scripture. Orthodox Jews tend to take the scriptures literally and therefore are strict in obeying the laws of Torah, as well as the Talmudic commentaries. Conservative Jews believe in both human authorship and divine inspiration. Most followers of this sect accept biblical scholarship and are willing to adapt the Jewish practices to culture, but only cautiously. Reform Jews usually lean toward human authorship rather than divine and are therefore quite liberal in adapting Jewish law to modern times or even setting the laws aside altogether. They are willing to accept that much of the narrative in the Hebrew Bible is mythical and can be interpreted with literary tools.

Catholics have had their own tug-of-war over the literal vs. literary reading of the scriptures. As early as the 19ᵗʰ century, Pope Leo XIII encouraged the literary, mythical approach. This method was opposed by the Vatican at the opening of the 20ᵗʰ century, but found approval from Pius XII in 1942. After decades of struggle, the literary approach was given full support by the Second Vatican Council. However, many Catholics continue to read their scriptures from a literal point of view.

Most mainline Protestants are comfortable with the mythical approach to scripture, but evangelicals are usually literal in their approach. As a result of their literal reading of the creation stories, many evangelicals have a difficult time with the findings of modern science regarding the development of the universe or the evolution of living things.

Today, many scholars, as well as university students and bible study groups, approach the Bible using the tools of archeology, linguistics, literary form and contextual criticism. They usually sustain the belief that the scriptures are "inspired revelation," but at the same time view these writings as the works of human authors. These authors used their own style and creativity to convey the revelation held by the religious communities in which they lived. From this perspective, the Gospel of Mark would not be an account of Jesus' historical words and deeds. Rather, this gospel would be viewed as a unique piece of literature written in Rome several generations after the death of Jesus. While based on traditions about what Jesus said and did, this gospel narrative would have been composed to reflect the faith of an early Christian community in Rome.

Islam presents a unique challenge when it comes to literalism. Since Muslims believe that the Qur'an is actually the words of God dictated to Muhammad, there is little room for literary analysis. Over the centuries, Islamic scholars have produced many interpretations and commentaries on the Qur'an, but most do not challenge its literal nature. Whereas Jews and Christian refer to the "*Word of God*," Muslims speak of the "*Words from God*."

The Use of Myth in Religious Texts

An understanding of myth is key to reading sacred texts. By myth, we do not mean the common meaning of "untrue" or "false," like the "myths about the Civil War." That understanding of myth goes back to the ancient Greeks, who distinguished between myths (implausible stories) and *logos* (propositional statements that can be proved). Early scholars of religion in the 18th and 19th centuries added further pejorative meaning to the word "myth" when they identified it with primitive attempts to explain natural phenomena.[16] As science explained these phenomena, such myths were to be discarded as primitive. A good example was the move to "discredit" biblical creation stories once Darwin published his theory of evolution. The atheists of the time, such as Marx, Lenin and Freud, rejoiced because it was now clear to them that religious beliefs in a Creator had been clearly shown to be false and illusionary.

Today, great strides have been made in both valuing and understanding the positive power and contribution of myth. The work of Carl Jung on archetypes and the collective unconsciousness has revealed that deep within the human psyche there are symbols and stories that tell us much about human nature and its shared history. Joseph Campbell has shown the great influence that myth has had in the search for meaning throughout history. His work helps us to better understand why ancient myths are valuable and why modern myths like Star Wars and Harry Potter can hold such a grip on contemporary culture.

As for religious myth, the work of Paul Ricoeur has shown how myths offer access to origins in a "primordial time" as opposed to everyday time. He suggests that a myth is a symbolic story that "gives rise to thought" and in fact shapes thought.[17] The research of Mircea Eliade has helped us understand how important myths are for understanding the deep meanings of human activities, as well as their central role in religions.[18] We now realize the importance of myth in religion; how it puts humans in touch with the sacred and reveals deep truth about reality and the human.[19]

Whether reading the creation myths of Hinduism, Judaism or the Native Americans, the trained reader can strive to get to the heart of the story and be put in contact with the religious truths that are being conveyed. The literalist, on the other hand, often becomes preoccupied with facts and events and is likely to miss the religious truth conveyed in the narrative. For instance, one's understanding of God could be much different from reading the violent battle scenes of the Bhagavid Gita or Deuteronomy literally than from viewing these stories as myth. The literal reading often describes a God who is violent, cruel and vengeful. The mythical approach sees these stories as describing the saving powers of the divinity and the ultimate victory that love and justice have over evil.

Some scriptural myths, such as those in the Hebrew stories, place the events in a historical context to show that God works within history. Some of these narratives do have a historical core (the Maccabean wars), others are fictional (the battle with the Egyptians at the Red Sea). Either way, their purpose is not to tell what happened but to teach about the protective and saving power of God.

When examining the use of myth in the gospels, scholars are divided. Some follow the lead of Rudolf Bultmann and see the gospels as mostly fictional myths designed to teach about the meaning of human life. Others view the gospel stories as narratives constructed around things that Jesus actually said and did, but raised to a level of myth in order to convey the meaning of Jesus' life and teaching.

John Barton of Oxford University has set down some valuable principles for reading sacred texts. He says that such texts should be approached as literature, with an eye for literary forms. The reader should: 1. be open to the lack of historicity in such texts (the text should be approached critically, but not with a sense of skepticism) and 2. be open to the truth that is disclosed in the text (there should be an openness to what the text says objectively and no hidden meaning should be forced on it).[20]

Myths are often integral to religious texts. Religious myths are sacred narratives or stories, sometime created around a historical core, sometimes made out of purely imaginative cloth. Their purpose is not so much to tell "what happened," but to teach some religious truth through story and metaphorical writing. For instance, from this perspective the Genesis I story of creation does not tell how creation came about. Rather it tries to get at the mystery of "who" brought all this about and to teach that creation is basically "good." It is a story about the ultimate source and quality of reality, rather than one about astronomy or ancient history.

By the same token, the two nativity stories in the gospels (Mt 1-2/Lk 2:1-20) would be considered to be mythical - composed to convey the meaning of Jesus' birth rather than actual events. Similarly, the four gospel accounts of the suffering and death of Jesus would be viewed as "plays" written to convey the meaning of the passion of Jesus. The difference between those stories and the nativity myths is that the passion stories are based on an event that was public and broadly witnessed.

The Hindu texts present a special challenge for the faithful with regards to the use of myth. The tradition is filled with countless stories of the gods and goddesses, which teach profound lessons about the divine and its interaction with humans. The epics are drawn large on vast canvases of history and warfare. Gandhi, who was committed to non-violence complained in his youth about the violence and warfare in the Gita. Only later on did he come to realize that these were symbolic narratives (myths), designed to teach about divine protection, duty, and how to live godly lives. He realized that these stories were not teaching about war or the military prowess of the gods and goddesses, but about the immutable nature of the divine. The following passage from the Gita demonstrates this: "Indestructible is the presence that pervades all this; no one can destroy this unchanging reality. Our bodies are known to end, but the embodied self is enduring, indestructible, and immeasurable."[20]

The Rig Veda (1500 BCE) contains a number of mythical hymns and their meaning continues to be explored today by learned Hindus. With the emergence of the great Hindu epics, there is a great deal of mythology. The Ramayana describes the hero Rama (an avatar of Vishnu) and his slaying of the demon Ravana in order to rescue his wife. Clearly this myth deals with the gods' powers to overcome evil. Similarly, the Bhagavad Gita presents many myths surrounding the hero Krishna (an avatar of Vishnu), and contains many of the treasured teachings of Hinduism. The later epics in the Puranas (c 200 CE) contain myths about the exploits of Vishnu, Shiva, Brahma and Devi, which convey many valuable teachings. Each of these narratives is believed to convey an aspect of "the Eternal Truth."

Much of the Buddhist scripture is plain teaching, and often the texts apply to how monastic life is to be led. Myth is also used in the Buddhist texts, as in the case of the miraculous conception stories of the Buddha (e.g. a white elephant enters his mother's side before he is born) as well as the stories about the temptations Siddhartha endured before his enlightenment and the miracles surrounding his life. In the canon, many stories about the Buddha's life and mission are constructed to convey his teachings in the dialogue. In addition, simple stories are told by the Buddha to teach lessons. In one, a heron offers to carry some fish and shrimp from a swamp to fresh waters. As he takes each one, he eats them. A crab insists that in the flight he wants to hold the neck of the heron with his claws, and when the crab sees that he is to be eaten he chokes the heron to death. The lesson: "if we treat others kindly, we will be treated kindly in return; but if we treat others cruelly, sooner or later, we will suffer the same fate."[22]

Beliefs

The word "belief" first gained currency in the Middle Ages, and was derived from the German word "glauben," which originally meant "to hold dear" or "to love." Here, belief came more from the heart and was motivated by faith, which is relational and involves commitment.[23]

With the arrival of the Enlightenment, or Age of Reason, belief took on a more cognitive dimension and could now be put to the test by reason and science. We can see this today, when the young (and more and more the old) ask themselves if they really believe the things they were taught to hold by reason to be true.

Every religion has specific beliefs that are propositions derived from its scriptures and great thinkers, and that are often expressed in its rituals. For instance, Christians have a belief in the Trinity, One God and three Persons. This belief derived from the mention of these three in the scriptures, was formulated by early church fathers, including St. Augustine, and is expressed each time a Christian makes the sign of the cross. Buddhists believe in the power of meditation to transform the consciousness and liberate humans from suffering. Muslims believe that Muhammad is the final prophet and the messenger of God's final revelation

Though each religion has numerous beliefs, there is a certain "hierarchy" of beliefs, wherein some carry more weight and importance than others. In the Hindu tradition there are countless beliefs, but beliefs such as rebirth, karma and ahimsa are at the core. In the Jewish tradition, there are numerous beliefs but belief in the one God and the covenant with that God are paramount. Christians have a tradition filled with beliefs, but the divinity/humanity of Jesus Christ is non-negotiable. For Catholics the real presence of Jesus in the Eucharist is central.

Some beliefs are held for a long period and then set aside or changed. For many centuries, Catholics believed that unbaptized babies went to limbo. That belief was challenged recently and eventually, Benedict XVI declared that limbo is no longer part of the tradition. In some cases, beliefs change. The practice of ordaining Buddhist nuns, although performed early on, was discontinued and for centuries it was believed that nuns should not be ordained. Now the practice of ordaining Buddhist nuns is once again acceptable.

Beliefs are usually taken on authority. We often accept the truths of beliefs because we are told them by those we trust: parents, relatives, priests, ministers, or rabbis. We take their word for it that the beliefs they teach are true. Beliefs also might be "caught" by watching parents or experiencing a community reciting a belief. Images, statues, and symbols that refer to beliefs can be influential. For instance, the Christmas crib encourages the belief that Jesus was born in a manger surrounded by animals, shepherds and angels.

There are also feelings involved in belief. We might feel affirmed by others for believing, feel secure by having a belief, or feel hopeful and happy as a result of a particular belief. A dying person can possibly be accepting of death through the belief that dying means being reunited with departed loved ones. And there is a social dimension to beliefs. We feel confident in our beliefs when we are surrounded by those we know and love who share our beliefs, and we feel secure and accepted in a community that accepts and supports us in our beliefs.[24]

Often, beliefs remain predominantly cognitive, without solid perception, emotional experience and community support. Such beliefs can easily fade into meaninglessness. For instance, if belief in the real presence of Eucharist is simply the acceptance of a proposition, without some real experience of this presence in the midst of a vital community, it can easily wither. Such a belief can remain purely a cognitive reality and have little effect on one's life.

Religious traditions sustain systems of beliefs. Some of these beliefs are ancient perspectives, taken to be part of eternal truth. At the same time, there are always different ways that these beliefs can be interpreted and accepted. In the Dharmic traditions, there are diverse ways that karma, rebirth, ahimsa, moksha, nirvana are understood. Yet, such diversity seems to be acceptable and not necessarily a source of alienation among Hindus, Buddhist, or Jains.

Among Muslims, there are perennial differences between Sunnis and Shias over how authority is passed down from Muhammad. The Sufi mystics have never been acceptable to many Muslim communities.

There has always been diversity in Judaism, and as a tradition it is known to be tolerant of differing positions. There is a saying that when you have three Jews you have four opinions! In the time of Jesus we see Jews divided, with the Sadducees denying the oral tradition and the Scribes holding onto it. Neither the Essenes nor the Samaritans accepted the legitimacy of the Temple Judaism in Jerusalem. After the destruction of Jerusalem and the Temple in 70 CE, a new rabbinic Judaism was formulated with different beliefs regarding temple, sacrifice and priesthood. Today, even with the division among Jews into Orthodox, Conservative, Reform and others, there is a still a strong solidarity among Jews as a people.

For Christians, however, difference in beliefs has often led to deep alienation and even violence. There is still a strong tendency among some Christians to see orthodoxy as a pre-requisite for salvation. Christians tend to have "doctrines," and have often classified those within their doctrine who disagree with them as "heretics." Traditionally, such heretics have been kicked out of the community or even executed. The Catholic Church often takes an absolute position on belief in certain doctrines and, at times, pressures its people and theologians to accept these beliefs. In recent decades, theologians have been censured for their views on infallibility, moral issues, liberation theology and the ordinations of women.

Doubt

Doubt is integral to any cognitive activity. Even in science, there are doubts about the accuracy of the measurements of the universe, the number of universes, the causes of climate change, and details in the process of human evolution. Some scientists today even have doubts about the correctness of Einstein's famous theory of relativity $E=MC^2$, which has been the cornerstone of modern physics.

Doubt is also integral to religious beliefs. A recent survey of more than 35,000 Americans asked people whether they believed in "God or a universal spirit" (92 percent did). The believers in God were then asked if they were "absolutely certain, fairly certain, not too certain, or not at all certain." While 71 percent replied "absolutely certain," a sizable portion (17 percent) fell into the "fairly certain" category.[25]

Religions often look at doubt as a weakness and even at times consider doubt to be sinful. Such positions don't seem to take into account that in this post-modern era, where there is a reluctance to consider anything absolute, some degree of religious doubt is understandable. In fact, doubt can be a be a sign of a sincere effort to better understand one's beliefs, an indication of vitality in the commitment to beliefs.

Monika Hellwig, an important contemporary theologian, has discussed a "healthy doubt" where the mature believer puzzles over and challenges beliefs. She distinguishes between destructive doubt and constructive doubt. Destructive doubt is cynical and rebellious and has little openness to new ways of interpretation and understanding. It often involves an "I don't know and I don't care' attitude that simply pitches beliefs overboard with little effort to evaluate or better understand. Constructive doubt, on the other hand, sincerely searches for new data, fresh interpretations and deeper understanding of beliefs.[26]

Some traditionalists discourage doubt, pointing out that it is indicative of a weakness in faith. Paul Tillich, however, insists that doubt is integral to religious belief, and is an indication of a vital and maturing religious search.[27] Tillich also points out that beliefs are limited statements about the unlimited Mystery of God. God is a Mystery, a reality beyond comprehension, beyond analogy, metaphor, beyond verbal or written formulations. Therefore, the believer must constantly reach beyond the formulations of beliefs to the Divine Reality itself. For Tillich, this "reaching" is the territory of doubt.[28]

Theology

The word "theology" comes from the two Greek words "theos" (God) and "logia" (discourse). We might then describe theology as "discourse on God and things divine." Of course, theology is also about human beings, because they are the recipients and interpreters of divine revelation.

Theology has been defined as a "disciplined consideration and exploration of the content of divine revelation."[29] Theology is a methodical *process*, which uses the human tools of reason and imagination to analyze, explain and interpret a religious revelatory tradition. Theology is also a *product* of ordinary believers as well as expert scholars. But theology is not just an individual endeavor. It also comes "from relating to other people and to God. Above all, as it engages with the past and present for God's future, its creativity depends on many types of belonging."[30]

Anselm of Canterbury's classic definition of theology as "faith seeking understanding" has survived the test of time. Theology studies a faith tradition and has as its purpose the strengthening of the faith of individuals and communities. The theologian is a searcher, a person of faith with a drive to better understand and interpret a tradition for self and others.

Edward Schillebeeckx, one of the great Christian theologians of the

20th century, has shown how theology is linked with faith and is a dynamic process: "Theology is faith itself, alive in a thinking spirit. This thinking on the part of the human spirit is never finished. The growth of human consciousness is always continuing, and something new is gained in ever age."[31]

Schillebeeckx also points out the balance that must be kept in theology between reason and faith. If theologians put too much emphasis on reason or philosophy they can lose touch with faith as well as with the Mystery they are examining. On the other hand, if too much emphasis is given to faith and the absolutizing of doctrine, the very intelligibility of the revelation can be lost.[32]

Like all believers, theologians are searchers; humans open to new experiences and insights. Their offerings are tentative and hypothetical, so they need to be given leeway to offer fresh insights. It takes time for their views to be tested by the community of experts and also by the faithful themselves. Even some of the theological work of Thomas Aquinas was condemned shortly after of his death, and it took centuries before his work was recognized and acclaimed as a standard for theological thinking.

The theologian can be a bridge-builder, linking religious traditions with the changing cultures in which they live. As one theologian observes: "the task of theology in assisting the church in the formulation and application of its faith commitments in the varied and shifting context of human life and thought is an on-going enterprise."[33] Paul Tillich, who was an expert on the relationship between culture and religion, observed that cultures ask the questions and religions provide answers.[34]

A noted contemporary theologian, David Tracy, went beyond this and proposed that cultures and religions both propose questions and offer answers.[35] In light of this, Tracy assigns theology the task to "establish mutually critical correlations between an interpretation of the Christian tradition and an interpretation of the contemporary situation."[36]

Christian Theology

Christian theology has a long history. Early on, the first disciples reflected on their experience of Jesus of Nazareth in light of their newly found resurrection faith. A number of traditions were formulated orally and then written down in "gospels" - some eventually accepted as authentic, others rejected (e.g. the Gnostic gospels). Even before these gospels were composed, the apostle Paul developed a Christian theology that would be intelligible for Gentiles (non-Jews).

After the church was accepted into the Roman Empire, Christian theology developed through the lens of Roman and Greek thought, and this perspective was used in the early Christological definitions at the Councils of Nicea and Chalcedon.

In the century that followed the great councils, theology was articulated by important bishops: Augustine, Basil, Gregory of Nyssa and Gregory Nazianzen. With the dissolution of the Empire, the theological craft shifted to the monasteries, with important thinkers like Bernard and Bonaventure. During that time a new audience emerged: the prevailing tribes, including Germanic, Frankish and Celtic.

New struggles with "heresies" and the dominance of Islam brought forth a defensive and exclusive theology that undergirded the movement of the crusades and inquisitions. These movements were brutal in their treatment of non-Christians as well as Christians that were considered to be heretics.

The medieval period produced the great cathedral schools and universities, along with theological giants like Albert the Great and Thomas Aquinas. Aquinas produced his classical overview of the Christian tradition in his greatest work, *Summa Theologica*, where he used the categories of Aristotelian philosophy to explain the doctrines of the Church.

A certain unity prevailed in Christian theology until the Protestant Reformation, when there was an explosion of confrontational and powerful theology from Luther, Zwingli, Calvin and others. These theologians took up such issues as the Bible, justification, the sacraments, the papacy, hierarchy and priesthood, and challenged the basic positions of classical Christian theology.

With the advent of the Enlightenment (the Age of Reason), the Christian tradition was subjected to a thorough and rigorous rational critique. The Bible itself underwent scientific scrutiny and its inspired character was challenged.

Roman Catholic theology distanced itself from Protestant theology and the advances of the Enlightenment and biblical criticism until the middle of the 20th century. Pius XII approved biblical criticism, but condemned the progressive "new theology" that was emerging post-World War II. The coming of the Second Vatican Council opened the floodgates and allowed progressive Catholic theology to gain broad exposure. Theologians such as Karl Rahner, Yves Congar, Henri de Lubac, Bernard Haring, and John Courtney Murray gained international recognition and set the standards for the development of a progressive theology.

The Council's encouragement of interfaith dialogue produced a rich exchange among churches and religions, brought about a new awareness of the truth and saving power of all religions, and developed a valuable comparative theology.[37] Ecumenical theology, theology developed through the dialogue among the various Christian churches, made possible the influences Karl Barth, Dietrich Bonhoeffer and Paul Tillich had on Catholic theology.

Classification of Christian Theology

Christian theology has been classified in various ways. Some divide theology into **academic**, which would include theology that is done with professional research and carried out in dialogue with other professionals; **practical**, which involves applying theology to particular situations (political, moral, social etc.); and **contemplative**, which deals with prayer, ritual and sacraments. Another standard division is: **Biblical theology**, a theology derived from the study of scripture; **Fundamental theology**, which is concerned with topics such as God, Trinity, Revelation, Bible, Church and Tradition; **Historical theology**, which attempts to reconstruct the historical process in which the tradition was formed; **Systematic theology**, which considers how the various areas of doctrine relate to each other and how they can be newly interpreted (Protestant theology studies doctrines under the heading of Dogmatics); **Practical theology**, which applies theology to specific pastoral needs (rather than specific situations); and finally **Moral theology**, which deals with specific ethical questions, both personal and social and how they can be applied.[38]

The development of new trends in theology has challenged the usefulness of these traditional classifications. First of all, theology has become more interpretive and innovative. For centuries, the study of Catholic theology meant examining and explaining official church teaching. Especially since Vatican Council II (1962-1965), theology has begun to critique, reinterpret and offer new insights into the tradition with an authority of its own. Secondly, some movements in modern theology bypass traditional doctrinal concerns and deal with fresh issues such as ecology, women's issues, and social and political issues.

The authorship of theology has also broadened. As late as the mid-twentieth century, theologians were predominantly male clerics. Now the profession not only includes, but is dominated by, lay women and men, as well as people from a variety of cultures. Today, theology is contextual in that it arises out of the contexts of history and cultures. This was true also in the past. Some of the theology of the gospels and the letters of Paul were shaped by the Jewish context in which they were conceived. During subsequent periods, Christian thinking took on the mindset of the Hellenistic world, then the Franco-Germanic, the Medieval, Renaissance, Enlightenment and then the modern period. Today's theology is influenced by post-modernity, a slippery term but one that seems to advocate relativization of absolutes, a reconstruction, if not deconstruction, of familiar narratives, and a challenge of many modern assumptions.[39] If anything, the postmodern approach has helped scholars to be "more aware of what has shaped us, such as origins, contexts, interests, perspectives and limitations."[40] In the following sections, we will consider some of these contemporary theological movements.

Women and Theology

The feminist movement and the recognition of the equality of the "people of God" brought about a vigorous feminist theology, which then initiated a Womanist theology from the experience of Black women, a Mujerista theology that represents the unique insights of Latina women, as well as a rich theology from the women of Africa, Asia and many indigenous cultures. Female biblical scholars reread and reinterpreted the scriptures, and female theologians opened up new and challenging interpretations of the Christian tradition.[41] The feminine eye has revealed how one-sided the presentation of the tradition has been and opened previously undiscovered insights and perspectives on Christian belief, moral thinking and spirituality. In an innovative approach to this dilemma, Tina Beattie points out: "If feminists are to understand and then challenge the misogyny that forms a dark undercurrent of the Catholic theological tradition, we must go beyond politics in order to ask why the Catholic hierarchy is so resistant to acknowledging the sacramentality of the female body in its capacity to reveal Christ. There is a profound fear of female sexuality that infects the celibate Catholic imagination, and I believe that this lies behind many of the Church's other failings, not least her failure to challenge war or violence with the same unyielding absolutism with which she challenges abortion and contraception."[42]

Liberation Theology

A new stream of liberation theology also entered the growing flow of theological thinking. The roots of linking the Christian tradition to freedom can be linked to the struggle of slaves to be free of oppression and the later efforts of African Americans to gain their civil rights in the United States.

Theologians such as Martin Luther King Jr. and James Cone developed a Black Theology that mined the Christian tradition to free their people from oppression and prejudice.[43]

In 1968, the very year that King was murdered, the Latin American bishops held a historic meeting in Medellin, Columbia and decided to be in solidarity with the poor and oppressed in their countries. They coined the phrase about the church's "preferential option for the poor." Gustavo Gutierrez, a Peruvian theologian, wrote a classic formulation of this perspective in *A Theology of Liberation*. His work produced an avalanche of articles and books on liberation theology, a "theology from below," derived from the experience of poverty and oppression in the Central and Latin American countries. The theology which "seeks to uncover oppression, exploitation, alienation, and discrimination" then diversified to reflect the experience of the oppressed throughout the world and began to apply Christian teaching to the liberation of women, political prisoners, victims of sex abuse, gays and lesbians, the elderly. Liberation theology has spread through African, Asia and many other areas of the world.[44]

Eco-theology

Christian concern for the environment was given a strong impetus by Lynn White's charges in 1967 that Christians bear responsibility for environment devastation. He maintained that the Christian belief that God created the world to be ruled and used by humans was at the root of the crisis.

First Protestant, then Catholic theologians, turned their attention to ecological matters and an enormous body of literature was produced. Christian leaders from the World Council of Churches in 1991, the Conference of European Churches in 1995 and Catholic Bishops Conferences around the world turned their attention to ecology. Pope John Paul II alerted the world to this crisis in 1990 and Pope Benedict XVI gained a reputation as "The Green Pope" with his many teachings on conservation.[45]

Rich as all these developments are, some experts caution fragmentation in theology, that is, the possibility of each perspective going off on its own and not being in dialogue with the others.[46] Another challenge will be to integrate these new perspectives into the tradition. For example, The Catechism of the Catholic Church, in attempting to offer a summary of Catholic teachings and narrow the theological boundaries, bypassed feminine, liberation, ecological and many other recent theological advances.

On a more positive note, David Ford points out that with the failure of modern ideologies like Communism and Fascism, many might turn to religion as the integrating factor throughout the globe. His hope is that interfaith dialogue can help fix the fragmentation and upheaval in today's world. Ford points out: "The religions' new prominence has not only highlighted their problems and pathologies, but has also stimulated them to engage afresh with each other... Inter-faith theology is perhaps the analogy to feminism and ecumenism in the 20th century, inviting Christians into a change of consciousness regarding many millions of their fellow human beings."[47]

It is obvious from the development of theology that there has been a major shift from orthodoxy to orthopraxis, from "believing correctly" to "acting correctly," to putting one's belief into action. And today liberating action is at the forefront of theology. As one scholar puts it: "The great religions are concerned above all with liberating humanity from worldly suffering!"[48]

The Future of Christian Theology

The later part of the 20th century saw tremendous development in Christian theology. Giants like Paul Tillich, Karl Barth, Dietrich Bonhoeffer, Karl Rahner, Henri de Lubac, Yves Congar, Hans Urs von Balthasar, Bernard Haring and David Tracy changed the landscape of theological thinking. Today, the question is: "Who will be the great contributors in the future and from what part of the world will they come?"

Let us consider some of the possible future trends in Christian theology:

Future Christian theology will be more accessible. Much of academic theology is quite specialized and technical. To make theology more "user friendly," it will have to be written in language for the ordinary reader. Moreover, contemporary theology, if it is to have more broad appeal, will have to address issues that are more practical and more geared toward action.

More conscious of the theological perspectives of other religions. Much of Christian theology is still confessional or at best ecumenical, but often lacks sufficient awareness of the perspectives of other religions. David Ford puts it this way: "The religions' new prominence has not only highlighted their problems and pathologies, but has also stimulated them to engage afresh with each other. Can they be partners in difference? Do they have the resources to serve the common good together? What about all the conflicts, bad histories? The present century not only unavoidably presents those sharp questions to religions; it is also already testing the resources and qualities of each faith."[49]

More "engaged." Theology will be more involved in cultural trends such as secularism, post-modernism, technology, and science. Contemporary theology will also be more engaged with pressing social issues such as poverty, the plight of refugees, violence, nuclear proliferation, discrimination, economic and political corruption, ecology, and women's rights.

Theologies of Some World Religions

Traditionally, the term "theology" was used largely in a Christian context. Now that the scriptures from many other religions are less frequently viewed as direct revelation from God than they are viewed as inspired human composition, the term is also applied to the religious thinking of other religions. The literature now speaks of Buddhist theology, Hindu theology, etc.

Hinduism

From this contemporary perspective, Hindu theology would be reflected in the early Vedas and Upanishads insights on creation, ultimate reality, the gods and goddesses, karma, rebirth and soul. The later Bhagavad Gita provides a context for the teaching of Krishna, which is foundational to the Hindu tradition. Krishna, who is an avatar of the god Vishnu, a direct descendent of the divine, comes with his creative and changeless energy to teach righteousness and offer protection to those who follow the path of goodness.[50]

Since Hinduism comes in many diverse shapes and forms, the student of Hindu theology is severely challenged. The Hindu tradition is "a set of human, cultural and religious energies developing, complexifying, adjusting over time," so the student will encounter a wide-array of theoretical developments, expansions, exegesis and discourses. Hindu thinking has also been influenced by Islamic thinking, colonial interpretations, and contemporary scholarship.[51]

Buddhism

Since theology is the study of God, speaking of a Buddhist theology, a religion without god-talk, seems to be a misnomer. However, today's notions of theology have broadened to the degree where considering a Buddhist theology might be acceptable. David Tracy notes that "to speak of a 'theology' is a useful way to indicate the more strictly intellectual interpretations of any religious tradition, whether that tradition is theistic or not."[52]

Many Buddhist practitioners in the East resist all the use of scientific tools and intense reasoned research being applied to their religion. Consequently, much of the theology of Buddhism has been a Western endeavor. At the same time, more Buddhists are coming to realize that their teachings have to be made relevant to today's cultural demands and therefore must bear more intense scrutiny and re-interpretation.[53] Buddhist theological studies thus consider how to apply biblical criticism, historical consciousness and interpretive tools to the tradition. There is also an increasing growth of research on Buddhist connections with ecology, peace, women's issues, and human rights.

Judaism

Jews have also in recent times begun to use the term "theology" with regard the study of their tradition. As early as the second temple period (500 BCE-70 CE), there was a rich prophetic and wisdom tradition in Judaism. The Pharisees and Sadducees argued over the resurrection of the body and the validity of the oral tradition. Great teachers such as Hillel and Shammai emerged and are still influential. The Essenes produced a rich tradition in their so-called Dead Sea Scrolls. During the rabbinic period after the destruction of Jerusalem, Judaism reinvented itself and recorded the teachings and interpretations of Torah in the Mishnah. During the medieval period, great scholars like Judah HaLevi (1075-1141) and Moses Maimonides (1135-1204) produced magnificent commentaries on Torah. In the 18th century, Moses Mendelssohn (1729-1786) encouraged his people to have a sophisticated and learned understanding of Torah and to adapt to the countries in which they lived. In modern times, the Orthodox, Conservative and Reform movements have carried on lively debates among themselves as well as with contemporary scholarship. Great Jewish thinkers like Abraham Heschel, Elie Wiesel and Jacob Neusner have made great contributions to the understanding of the Jewish tradition.

Jewish theology today often focuses on restoring the mission of the Jewish people in the modern world. Rabbi David Wolfe points out that Jews should no longer see themselves as against other religions or modern concerns. He advises that Jews today be conversant in the modern disciplines, lest they become irrelevant. In addition, Jews must see themselves as part of and not against: "Ultimately the thread that binds Jewish teaching together is relationship. The Jew must establish a relationship with God, with self, with other Jews, with the non-Jewish world, with the land of Israel and even with the marvel of creation."[54]

Islam

Muslims refer to two kinds of religious reflection: *falsafa*, which is akin to philosophy, and *kalam*, which would be equivalent to theology. Of course, the central text for Islam is the Qur'an, which as we have seen is accepted as the words of God given to Muhammad the Prophet. Even though the Qur'an is considered to be the words of God, it has been subject to study, interpretation and application since the beginning. Besides the Qur'an, Islam reverences the Hadith, which is a collection of the words and deeds of Muhammad and some of his original followers. The Hadith addresses new circumstances as they arise and reflects on rituals, beliefs and practices. Many passages in the Hadith reflect application of the Qur'an to later social and political situations. The Sunni (the majority) Muslims and the Shia (the minority) each have their own collections of the Hadith. There are also the reform traditions of the Kharijites and the mystical tradition of the Sufi. The medieval period produced great scholars and religious thinkers like Abu al-Ghazali (1055-1111), who was a confidant to the Sultan and a renowned professor in Bagdad. He was a strong defender of the Sunni tradition, an admirer of Sufiism, and he integrated Aristotle's thought into Islamic theology.

Today, there is a vigorous Islamic theology, searching for Muslim identity in the modern world. 9/11/2001 brought much prejudice and suspicion directed towards Muslims and has often moved them to a re-examining and clarification of beliefs such as Jihad, sharia law, and Arab and Muslim unity. The "Arab Spring" revolutions have continued in Libya, Yemen, Egypt, Saudi Arabia, Syria and other countries. Many of the young, as well as many of the older Muslims, want to embrace an Islam that honors freedom, democracy and equal opportunity. Many Muslim women call out for freedom and equality and some have become so desperate that they have set themselves on fire to escape their homes.[55] Muslims are even in the process of developing their own liberation theology.[56]

Moral Codes

Religions appeal to the "better angels" of humans and set down guidelines and rules to be followed in order to lead good lives. Religions propose "ways" or "paths" that lead to fulfillment and happiness in this life and in the "hereafter."

Fundamental to the moral code of most religions is the "Golden Rule." For Christians, this is: "Do unto others as you would have them do unto you" (Mt 7:12). In Hinduism, the rule reads: "Do not unto others what you would not have them do unto you"[57] and in Buddhism it declares: "Hurt not others in ways that you yourself would find hurtful."[58] The Jewish Talmud commands: "What is hateful to you, do not do to your fellowmen," and the Muslim teaching is: "No one of you is a believer until he desires for others that which he desires for himself."[59]

Hinduism

Each religion also has a specific moral code. For the Hindus, one of the oldest sources of law is the Laws of Manu, which includes 13 chapters and thousands of teachings, laws, specific duties of leaders, castes, gender, family roles, occupations in life, rituals, diet and crimes. The Laws of Manu (200 CE) has had a profound influence on Hindu life, but in recent times it has been criticized for some of its extreme positions on caste and for its emphasis on the sovereignty of men over women.

In Hinduism, Dharma is the "Eternal Law" and karma is at the center of morality. Karma refers to one's actions, good or bad, that shape one's being and one's life. The Upanishads teach, "As one acts and as one behaves, so one becomes."[60] It is one's karma that determines the nature of one's rebirth after death, which generally is a long cycle.

Buddhism

For Buddhists, the main moral guide is the Eightfold Path, which is the way to avoid suffering and achieve nirvana or moksha, which is liberation from desires and toxic feelings such as anger, greed, lust or hatred. The goal is to achieve a "no self" which is dedicated to loving kindness and compassion.

The eightfold path pertains to the achievement of wisdom, good morality and proper meditation. Wisdom is achieved by right vision, purpose and speech. **Right vision** overcomes ignorance as one learns the causes and cures of suffering. **Right purpose** is directed at "ahimsa," whereby no harm is done to sentient beings, and **right speech** avoids lies and cruel speech. Good morality is achieved by **right actions**, avoiding stealing, anger, violence and lust. This involves also choosing a **right livelihood** or profession that will not harm or exploit others. And finally, effective meditation requires **right effort** (mindfulness), **right awareness** of one's body, feelings and attitudes during meditation, **and right concentration** during meditation.

Karma is also part of Buddhism's moral equation, but Buddhist notion differs, in that by one's own efforts the endless cycle of rebirths can be broken as one achieves moksha.

Judaism

For Judaism, the moral code comes from the Torah, which contains the commandments, specific laws on particular situations (Lev 7:2), and a summation of all the laws (Deut 4:44). All in all there are a total of 613 laws (*mitzvot*). Jews also honor the two great commandments: "Thou shalt love the Lord thy God with all thy heart, and with all thy soul, and with all thy mind" (Deut 6:4-5) and "Thou shalt love thy neighbor as thyself". (Lev 19:18)

Christianity

The Ten Commandments are the basic laws for Christians, but they do not recognize the 612 laws of Torah. Christians see the "law of Christ" as the law of love and also deeply honor the Beatitudes:

"Blessed are the poor in spirit,
for theirs is the kingdom of heaven.
Blessed are they who mourn,
for they shall be comforted.
Blessed are the meek
for they shall inherit the earth.
Blessed are they who hunger and thirst for righteousness,
for they shall be satisfied.
Blessed are the merciful,
for they shall obtain mercy.
Blessed are the pure of heart,
for they shall see God.
Blessed are the peacemakers,
for they shall be called children of God.
Blessed are they who are persecuted for the sake of righteousness,
for theirs is the kingdom of heaven."
— Gospel According to Matthew, 5:3-10

From Law to Gospel in Christianity and Islam

Since the medieval period, church law, also known as canon law, has provided norms for church morality. Until recently, canon law was the basis for Catholic moral theology. Bernard Haring, the renowned moralist working out of the Tubingen school, was instrumental in shifting the basic source of Catholic morality to the New Testament in his monumental work, *The Law of Christ* (1954). Today, Catholic moral theology also takes into consideration other disciplines such as sociology, science and psychology as well as covering a wide range of areas including bioethics, sexuality, war, social ethics.

The Catholic Church has a treasured tradition of social teaching, beginning with Leo XIII and continuing to the present day. This tradition has stressed human dignity, human rights, the link between faith and justice, solidarity with the oppressed and poor, as well as a strong commitment to non-violence and the common good. Some of the more recent issues addressed are criminal justice, migration, child sex-abuse, and business ethics.

The Islamic moral tradition, which is similar to Christianity's in many respects, is summed up in the Five Pillars of Islam. These Pillars are as follows:

The first pillar represents the Muslim's life commitment. It is the *Shahada*, a daily prayer that gives testimony to the one God, Allah and to his prophet Muhammad. It states: "I testify that there is no God but God. I testify that Muhammad is the Messenger to God."[61]

The second pillar (*salat*) is the obligation to pray five times a day, preferably communally, wherein one places oneself in the presence of Allah and offers praise and thanksgiving. Prayer is believed to purify practitioners from sin and offer the grace and strength to be faithful to Allah.

The third pillar is the giving of alms to the poor (*zakat*). It represents a resolve to avoid greed and hoarding as well as a commitment to be compassionate to the poor.

The fourth pillar is the month long fast during Ramadan (*Sawn*). Here, there is a fasting from food, drink and sexual intercourse from sunrise to sundown. It is a time to reflect on Allah's blessings, be mindful of the poor, and enjoy family and friends in the breaking of the fast at sundown, especially at the final night of Ramadan.

The fifth pillar is the pilgrimage to Mecca (*Hajj*) once in one's lifetime. This is a time of intense preparation and deep experiences of devotion amidst throngs of other Muslims.

Sharia is Islamic law. The word "sharia" means "the path worn by camels getting to water." For Muslims, it is the systematic description of how they should live. Its laws are derived from the Qur'an and the Hadith, although later cultures have added interpretations. In recent times, we have seen some extreme practices in countries like Afghanistan, Saudi Arabia, Pakistan and Iran, especially with regard the laws for women and laws prejudiced toward other religions. In Sharia, actions are classified as: obligatory, meritorious, indifferent, reprehensible and forbidden.

Ritual

The final component we will discuss is ritual. Rituals are an integral part of human life. One remembers the great tragedy of 9/11/2001, when pictures of those who were missing or who had died were posted at ground zero, along with tear-stained letters, flowers, firemen's gear, police badges and other mementos. Thousands of memorial services were held for the deceased. Who can forget the hundreds of funerals held for the firemen killed, which usually involved highly-charged liturgies with fire engines outside, their ladders raised and draped with flags? Here, people seemingly were compelled to memorialize their loved ones. Many more deeply moving rituals were to follow.

Rituals are integral to all religions, ranging from the lively singing and dancing of African or Native American tribes to the silent and prayerful sitting of the Quakers.

The word "ritual" comes from the Latin word "ritus," which prescribed ceremonial order for the celebration of a religious service. Christians often use the word "liturgy," for their worship services. Liturgy comes from the Greek word "leitourgia," which refers to the "work of the people in the service of God."

Authentic ritual involves the whole person.[62] Cognitively, it expresses the beliefs of the individuals and community celebrating. Physically, the postures and gestures express the goals of the ceremony whether they be joy through singing, awe in kneeling, or hope in extending the hands in prayer. Emotionally, ritual expresses feelings appropriate to the ceremony: joy at a wedding, grief at a funeral, or awe at a great feast like Christmas or Passover. Imagination is stimulated by sacred symbols, whether it be the OM at a Hindu ceremony or the cross at a Christian celebration. Imagination is further stimulated as the great narratives of a religion are proclaimed: Buddhist monks chanting tales of the Buddha, a Jewish congregation re-living the exodus, or Christians commemorating the passion and death of Jesus.

Communities are bonded by ritual as they celebrate their histories, beliefs and traditions. They are drawn closer to each other and to their Ultimate as they worship, listen to their texts and to sermons, sing, commune, petition and meditate together.

Finally, congregations or gatherings are moved to action, whether these involve improving their lives or serving others. Christian liturgy is often described as "the source and summit," which applied to all religious ritual would mean that ritual is where the people of God find the source for all their spirituals needs and also the place where they gather all that they have and meet their God on the summit for praise and thanksgiving.

Sacrifice

Sacrifice has traditionally been a part of religious ritual. The word "sacrifice" comes from the Latin *sacra* and *facere* (to make sacred). Here, the offering is rendered sacred and becomes a means of communing with the divine. At its most extreme, this involved human sacrifice in early pagan religions of the Middle East and in the Inca and Aztec religions of Peru and Mexico. In the Temple period of Judaism, lambs or doves were sacrificed by priests on the altar of the Temple in Jerusalem. Once this temple was destroyed by the Romans, both the priesthood and animal sacrifice disappeared from Judaism. As rabbinic Judaism was formed, the offering of the people now became repentance in their own lives as well as acts of love and kindness.

For Christians, the notion of sacrifice became a point of controversy during the Protestant Reformation. For centuries, tradition described the Mass as the reenactment of Calvary. During the Reformation, this understanding of the Mass was challenged, along with the "real presence" in the Eucharist. Many denominations substituted a "service," which placed the scriptures and preaching at the center of the ritual and often reduced communion to a mere symbolic gesture.

The Catholic Church has continued to insist on the "real presence" of Jesus Christ in the Eucharist. The Mass is still viewed as commemoration of the Last Supper, of Jesus' loving sacrifice for all on the cross and of communion with the saving power of Jesus' risen presence.

Seasons and Life Events

Religious rituals are partly seasonal: Ramadan, the Muslim feast, is celebrated in the 9th month of the Islamic year and is a time of intense fasting and prayer. Jews celebrate the High Holy Days at the beginning of the Jewish New Year Rosh Hashanah, and begin ten days of self-examination and repentance ending with Yom Kippur, a day of fasting and prayer in which one seeks God's love and forgiveness. Christians celebrate Holy Week in the spring, commemorating the Last Supper on Thursday, Jesus' passion and death on Friday, and the Resurrection on Easter Sunday.

Other religious rituals mark certain passages in life. Christians use water and anointing with oil to highlight birth or conversion with baptism. The baptism is sealed with another anointing with oil, called "Confirmation." Jewish males are circumcised and when the children reach adolescence there is a ceremony to mark that passage: Bar Mitzvah for boys and Bat Mitzvah for girls. Hindus celebrate a boy's coming into puberty with the sacred thread ceremony. Friends and relatives are invited and as music plays, the young boy has his head shaved. He is presented to the god of the household (e.g. Ganesha) and is given the sacred thread, which he wears on his body to represent that he has now come of age. Various kinds of threads distinguish one's caste. At times young boys are initiated into communities of monks by shaving their heads, pouring water over them and dressing them in monk's robes.

Other rituals denote a new state in life. Weddings of course are celebrated in all religions, with ceremonies ranging from the simple Christian exchange of vows and rings with the kiss and the blessing, to the elaborate Hindu ceremonies that last for days. Likewise, funerals range from Black high-spirited, jazz-accompanied marches in New Orleans and solemn Masses for departed Catholics to the moving Hindu cremation ceremonies on the shores of the Ganges.

Religions have developed special ordination rituals. Buddhist monks and nuns are ordained in a ceremony where their heads are shaved and washed, their robes are donned and they recite the Three Jewels of Buddhism: "I take refuge in the Buddha; I take refuge in the Dharma; I take refuge in the Sangha." Catholic priests are ordained by a bishop in an elaborate ceremony at Mass, which involves the candidates prostrating, and being ordained by the laying on of hands and an anointing of their hands.

Use of Symbols in Religious Ritual

Rituals are highly symbolic celebrations. Material things commonly take on spiritual meaning in Christian "sacraments." Water is used in Christian baptisms to symbolize cleansing. The early baptismal pools were deep enough that the convert could be submerged and then be brought to the surface to symbolize going down into the death of Jesus and then rising to new life. Christians use bread and wine at Eucharist or communion services to symbolize the spiritual food of the sacrament. Soothing and strength-giving oils are used for healing and ordaining. Rings are exchanged to symbolize the eternal circle of promise. Sacred fire is kindled at a Hindu wedding and is circled seven times by the couple to honor and ask the blessings of the ancient Vedic god of fire, Agni. A Jewish couple is married under a Chuppah, a wedding canopy that symbolizes the new home they are building for each other. At the end of the ceremony, the groom smashes a glass with his right foot and the guests shout *Mazel tov!* (Good luck) perhaps wishing the couple good fortune in the broken parts of their lives together.

Verbal symbols are normally an important part of rituals. For Christians, there are the formulas: This is my body, This is my blood; Your sins are forgiven; I pronounce you husband and wife; May you be blessed. There are proclamations of the sacred Torah in synagogue, the gospels in churches, the sacred revelations of Nanak at Sikh services. During the service at Muslim mosques five times a day, there are the moving prayers in praise of Allah and the readings of the Qur'an by the Imam.

There is physical involvement in ritual: bowing, kneeling, standing to pay homage to God, holding arms open or hands out to symbolize prayer, raising sacred texts to honor treasured revelations, and dancing to show the joy of celebration.

Some Major Shifts in Religious Ritual

Catherine Bell, an expert on ritual, points out that major shifts are going on with regards to ritual today. First, whereas ritual or liturgy shaped lives in the past, our lives and experiences are shaping our rituals now. One sees this in the increasingly popular mega-churches, where the symbols, rituals and topics are more contemporary and relevant. Bell points out: "Religion does not define the nature of human beings, humanness defines the nature of religion... Rituals and symbols are less clear-cut, more tentative, experimental, and open to individual appropriation... While many people affiliate with religious institutions, they are less concerned with issues of doctrinal orthodoxy and more with issues of personal meaning and fulfillment."[63]

In the past, it seems as though traditional beliefs and rituals shaped the lives of individuals and communities more that they do today. In the contemporary era, a reversal is taking place whereby present human experiences are more likely to shape beliefs and rituals.[64] Since human life today is so unpredictable and diverse, past beliefs and rituals can be seen as irrelevant. Thus, religions which cling to absolute positions on their beliefs and rituals soon find a loss in membership, especially among the young.

Another shift is in the absence of understanding followers have of traditional religious symbols as well as their lack of faith in the power of symbolic rituals. This perhaps began at the time of the Protestant Reformation when there was a move from symbol and sacrament to devotion to the Word. In reaction, the Catholic Church held on firmly to all seven of its seven sacraments as the main means of salvation. As Protestant groups moved more to the left, religious symbols became less and less important. With the advent of secularism, they lost even more of their intelligibility. Now, this phenomenon has also affected Catholicism.

Christian Eucharist: Many Shifts in Meaning

Christian Eucharist is a valuable case study on how a central ritualistic symbol's meaning can evolve. The Eucharist has always been the central ritual for Catholicism. The earliest reference to this ritual was written by the apostle Paul in the 50s CE. Early on, the followers of Jesus still worshipped in the Temple and synagogues, but always had to observe their Christian rituals privately in homes. As Jews and Christians separated, the latter no longer attended Temple or synagogue. Their simple home rituals included readings of sacred texts, as well as traditional chants and songs. Here, the simple "breaking of the bread" was celebrated in the context of a larger community meal called The Agape, or love feast. From the beginning, this ritual was a commemoration of the last supper Jesus shared with his disciples and was closely associated with Jesus' suffering and death. (1Cor 11:23) Since Christians in the early centuries were not acceptable to the Roman authorities, they had to celebrate the "the breaking of the bread" in private homes, first in the rural areas and then in the cities as Christianity became more urban. As Christianity moved into Gentile communities and spread through modern day Syria, Turkey, Greece and Italy, the worship became less Jewish and more Hellenized.

As the communities grew, their meetings expanded into the larger homes of the wealthy, who often remodeled parts of their homes to serve as places of worship.[65] This type of venue, along with many variations of Eucharistic rituals and ministries, prevailed for the first few centuries of the Jesus movement. Edward Foley, of the Catholic Theological Union, points out: "There was no primitive Christian rite promulgated early in the first century that eventually became more diverse with the passing of time. Rather a rich variety of worship forms and styles has existed from the start. Such an awareness is of immeasurable value as we forge prayer for the diverse communities of the 21st century church."[66]

We get a peek into these rituals in the famous letter of Pliny to the Emperor reporting Christian activities. He wrote: "They used to gather on a stated day before dawn and sing to Christ as if he were a god, and they took an oath not to involve themselves in villainy, but rather to commit no theft, no fraud, no adultery; not to break faith, nor to deny money placed with them in trust. Once these things were done, it was their custom to part and return later to eat a meal together, innocently, although they stopped this after my edict, in which I, following your mandate, forbade all secret societies."[67]

A History of Catholic Ritual from Home Liturgies to Royal Ceremonies

From the end of the 1st century to the end of the 3rd, the number of Christians grew from 20,000 to 7 million. They had become a sizeable minority of 5% in an Empire of 60 million.[68] As this growing minority became more influential and continued to reject the Roman religion, it was subjected to severe persecutions under emperors such as Nero (d. 68), Domitian (d. 96), Trajan (d.117), Marcus Aurelius (d. 180), Decius (d. 251), and Diocletian (d. 305).[69]

To the amazement of many Christians, a seismic event occurred in the Empire. Constantine, the Roman Emperor, was converted to Christianity and suddenly the movement was deemed acceptable by imperial decree in 313. Even more amazingly, by 380 Christianity was declared to be the official religion of the Roman Empire. The numbers increased quickly and Christian ritual took on new forms.

The Eucharistic meal expanded into large Roman buildings (*basilicas*). Rituals became more formal, were more uniformly organized and were led by ordained bishops and priests. In the 5th century, the "barbarian tribes" began to roam over the Empire, crushing the Romans, and Christianity now had the challenge of dealing with these unruly and pagan groups, many of whom were gradually converted. In 498, Clovis was converted; eventually the Frankish empire was established by Clovis and then Pepin, and then was solidified by the great Charlemagne, who wedded the empire with the Church and supported great reforms in the church, including its liturgy. As Christianity spread through Europe, large churches were constructed which became the magnificent cathedrals of the medieval period. The liturgy was standardized by councils as Rome and the Pope now dominated the Church.

By the middle ages, the Mass was now a ritual of the clergy, with the laity standing by as passive spectators. It was celebrated with grand solemnity in Latin, and the focus was on an extremely literal notion of the real presence. The ability to stare at the Host as it was raised or carried about in a monstrance was treasured, and often this vision of the Host was thought to have healing or even magical powers. Communion for the faithful became more rare and was received on the tongue. The chalice was only allowed to the clergy.

The late middle ages saw much upheaval in the church. In the 14th century, there were three rival popes and corruption in the papacy. (Alexander VI [d. 1503] was known for his affairs and his many illegitimate children). Popes maintained their armies and were at times warriors themselves. Many superstitions now surrounded the Mass, and for many priests, the saying of numerous Masses became a commercial enterprise. There was also increasing confusion about the real presence. Some were quite literal and viewed the priest as "breaking bones and drinking blood," while others saw the real presence as symbolic. The use of Latin at Mass and in the bible, as well as the screens separating celebrants from the people, rendered the laity quite passive and confused about liturgy.

The Protestant revolt began with a young friar, Martin Luther, who objected to church corruption and the selling of indulgences. Ultimately, his position led to a denial of priesthood, the hierarchy, papacy and church authority. More radical Protestant thinkers like Zwingli and John Calvin went beyond Luther's objections and denied the real presence in Eucharist. Zwingli gutted his church in Zurich of everything but the place for the scriptures, gave the pulpit and bible center position, and threatened to drown anyone who opposed him.

In 1563, the Roman Catholic liturgy was firmly set and prevailed until reform began to percolate in the 19th and early 20th centuries. Historical studies provided reasons for change, and suggestions were made to move toward the vernacular, with more emphasis on scripture and more participation on the part of the laity.

Such reforms, along with other innovations, were given approval at Vatican II. Altars were turned around, the priests faced the people, Latin was replaced with the vernacular, modern music was permitted, the laity were encouraged to participate, and both women and men were given roles as readers and distributors of communion. A great deal of exhilarating experimentation was allowed, with dialogue homilies, home Masses, and priests concelebrating rather than saying stipend Masses on their own.

With the election of John Paul II, experimentation was discouraged and there was a gradual return to uniformity. One can see this pattern in the recent enforcement by Rome of the new translations and responses for Mass. In some churches, Latin has been restored and communion with the chalice has been eliminated with communion once again being given on the tongue. There has also been a shift regarding the laity's role in the church and therefore in the liturgy. As Edward Hahnenberg points out: "Some church documents have hardened the divide line between the secular laity and the sacred priest."[70]

Catholic Ritual Today

Today, there is a noticeable lack of understanding of the sacraments and liturgy, as well as a yearning for more meaningful experience. The sacraments of initiation, as well as first communion and first penance, are usually celebrated before young people have the capacity to understand them or experience them in a meaningful way. The celebration of the sacrament of reconciliation is in serious decline. There is much confusion with regard to the sacrament of the sick and a marked shortage of priests to administer it in homes, hospitals, hospice and nursing homes.

Catholic and mainline Protestant churches that put some premium on traditional rituals have seen a significant decline in attendance. Pentecostal churches, mega-churches and evangelical congregations have increased in their numbers and participation. Church attendance in France and Holland is very low and on the decline in Ireland, Germany and Spain. One question that puzzles many scholars is: "Why the lack of interest in sacraments and rituals in the academy?" as evidenced by the lack of publications on this topic. Along the same lines, the question for church leaders is: "Why the lack of interest in ritual, especially among the young?" Christine Hall observes: "sacramental theology, as traditionally conceived, seems to feature less and less on academic teaching and research programs in many parts of the world... Churches with an overtly sacramental approach are losing adherents... At the same time, it is arguable that in many places the Church has withdrawn from large areas of human experience that have previously been its concern, and that those who are leaving it or are not attracted to it are seeking a wide range of alternative "sacramental" experiences."[71]

With the growing shortage of priests and the continuing closing of parishes, many Catholics ask: "Will we now return to having house churches, with liturgies led by lay people?" Many are taking the "priesthood of the laity" as well as the ordination of women very seriously, which might indicate some radical changes with regard ritual in the future church.

Summary

We have given an overview of the many components of religion. We began with the perennial and consistent drive on the part of Ultimate Mystery or God toward self-**revelation** and how that has been received in so many diverse ways. Many **founders**, whether they be anonymous sages or famous prophets, have received these revelations and passed them on to followers as individual religions began to form. Revelations are at first in oral form, but are then written into **texts** that are collected and given a range of authenticity. Each religion has its own set of sacred texts which it honors, studies and observes. Today, religions struggle with conflict between those who approach these texts literally or contextually, and struggle with how to deal with the mythology that is so much a part of these texts.

From these sacred texts a wide variety of **beliefs** emerge. Religions approach their beliefs differently, ranging from the Buddhists who see their beliefs as teaching tools to some Christians who absolutise their beliefs and make them essential to salvation.

Each religion recognizes a **theological** endeavor, which explains, interprets, and even critiques beliefs. The variations in these interpretations have led to much controversy within each religion as well as among religions themselves. There are traditional classifications of Christian theology, but today these have to be modified to take into consideration a broadening of theology in its interests as well as its participants.

All religions have their **moral codes** that form guidelines for how to live a faithful and happy life. Fundamental to all these codes are the values of love, kindness and justice. Today, there is a resistance to blind obedience to these codes and revisions are being made to accommodate them to modern cultures.

Ritual is integral to human life as well as to religious practice. Rituals are symbolic ceremonies whereby religions celebrate their beliefs and build strong communities. Rituals consist of words and actions through which religions worship, remember and celebrate valued historical events, seasons and human passages. Today's experiences are challenging traditional symbols and rituals, and many believers are seeking those that are more relevant to their lives.

Religions are learning that if they are to remain healthy, all their components must be attended to, modified and kept vibrant.

SUGGESTED READINGS

Bieler, Andrea, and Luise Schottroff. *The Eucharist: Bodies, Bread & Resurrection*. Minneapolis, Minnesota: Fortress Press, 2006.

Chan, Simon. *Liturgical Theology: The Church as Worshiping Community*. Downers Grove, Illinois: IVP Academic, 2006.

Dabashi, Hamid. *Islamic Liberation Theology: Resisting the Empire*. New York: Routledge, 2008.

Giles, Richard. *Creating Uncommon Worship: Transforming the Liturgy of the Eucharist*. Collegeville, Minnesota: Liturgical Press, 2004.

Jackson, Roger R., John Makransky. *Buddhist Theology: Critical Reflections by Contemporary Buddhist Scholars*. Surrey, UK: Curzon, 2000.

Rowell, Geoffrey, and Christine Hall. *The Gestures of God: Explorations in Sacramentality*. New York: Continuum, 2004.

Salamone, Frank A., ed. *The Routledge Encyclopedia of Religious Rites, Rituals and Festivals*. New York: Routledge, 2010.

VIDEOS ONLINE

Buddha - A Documentary About Buddhism
   https://www.youtube.com/watch?v=dLMZNmxFUZU

Campbell, Joseph. Myth As the Mirror for the Ego
   https://www.youtube.com/watch?v=VgOUxICCHoA

Chomsky, Noam. on the Assassination of Oscar Romero and Liberation Theology
   https://www.youtube.com/watch?v=aeaqOfvPiMc

———, on Religion
   https://www.youtube.com/watch?v=SNDG7ErY-k4

Curran, Rev. Dr. Charles. (on theological dissent)
   https://www.youtube.com/watch?v=ehC3YlcFieU

Ecology: Religion and a new environmental ethic
   https://www.youtube.com/watch?v=BG0bQ3SwDI8

Iligabiza, Immaculee.
   https://www.youtube.com/watch?v=Q7Od6V6Z3ug

Islam: Empire of Faith. Part 1: Prophet Muhammad and rise of Islam;
https://www.youtube.com/watch?v=yX3UHNhQ1Zk

Jesus of Nazareth (parable of the prodigal son from the film); https://www.youtube.com/watch?v=14epxvU8XIA

Ritual Music of Tibetan Buddhism
https://www.youtube.com/watch?v=kdBSTAw_cKY

Remembering Edward Schillebeeckx
https://www.youtube.com/watch?v=zmltUL05xPU

Theology: What is Systematic Theology and Why?
https://www.youtube.com/watch?v=UH223pSw1ZM

Varanasi (evening prayer to the Ganges)
https://www.youtube.com/watch?v=mDFtqJ57Fh4

📽 NOTES

1. Vatican I: DS 3016, quoted by Avery Dulles, "Faith and Revelation," in *Systematic Theology: Roman Catholic Perspectives, Vol. I.*, ed. Francis Schüssler Fiorenza and John P. Galvin (Minneapolis: Fortress Press, 2011), 84.

2. Pope Paul VI, *Nostra Aetate: Declaration on the Relation of the Church to Non-Christian Religions.* October 28, 1965.

3. Avery Dulles, "Faith and Revelation," in *Systematic Theology: Roman Catholic Perspectives, Vol. I.*, ed. Francis Schüssler Fiorenza and John P. Galvin (Minneapolis: Fortress Press, 1991), 86-87.

4. Ibid., 88.

5. Urgyen Sangharakshita, *The Eternal Legacy: An Introduction to the Canonical Literature of Buddhism*, Birmingham: Windhorse Publications, 1985), 225.

6. Dan Cohn-Sherbok, *Judaism: History, Belief and Practice.* (New York: Routledge, 2003), 392ff.

7. The Midwest Dialogue of Catholics and Muslims, co-sponsored by the Islamic Society of North America and the United States Conference of Catholic Bishops, *Revelation: Catholic and Muslim Perspectives.* (Washington, DC: United States Conference of Catholic Bishops), 8.

8. Mustansir Mir, "The Quran, The Word of God" in *Voices of Islam. Vol 1.*, ed. Vincent. J. Cornell (London: Praeger, 2007) 45ff.

9. USCC, *Revelation*, 26.

10. Albert B. Randall, *Strangers on the Shore.* (New York: Peter Lang Publishing, 2006), 25.

11. Thich Nhat Hanh, *Old Path White Clouds: Walking in the Footsteps of the Buddha.* (Berkeley, California: Parallax Press, 1991), 576.

12. Bradley S. Clough, "Buddhism" in *God*, ed. Jacob Neusner (Cleveland: The Pilgrim Press, 1998), 60ff.

13. Watanbe Shoko, *Bukkyo* (Tokyo: Iwanami Shoten, 1974) p. 26.

14. Robert E. Van Voorst, *Anthology of World Scriptures.* Belmont CA: Wadsworth Pub. Co.,

1994), pp. 28-29.

15. See Norvene Vest, *Re-Visioning Theology: A Mythical Approach to Religion*. (New York: Paulist, 2011), 2ff.

16. Robert A. Segal, "Myth" in *The Blackwell Companion to the Study of Religion*, ed. Robert A. Segal. (Oxford: Blackwell Pub, 2006), 339ff.

17. Paul Ricoeur, *The Symbolism of Evil*. (Boston: Beacon, 1967), 348.

18. See Mircea Eliade, *The Sacred and the Profane*, trans. Willard R. Trask. (New York: Harvest Books, 1968).

19. Willi Braun and Russell T. McCutcheon, eds., *Guide to the Study of Religion*. (New York: Continuum, 2000), 197ff.

20. John Barton, *The Nature of Biblical Criticism*. (London: Westminster John Knox Press, 2007), 5-6.xxi.

21. Robert E. Van Voorst, *366 Readings from Hinduism*. (Cleveland: Pilgrim Press, 2000), Gita, 2, 15-20.

22. Thich Nhat Hanh, 201.

23. Andrew Newberg, *Why We Believe What We Believe*. (New York: Free Press, 2006), 25.

24. Ibid., 22.

25. Peter Steinfels, "*Uncertainties About the Role of Doubt in Religion*," New York Times, July 19, 2008, http://www.nytimes.com/2008/07/19/us/19beliefs.html?_r=1&ref=petersteinfels.

26. Monika Hellwig, *Understanding Catholicism*. (New York: Paulist Press, 1981), 4ff.

27. Paul Tillich, *Dynamics of Faith: Faith and Belief and What They Are*. (New York: Harper & Brothers, 1957), 16ff.

28. Arne Unhjem, *Dynamics of Doubt: A Preface to Tillich*. (Philadelphia, Pennsylvania: Fortress Press, 1966), 33ff.

29. John R. Franke, *The Character of Theology: An Introduction to its Nature, Task, and Purpose*. (Grand Rapids, Michigan: Baker Academic, 2005).

30. David F. Ford, *The Future of Christian Theology*. (Oxford: Wiley-Blackwell, 2011), 84.

31. Edward Schillebeeckx, *The Schillebeeckx Reader*, ed. Robert J. Schreiter (New York: Crossroad, 1984), 89-90.

32. Ibid., 91.

33. Franke, 113.

34. Francis Schussler Fiorenza, "Systematic Theology: Tasks and Methods" in *Systematic Theology*, ed. Fiorenza and Galvin, 42.

35. David Tracy, *Blessed Rage for Order: The New Pluralism in Theology*. (New York: Seabury, 1975), 240ff.

36. Robert M. Grant and David Tracy, *A Short History of the Interpretation of The Bible*. (Philadelphia, Fortress Press, 1984), 170.

37. See Francis X. Clooney, *Comparative Theology: Deep Learning Across Religious Borders*. (Oxford: Wiley-Blackwell, 2010).

38. Franke, 200.

39. Ibid., 15ff.

40. Ford, 10.

41. A foundational book here is Elisabeth Schussler Fiorenza, *In Memory of Her: A Feminist*

Theological Reconstruction of Christian Origins, ll. (New York: Crossroad, 1984).

42.   Tina Beattie, *New Catholic Feminism: Theology and Theory*. (New York: Routledge, 2006), 4.

43.   James H. Cone, *A Black Theology of Liberation*. (Maryknoll, New York: Orbis Books, 2010).

44.   Francis Schussler Fiorenza, "*Systematic Theology: Tasks and Methods,*" 48.

45.   For an overview, see Celia Deane-Drummond, *Eco-Theology*. (London: Darton, Longman and Todd, Ltd., 2008).

46.   David F. Ford, *The Future of Christian Theology*. (Oxford: Wiley-Blackwell, 2011), 10f.

47.   Ibid., 12.

48.   Clough, 75.

49.   Ford, 12.

50.   Van Voorst, *Anthology of World Scriptures*, p. 52.

51.   Clooney, *Comparative Theology*, p. xx.

52.   David Tracy, "Comparative Theology," *The Encyclopedia of Religion*, Vol. 14., ed. Mircea Eliade (New York: Macmillan,1987), 446ff.

53.   Roger R. Jackson and John J. Makransky, eds., *Buddhist Theology: Critical Reflections by Contemporary Buddhist Scholars*. (Surrey: Curzon, 2000), 6ff.

54.   Rabbi Elliot J. Cosgrove, ed., *Jewish Theology in Our Time*. (Woodstock, VT: Jewish Lights, 2010), xi-xii.

55.   See John J. Donohue and John J. Esposito, eds., *Islam in Transition: Muslim Perspectives*. (New York: Oxford University Press, 2007); Roy Olivier, Globalized Islam. (New York: Columbia Univ. Press, 2004).

56.   Hamid Dabashi, *Islamic Liberation Theology: Resisting the Empire*. (New York: Routledge, 2008).

57.   *Mahabharata, Anusasana Parva* 113.8

58.   *Sutta Nipata*, 705

59.   *Forty Hadith of an-Nawawi* 13

60.   Upanishads, IV 4, 1-7

61.   Qur'an 4,19; 48, 29

62.   Catherine Bell, "Ritual," *The Blackwell Companion to the Study of Religion*, ed. Robert A. Segal. (Oxford: Blackwell Pub, 2006)

63.   Catherine Bell, *Ritual: Perspectives and Dimensions*. (New York: Oxford University Press, 1997), 182.

64.   Geoffrey Rowell and Christine Hall, eds., *The Gestures of God*. (New York: Continuum, 2004), 49.

65.   Edward Foley, *From Age to Age*. (Chicago: Liturgy Training Publications, 1991), 27ff.

66.   Foley, vi.

67.   Robert L. Wilken, *The Christians as the Romans Saw Them* (New Haven: Yale University Press, 1984), p.13.

68.   Foley, 26.

69.   Ibid.

70.   Edward P. Hahnenberg, *Ministries: A Relational Approach*. (New York: Herder and Herder, 2003), 23; See Nicolas Lash, "Vatican II: Of Happy Memory—and Hope?" *Theology for Pilgrims*. (Notre Dame, Indiana: 2008), 227ff.

71.   Rowell and Hall, xiv.

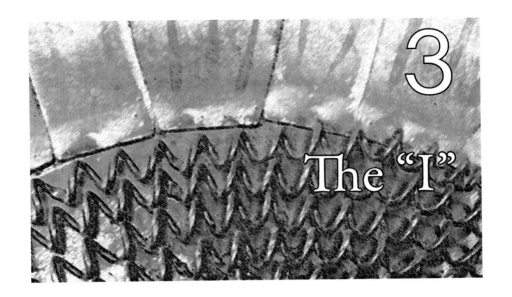

Stages of Personal Development, Gender and Personality Types

The religious false self can even justify racism, slavery, war, and total denial or deception and feel no guilt whatsoever.
— Richard Rohr

"The secret of Buddhism is to remove all ideas, all concepts, in order for the truth to have a chance to penetrate, to reveal itself."
— Thich Nhat Hanh

In this book, we are pursuing an integral approach to religion; that is, a holistic and inclusive approach that looks at religions through many lenses and from many perspectives. Ken Wilber, one of the main proponents of the integral approach to reality, proposes a model of four quadrants or views of reality. From his perspective, the "I," "Thou," "We," and "It" are four contours that enable one to "feel into the texture of the Kosmos and find your very Self in every warp and woof of a universe now arising as the radiance of the Spirit that can never be denied."[1] We will use these four quadrants in the next four chapters as useful tools for looking at religion integrally, that is, from many diverse points of view. Two of these quadrants are subjective and include the "I" perspective and the "We." The other two quadrants are objective and include the "Thou" and the "It."

Here we discuss the "I" point of view. We will examine the stages of personal development, gender, and personality types and observe how each of these personal aspects relates to religion. You will find that these systems have their own limitations, and at times provide competing and even at times contradictory perspectives. Yet, each system in its own way provides valuable insights into the mystery of the human ego. Each can help us better understand the "I" that is so central to the religious response.

I encourage you to explore each model and see what is valuable for your self-understanding and your own position with regard to religion.

Stages of Personal Development

Over the last half-century, we have learned a great deal about the developmental stages of human life. An early developmental psychologist, Erik Erikson (1902-1994), produced groundbreaking work in *Identity and the Life Cycle* (1959) and initiated discussion about the psychological changes that occur throughout a human lifetime. James Fowler (b. 1940), Professor of Theology and Human Development at Emory University, made a great contribution to the study of the stages of faith development. Lawrence Kohlberg (1927-1987), a brilliant professor at both the University of Chicago and Harvard University, made great progress in the understanding of the stages of moral development. Specific differences in gender development were also revealed with Carol Gilligan's (b. 1936) research on women and with work on men by authors such as Robert Bly (b. 1926) and Richard Rohr (b. 1943). There is an enormous amount of literature in these areas and much debate about the literature's validity. Here, we will provide an overview of the highlights of these theories and integrate them into the discussion of religion.

Erikson's Stages of Development

Erikson outlines eight stages of human development: four for childhood, one for adolescence, two for young adulthood and middle age, and one for old age. People must achieve certain tasks in each stage, and if they face developmental setbacks, they will return to a previous stage and complete the tasks again.

Erikson's Stages of Human Development		
Stage	Age	Development
Infancy	0-1	trust
Early Childhood	2-3	autonomy
Childhood	3-6	initiative, independence and competence
Childhood	7-12	social and intellectual skills, work ethic
Adolescence	13-18	puberty, role models, rebellion, identity, questioning
Adulthood	19-40	career, committment, stability
Middle Age	40-65	stability, dedication and service
Final Stage	65+	integrity, deterioration, spiritual

During the **first stage of childhood** (0-1 years old), the child lays the foundation for trust, which is accomplished through care, attention and protection, largely on the part of the mother. Neglect or abuse at this vulnerable stage can produce feelings of mistrust and fear which can later affect the individual's relationships with others, including with God and religious communities.

In the **second stage** (2-3 years old), children begin to achieve autonomy over their bodies; they walk, run, climb and gain control of their bodily functions. They gain power by eliciting responses from those around them and learn how to gain praise as well as disapproval. Over-strictness here can provoke shame and self-doubt. At this point, children begin to distinguish between right and wrong and develop the beginnings of conscience and a moral sensibility. Children who at this point are exposed to violence and abuse may well have a skewered sense of morality later on. Openness to religious moral values can be deeply affected at this stage.

In the **third stage** (3-6 years old), the child begins to develop personal initiative, independence, social skills and competence. At this time, encouragement is needed, lest the child lose self-confidence. Too much punishment at this time can cause a sense of guilt and a loss of initiative. With regard to religion, this focus on guilt can be further inculcated by too much emphasis on sin and punishment. Many older Catholics observe that they still carry a serious preoccupation with guilt from their childhood.

In the **final stage of childhood** (7-12 years old), it is important to achieve social and intellectual skills, belong to peer groups, and become independent in learning and play activities. Here, cooperation and a work ethic can develop. This sense of belonging can be translated into a healthy relationship with a religious community, which can assist in the development of social, cognitive and affective skills, as well as opportunities for serving others.

The **fifth stage**, adolescence, is for Erikson a time when teens must deal with the onset of puberty, biological and hormonal changes, and a new sense of identity. This identity is achieved in the midst of taking on assigned identities from peers (you are cool or you are a nerd), striving to be like celebrity role models, and engaging in conflicts with parents, teachers and employers. This period is characterized by experimentation on many levels. Religiously, teens often begin to question the beliefs passed on from parents and teachers and to resist the adult church community. Self-worth is fragile here, and this can be further aggravated by a religion that is rigid and controlling. Evangelical communities, who usually pay close attention to youth during this period, often maintain loyalty from their youth. Catholic communities, who often pay little attention to their teens or who approach them with absolute positions, can lose their youth during this period.

The **sixth stage** is adulthood (19-40), a time to master the skills needed for intimacy, for commitment to another, perhaps in marriage, and for establishing one's vocation or work. During this period, those who marry can make a renewed religious commitment, especially in order to share faith with their children. For Erikson, this is the time for investment in a stable life and mature beliefs. Neglect here can leave one isolated and rootless.

In the **seventh stage**, which is mature adulthood (40-65), the task is to move from a solid base with family and career to a dedication to one's children and other young people, as well as work and the service for others. Not dealing with the tasks of this stage can result in stagnation (the "couch potato" or "grouch"). With regard to religion, this period is sometimes characterized by adding volunteer church activity to one's occupations, coaching youth, teaching religion to teens, or traveling to developing countries to serve the needy.

The goal of the **final stage of human development** is integrity, which involves dealing well with relationships, accepting physical and mental deterioration, and developing a good perspective on the past, a sense of personal worth, and an acceptance of death. This stage is often characterized by renewed spiritual and religious activities, meditation, and sharing wisdom with the young. Those who don't deal with this stage's tasks well often experience emptiness and even despair. As death approaches, they need help with their anxieties, unresolved issues, fears and difficulty with prayer.

Keep in mind that each individual is different and there are many varying circumstances both cultural and experiential that affect human development. However, Erikson has provided an extremely valuable model against which each human life may be compared, and his depictions of what characterizes each stage of life seem to be born out in the experience of those who have used these models over the years.

Fowler's Stages of Faith

Fowler describes seven stages of faith development. He points out that these stages are not "matters of the content of faith," but are instead "ways of being in faith." They are ways of knowing and valuing.[2] Fowler's stages are as follows:

Primal faith. Life begins in the womb amidst a wonderful symbiotic relationship. Birth, however, is traumatic. We are "bruised and squeezed into life; we gasp our way into community."[3] The first year is normally engaged in bonding and attachment, the beginnings of a selfhood, the tension between trust and mistrust as our needs are or are not met. The powerful images of our caregivers lay down the foundations for later images of God. For instance, those who have been abandoned by their fathers might have difficulty with a prayer such as the "Our Father."

Intuitive-projective faith. Around age two, language begins to emerge and the process of communication begins. The world of meaning emerges as words match objects and feelings, as the imagination encounters stories, symbols and images. Toddlers are the center of the world and as they are told about God they begin to grasp this notion by intuition and imagination. They are often told that this God knows all, is everywhere and controls everything. This can be comforting for some or fear-inducing for others. Children begin to have questions and fears about the mysteries of creation, life and death.

Mythic-literal faith. As school age arrives, children begin to move from fantasy and feeling to space, time and causality. Their world becomes more orderly and predictable. Stories now bring them literal meaning about right and wrong. "Faith becomes a reliance on stories, rules and implicit values of the family's community of meanings."[4] They begin to adopt the faith of their parents or caregivers and accept these beliefs literally and completely.

Fowler's Stages of Faith		
Stage	Faith	Description
1	Intuitive-Projective	grasped by intuition, faith from another
2	Mythic-Literal	learn from stories- faith from another
3	Synthetic-Conventional	can abstract and challenge/question, but not seriusly reconstruct
4	Individuative-Reflective	reconstruct and develop one's own faith
5	Conjunctive	can deal with ambiguity, paradox, and mystery
6	Inclusive	open to other faiths; other-centered

Synthetic-Conventional faith. This is typically the faith of early adolescence, when faith becomes more complicated and the ways of knowing and valuing more challenging. Earlier images of God begin to break down and adolescents begin to observe from their experiences that the divinity is not as powerful as they thought. They learn of horrible physical and moral evils over which God seems to have no control. This faith is called "synthetic" because this stage marks the beginnings of the capacity to abstract and then synthesize various perspectives into a unified thought. The faith here is conventional because the faith outlook that adolescents are beginning to challenge is the one received in their childhood. It should be noted that some individuals remain at this stage for the rest of their lives. They might have questions, but they never seriously critique or challenge the faith they have been given.

Individuative-reflective faith. This stage seems to develop as individuals get in touch with their true selves and their authentic identities. Now they are capable of choosing their own beliefs and values through a process of critical reflection. This faith may not be the same faith that was given to them as children, but it is now their own. This stage often requires years of searching, serious critique of beliefs, and even perhaps a range of choices made and changed. A good example of this stage is Jake, who was brought up in a conservative Catholic family and required to attend Mass every Sunday. Once he got to college he stopped going to church and dropped out of his religion. He said: "All they talk about is salvation or spending money. They don't talk about the things I am interested in: music, school, girls, sex etc." Recently a friend brought Jake to a megachurch where there is a coffee gathering before the service, lots of high-tech images and contemporary music. Now Jake has become a member, and will travel with a group this summer to build houses for a poor neighborhood in Africa.

Conjunctive faith. This stage often occurs in midlife. It is called conjunctive because it struggles to conjoin things that are opposites, paradoxical and contradictory. Experience and acquired wisdom moves people to see that the boundaries they have established around things in their life have moved- life is much more complicated than they ever realized before. The mysteries of suffering, life and death seem to be beyond understanding. Many beliefs they thought were unchangeable now seem to be challenged. On one side, they might have elderly parents approaching the end of their lives. On the other side, they have their grown children with stresses and anxieties. Adding to that are the grandchildren just beginning their lives with their own unique drama and challenges. In the midst of all this turmoil, some middle aged adults find their church's positions on many issues too rigid and uncompromising. The varying lifestyles of the young and their new attitudes toward sex, living together, gay and lesbian marriage and other issues challenge the moral values they hold. One middle-aged mother put it this way: "We are told that the gospels are faith stories or myths! After all these years, just when I thought I had it all together, I am surrounded with challenges and contradictions that I have to figure out. I turn to my church for answers and find that the leaders are living in some other era! I find myself turning to other religions in search of truth. Often I just figure it out for myself."

Universalizing faith. Older people often evolve to this stage. They move from focus on their own faith toward openness to the faith of others and other religions in a way that is no longer threatening to them. They see the limitations of truth and the ineffability of mystery, and they become at peace with their limits to understanding, as well as with the diversity of viewpoints. People at this age often achieve a certain wisdom whereby they can accept chaos, life's messiness, and the faults of others. They can resist judgment because they recognize the same faults and failings in themselves. They can be understanding of the beliefs of others while still holding onto their own. This stage moves away from a position where the self is at the center and can now "participate in the valuing of the Creator and values of other beings... identified with the love of the Creator for creatures."[5]

Kohlberg's Stages of Moral Development

Kohlberg designs his stages of moral development on three levels: **preconventional, conventional** and **postconventional**.

Kohlberg's Stages of Moral Development		
Morality	Stage	Focus
Preconventional	1 - Obedience	reward / punishment
Preconventional	2 - Individualism	personal needs
Conventional	3 - Interpersonal	influenced by peer groups
Conventional	4 - Maintain Social Order	being a good citizen / church member
Postconventional	5 - Social Contract, Rights	common good
Postconventional	6 - Universal Principles	self-chosen principles; sometimes heroic and counter-cultural

The **preconventional** level has two stages: *reward and punishment* and *individualistic*. Young children are usually in the reward and punishment stage. Here, the good or bad of an action depends on what people in authority will do to punish or reward. The child does not steal from Mom's purse because she knows she will be spanked or given time out. Even adults can be at this stage and avoid speeding solely to avoid getting a ticket. The moral authority here is outside the individual making the decision.

The second stage of preconventional morality is individualist, meaning that the motivation now comes more from the wants and needs of the individual. At this point, the morality can also be determined by mutual agreements. For instance, students agree to avoid cheating on tests because they accept the syllabus of the course they are taking. A husband promises his wife that he will not stop at the bar on payday and squander his wages.

Conventional morality is determined by social groups like family, peers or religions. Conventional morality also has two stages: the first responds to *interpersonal relationships* and the second to *social systems*. At the interpersonal stage, morality is determined by the expectations of one's social or peer group. Here, loyalty to the group and a desire to belong determines morality. Teens and young adults are often at this stage. A young female student may feel pressured to have sex because it is not "cool" to be a virgin. A young male might binge drink in order to keep his place in the frat house.

The second stage on the conventional level responds to social systems and social order. Here, one's morality is determined by a motivation to be a good citizen or a good church member. Duty is the key word here and obligation is at the heart of this morality. This is also described as "the morality of law and order." One example is a young Catholic couple who is obedient to the authority of their church and therefore will not use artificial birth control. Another example is a young man who volunteers for the military because he believes that he has the obligation to protect the freedom of his country.

The final, **postconventional**, stage of morality is a morality determined by one's commitment to reason and justice. It also has two stages: the *morality of social contract and rights* and a *morality determined by universal principles*.

Morality determined by social contract or rights follows general norms like freedom and liberty and is concerned about what is best for the common good. These norms often take precedence over laws. For instance, an "Occupy" group decides to camp in a public park, risking arrest, in order to demonstrate against corruption on Wall Street. Or, during "the Arab Spring," many gathered in Cairo to protest the Mubarak government.

The stage of morality of universal ethical principles would apply to individuals who follow self-chosen principles, which may or may not coincide with the law. Morality here is derived from comprehensive thinking and a universal mindset, and is concerned with protecting human rights. Here, even stealing food would be justified to provide food for starving people. An example of this would be the individuals during World War II who risked their lives by providing hiding places and forged documents to Jews who were threatened by the Nazis with imprisonment and death. This stage has moved many religious persons to become intensely involved in peace and justice movements late in life, such as when the older Religious Sisters were arrested after protesting at nuclear facilities.

Obviously this stage theory does not represent a mechanical movement from one stage to another. At different points of one's life and in individual situations, one stage or another might apply. What is useful here is that it gives us a model against which to discuss our own approaches to moral decisions.

The Emerging Adult Stage

Current developmental literature today speaks of "the emerging adult," apparently a newer phenomenon of young adult development. First of all, this stage of beginning adulthood often lasts longer than is did in the past, due to the need for extended education, the difficulty in finding employment, a delay in getting married and raising a family, and other factors. As a result, many young people don't fully emerge into responsible and independent adulthood until they are in their thirties.

Young adults find themselves in times that are rapidly changing, often unexpectedly. They often find themselves surrounded by events over which they have little control. In addition, the complexity of these developments seems to make it difficult for many young adults to find mentors who are capable of helping them deal with these challenges. Wars, terrorist attacks, financial collapse, and political stalemates can come without warning. There is now a global economy in which the strength of one or another country affects that of all the others. It is often difficult to know who owns or will own the company one works for. Companies come and go, young adults find themselves changing jobs often, and employers and employees have often lost any sense of trust in and commitment to each other. Those with inadequate economic and educational opportunities often find themselves with children before marriage or in early marriages with few employment opportunities. Many find themselves caught up in drugs, alcohol and crime and possibly end up in prison. Those who can afford higher education come out of college with their degrees, sometimes with few applicable skills, few available jobs and saddled with huge debt. As one young adult commented: "I won't consider myself an adult until a have a life, and I certainly don't have one yet."

The period of emerging adulthood can be a challenging time in one's life. For some, it is a time for partying, play, sexual experimentation and study. For others it is a time to serve in the armed forces and to experience the atrocities of war. As one student remarked when he returned from Afghanistan: "I have seen many horrible things in my life; much more than someone my age should have to witness. I am just not in the same frame of mind as these other students." Some young adults suffer serious debilitating injuries in wars, car accidents or in sports. Others have major health problems, which prevent them from working and put them in serious debt.

Emerging adults live in what some call a "post–modern" age, where there is thought to be no absolutes and all is relative; a time where the traditional wisdom about life has been "deconstructed." We live in an era of economic instability, terrorism and environmental crisis. Our American culture is becoming more diverse, which often results in alienation and division in politics and religion. The political right pulls young adults one way, the left the other and the moderates does not seem to be on stable ground.

Emerging adults have grown up in a technological age. Over the last decade, we have moved from cell phone to smart phone, from laptop to iPad, and from book to Nook. We are developing generations of "screen people" who text, Facebook, Tweet, Blog, Skype, listen to tunes, play videogames and stream videos online. Social life, education, publishing, politics, warfare, transportation - indeed nearly every aspect of modern living - has been affected by technology. In 2010, we even saw a series of revolutions parts of the Arab world, such as Tunisia and Egypt, that were started through social media.

This period of emerging adulthood is indeed a crucial stage of human development, and how one negotiates it affects the rest of one's life. Often, our society focuses on the turmoil in teen stages and misses the extreme challenges that are faced in young adulthood. This is a unique time in which those moving toward adulthood have to navigate "the experience of the birth of critical awareness and consequently the dissolution and recomposition of the meaning of the self, other, world and 'God.'"[6]

It is a time to begin searching for meaning in life, or one's "calling" (as opposed to just a job). Young adults face the crucial task of linking their sexual life with moral values or religious beliefs. It's a period for examining one's religion and beliefs - a time to decide whether or not to accept the religion handed down by parents, make one's own religious choices, or simply walk away from the whole enterprise. We will deal more with this in the chapter on faith.

The Journey Model of Development

It is worth noting here that some contemporary scholars have moved beyond describing human development in the "stage" model that we talked about earlier. They suggest that with all the complexity and circling back during life, the stage model might be too mechanical. Instead, the "journey" model is becoming more commonly used.[7] In this paradigm, young adults, like everyone else, move through life searching for purpose and meaning. They are at a point where there is a lot of future ahead and they are usually filled with hope of success and expectation of opportunities. They are crossing over, moving past the adolescence and past control by their parents and churches. They are at the beginning of a great adventure at a time when they search for the right decisions that will influence the rest of their lives. They make decisions about education, friends, and lovers. Some scholars have compared young adults at this point of their lives to immigrants who enter new lands, knowing that they will never return.[8]

This youthful journey is usually somewhat different for men than it is women. For men, the "central task in becoming a self is separation or differentiation." For women "the task of becoming self requires identification with attachment and connection."[9] For both, there is a letting go of dependency on parents, a freedom from past authorities, and a movement toward new relationships, new places of belonging and new dreams. It means leaving one home and settling into new dwelling places, often to establish a new home for the self and new loved ones. It is a time for testing new commitments, usually temporary at first, before settling more confidently into more permanent ones. There are now new "tribes," from school or work, from old high school or college friends, from parties and travel. As young adults grow older, they are opened up to larger worlds.

This journey is uniquely described in the Quaker religion as moving from childhood piety to youthful frivolity to a divided self, where one struggles between the Quaker ways and the broader culture. This journey is usually resolved in the late twenties. Those who have chosen the way of the "Inner Light" and Quaker beliefs are now described as being "at one." They have resolved the struggle between Quaker values and the values of the wider culture.[10]

Young adulthood is an intense period spent imagining what one will be, what one will do and what one's world will be like. It is a time for optimism, hope and ambition. On this period of the journey, there are many questions: Who am I? How do I find my true self? Does my life have a purpose? How could it be that one of my young friends died? What are my values? Why was I betrayed and will I get over it? What are my talents and am I using them? Do I really need religion? Why is there so much violence and injustice? Who can I trust?[11]

The emerging adult needs mentoring. Sometimes this guide can be a parent, an older brother or sister, or a teacher. It is often someone closer in age who has recently navigated this same period themselves and who has some lessons to share.

There can be many unique tensions during this part of the human journey such as discomforts with family, the church, the self, or with adult culture and its laws and authority. Young adults may find tension over sexual practices, drug use, risk-taking, sketchy friends, dress, etc.

The Emerging Adult and Religion

Recent studies have revealed a wide-range of attitudes toward religion on the part of today's emerging adults. Though many at this point are not strongly involved with religion, they are still comfortable talking about religion when the topic comes up. Though the topic seldom comes up in social settings, it can easily come up in a class dealing with religion.

Reactions to the discussion of religion in classroom settings vary. Most students are willing to share their views and eager to hear the perspectives of their peers. Some might be reticent at first because they feel slightly guilty for not being much involved with religion.[12] Some draw a blank on the topic of religion because they simply have no background in this area. Others have just been too pre-occupied with other matters to have given religion much thought. As one student put it, "Right now I have too many other things on my plate: school, working, friends, partying. I just don't have much room for religion right now."[13]

It is common among emerging adults to think that all religions are pretty much the same. From this point of view, all religions hold that you are supposed to be a good person and stay out of trouble. For many young people, they can do this by belonging to any religion that is handy or even by not having anything to do with religion.[14] Some get impatient with all the disagreements among religions and just wish that religious leaders would all come together and agree. As for themselves, entering into the conflicts would just cause them too much unnecessary frustration.

There are some religious young adults who are fervent about their commitment and believe that their religion is the only way to go. These are usually Mormons, Pentecostals, Evangelicals and possibly a small number of Catholics. They stand firmly with their church or denomination and are often committed to converting others. As one student said, "You can only be saved by giving your life over to Jesus Christ." For those of this mentality, believers such as Buddhists, Jews and Hindus are completely beyond hope unless they convert.

One study has concluded that many emerging adults are affiliated with "a new, de facto religion: moralistic therapeutic deism (MTD)".[15] MTD is a "religion" that holds that God is far in the sky and has created everything and watches over it. This God wants everybody to be nice to each other. The goal is to be happy, feel good about yourself, and then be rewarded with heaven after death. The God of this religion is a sky-God who is not usually much involved in life, but who can be counted on when one has a personal problem, an exam to pass, or a game to win. Then you pray hard! This study maintains that this "religion" often begins in the teens and continues into young adulthood. In this latter stage, it becomes better nuanced, further shaped by real life experience, more complex, and usually independent from the religion of their parents.[16] At this point, emerging adults, if they are at all interested in religion, are often drawn to megachurches. At megachurches, they often find less concern for tradition, more socializing, more sermons on topics that are relevant to their lives, and commitment to service of the needy.

Emerging adults today often pay little attention to doctrinal or moral authority in religion. Religious truth, indeed all truth, is relative for them. One graduate student put it this way: "I believe what I think to be true and you can believe what you think is true. It is up to each person to decide."

As we have seen, young adults have been brought up in an information age and have been exposed to so many conflicting opinions that they have often concluded that there is no way to know what is true.

Smith and Snell have sorted out six major religious types among emerging adults and have given percentages:[17]

%	TYPE	DESCRIPTION
15%	Committed Traditionalists	Committed with a strong faith to some religious tradition
30%	Selective Adherents	Accept certain beliefs and values of a religious tradition but set aside others
15%	Spiritually Open	Not committed to any one religious tradition; are somewhat open to exploring religious ideas and movements
25%	Religiously Indifferent	Are not involved by religion at all; are not interested in religious topics
5%	Religiously Disconnected	Have had no exposure to religion or religious beliefs; are not able to carry on a conversation about religion because they don't have the necessary vocabulary or understanding
10%	Irreligious	Skeptical or even downright opposed to religion; some are angry, others are sarcastic or think that the whole endeavor is without purpose or meaning

Increased Relativity in Contemporary Moral Matters

Relativity seems to characterize the young adult's approach to moral matters. Studies show that emerging adults, even if they are religious, often make no connection between their moral decisions and their religion. They are often quite "situational" in their ethics. If a certain action seems good to them at the time, they do it. If the situation turns out badly for them, they take their losses and move on. Has this relativity been influenced by Joseph Fletcher's well-known "situational ethics" of the turbulent 1960's? Or is it a product of increasing secularization, which often severely separates religion from moral questions?

This pragmatic and situational approach to morality often applies to their sexual lives, as in the recent "hook-up" culture on many campuses where one can engage in "making out," oral sex or intercourse without any personal commitment. Here, the situation is morally neutral. If all goes well, no problem. If someone gets hurt (often the female), lessons are learned and participants move on.

For many Catholic and mainline Protestant young adults, what little they know about their churches' teachings on sexual morality is simply not relevant to them. They do know that in general religious teaching opposes sex outside of marriage and living together, but they see this position as outdated, written for another time in the foggy history of the past. Donna Freitas, who has done a recent study of sex on college campuses, says "When I set out to test the relationship between sex and the soul among American college students, I had no idea how marginal an influence religion has become in sexual matters among students. Evangelicals aside, most students live their sexual live as if they are religiously unaffiliated—as if their religious and spiritual commitments simply do not matter."[18]

Influence of Post-modernism on the Emerging Adult

The so-called post-modern culture seems to have deeply affected young adults' approach to religion. This is a culture which places little value on tradition and which "deconstructs" religious narratives and symbols, often leaving them empty of meaning. Post-modern youth seem to have taken the approach to a new level in that they aren't even interested in de-constructing past narratives and symbols, and they often simply discount them altogether. Often, these young adults are "now" people, "reality show" fans, with little interest for myth-making or the past. As one student put it, "Reading religious stories is like reading Harry Potter. It can be entertaining, but has little use for my everyday life."

This attitude surely puts the value of religious tradition in serious jeopardy. It can empty sacred religious myths of their invaluable ageless wisdom and reduce them to curious fairy tales. It can reduce treasured religious traditions that have affected human lives for millennia to irrelevant museum artifacts.

Differentiated Religious Vocabulary

In addition to a shift in attitude toward moral matters, young adults have developed new views toward religion, faith and belief, and it is useful to distinguish between them. Religions are organized movements and communities dedicated to particular traditions. Faith can refer to the content to the religious tradition, but is more properly the relational trust that one puts in God and his revelation. Beliefs are religious doctrines or values, which can be embraced cognitively or personally.

Religion

Recent studies show that there exists a wide range of attitudes toward religion among emerging adults in this country. In evangelical communities, which seriously attend to and nurture their youth, young adults often continue on with their religion through college and beyond. For many Catholics and mainline Protestant emerging adults, it is a different story. Here, religion can take on the image of something archaic and unchanging, something in opposition to the lifestyle they are living. As we have seen, emerging adults are often solidly linked to the present and for them, religion seems to have little relevancy to present concerns. Generally, young adults are hopefully looking forward to the future and religion seems to be largely concerned with what happened in the past and how to preserve it. By its very definition, religion is supposed to link it followers with the divine and present them with many role models of how to lead a good life. Instead, many young people get the impression that religion is more concerned about taking up collections, investigating and judging others, and preserving things that are no longer useful. Many Catholic young adults look at their church's hot-button issues - a married clergy, the ordination of women, living together, accepting gay and lesbian marriage - and simply say "Why not?" They are usually uninformed about all the complications in these controversies and take a common sense approach to them all. Frustrated prelates might say: "If only we could properly educate them in the faith." However, education does not seem to be the issue here. Young people today are of a very progressive generation and see things quite differently from their religious leaders. They have confidence in their own opinions and have a built–in resistance to brain-washing.

Hostility toward religion

Some emerging adults are downright hostile toward religion, such as in the classic objection to the "hypocrite in the parking lot." Some critics say "Yeh, they go to church to show off their piety and then they cut you out and curse at you leaving the church parking lot!" Some have concluded that the church is all about collecting money to build luxurious churches and rectories. Others, especially young Catholics, are appalled by the clergy-child sex-abuse scandal and the cover-ups by the religious hierarchy.

Faith

For many young adults, "faith" connotes being blindly attached to a set of unchangeable and absolute beliefs. In their world of constant change that subjects every idea to the bar of reason, such faith is not very attractive. These young adults are used to having clear evidence of things presented to them as truths, and have no interest in ideas that cannot be proven.

Other young adults view their faith as personal, trusting, relational and evolving. They see faith as commitment to someone or something that pertains to "deep down things." They have learned that faith is linked with love of those around them and hope in their future. Many young people today find the "sacred" in their families, their grandparents, or in their own children. That is where they put their trust, rather than in religion. Some have learned that faith involves the search to understand the unseen and the mysteries of life and death. Some have gone to far-off lands to live in solidarity with the oppressed and the poor to better understand the "deep down things."

Beliefs

Many emerging adults have been taught that beliefs are propositions to which they are to give cognitive assent. They were taught many of these beliefs as young children, which was long before they had sufficient cognition to understand them and long before they could abstract to analyze them. Once the young acquire more advanced cognitive powers, they often begin to see that much of what they have been taught in religion is difficult for them to accept. If they are fortunate enough to take some classes in theology in college, they come to see the context for these beliefs and the wide range of possible interpretations.

In an earlier era, belief was not as much about cognition and blind acceptance. Back then, belief meant "to hold dear," "to love," and "to value highly." From this point of view, believing is not blind rational acceptance of a set of propositions. Rather, belief is holding dear and loving the realities behind these propositions, awkward as they may be. This form of belief includes the limitations these propositions have in dealing with ultimate and incomprehensible realities.

Many young Christians, especially Evangelicals, hold dear their loving and saving God, Jesus Christ, as well as the members of the faithful communities to which they belong and depend on for support. Many young Christians hold dear their families, children, friends and lovers, all made in the image of God. One of my students, a 19 year-old single mother, told me that it is her baby she believes in—holds dear. That is where she finds the presence of the divine.

Emerging adults are too savvy to think that religions have the last word on truth.

The culture young adults live in accepts evolution and experiences on-going change on all levels. In their world of diverse religions, manifold cultures and a wide range of views on every issue, it is understandable that emerging adults fail to accept absolutes with regard to religious beliefs.

Gender's Impact on Religion

Gender is a key factor that affects the "I" perspective and one's personal identity. In this next section, we will discuss the feminine and masculine gender and their implications for religion.

The Feminine Gender

The late 1960s and 1970s marked a turning point for the woman's movement. This was the time when the so-called "second wave" of the women's movement swept through the United States. (The "first wave" began in the 19th century and focused on equality and obtaining woman's right to vote, which was recognized in the US in 1920). Books such as *The Feminine Mystique*, by Betty Friedan, challenged many of the traditional images and roles of women. Organizations such as the National Organization for Women were formed to gain equality for women, and many women made their voices heard during this period. They participated in the demonstrations against the Vietnam War, disrupting political conventions and even forcing universities to shut down. During this period, the work of scholars like Carol Gilligan and Nancy Chodorow made ground-breaking observations on women's identity. [19]

Gilligan's studies reveal several unique characteristics of women that still hold in today's understanding of the feminine. First, she points out that women usually describe their identity in terms of intimacy and relationship. As infants, female identity is usually shaped by identification with the mother and carries a responsibility to nurture, care for, show kindness, avoid hurting.[20] This often puts females deeply in touch with their emotions and with the affective dimension of relationships. Young men often find this affectivity difficult to understand and can become frustrated when their girlfriends closely monitor their relationship and want to be in touch regularly. This can result in a stand-off, where the male says "What does she want from me?" and the female answers, "He just doesn't get it." Parents can also be puzzled by the affectivity of their daughters and can be disturbed by the "drama" in their daughters' lives.

Gilligan's second key observation centers on relational errors that can be made by males and females. She maintains that men tend to find their identity from inside themselves. This can give men a certain arrogance and overconfidence in their views about themselves as well as about women. Women, on the other hand, often derive their identity from those outside themselves. This can result in self-doubt, a reluctance to find their own voice, and possibly too much dependence on males and cultures dominated by the male perspective.

This dynamic can result in two relational errors. One is "for men to think that if they know themselves... they will also know women" and the other is "for women to think that if only they know others, they will come to know themselves."[21] In this scenario, neither men nor women are really in touch with authentic feminine identity or experiences. As a result, men often feel disconnected from women, while women can feel dissociated from themselves.[22]

For several years, the Catholic hierarchy has been investigating Catholic nuns in the United States. The prelates understand themselves to be rule-makers and truth teachers and expect the Sisters, whom they view as unequal, to be compliant, subservient and obedient. Many of the nuns, on the other hand, have found their own voice and their feminine identity as equal disciples, servants of the poor and critical thinkers. Thus, the prelates feel disconnected from the nuns whom they perceive as "radical feminists" and "dissenters." The Sisters are at a critical point where they either enter self-doubt and concede to further investigations or insist on preserving their hard-won self-identity.

The so-called "third wave" of feminism, which began in the 1990s, seems to be not so much of a movement as it is a new awareness of the diversity of the experiences of women. Many women have found their own voices, but in the process have discovered that their voices differ, ranging from Black Womanists and Latina Mujeristas, to women in various parts of Africa, Asia and other parts of the world. Women garner their experiences now from many different cultural, religious and socio-economic backgrounds. In addition, there are as many different feminine experiences as there are individual women. In other words, there is no "one-size fits all" in the women's movements. There is now a new awareness that equality must not only honor the genuine differences between women and men, it must also recognize the differences among women themselves. As Luce Irigaray puts it, "I am a woman; a woman who favors difference, even though I understand that equality can, and sometimes must, come first in order that the differences can be seen for what they really are. To be supportive, for example, of the difference between man and woman cannot be interpreted as a return to a hierarchical situation; instead, we have come to a new era, in which it is recognized that the irreducible core of community is to be found between a man and a woman who respect each other in their differences."[23]

In the post-modern age, it becomes increasingly difficult to hold on to classical definitions of the feminine. Nor is it still fashionable to identify the enemy as patriarchy. Many younger women do not want the path to equality to be conflictual or alienating. They would rather encourage each woman to solidify her own identity and experience as a woman, and to achieve this without denigrating men. Nancy Chodorow maintains that sorting out the feminine must "begin from experience, a freedom to challenge, a view that knowledge is perspectivial and embedded in power, and an awareness of the multiple constituents of individual genders and sexualities.[24]

There are many religious implications attached to women discovering their own identities rather than accepting identities thrust on them by tradition or culture. First of all, since the feminine identity is often characterized by intimacy and relationships, women are specially qualified to build community within religions, to reach out to the needs in the community and to be compassionately concerned about those who are oppressed and neglected. As Jean Donovan, a lay missionary who was killed for her work with the refugees in El Salvador, wrote to a friend: "Several times I have decided to leave El Salvadore. I almost could except for the children, the poor, bruised victims of this insanity. Who would care for them? Whose heart could be so staunch as to favor the reasonable thing in a sea of their tears and loneliness? Not mine, dear friend, not mine."[25] Women are specially qualified to develop an "ethics of care" in their religious communities and to be active servant-leaders in the areas of peace and justice.[26] Moreover, women are often gifted to lead others in the spiritual life as well as in prayer. It might be said that "Women are the shapers of the soul. Their nurturing, healing, creative and compassionate abilities promote transformation. Women's relational natures ignite changes in the soul at both individual and collective levels."[27]

The Catholic Asian bishops, who have now become a significant voice in the Catholic Church, are convinced that for a renewed church to come about, both men and women must be empowered and viewed as sharing in "the freedom of the children of God."[28]

Johanna Stuckey proposes a number of reasons why feminine spirituality should be recognized. First, spirituality is central to women's lives, offering a treasure of multiple and diverse approaches. Second, feminine approaches to spirituality can offer much needed correctives to contemporary political and economic perspectives; a way to sustain equality within religious traditions. Third, the richness and the diversity among the spiritualities of women offer much to world religions.[29]

The Masculine Gender

Gilligan's studies also examine the masculine identity. Her studies suggest that males begin their identification by separating from the identity of the mother, rather than bonding with it as females do. Men often follow an ideal of masculinity that encourages men to be "independent, self-sufficient, rational, active, controlling, emotionally restrictive and competitive."[30] Gilligan explains that the male identity is often "clearer more direct, more distinct and sharp-edged."[31] Men are often aggressive and goal-driven. They frequently have only a narrow circle of personal friends and are not that close with many other males. Men are often not given to permanent attachment and can be isolated, even to the point of indifference. [32] Their separateness can turn into arrogance or haughtiness. To a woman hurt by them, men can appear to be unconcerned, even uncaring, while in truth they might simply be having difficulty dealing with feelings.

Many men are "without fathers," meaning that they are over-mothered or their fathers did not have time for them or deserted them.[33] Although this trend seems to be changing, when fathers of the past were in the home they were often silent figures who came home tired and said little to the family. Many men comment that they really don't know their fathers nearly as well as they do their mothers. Rohr says that this lack of fathering can have an unhealthy effect on both genders. It can produce "boys who never grow up and want to marry mothers, and girls who want securing and affirming daddies instead of risk-taking partners. Neither gender is ready for the work and adventure of a full life."[34] From the more positive side, there are many fathers today who are seriously attempting to nurture their children and do their share of parenting.[35] This shift in gender roles in families will no doubt have deep effects on the way men and women will live their lives in the future.

It appears that the culture in the United States is often not healthy for males, especially minority males. Among minority males, there is a marked level of drug abuse, alcoholism, violence, depression and suicide. Over 90% of those in prison are males, males live an average of seven years less than women, and over 80% of suicides are men.[36] Men seem to be falling behind in the work force; they are beginning to make less than women, and are now outnumbered and often outscored by women in colleges. 70% of the valedictorian addresses are being given by women. Thus, some researchers question whether or not many men in this country are losing the initiative, drive and toughness to succeed.[37] Other researchers observe that there are still many young men of high energy and good abilities who are filled with hope and idealism, yet at the same time need mentoring and solid role models if they are to succeed. Others observe that many young men, and often young women as well, are being raised in comfort, are privileged, and are having little demanded of them. There seems to be a new sense of "deserved entitlement" among young adults that seems to come in part from being told: "you are special, "good job," "you are #1," when in fact they may have done little to deserve such affirmation. In addition, education seems to have been "dumbed downed" by "teaching for the test," grade inflation, and passing on students who have not merited it. The fact that the United States is ranked 28th in the world for education has to say something about the utter wrongness of our approach. Many people ask: "Are we producing a work force that does not have the motivation to be competitive with world markets?"

Since religion is often associated with interiority, connectedness, emotion, relationship with God and community, it is no wonder that many young men tend to keep their distance. Historically, we are faced with the irony that most religions have been inspired, organized and led by men, but have had more enthusiastic participation by women! Catholicism is a classic example: its founder was a man; its hierarchy and priests are celibate men; its doctrines, laws, and until recently, its theology has been written by men.

Despite that, the followers most devoted to the services are often women, and most of the church work (some say 80%) is done by women!

Spiritual, Not Religious

Studies of young college men indicate that while many of them are not affiliated with any religion, the majority of them are interested in spirituality. Many have moved from being in a church to a more independent and private search for the beliefs and values that are relevant to their lives. Their spiritual quest is often for meaning, purpose in their work and social milieu, concern for living good and authentic lives, and getting in touch with their "best selves.[38] Some have found it useful to belong to all-male groups on campus, where they are more free to examine their male identity among peers and can get in touch with their "softer side" in a safe environment. We will discuss this issue of being "spiritual but not religious" in chapter 7.

Megachurches

As mentioned earlier, some young males are being drawn to the megachurches, which do not have enforced doctrines or rigid authority, are social and informal, and discuss topics relevant to young adults. Often, these churches provide inspiring models and opportunities for social service as well as small group experiences wherein relevant topics are discussed.

In the past four decades, women have done much to reclaim their voice, redefine their self images, and make headway towards equality in what has traditionally been a "man's world" with "male-dominate" religions. The next challenge is for men to adjust to these seismic shifts and make serious efforts to find authentic voices and self-images so that than can comfortably fit into this new world where new religious movements are emerging.

The Enneagram Personality Types

The Enneagram has become increasingly popular as a tool for understanding personality types. Enneagram ("any a gram") comes from two Greek words, Ennea (nine) and gram (drawing). This refers to a drawing with nine points: the nine types of personality. The origins of the Enneagram are not clearly known, largely because it appears to have been handed down orally. We do know that it was brought to the West from Afghanistan by an Armenian mystic, George Gurdjieff (1870-1949) in the early 20th century. He taught that tradition had levels of meanings but he did not apply it to nine personality types.[39] The Enneagram was formulated into a map of inner experience by a Bolivian mystic, Oscar Ichazo, in Chile in the early 1970s. One of Ichazo's students, Claudio Naranjo, then brought it to the United States. Naranjo was a psychiatrist and worked intensely on the Enneagram with a group in Berkeley, California to integrate the map with Gestalt therapy, the type psychology of Karen Horney, and many of the traditions from the Eastern religions. The models worked out at that time have been largely used for both psychological and spiritual efforts to this day. Several American Jesuits, including Fr. Robert Ochs, have been instrumental in integrating the Enneagram into spiritual direction, and a Franciscan, Fr. Richard Rohr, has been influential in popularizing the model with Catholics and others.

From the outset, it should be noted that the Enneagram is not for the purpose of mechanically classifying people or pigeonholing them with some "number" or "type." Rather, the Enneagram is a means for helping us understand ourselves and others. It is a sophisticated tool that can help us understand how we have constructed our self-image early on through the many inner and outer influences around us. It can help us to better understand our strengths as well as our weaknesses. It can assist us in growing and transforming ourselves; in discovering our true selves. As Richard Rohr points out, "The Enneagram can help us to purify our self-perception, to become unsparingly honest toward ourselves, and to discern better and better when we are hearing only our inner voices and impressions and are prisoner of our prejudices—and when we are capable of being open to what is new."[40]

The Enneagram looks into the frameworks we build when we are young, which establishes patterns of behavior. These patterns are connected to our abilities and to our family and cultural background. Our self-image usually consists of roles we play, masks we wear, names that we have been called, inner tapes that tell us what to do. Knowing our type enables us to understand this framework and be able to move on to further self-development. It can help us better understand our outer shell so that we can move inward to transform our true inner selves. That is why it is important that each interested person works to select his or her own type and not allow others to impose a given type on them.

In the following section, we will describe the nine types and how each relates to religions. We ask you to read them all and try in a very preliminary way try to discern which type best describes you. If you want to work more to discover your type, you can consult the book *The Essential Enneagram* or the website Free Enneagram Personality Test (similarminds.com/test.html).

#1 The Perfectionist

Perfectionists are highly principled, conscientious persons who live up to high ideals. They are ethical, law-abiding, fair and self-disciplined. ONES are dutiful and responsible, punctual and serious (they don't usually like to tell jokes). They have a puritanical bent and can be hard on themselves and others. They can also get angry with themselves and others for not being perfect. ONES like to have things orderly and neat, and can be anxious when things are out of order. Perfectionists have a difficult time coping with wrongness or incorrectness in themselves or others. They often react strongly to any kind of negative feedback regarding themselves or what they have done wrong, yet they often judge themselves rather harshly. They tend to be uncomfortable with complainers and often encourage others to look at the positive side of things. ONES try hard to make things better for others because they have a deep sense of right and wrong, perfection and imperfection. Courtesy and correctness are high values for perfectionists. They are idealists and often tend to correct others, and can even in the extreme be crusaders or zealots. This can also lead them to be controlling and judgmental. At the same time, ones can be open to self-hatred, which can lead them to performing out of their dark side and behaving untypically immoral (e.g. parents or even priests who abuse children). Their impatience with criticism or clutter can lead them into anger, tirades and annoyance with others.

With regard to religion, perfectionists can often feel that God is on their side as they crusade for perfection and can even be led to persecute those who are in error or sin. They sometimes prefer a church that is legalistic and keeps them in line. They have the potential to be "inquisitors" and persecute people that they perceive to be heretical or non-conformists. At times, Vatican declarations or investigations seem to arise out of perfectionist types. Religious perfectionists can be very saintly in their lives, but they can also repress their natural desires and become extremists. The ancient concern for "uncleanness" in the Jewish tradition seems to come from these types. Certain foods were considered to be unclean, women were thought to be unclean because of menstruation, and lepers and the diseased were segregated for their contamination. Perfectionists can be open, honest and truthful, or in the other extreme can be rigid, greedy and tight-lipped. They have little tolerance for chaos (which makes it difficult for them to visit a country like India!) and their need to be correct can lead them to great efficiency and competency. Or, it can lead them to scrupulosity and obsessive behavior. They can relate well to an orderly and good God, but they struggle with the question of why bad things happen to good people. They can be aligned with a Church that is rigid and enforcing, or they can be turned off by how the harmony and order of the community is disturbed by the injustice and oppression that can be caused by such a church.

ONES are usually loving, prefer a loving God, are close to nature and can find God in nature as well as in beautiful music. They like orderly, well-planned liturgies and can be impatient with poorly prepared and rambling sermons.

#2 The Helper

Helpers are sensitive, nurturing and concerned about the needs of others. The helper is loving, positive, empathetic, generous, and caring. They can also be too demonstrative, overly solicitous and possessive. They like you to be interested in them, to make them feel special and be appreciative. They don't take criticism well. TWOS can be easily hurt, dependent, and overly involved in helping others. They need to give more attention to themselves and often have to learn to say no. They do not take snubs well or lack of gratitude. TWOS often have many friends, but can have low self-esteem and feel drained from helping. They often don't trust the way things are going and micromanage to make things happen. TWOS are often drawn to some special other that they hope will complete them and rescue them. Often they are pleasers and want above all to be loved. If things don't work out as expected, they might feel rejected or devalued. TWOS often divide people into those that are superior or inferior to them. They can be submissive to those who are superior and haughty towards the inferior. They often feel guilt for not living up to what others expect of them. Their self-sacrifice can lead them to think of themselves as martyrs. Their emotions can be dramatic and at times they are given to crying. They often have to hide their neediness and feelings of being deprived or abused.

TWOS are invaluable in campus ministry or parish activities. They are good organizers, generous with their time and very good at serving others. (But they need to be appreciated!) Women TWOS, of which there are many in parish work, give tirelessly of their time in the service and ministries of the parish. At the same time, many of them do not feel that the Church recognizes them or considers them equal to men. Many TWO women would like to serve as deacons or priests in the Catholic Church and have some say in their churches, but this is firmly not allowed. Some today are actually being ordained "Roman Catholic Women Priests" and are willing to endure excommunication for being ordained.

Sometimes TWOS are so efficient and capable that they really don't feel a need for God. At times it seems that "God needs them."[41] Many TWOs struggle to be humble and to admit that they need God to assist them in their efforts. They have to struggle with helping others so much that they don't have time to pray. A TWO who seemed to acquire a balance in this regard was Mother Teresa, who tirelessly served others and yet was always dedicated to prayer.

#3 The Achiever

Achievers are team-players, good at being "company people," getting things done and being successful. They are people of high energy and self-assurance who like to set and accomplish goals. They are very productive and seek to be successful. They are good networkers and get along with people easily. They are always busy and finish the jobs they undertake. At the same time, they expect recognition for what they do. Often, they do not receive due praise because they seem so confident and self-assured. Unlike the TWO who asks, "Do they like me?" the THREE asks "How am I doing?" and requires recognition. THREES don't talk a great deal about their personal lives or the job. They need their quiet time, as well as time for socializing, sports activities and fun. They are never bored because they are always finding things to do. THREES present themselves well, like praise, are playful, responsible, and well regarded. They can be overly competitive and at times vain, self-centered and moody. They can be defensive and curt, especially when they become exhausted from being "on." THREES are usually neat and cool, and they like to keep their bodies in good shape.

THREES are attracted to religions and churches that are relevant and contemporary. Many young THREES move away from the Catholic Church, seeing it as slow-moving, out of touch and concerned with issues that are irrelevant to the young. For them, the Church may not project youth, vigor or energy. They see that the bishops, priests and sisters are for the most part elderly and out-of-touch with their concerns. Thus, they are often drawn to megachurches that use technology, youthful leaders in blue jeans, and concern for personal and social issues.

It is said that THREEs need to step back and learn to pray and meditate. They are often so busy being successful that they neglect dealing with their inner life. Many of them find that serving the poor and less fortunate gives more balance to their lives.[42] Dorothy Day might be an example of a THREE because she was a strong, efficient and extremely talented woman, who found her true self in prayer and in serving the homeless and the poor. She founded the Catholic Worker Movement.

#4 The Romantic

Romantics are warm, empathic personalities who have very sensitive feelings. They are compassionate, introspective, intuitive searchers. FOURS can appear cheerful, but there is a tragic dimension to their inner selves. FOURS look for approval and try to stand out and be attractive, but their efforts can make them appear a bit too vivacious or even exotic. They sometimes wear odd or eccentric clothes and have unique eating habits.[43] They at times feel abandoned and alone and this might cause them to withdraw into themselves for periods of time. FOURS long for relationships but often have difficulty establishing lasting relationships. FOURS are idealistic and can easily be moved by the sufferings of others. They sincerely reach out to help others, but are often too preoccupied by their own hurts to effectively help others.

FOURS have the gift of intuition and can be visionaries about the future, but can have difficulty living in the present. They expect too much of life and often long for what others have and they don't. For FOURS, the grass is always greener on the other side. They can also envy what others have.

At times, they can live in the idealized past, pining over their loss of a better time. They may have hopes for the future, but have difficulty with the gloomy present. Romantics love beauty and long to be one with nature. They have good taste for art and music and are often good writers who can express themselves better and inspire others in the written word.

FOURS often feel cut off from God and might be concerned about eternal punishment. At times, they have difficulty believing that they are loved by God and sometimes live in fear of His wrath. They long for closeness to God but often feel disconnected. FOURS search for God in nature, art, and music. They love beautiful liturgical ritual and can be mesmerized by old cathedrals. They can feel misunderstood or alienated by the Church. FOURS have a need for meditation to explore their true inner selves and learn to affirm themselves. If FOURS are to establish an adult relationship with God, they need to see themselves as unique, but also as sharing the commonality of other children of God rather than being cut off from them. They need to know that beauty and art need not be substitutes for God, but can be paths to the Divine.[44]

Thomas Merton seems to have been a FOUR. His parents were artists and after their deaths he wandered Europe, fathered a child at Cambridge, and partied in New York. After his conversion, Merton went off to a monastery to search for his true self. After years of prayer and an amazing production of writing, Merton seems to have come in touch with his authentic inner self.

#5 The Observer

FIVES are called observers because they would prefer to study a situation rather than participate. They can appear cool or detached about the fray.

FIVES don't like small talk and prefer the big picture rather than the details. Observers are good listeners and often have the feeling of being empty and a need to be filled up with knowledge. They can be takers rather than givers. FIVES are introverted and curious, and they like to spend lots of time on their own. They are driven to know and understand and they approach knowledge analytically and objectively. FIVES like to think things through before taking action. They often consider themselves intellectually superior.[45] Some of the great philosophers have been FIVES: Aquinas, Descartes, Camus. It is said that the great scientists like Albert Einstein and Stephan Hawking are FIVES. FIVES also make good trainers and counselors.

FIVES are shy about expressing their feelings and find it difficult to ask for help. They don't like noisy or fussy situations. They can make good friends provided you don't expect them to take the initiative or be completely present to the relationship. Observers need their space and can be stingy with their time as well as with their possessions, afraid of losing what little they have. At times they can stock things up or even be hoarders. They can procrastinate, being reluctant to commit to anything.

FIVES are very perceptive and can appear to be arrogant or negative. They tend to learn from reading rather than doing. Observers don't like conformity but can be sensitive to criticism. They are not team players and they don't like to draw attention to themselves.[46] They can be socially uncomfortable, shy and awkward. FIVES can be self-sufficient and open-minded, but can also be inclined to be negative and withdrawn. They are usually calm in a crisis.

Because of their ability to withdraw, FIVES can be drawn to contemplation and mysticism. They are often called to move beyond knowledge to wisdom, to a deeper understanding of God and mystery, and to the realities beyond mere knowledge.[47] They need to move beyond isolation into action, beyond self-sufficiency to dependence on God.[48] They need to reach out more to others and give of themselves. FIVES can get lost in the theory of religion and cognitive beliefs and never get down to the practice.

ENNEAGRAM TYPES		
#	Type	Description
1	Perfectionist	conscientius, law-abiding, orderly, dutiful, self-judging
2	Helper	sensitive, nurturing, meets needs of others, sensitive to criticism, wants to be liked
3	Achiever	team player, competitive, high energy, playful, wants recognition
4	Romantic	warm, empathetic, can be tragic, wants to stand out as attractive, relational, idealistic
5	Observer	cool and detached, shy, distant, non-committal, self-sufficient
6	Questioner	reliable, witty, wants certainty and justice, fights for the oppressed, can be literal and conservative, possible abandonment issues
7	Adventurer	lively, confident, risk-taker, positive, idealist, wants better world, optimist
8	Asserter	powerful, self-confident, defender of weak, warrior, wans credit and appreciation
9	Peace-maker	upbeat, connected, put things off, doesn't like change, represses feelings

#6 The Questioner

The questioners are warm, reliable and witty. They can be far-sighted and bold. They like authority but at the same time can fear it. SIXES want security and sometimes experience fear of uncertainty. They can fear failure and even fear success. They long for certainty. Questioners can have a hard time accepting praise because they are not sure it is sincere. SIXES often follow a God of fear who rewards and punishes. They like a Church that can give them security and certain answers. They like infallible Popes and hierarchical structures. The Catholic Church today often seems to be split between Fives who want a conservative Church and others who want the Church to be liberal and more flexible. SIXES can often be drawn to fundamentalism in religion and to the literal meaning of scripture. If their church betrays them, questioners might withdraw for fear of being hurt again. SIXES have abandonment issues. They can give the same infallibility they attribute to religion to science.When organizations are corrupt, SIXES fight for those oppressed by corrupt hierarchies. Oscar Romero is an example of such a type. He took on his Church and government in order to protect the poor and oppressed.

#7 The Adventurer

Adventurers are lively, fun-loving, spontaneous, quick, confident, charming, curious and supremely optimistic. They have lots of energy, always look on the positive side of a situation, and often want to contribute to make a better world. SEVENS are risk-takers; they love excitement and travel, sailing, flying, and skiing. They are seldom bored, and are good to themselves, idealistic, at ease with groups, and enjoy travel groups and cruises. SEVENS are forceful in their arguments and say what is on their minds. They have grand visions and, always optimistic, enjoy the present and look forward to the future. SEVENS are generous, idealistic, and they easily forgiving because they don't like to dwell on the negative.

SEVENS can be loud and outrageous. They are playful and love children. It is said that they are "adrenaline addicts."[49] Adventurers don't like people who are weak, boring or whiners. They can have a hard time being compassionate or listening to another's troubles. They can cushion every trouble with a rosy attitude and call every tragedy a blessing in disguise.

SEVENS can get caught up in the idealism of religion and be blind to its corruptions and dark side. They can be dedicated to a Church while being blind to its failures, largely because of their resistance to seeing the dark side of anything. They can avoid the difficult peace and justice issues and bypass the horrendous conditions in the world because these factors are just too hard to look at. They can be so caught up in the joy of religion that they don't see the pathos of other people. SEVENS can avoid the pain of others because it simply demands that they take off their blinders. In the churches, SEVENS would have a very difficult time working "in the trenches" with the poor and downtrodden.

#8 The Asserter

Asserters are powerful, self-confident protectors, especially of the oppressed. They are direct, authoritative and energetic. EIGHTS can also be controlling, insensitive and rebellious. They are usually aggressive and individualistic and do not like to apologize. EIGHTS can get things done and you definitely want them at your side in a conflict. Asserters take delight in verbal sparring and they can be quick witted. EIGHTS can be vulnerable and loving with those they trust, and they will not tolerate a break in trust. They like to be acknowledged, and receive credit, but they don't like flattery. EIGHTS are assertive and sometimes yell and swear, intimidating people when they are just trying to be forceful. They know how to take charge, but are able to delegate. They like to surround themselves with people who appreciate them.

EIGHTS have trouble with authorities that are oppressive or threatening, especially where the defenseless are concerned. They often unmask falsehood and expose hypocrisy. EIGHTS often get opposition from authority, but can thrive on that. They can willingly absorb the hatred against them. Franklin Delano Roosevelt, who seems to have been an EIGHT, once said about his many political enemies: "They are unanimous in their hatred and I welcome their hatred... They have met their master!" Ernest Hemingway and Margaret Thatcher are possibly other examples of EIGHTS.

EIGHTS usually keep abreast of abuses in their churches and can get into trouble with church authorities. Hans Kung is a good Catholic example of an EIGHT. They are powerful representatives of the church's teachings on social justice and can be a force in defending the powerless. There is plenty of EIGHT energy in the liberation theology movement. They can be formidable opponents to the church's positions on moral issues, abuse of women, and homosexuality. On the other hand, when EIGHTS are in power in the church, they can be oppressive and can try to rule through fear and intimidation.

EIGHTS need to integrate action with contemplation. They need to use their power in serving others rather than in controlling others. EIGHTS who are critical of the church have to avoid bitterness in order to be effective in their opposition. They are usually counseled to avoid being alienated from those who disagree with them so that they can take part in constructive dialogue. They need to avoid being cynical about the official church or religion, lest they became alienated. EIGHTS, like all of us, have to realize that they also have their faults and their dark sides.

#9 The Peacemaker

NINES are good-natured and like to connect with others and support their needs. They are relaxed, easy-going and not easily upset. NINES tend to put things off and don't get easily disturbed.

They are pleasant, patient with the faults of others and generous with their time and goods. They like to hang out with family and friends.

NINES don't like change and they don't get easily excited. They tend to repress their feelings and can be indecisive.[50] Peacemakers don't have a lot of self-importance and don't like other people to rock the boat.

NINES accept others without prejudice and thus make good mediators and peacemakers. They tend to be generalists, who do a little of this and a little of that, but often don't master one thing. Peacemakers avoid conflict, but can be stubborn, especially when they think someone is going to take advantage of them. Many NINES are gifted but neglect to bring these gifts forward.

NINES like sermons that are simple and practical, not complex or abstract. They like religion to be relaxed and not dogmatic and they are comfortable with ambiguity in their doctrine. NINES take a long time to consider a ministry but once they are sold they jump in full force. They avoid conflict with their church and back away from dogmatism or threats. NINES can be very effective in work for social justice once they are convinced about a cause. They can also be fervently committed to work for peace. NINES can be strongly devoted to loving God and others once they are sure they are loved. It is said that the much-loved Pope of Vatican II, John XXIII, was a NINE. If churches can awaken their NINES to the importance of issues and give them motivation, they will find the NINES an invaluable resource.[51]

The Enneagram can be an invaluable tool for helping us understand who we are, what we can be, and how we can better relate to and experience religion and spirituality for ourselves and others. Do some research to discover your own type and how it affects your relationships and spiritual practice.

The Myers-Briggs Type Indicator

Another useful tool for understanding our personality as well as our attitudes with regard religion is The Myers-Briggs. It is named after Katherine Briggs (1875-1968) and her daughter Isabel (1897-1980) who used Carl Jung's book *Psychological Types* (1923) in their effort to understand personality profiles. In 1975, their work was published and has since become the most widely used personality assessment in the world today.

This instrument is based on Jung's observation that we are born with innate preferences and "that these affect the ways in which we perceive the world around us, take in information from the world, process it, and develop our responses to it - our actions and behavior."[52]

Again, we must note that the purpose here is not to put people in boxes. The instrument recognizes the complexity and individuality of human persons. At the same time, it offers a tool which can help us better understand who we are as people, as well as how we relate to religion. It also should be pointed out, as in the case of the Enneagram, no type is better than another. Each has its own strengths to develop and weaknesses to overcome. Though we may have one preference over another, we all have a blend of all the preferences.

The Myers-Briggs holds that we are born with a preference for four of eight personality traits: extravert or introvert, sensing or intuition, thinking or feeling, judging or perceiving. If someone prefers extroversion, intuition, thinking and judging, they are referred to as ENTJ. In total, there are 16 possible combinations or personality types. We don't have space to consider all the types, so we limit our consideration to the eight individual preferences. See which preferences best apply to you and remember that there is a wide range within each category. You might want to take a test online to acquaint you in a preliminary way with this tool. (http://www.humanmetrics.com/cgi-win/jtypes2.asp)

MYERS-BRIGGS PERSONALITY TYPES		
Dichotomy	Type	Description
Attitudes	Extravert	outgoing, friendly, stimulated by people, acts first then thinks, can think while talking
Attitudes	Introvert	quiet, reflective, thinks then acts, drained by people, needs to think before arguing
Judging	Sensate	relies on senses for information, practical, appreciates details, enjoys the experiential
Judging	Intuitive	works through intuition, big picture, vision
Perceiving	Thinker	logic, reason, facts, problem-solver, wants fairness and justice
Perceiving	Feeler	works out of heart and emotion, from inside and in-depth, likes praise
Lifestyle	Judging	likes structure and efficiency, planners, organized, makes lists, needs systems
Lifestyle	Perceptive	creative, innovative, not concerned with order or being on-time, informal

1. Extraverts

Extraverts are outgoing, comfortable with people, and they enjoy being on stage - they draw energy from being with others. Teachers are often extraverts. Extraverts enjoy a wide variety of experiences and they prefer talking their way to conclusions. When it comes to things to do, extraverts act first and think later. Extraverts are not hesitant to speak about themselves and they usually have many friends. Successful presidential candidates need strong extroversion energy.

Catholic Extraverts rejoiced when Vatican II described the Church as "the people of God." They like to belong, participate, share and be part of the action. They enjoy a vital communal liturgy where people participate and socialize before and after. They probably would avoid the quiet, low-key services. Extraverts enjoy participating in church programs and can usually be counted on to do the social planning. When service projects are suggested, extraverts often jump in to be of help without second thought. They like clergy who are outgoing and friendly, and they enjoy challenging sermons that motivate them toward some action. They often choose to be readers at the service, to teach religious education or to be leaders of renewal groups.

Extraverted Buddhists, like the Dalai Lama and Thich Nhat Hahn, value their quiet time and meditation, but they want to see Buddhists engaged in peacemaking and social issues. Another possible extraverted leader, Mahatma Gandhi, while he treasured his quiet time living on an ashram, dedicated himself to liberating his people from oppressive British colonialism. Rabbi Abraham Heschel, a serious scholar and teacher, marched alongside Martin Luther King Jr. for the civil rights of Blacks.

2. Introverts

Introverts are quiet and reflective people, so they need their space and their quiet time. They may like to party, but groups drain the energy from them. They find it difficult to speak in public or to be on stage and if they do these activities, they need time and space to recover their energy. Introverts have to do a lot of thinking before they are ready to talk. They are not good at "talking off the top of their heads." They also think things through before they act so they are known for their prudence. Introverts are slow to talk about themselves, preferring to speak about others that they care for when they are among a small intimate group of friends.

Christian Introverts don't like church officials who are pushy and dominating. They simply remove themselves out of range of such individuals.

They can be very effective in church ministries, but usually work behind the scenes and are low key. Introverts might prefer the quiet liturgy where there is a more silence and time for reflection. They would be uncomfortable with loud, boisterous "hell and brimstone" sermons. Introverts might think twice about going to large church gatherings or demonstrations, not because they aren't interested but because such attendance would take such a toll on them.

Introverted Hindus might prefer silently reflecting before the figure of a god or goddess in the Temple to the lively singing and dancing in a ceremony. Introverted Buddhists might be more inclined to silence and meditation in the forest to being engaged in social issues. The introverted Jew might prefer the quiet repentance of Yom Kippur to the elaborate costumes for the celebration of Purim. The introverted Muslim would be utterly drained joining 2 million Muslims for the Hajj to Mecca.

3. Sensates

These personalities rely on their senses of sight, hearing, touch, taste and smell to take in information. They like to work with blocks of information, one at a time. They are very practical people who are concerned about what is going on around them, so they would rather experience something than think about it. "Seeing is believing" is their motto. Maybe Doubting Thomas was a sensate! They are careful about details and facts and they work systematically and methodically. They are good at color and detail when looking at a painting.

Sensates would be good at planning or decorating for important feasts and would be good at designing colorful ceremonies. Sensates have a closeness to nature and would be helpful in creating programs connecting ecology and faith. They are good at details and can be counted on to carefully organize church events.

Sensates are good at the "now" and they want religion be relevant to the needs of today. They are usually activists. "Just do it!" might be their motto. By the same token, in the midst of the action, sensates always want to "take time to smell the roses." Sensates can experience the presence of God in the world and want to be part of the creative process.52 They are aware of their bodies and are usually adept at ceremonial dance. Catholic sensates like the "smells and bells:" holding the palm, feeling the ashes on their forehead and the oil on their hands, the washing of the feet on Holy Thursday. They like devotions and moving hymns.

The sensate Muslim enjoys the physical activities of standing, kneeling and bowing at prayer in the mosque. He or she would delight in the melodious sound of the Qur'an being chanted in Arabic or the frequent call to prayer by the muezzin from the minaret at the prescribed times of day. One would think that the Taj Mahal was designed by a sensate! Sensate Sufis enjoy colorful ceremonies and the Whirling Dervishes seem to be sensates, as they are able to move into mystical contemplation through dance.

4. Intuitives

These personalities work through their intuition, which is direct perception independent of reasoning, a keen and quick insight and an immediate apprehension. They work on hunches, using imagination. They prefer thoughts to actions. Intuitives are concerned with the big picture, but can miss details.

Intuitives are comfortable with a God who is wrapped in mystery. They are comfortable with images of God, and can easily imagine God as Force, Power, Energy, or as a reality beyond imagination. They are interested in the "big picture" so they can imagine creation, evolution, the past and the future. One would think that many of the prophetic individuals in religions have been intuitives.

Christian Intuitives are visionaries and are good at seeing where the church or parish is now and where it can go in the future. One must think that there were some intuitives present at Vatican II when the Church in the Modern World was written. They are good at thinking of ways in which the church, either local or global can serve the world. Intuitives are comfortable reading scripture in an imaginative way. They are seldom literalists or fundamentalists.

An intuitive Muslim can break out of the fundamentalism, that is locked in the past and see the relevance of the Qur'an today. They can have vision enough to see the value of other religions, the peace mission of Islam and the need to attend to women's rights. Certainly, Rumi, the renowned Sufi poet of the 13th century was intuitive and could envision the connection of nature with the human spirit. Tawakkul Karman, a Muslim woman activist, won the Nobel Peace Prize in 2011 for her revolutionary work for her country of Yemen. Tawakkul provided a vision of freedom and human rights for her people. Archbishop Desmond Tutu provided a similar vision of freedom and justice for his people in South Africa and was awarded the Nobel Peace Prize of 1984. Aung San Suu Kyi, the Buddhist woman leader in Burma who won the 1991 Nobel Peace Prize, spent many years under house arrest for her vision of freedom for her country. She has now prevailed and was elected to leadership in 2012. These are intuitives!

Quakers seem to have the intuitive spirit and have historically been ahead of their time in their opposition to slavery and war.

5. Thinkers

These people are reasoners, and are logical and precise. They approach problems rationally. Thinkers analyze all the facts and work through problems systematically. They are objective, not too concerned with the personal, and they have good powers of critical thinking.[53] Fairness and justice is their goal rather than harmony.

The thinking energy is apparent in the Catholic Church in the way it values organized doctrines. Its beliefs are often embraced cognitively rather than through the heart. Many theologians are thinkers and spend their lives looking into the history and interpretations of doctrines. Religious historians tend to be thinkers and are dedicated to organizing and interpreting the past. Thinkers like well-organized sermons and can be angered when sermons are ill-prepared, rambling or vague. They might be comfortable with ordered meditations, but uncomfortable with contemplation or centering prayer.

Many Orthodox Jews tend to be thinkers in that they interpret the Torah and Talmud literally. They are legalistic and precise in their following of traditional prescripts. Reform Jews are much more open in their interpretation and practice of the tradition. Many Muslims like the strict organization of Shariah law and the structure of the Pillars of Islam.

6. Feelers

Feelers act primarily out of their heart and emotions. They are very concerned about the feelings of others and are compassionate and empathetic. They value beauty and peace. Feelers are good at seeing things from the inside and considering them in depth. Feelers need recognition and praise for what they do, and they do not like criticism.

Christian Feelers are often attracted to church art, architecture, moving sermons and celebrations. They often minister to the homeless, sick and poor. The St. Vincent de Paul Society and the Salvation Army often attract people who are feelers.

Feelers can become distraught when there is conflict or disruption in their religious community. They like their religious experience to be harmonious and peaceful. The divisions in religions, whether it be Sunni and Shia, Orthodox and Reform Jews or liberal and conservative Catholics can make feelers quite uncomfortable and even drive them away.

7. Judgers

Those with this preference like structure and efficiency. "What is the plan?' they say and they want to get started on a project as soon as it is brought up. They make lists and follow them, value quick decision-making and want clear structures and well-run organizations. Judgers are punctual and like to set the time and the place for meetings. Judgers like structures, hierarchies, and systems. They value order and precise rules and regulations.

Catholic judgers are perfectly at home with the structures and systems in their church. They like the doctrines to be lined up neatly, the moral precepts to be clear and enforced. They oppose those who rock the boat with controversies over birth control, homosexuality or the ordination of women. "If they don't like the way the Church does things, why don't they just get out," is the position of many judgers. Nevertheless, when systems become unjust or corrupted, judgers become disillusioned and critical.

Muslim judgers want the Qur'an to be interpreted clearly and they want to know just what they have to do to be a good Muslim. Those who embrace a strict application of Shariah law in countries like Saudi Arabia and Iran exhibit the judger energy.

Orthodox Jews seem to have their share of judgers. They want the Torah to be consistently and strictly followed. If there are doubts about a situation, they want their learned rabbis to consult the Talmud. Theravada Buddhists want the ancient teachings of the Buddha to be followed. They avoid the "innovations" of the Mahayana Buddhists and resist such modern movements as the ordination of nuns.

8. Perceivers

This preference is not so concerned with order or with being on time. Perceivers are creative thinkers and thrive on new ideas. They don't make lists. They often pile things around and can have a difficult time finding things; they don't relate well to systems and rigid organizations with a hierarchy of chain of command. They often have a difficult time in the military since they like matters to be informal and casual, with common sense prevailing. They are not legalistic and have little concern about keeping rules carefully. They can easily change their minds and are good at improvising.

Christian perceivers are comfortable with informal home services that are spontaneous and not well-planned. They are put off when their churches become uptight or rigid and begin threatening to investigate or expel members.

Quakers seem to have the perceiver energy in their communities. Their services are spontaneous, silent and unstructured.

Buddhist tradition moves them to be in touch with their own suffering as well as the suffering of others. Their meditations prepare them to alleviate the suffering of others through loving kindness and compassion.

The Myers-Briggs Inventory can help us understand our innate preferences and how they shape our lives. It can assist us in understanding the choices of others with more compassion and insight. As we have seen, it can also be a tool to help us appreciate our own religious/spiritual tendencies as well as those of others.

Summary

The "I" is the subjective personal participator in religion. As we have seen, the more one knows about the self, the better one can choose to participate authentically in religion. An understanding of the stages of human development as well as the stages of faith and morals can help us better understand how people relate to religion differently at various times in their lives. Insights into gender can assist in understanding the dynamics of religious response to celebration, closeness in community and approaches to religious service. As we have also seen, comprehension of the variety of personality types can assist in comprehending both the attractions as well as the tensions with regard to religious participation.

◻◀ VIDEOS ONLINE

Erik Erikson
> https://www.youtube.com/watch?v=PsHXIPyG6yI
> http://www.youtube.com/user/ADLNational?v=3KyvlMJefR4

The Stages of Faith Development in Young Adults
> https://www.youtube.com/watch?v=f9QXMDdK1fU

Dr. Kohlberg's Theory of Moral Development
> https://www.youtube.com/watch?v=O7pQJ0ptjk0

Emerging Adults: *Clark University Prof. Jeffrey Arnett speaks about*

Emerging Adulthood
https://www.youtube.com/watch?v=n9Gzp0nIR9E

Carol Gilligan on '*In A Different Voice*'
https://www.youtube.com/watch?v=mG3_ZP6Drn0

The Feminine: *Awakening the Feminine Heart* Chameli Ardagh.
https://www.youtube.com/watch?v=tXJAj-JwDCQ

The 9 Enneagram Types at a Party
https://www.youtube.com/watch?v=ONUGotSc2nA

Myers Briggs: *Discover Your Personality Type*
https://www.youtube.com/watch?v=WQoOqQiVzwQ

NOTES

1. For Wilbur, all religions have attempted to reveal the ultimate secret: "namely that fully enlightened and ever-present Divine awareness is not hard to find but impossible to avoid." Ken Wilbur, *Integral Spirituality: A Startling New Role of Religion in the Modern and Postmodern World* (Boston: Integral Books, 2006), 208.

2. James W. Fowler, *Becoming Adult, Becoming Christian* (San Francisco: Jossey-Bass Publishers, 2000), 40.

3. Ibid., 41.

4. Ibid., 43.

5. Ibid., 56.

6. Sharon Daloz Parks, *Big Questions, Worthy Dreams* (San Francisco: Jossey-Bass, 2011), 8.

7. Parks, 66ff.

8. Parks, 65.

9. Nancy Chodorow, *The Reproduction of Mothering* (Berkeley: University of California Press, 1978,) 36.

10. Howard Brinton, *Quaker Journals* (Wallingform, PA: Pendle Hill, 1972), 6-68.

11. See Parks, 178-179.

12. Christian Smith and Patricia Smith, *Souls in Transition* (New York: Oxford University Press,2009), 125.

13. Ibid., 140.

14. Ibid., 145.

15. Ibid,, 154.

16. Ibid., 155.

17. Smith and Snell, 166-168.

18. Donna Freitas, *Sex and the Soul* (New York: Oxford University Press, 2008), 16.

19. See Carol Gilligan. *In a Different Voice*, (New York, Oxford University Press, 1999).

20. Carol Gilligan, *In a Different Voice* (New York, Oxford University Press, 1999),159.

21. Ibid., xx.

22. Ibid.

23. Luce Irigaray and Kirsteen Anderson, trans., *Democracy Begins Between Two* (London: The

Athlone Press, 2000), 24.

24.   Nancy Chodorow, *Individualizing Gender and Sexuality* (New York: Routledge, 2012), 89.

25.   Ana Carrigan, *Salvadoran Witness: The Life and Calling of Jean Donovan* (New York, Simon and Schuster, 1984), 218.

26.   Rosemarie Tong, *Feminine and Feminist Ethics* (Belmont, CA: Wadsworth Publishing Company, 1993), 88ff.

27.   Carole A. Rayburn and Lillian Comas-Diaz, eds., *WomanSoul* (Westport, CT: Praeger, 2008), 261.

28.   Elisabeth Schussler Fiorenza, *Transforming Vision: Explorations in Feminine Theology* (Minneapolis, MN: Fortress Press).

29.   Johanna H. Stuckey, *Women's Spirituality* (Toronto: Inanna Publications and Education, 2010).

30.   W. Merle Longwood, Wm S. Shipper, and Philip Culbertson, *Forging the Male Spirit: The Spiritual Lives of American College Men* (Eugene, OR: Wipf and Stock, 2012), 57.

31.   Gilligan, 160.

32.   Ibid., 163.

33.   Richard Rohr, *Adam's Return: The Five Promises Of Male Initiation* (New York: Crossroads, 2004), 12.

34.   Ibid., 13.

35.   Ronald F. Levant and William S. Pollack, eds., *A New Psychology of Men* (New York: Basicbooks, 1995), 51.

36.   Weldon Hardenbrook, *Missing from Action: Vanishing Manhood in America* (Nashville, TN: Thomas Nelson, 1987), 15.

37.   Christina Hoff Summers, *The War Against Boys* (New York: Simon and Schuster, 2000), 37ff.

38.   Longwood et al., 73.

39.   Susan Maitri, *The Spiritual Dimension of the Enneagram* (New York : Jeremy P. Tarcher/ Putnam, 2000) 4ff

40.   Richard Rohr and Andreas Ebert, Peter Heinegg, trans., *Discovering the Enneagram: An Ancient Tool for A New Spiritual Journey* (New York: Crossroad, 1990), 11.

41.   Rohr and Ebert, *Discovering*, 58.

42.   Ibid., 78.

43.   Ibid., 83.

44.   James Empereur, *The Enneagram And Spiritual Direction* (New York: Continuum, 1998), 97ff.

45.   Ellis and Bergin and Edward Fitzgerald, *The Enneagram* (Mystic, CT: Twenty Third Publications, 1998) 36.

46.   Rohr and Ebert, *Discovering*, 103.

47.   Ibid., 110

48.   Ibid.

49.   Ibid., 132.

50.   Bergin and Fitz, 40.

51.   Empereur, 191ff.

52.   Goldsmith, Michael, *Getting your Boss's Number* (San Francisco: HarperSanFrancisco, 1996 27.

53.   Ibid., 58.

The "Thou"

Realizing Others' Humanity in Religion

Healthy religion should be the most inclusive system of all, making use of every discipline, avenue, and access point for Big Truth.
— Richard Rohr

In this chapter, we consider the area of the quadrant that refers to the "Other," or the "Thou." Most religions have a teaching similar to the Christian commandment to "Do unto others as you would have them do unto you." Hinduism teaches: "Treat others as you would yourself be treated." Judaism says "Do to no one what you yourself dislike," the Buddha declares: "Hurt not others with that which pains you" and Islam teaches: "Do unto all men as you would wish to have done."

In the exercise of authentic religion, the I's love is to be extended to the Thou inclusively. According to Jesus, this love of neighbor is to be extended to the hated Samaritan, even to one's enemies. For Jesus, the love of self is the criterion for the love of neighbor. In his classic work *I and Thou*, Martin Buber (1878-1965), a Jewish philosopher, points out the importance of not relating to others as I-IT, where persons become objects and can be easily dismissed. Buber learned well from his experience of the Nazis in Germany that once people are viewed as objects, they can be excluded or even eliminated. For Buber, authentic relationships should involve personal encounters where we meet each person as he or she is and throw out any preconceived or formulated idea of their personhood.

In this chapter, we are going to discuss religion's intrinsic impulse to move people beyond the objectification of the other to a personal encounter with the Thou. We are going to discuss how authentic religion calls people to relate with so-called minorities in their midst: people of color, people from different religions or ethnic backgrounds, gay-lesbian-bisexual-transgendered persons, and the disabled. Authentic religions call their followers to "personify" all individuals and often to see them as created in the image and likeness of God (Judaism, Christianity and Islam) and even as bearing within individuals the divine itself (Christianity, Hinduism, and Buddhism). We will confine our discussion to some of the minorities that are most frequently encountered in American colleges.

A Changed Demographic Landscape

Many Americans still ascribe to the mythology that this country is a white Christian nation, composed of immigrants from Europe. The facts show otherwise. The 2010 census revealed that over one third of the population in the United States is composed of "minorities;" that is Hispanics, African Americans, Asians and others.[1] In 2012, the birthrate of the minorities (Blacks, Asians, Hispanics and others) exceeded the birthrate of the white majority. It is projected that by 2050 those who are now considered to be the minorities will in fact be the majority of American citizens.[2] At the same time, there is a significant growth of religions other than Christianity in the United States: Islam, Hindu, Jewish, Sikh, Jain, Buddhist and others are all on the rise. In short, for the religious person, the "other" is becoming more complicated and challenging. This increase in diversity makes it more difficult for religious persons to understand the "other" and perceive them as fully human.

Minorities

There are three main racial and ethnic minorities in the United States: African Americans or Blacks, Hispanics or Latinos, and Asians. Let's look at these minorities from both cultural and religious perspectives. Much more attention has been given the Black racial minority than the ethnic Hispanic and Asian minorities, largely because of the stormy history of African Americans and the deep racial prejudice that still prevails in this country.

African Americans

In the last fifty years, African Americans have moved from legalized segregation to securing their civil rights. Spurred by the movement led by Martin Luther King, Jr. and many others, new legislation eliminated segregation and accorded Blacks their rights. Affirmative Action, a policy that attempts to level the playing field in employment, business, and education for the minorities, has helped Blacks move into prominent positions in government (Barack Obama, Condoleezza Rice), the military (Colin Powell), sports (Venus and Serena Williams and the many Blacks in baseball, football, basketball and track), literature (Toni Morrison and Maya Angelou), entertainment (Bill Cosby and Oprah Winfrey), and education (Cornel West and Henry Gates.) Blacks have also continued to shape American music with jazz, hip-hop and rap, and they have made major contributions to opera (Leontyne Price, Simon Estes, and Kathleen Battle).[3] At the same time, the Black community suffers from unemployment, poverty, homelessness, imprisonment, addictions and gang violence.

Blacks are the second-largest minority in the United States. There are 42 million Black Americans; in fact one in seven Americans are Black. (By contrast, there are 50 million Hispanics in the U.S. and they are the fastest growing minority). 55% of Blacks live in the South; the majority of the others live in either the Northeast or Midwest. Most are urban.

Many Blacks are concerned with the breakdown of family structures. Only 37% of Black men and 28% of Black women are married. Married couples head only 29% of Black households and among Black children under age 18, only 36% live with married parents.[4] Research has demonstrated that households headed by a married couple have much higher median incomes and the children have more educational opportunities.[5] Blacks have especially been hit hard by the recession and their unemployment rate is 16% contrasted with the 8.5% national average.

Black students are often disadvantaged when it comes to education. Their schools are underfunded and ill equipped to prepare them for the work force or for college. The majority of Black students graduate from high school and go on to college, but many never finish. Only 20% of blacks have a college degree, as opposed to 30% for the general population. The excessive cost of higher education is an important factor in hindering Blacks students from achieving a specialized degree.[6]

Racial Prejudice

African Americans are often subjected to racial prejudice. Such discrimination seems to date back to when Africans were brought to this country as early as 1619 to be worked as slaves. Slaves were of a different color, spoke different languages, were not Christian and were thus deemed inferior. Their state was worsened by the horrible conditions to which they were subjected and the fact that they were not permitted to be educated. Often the birth dates of slaves were not recorded and they were sold on the block like farm animals. Their "inferior" status was even given scriptural backing. White Christians told black people that they were the cursed descendents of Noah's son Ham and that they were not created in the image and likeness of God, who they thought was obviously white. Slaves were told that both Jesus and the apostle Paul approved of slavery or quoted Paul's injunction that slaves should be obedient to their masters.

Racial prejudice usually includes color, gender and class. Thus, a Black woman from the poor class suffers from three layers of prejudice.[7] Curiously, the notion of race is somewhat recent. Michelle Alexander points out that "The concept of race is a relatively late development. Only in the past few centuries, owing largely to European colonial imperialism, have the world's people been classified along racial lines." Here in America, the "idea of race emerged as a way of reconciling chattel slavery- as well as the extermination of American Indians—with the ideals of freedom preached by whites in the new colonies."[8] Race was "invented" so as to demote certain groups from humanity and then either enslave them or eliminate them. The Native Americans were reduced to "savages" and then killed or sold as slaves to the Caribbean. Later, they were driven into reservations. The African Americans were reduced to inferior animalistic creatures in the eyes of White society and were subject to domination and enslavement because they were not thought to be created in the "image and likeness" of the White God.

This view on Black racial inferiority is reflected in the famous Dred Scott decision from 1857, which declared that slaves could not be citizens because blacks were a "subordinate and inferior class of being." Slaves had no rights and were to be treated "as an ordinary article of merchandise and trafficked, whenever profit could be made." As for the Declaration of Independence's statement that "all men are created equal," politicians made sure that slaves were not included. In other words, they were not considered to be human.

The Dred Scott decision was one of the events leading up to the Civil War. The American Civil War began as a war over succession of southern states opposed to Lincoln's position on slavery, but ultimately turned into a war over the legitimacy of slavery itself. In 1863, during a particularly rough part of the war, President Abraham Lincoln issued the Emancipation Proclamation, which freed the slaves in the Confederacy but remained unenforceable until the South was defeated. In 1865, the 13th Amendment of the Constitution abolished slavery in the United States. Most freed blacks remained in the South, but were subjected to draconian Jim Crow laws of segregation.

During the two world wars, many blacks migrated to the northern cities for work in factories. Here, they often endured the same racial prejudice experienced in the South. After the 1950s, many whites fled to the suburbs, leaving the inner cities to fall into decay around the black residents left behind.

The Civil Rights movement was sparked in 1955 by Rosa Parks' refusal to move to the back of the bus to make room for a white passenger. She was arrested and charged. Soon after this event, Rev. Martin Luther King Jr. led the movement against segregation through a series of sit-ins and marches. Perhaps the high point of the movement was King's "I have a dream" speech in front of the Lincoln Memorial in 1963. Five years later, Dr. King was assassinated. In 1964, the Civil Rights Act was passed that banned discrimination in employment practices and public accommodations. In 1965, the Voting Rights Act restored voting rights for Black Americans, and the Civil Rights Act of 1968 banned discrimination in the sale or rental of housing.

Racial prejudice became ultimately related to skin color. According to genetics and blood type, all humans across the board are the same. Skin color seems to correspond to pigmentation resulting from differing ultra-violet rays in certain latitudes. Sub-Saharan Africans, Tamils of southern Asia, and Melanesians from the Pacific all have very dark skin. Those from higher latitudes have lighter skin. Anthropologists point out that "we are all Africans," in that homo sapiens evolved in Africa and migrated to other parts of the world around 50,000 years ago.[9]

Blacks and Liberation

The notion of Jesus as liberator goes back to the days of slavery. Blacks identified with the persecuted Jesus in his courageous struggle to bring freedom to his people through his suffering. The slaves identified with Jesus' redemptive suffering when they sang the plaintive "Were You There (When They Crucified My Lord?)" Those who rebelled and escaped slavery often saw Jesus standing with them. These communities thought of themselves as the real churches of Jesus Christ, and not the "hypocritical" churches that enslaved other human beings.

The civil rights movement was born out of religious conviction. King spoke of "the long night of captivity" of African Americans reaching out for the daybreak of freedom, justice, and equality. He reminded Americans that Christianity involved both love and justice and that their nation was under God and dedicated to freedom and equality. His movement was strong but peaceful. It followed the non-violent teaching of Jesus to love the enemy, turn the other cheek and put away the sword. He believed that suffering that was unearned and unjustly inflicted had redemptive power—that the cross contained the redemptive power of God.[10]

Many black scholars have been in the forefront of the liberation movement. Theologians like James Cone have developed a black theology that is critical of the way white theology has ignored racism. This is a theology of a black Jesus who stands in solidarity with the suffering and struggles of Blacks against prejudice and oppression.[11]

Black "Womanist" scholars distinguish themselves from feminists and expose the oppression of black women throughout the world. A growing Womanist movement represents Black women, who note that they have experienced oppression throughout the world and struggle for human dignity against great odds. These women point out how racism is a crippling blindness and a moral failing that places entire groups, especially women, outside the sphere of care and concern. Racism dehumanizes and robs people of their human dignity and freedom.[12] Shawn Copeland, a leading Christian Womanist theologian, emphasizes how oppression of Black women, indeed of any women, rejects the notion of all human beings created in the image of God and the belief that the incarnation of Jesus gives dignity to all human flesh.[13]

Kelly Brown Douglas, Jacquelyn Grant and others more recently have given voice to black women who struggle for dignity in their churches and their communities. They speak of the Black Christ who stands in solidarity with black women as they raise their children, often alone in poverty, and as they grieve for their young who are shot down in the street, hauled off to prison, or killed on the battlefield.[14]

While Blacks in America have made great progress and are protected in their civil rights, some think that there are new forces to keep them segregated and suppressed. Alexander points out that the criminalization of drugs has resulted in the incarceration of many young Black men. As a result of other laws, such as those against the employment of felons, forbidding felons to vote, depriving them of food stamps and rentals in public housing, and the 3 strikes policy which imprisons them for life after their third offense, many Black men have been ostracized from society. It must then be asked: "Do we now have a new set of Jim Crow laws put in place to separate Blacks from American society?" Alexander powerfully predicts: "When the system of mass incarceration collapses (and if history is any guide, it will), historians will undoubtedly look back and marvel that such an extraordinarily comprehensive system of racialized social control existed in the United States. 'How fascinating,' they will say, 'that a drug war was waged almost exclusively against poor people of color... They were rounded up by the millions, packed away in prisons, and when released, they were stigmatized for life, denied the right to vote and ushered into a world of discrimination. Legally barred from employment, housing, and welfare benefits—and saddled with thousands of dollars of debt—these men were shamed and condemned for failing to hold together their families.'"[15]

While it is true that Black Americans have made great progress in this country, racial prejudice is still prevalent. Moreover, the charge that there are new efforts afoot to once again separate and dominate Blacks must be addressed.

Blacks and Religion

The first black people brought to America as slaves were stripped of their indigenous religions because these religions were thought to be "heathen and false." During much of the slavery period, slaveholders objected to slaves practicing religion, thinking that this might be a way toward literacy and education, and a means of dangerous congregating.

By 1700, the Church of England launched an effort to Christianize slaves. Evangelization was not very successful, largely due to the stiffness of the English liturgy and the complicated doctrinal aspect of the tradition. Eventually, Baptist and Methodist circuit riders realized more success in converting slaves with their themes of human dignity and freedom. These denominations allowed for more emotional and charismatic expression in ritual and were more centered on the Bible than on doctrine.

At first, slaves were gradually allowed to worship in white churches, but had to sit in the balcony or in a separate section of the main floor. The ministers were usually white, and if a black minister was allowed to preside it had to be clear that his sermons supported the status of the slaves.[16]

In the North, free Blacks established their own churches where they would be free to worship and speak out of their own culture. Some of these churches served as centers of abolitionist ideas or even stations for the Underground Railroad. As one scholar points out: "The religion of African Americans has constituted the one ongoing positive force in their history from the earliest times up to the present day. It has both saved the people from falling victim to fatalism and despair, and given them the theological grounds for their claim that suffering will end because God is on their side and desires their deliverance.[17] After the Civil War, the freed slaves in the South established their own churches which became centers for social organization. The ministers often became political leaders in addition to religious leaders. Once white supremacy was established in the South, however, it was clear that the black churches would be tolerated only if they toed the line. The black minister was often "the accommodating Negro leader," or the mediator between the black and white communities.[18] Perhaps that is why, when Martin Luther King Jr., the minister of a Black Baptist Church, took over the leadership of the civil rights movement, he found that he often did not receive strong support from the other black churches. He came to realize that many of the black churches were so concerned with otherworldly matters that they ignored social issues and actually became a party to segregation. At one point, he said "Sunday is the most segregated day of the week." The black churches of the North were not militant forces against segregation either.

Today, the black churches provide solid bases for black worship and socialization. In many ways, these churches provide an effective means for social organization and expression of individual and cultural needs. With regard to religion, African Americans today are more likely to be affiliated with a church than whites, and they spend more time on religious activities than the average person. The majority of Blacks believe that the Bible is the actual word of God and thus do not believe in evolution or same-sex marriage. The majority identify themselves as Protestants and consider themselves as either very or moderately religious. Most Blacks think that prayer and the Bible belong in public schools. 50% think that pre-marital sex is not wrong, but 66% think that homosexual relations are wrong.[19] The majority of Blacks support abortion and euthanasia, but oppose the death penalty.

Hispanics

Hispanics (Latinos/Latinas) are an ethnic group rather than a race. Most consider themselves to be white, but others categorize themselves as black, multiracial or "other."

There are 50 million Hispanics in the United States, 16% of the U.S. population, and they are the fastest growing minority. In the last ten years, their numbers have grown 43% because of immigration and because of the larger number of children in each family. They spend more time than the average American caring for their own children and tending to the household. 26% of children under 5 in the U.S. are Hispanic. 62% of Hispanics were born in the U.S. and therefore speak English as their native language. 26% are foreign born and are not citizens. 65% have traditional ties with Mexico, 10% with Puerto Rico, and 30% with other countries. Nearly half of Hispanics in the U.S. live in either California or Texas. Their median income is about $10,000 less than the average in the U.S., and they have little wealth on the whole. Hispanics have less education than most Americans and many do not have health insurance. Their participation in the labor force is growing very rapidly, but at present, their share of the poverty level is higher than the Blacks. Almost half of Hispanic households have children and are family oriented. The divorce rate is low among Hispanics, but separation is common.

Hispanics are generally optimistic, but few are trusting of those outside their group. They identify with the working class and only 25% consider themselves to belong to the middle class. The majority consider themselves to be better off than their parents, but few are satisfied with their financial situation. Most vote Democratic. Overall, they are hardworking people and depend on their own efforts to get ahead. The vast majority believe that their children will be better off than they are.

Hispanics strive for better education, but only 63% have high school diplomas and only 14% have college degrees, which is well below the national average of 30%.

Many Hispanics have health problems and one third of them have no healthcare, yet their life expectancy is longer than the average American. About half of Hispanics own their own home, and they are inclined to be more mobile than the average citizen.

Hispanics and Religion

The majority (63%) of Hispanics are Catholic; most are affiliated with a religion and consider themselves to be moderately or slightly religious, but spent less time than others in religious activities. For the most part, Hispanics are religiously conservative and stand in opposition to issues like same-sex marriage. The majority believe the Bible is the word of God and most disapprove of the government's ruling against prayer and Bible reading in the public schools. Almost half hold that pre-marital sex is not wrong, while 25% believe that such sex is always wrong. Most are opposed to abortion but favor the death penalty.[20]

It is said that Hispanic women are generally more religious than the men and normally are the ones responsible for inculcating religious values in their children. Their relationship with God is personal and intimate and they are given to prayer, devotions (especially to the Virgin of Guadalupe) and the saints. Many have turned to liberation theology to help free them from the male dominance in their church and culture. Although they are not allowed leadership positions in their official church, many are involved in strong grassroots movements. Women theologians, called Mujeristas, have published widely on Latina issues in the church.[21]

In the United States, there are a wide variety of religious practices among Hispanics. There are actually Spanish-speaking synagogues in the U.S., where Sephardic Jews who are descendents of those expelled from Spain in 1492 worship. There are also Jewish Hispanics who fled from the Nazis to South America during WWII and who have now migrated to the United States.

There are the great religious celebrations in El Santuario de Chimayo, possibly the most visited church in New Mexico. For nine evenings before Christmas, the posadas (lodgings) reenact the search of Mary and Joseph for a place to stay. Tepeyac, the church in Mexico City where the Virgin of Guadalupe is said to have appeared to a peasant Juan Diego, is a most popular place for devotion and healing.

There is also a growing appeal among Hispanics for Pentecostalism. After

Roman Catholicism, it is the second largest religious group among Hispanics in the United States. The Pentecostal churches go out of their way to provide transportation and assistance and are open to the spontaneous and expressive ways of Hispanic worship. Pentecostal churches also seem to be vigorously involved in immigration issues.[22]

Asians

There are more than 17 million Asians in the U.S., which is 6% of the entire population. While small in number, the Asians are quite influential because of their high degree of education and wealth. They are one of the fastest growing new immigrant groups in the United States. Nearly one quarter of the Asian population here are Chinese, with those from India and the Philippines nearly 20% each. Only one in three Asian Americans have been born in the States; most have become naturalized citizens. In the last ten years, the Asian population has grown by 44%.

More than 50% of the Asians in this country live in five States: California (1/3), New York, Texas, New Jersey and Hawaii. There are 1 million Asians living in three cities: New York, Los Angeles and San Francisco.

The household incomes of Asians are 31% above average, which is largely because most have jobs and are highly educated. Most Asian households are headed by married couples and have strong family values. They usually delay having children until after age 30 and limit their families to two children. Asians have only a 10% rate of divorce, in contrast to the 50% nationally.

Most Asians are optimistic and are more trusting of others than many minorities. Most think that they are better off than their parents, though this belief has dropped 10% in the last ten years. Many Asian women work outside the home, yet are seriously dedicated to their children. A higher percentage of Asians are satisfied with their incomes than other minorities and they spend about 15% more than the average American. They are progressive for the most part; they're favorable toward science, believe in evolution, and over 70% approve of same-sex marriage. Like the other minorities, Asians hold that there is more reason to worry about the economy than the environment. Most Asians vote Democrat.

Asians believe that hard work in school and one's job is the key to success. They spend most of their time working and caring for their children; little time is spent watching TV. Whereas Blacks and Hispanics often call themselves working class, Asians identify themselves more with the middle class.

Asians are usually better educated that the average American. They attend school well into their twenties and a majority of them has bachelor degrees. Many are drawn to science; Asians hold 1 in 5 degrees awarded in dentistry, medicine, optometry and pharmacy. Rather than taking away jobs, the Asians have improved the quality of the labor force and have in fact created jobs through their investments and business start-ups. The large groups of refugee Cambodian, Laotian and Vietnamese who migrated here quickly adapted to the culture, worked hard, became educated and depended little on welfare assistance. Their restaurants have brought healthy food to Americans and their practices of yoga, acupuncture, Tai Chi and herbology have contributed to the well being of Americans. Asians have a very low rate of crime and incarceration. Asians are noted for assimilation with regard to language, socialization and economics.[23]

Asians and Religion

Unlike the majority of Americans, only one third of Asians claim to be at least moderately religious. Many of those who are involved in religion consider themselves to be Buddhist. Some are Hindus, Muslims or Shinto. 36% have no religious affiliation. Upon coming to the United States, many Asians were converted to Christianity. Protestantism has been popular with Koreans, while the Filipinos have favored the Catholicism they brought over from their native country and the Vietnamese seem to favor the Buddhism they brought with them.[24] More than half of Asian Americans do not think the Bible is inspired, and most think that prayer and the Bible should be excluded from public schools.

Most Asians are progressive on moral issues. 66% see nothing wrong with sex before marriage and the majority can endorse sex between two adults of the same sex. The majority support abortion rights and favor the death penalty and gun rights.[25]

Gays and Lesbians

The contemporary notion of homosexuality as an orientation is rather recent. The word homosexuality was first published in a German pamphlet in 1869 and appeared in English several years later. At that time, and until the 1970s, homosexuality was often viewed as a mental disease or disorder. In the 1970s, the American Psychiatric Association (1973) and the American Psychological Association (1975) declared that they no longer held homosexuality to be a mental disease or disorder. Since that time, homosexuality became gradually more acceptable and after 1990 the public's views began to change significantly.[26]

There is evidence that individuals had intercourse with those of the same sex in earlier times. Plato speaks of men in Greece who had wives and children but at the same time enjoyed sex with younger men. In the mid 18th century, French missionaries reported that Native American men sometimes dressed as women and took men as their sexual partners. In this century in New Guinea, there is evidence of sex between boys that is part of family and tribal customs. None of these accepted practices were called homosexuality and they seem to be connected to quite different notions of sexuality.[27]

Today, homosexuality usually describes individuals who are drawn to intimacy with others of the same sex. These women are called lesbians; these men are called gay. Individuals who are sexually involved with both genders are called bi-sexual. Transgendered persons are those who carry both sexes within themselves. Usually the transgendered do not identify personally with the gender assigned them but can at times move from one gender to another. The abbreviation now used for all four groups is LGBT. The current figures for homosexuals (which are very difficult to cite accurately) are 9% of the men for gays and 4% of women for lesbians.[28]

As late as the 1960s, it was quite dangerous to be gay or lesbian in the United States. Public school teachers of this orientation could lose their jobs, bars were forbidden to serve them drinks, dancing with another person of the same gender was restricted, and propositioning someone of the same sex was considered a sex offense that was punishable with imprisonment. Gays and lesbians were often insulted or assaulted, brutalized by police, and even imprisoned.

During the 1960s, there was a "Lavender Scare" comparable to the "Red Scare" against Communists. Government officials, businesses, schools and universities came under scrutiny for homosexual activities.[29]

Today, things have changed a great deal. Young people are much more comfortable discussing homosexuality and socializing with those of this orientation. Many more gays and lesbians now feel safe "to be out," can marry in an increasingly number of States, and are parenting children. Homosexuals are legally protected by both the First and Fourteenth amendments, which gave homosexuals the right express an identity as well as a right to be treated equally under that identity.[30]

The military has offered recent leadership toward the acceptance of gays and lesbians. First there was the "Don't ask, Don't tell" policy which allowed only closeted individuals to be active in the military. That policy has now been dropped and people who are openly gay or lesbian are now permitted in the military. The next question that is being addressed is same-sex marriage in the military.

Same-sex marriage has become a burning issue in politics. Same-sex marriage is now allowed in Massachusetts, Connecticut, Iowa, Vermont, New Hampshire, New York and Washington, DC. In 2012, Barack Obama became the first American President to state that he favored same-sex marriage. Increasingly, there is an acceptance of homosexuality as a legitimate orientation rather than as a corrupted and sinful state. A person's need for love and attachment is fundamental to the human experience and central to the person's identity, and is an orientation that may be altered only at the expense of damage to the person's sense of self.[31] As a result, homosexuality is being discussed much more openly in American culture. Leading media figures such as Ellen DeGeneres, Suze Orman and Rachel Maddow; entertainers like Neil Patrick Harris and Ricky Martin; and politicians such as Barney Frank have helped make the public more comfortable with lesbians and gays.

At the same time, there are still dangers for gays and lesbians. In 2008, a fifteen-year-old gay teen was shot and killed in class just days after he came out. Bullying of gays and lesbians has also resulted in a number of suicides.[32]

Religion and Homosexuality

Today, homosexuality is a burning question among some religious congregations in the United States. The Southern Baptists and the Catholic Vatican take a strong position against same-sex partnerships and consider such relations to be sinful. The Vatican has even gone so far as to block United Nations efforts to protect the human rights of homosexuals.[33] The Presbyterian Church USA, United Methodist Church and Episcopal Church USA are seriously divided over this issue. A number of Episcopal clergy and laity have become Roman Catholics rather than give into the election of gay bishops.

Many religious leaders hold that this is a time for serious study of homosexuality and dialogue as well as personal contact with those in the LGBT community. There is nothing so effective in breaking down prejudice than to see that lesbian and gay "thous," whether married or single, live their lives just as we all do!

In the following section, we will give an overview of how some religions deal with homosexuality. It has been observed that religions that are strongly patriarchal are the most vehemently opposed to homosexuality. Perhaps these religions require a sharp division between male and female in order to sustain their patriarchal domination. Homosexuality tends to blur the differences and thus can diffuse patriarchal authority.[34]

Christianity

This analysis might hold true for Roman Catholicism, which remains adamantly opposed to homosexuality and views the orientation as "objectively disordered" and homosexual relations as "intrinsically evil."

From early on, Christianity attempted to limit sexual relations to procreation. Female virginity was deeply honored, and from at least the medieval period, celibacy was required for clergy. During this same medieval period, the church began to persecute "sodomites" through the Inquisition. The Papal Inquisition enlisted the secular authority to have sodomites tortured and burned at the stake while the Spanish Inquisition persecuted sodomites as heretics, both in Europe and among the indigenous people of the New World. In the 13th century, the Cathars were accused of sodomy and heresy and annihilated. In 1307, the Inquisition accused the Knights Templar of sodomy, heresy and witchcraft, and its members were tortured and burned. After the Reformation, most divisions of Christianity continued to condemn sodomy. By the late 19th century, the "sodomite," considered a morally corrupt sinner, was replaced by the "homosexual," a medical and psychological type that was usually considered to be pathological.[35]

In today's Christianity, there is the tension between those who see homosexuals through a religious lens as sinners, and those who view homosexuals as human persons worthy of respect and civil rights protection.

The Bible

Christian churches approach homosexuality in diverse ways. The churches that take a literal view of the scriptures, which would include the evangelical churches, strictly oppose homosexuality. The churches that interpret the scriptures contextually and through the lens of modern biblical criticism, which would include many of the mainline Protestant churches, hold more liberal views on homosexuality. The anomaly is the Roman Catholic Church, which, though it accepts biblical criticism, exerts its own authority in judging homosexual acts to be sinful.

There are a number of biblical passages that are cited with regard to homosexuality. The main text used from the Hebrew Scriptures is in Genesis 19: the story of Sodom and Gomorrah. Lot, a relative of Abraham and a resident of Sodom, offers hospitality in his home to two angels disguised as men strangers. In the evening, some of the men of the town come to the house, apparently to do sexual violence on Lot's guests. Lot offers his daughters in the place of his guest. The two angels blind the evil men and Sodom and Gomorrah are destroyed for the sins. Traditionally, the townsmen who wish to "sodomize" the guests are seen as homosexuals and the destruction of the towns is read as the consequence for that evil. Modern interpreters see the main issue here to actually be the sanctity of hospitality and that the sexual violence abuses that sanctity. This interpretation does not associate homosexuality with sexual violence.

There are also two passages in Leviticus that seem to argue against homosexuality. Leviticus 18:22 says "If a man lies with a male as with a woman: it is an abomination. And Leviticus 20:13 says "If a man lies with a man as with a woman; both have committed an abomination and should be put to death; their blood is upon them." Taken literally, these passages seem to be straightforward, although they do not mention women with women, nor can we conceivably think of executing people today for such action. In context, these passages seem to be part of the Holiness Code, distinguishing Jews from Canaanites. The Code also forbids the cross-breeding of animals, sowing two kind of seeds in one field, wearing garments of different fabrics and certain ways of cutting hair and beards. None of these are interpreted today as forbidden by God. So is the passage in fact dealing with homosexuality at all? If so, does it apply to today's much better understanding of homosexuality?

In the New Testament, Jesus does not address homosexuality, although he does specify that marriage is between a man and a woman. In Paul's letter to the Romans, he says that sex between women or between men is "unnatural" and "shameful."[36] In context, Paul might well have been talking about sexual relations related to Gentile idolatry and in the Greek context of male prostitution, slave prostitution and sex with young boys. In 1 Corinthians 6:9-10, Paul names sodomites in his vice list, but again, this may well be referring to male prostitution.[37] To sum up, one has to wonder whether the ancient world interpreted homosexuality the way we do today.

Christian churches are divided over whether these biblical passages should apply. Some Christians argue that homosexuality is a choice that can be overcome, others argue that it is a God-given orientation that must be respected. Some argue for rejection, others for compassion and love. At present, the Church of England and its counterparts, the Anglican Church of Canada and Episcopal Church of the United States, are deeply divided over this issue. [38] In Africans countries such as Nigeria and Uganda, some Anglican bishops have advocated the death penalty for homosexuality.[39] For the most part, The Evangelical Movement opposes homosexuality and rejects the ordination of gay clergy. At the same time, there are those in the tradition with more liberal views and many members who are gay and lesbian.[40] The Methodist Church's campaign of "open hearts, open minds, open doors" is indicative of the inclusivity of this Christian denomination.

The Presbyterian churches have conducted many studies of homosexuality and have made numerous efforts to address this issue. At present, these churches still suffer serious division among members and among the various groupings. The tension lies in the need to be faithful to the scriptures and past traditions, and at the same time be open to contemporary views and needs in the community.

The Roman Catholic tradition has not had to deal with the Protestant question of whether or not to ordain actively gay or lesbian clergy or bishops because Catholic clergy are required to be celibate. Holding to the position that sexual relations are meant to be procreative, the Church has adamantly opposed homosexual acts as well as same-sex marriage. The Vatican has declared that the "homosexual inclination" is "objectively disordered" in that it is a tendency toward intrinsically evil acts.[41] The Vatican is clear that it does not condemn those who have this "deep-seated" and "not chosen" disorder, but it does forbid same-sex sexual acts.[42] While the Vatican views homosexual acts to be objectively wrong, it admits that subjective circumstances can diminish culpability. The Vatican does not label individuals as homosexuals, but sees all as children of God. They recommend pastoral care and condemn prejudice, discrimination or violence against those of this orientation.[43] In 2005, the Vatican declared that those who practice homosexuality cannot be admitted to the priesthood.

Judaism

Traditionally, Judaism has been opposed to homosexual activity largely because it is not procreative and is associated with pagan cultures. Yearly readings disdaining homosexual acts on Yom Kippur reinforced this law. In the modern era, rabbinic teachings have been more understanding of homosexuals, and Jewish scientists led the way to removing it as a pathological condition. Gay activists began to form their own synagogues in the 1970s in San Francisco and New York, and were mostly associated with Reform Judaism, which, since the 1980s, accepted homosexuals as members and rabbis as well.[44] Israelis have been able to remove the law forbidding same-sex actions and have gained approval for same-sex marriage.

Reconstructionist and Renewal movements have been very liberal toward homosexuals. The Conservative movement welcomes gays and lesbians as candidates for the rabbinate. The Orthodox movement is conservative with regard homosexuality, but at times adopts a "don't ask, don't tell" attitude. Of course, this policy does not allow for same-sex marriage, and at times gays and lesbians are subjected to "conversion therapy". At the same time, many in the Orthodox movement seem to be edging toward acceptance.[45]

Islam

The Koran has little to say about male homosexuality and says nothing about sex between women. Its punishment for adultery is much harsher. In the Hadith, which is thought to be teachings of Mohammed, same-sex actions can be punishable by death. At the same time, in many Muslim communities, sex between men has been tolerated and even practiced by Caliphs and celebrated by Muslim poets. Today, it is acceptable in Muslim communities in parts of Pakistan and in sections of Kenya, Tanzania and Sudan in Africa.[46]

Hinduism

The law of Manu, a central Hindu collection of laws, forbids and recommends punishment for same-sex actions, especially for women. Until recently, there have been severe punishments for homosexuals in India and Nepal. A position has begun to take hold that suggests homophobia came with the British occupation and that authentic Hindu traditions are more accepting to homosexuals. In 2007, Hindu Nepal legalized homosexuality and accorded equal rights to gays and lesbians. In 2009, a court judgment set aside the legal ban on sex between men.[47]

Buddhism

The teaching of the Buddha is more concerned with the celibacy of his monks and sexuality that does no harm to others than with homosexuality. In the monastic teaching, when same-sex is mentioned between nuns or monks it is in the context of a breach of celibacy. Homoerotic actions are mentioned among the Tibetan monks, and the Japanese Mahayana literature speaks favorably about same-sex actions that become spiritualized between older and younger monks. Buddhism has adapted to other cultures. In Cambodia, which practices mostly Theravada Buddhism, there is religious freedom and same-sex marriage is allowed out of compassion. There are no laws against homosexuality in Thailand, whereas it is strongly opposed in Sri Lanka. Buddhist leaders such as the Dalai Lama of Tibet and Thich Nhat Hanh of Vietnam express influential views about homosexuality. The Dalai Lama has been ambiguous, at one time repeating the Buddhist prohibition of nonprocreative sex and at another time supporting gay civil marriage. While he sometimes points out that homosexuality might be against Buddhist teaching, he does not approve of any national laws opposing it. Thich Nhat Hanh, a widely read spiritual teacher, also supports gay marriage, is willing to ceremonialize it and applies the same moral rules of heterosexuals to homosexuals.[48]

The Disabled as "Thou"

The disabled are too often set apart as an "other" to be avoided, shunned or excluded. Ally Bruener is a twenty-three year-old young woman who, since age three, has suffered from the crippling disease, muscular dystrophy, which results in a deterioration of the muscles. Ally has been in a wheelchair since she was 7, but successfully graduated from high school and won a scholarship to college. After several years, she decided to leave college and take up a career as a comedian, where she could entertain people about disabilities and break down stereotypes. She observes: "people think that because I am disabled I am mentally deficient and somehow less human. They are often uncomfortable with me and are often surprised at the witty remarks. When my assistant introduces me in a comedy club by saying: 'Do you want to laugh at the crippled girl?' they get uncomfortable. But once I start my routine, they relax and laugh at my jokes."

The Disabilities Act of 1990 defines a disability as "a physical or mental impairment that substantially limits one or more of the major activities of life." This includes physical, cognitive and psychological impairments, and it is estimated that over 51 million Americans, or 18% of the population, has such impairments.[49] Each disability has its own challenges, and women are thought to have the most difficulties with managing disabilities financially. Many disabled people object to being classified as "problems" or "liabilities." They do not want to be defined by their disabilities but rather want to sustain their own unique identities as individuals. This is a very important point to remember when relating to persons with disabilities since they are citizens like everyone else.[50]

Persons with disabilities experience a wide range of reactions. Some experience that others fear them, and anticipate some violent outburst or even think that they carry something that is contagious. Many people have had little or not experience with those who are disabled, are at a loss about how to react, and just turn away in awkward silence. Some are filled with pity and just look at them as though they are helpless. Some might laugh behind their backs and make some comment like "retard."

Disabled people often experience a kind of domination by well-meaning people and even by family members. They might be given assistance that they really don't need, or decisions might be made for them for employment or leisure activities without consulting them. The disabled are often treated as though they are incapable of speaking for themselves. A waiter might ask a family accompanying someone in a wheelchair: "What will he want to eat?"

Language with regard the disabled is often extremely offensive to them: words like "idiot," "spaz," "crippled," "deaf and dumb," or "deformed" can deeply hurt the disabled. Persons with disabilities are often put in a category of "other" that is set aside from the norm and viewed to be inferior.[51]

Such prejudice against the disabled has a long history. Historically, many disabled people were institutionalized in extremely poor conditions and treated as though they were subhuman. Often, they were physically and sexually abused in these institutions. In the early 1970s, Senator Robert Kennedy visited the now infamous Willowbrook Institution where many mentally disabled people were "warehoused." Kennedy, whose sister was mentally disabled, remarked that the place was "less comfortable and cheerful than the cages in which we put animals in the zoo."[52] Willowbrook was closed in 1972, as were many other such institutions, and the residents were moved to better living situations. The following year, the Rehabilitation Act was passed in Congress, which forbade Federal funds being used for programs that discriminated against people with disabilities. This bill also provided funds for the training and placement of disabled workers. In 1975, the Education of All Handicapped Children Act was passed which provided good education for such children and promoted the field of Special Education. In 1990, the Americans with Disabilities Act freed disabled persons from discrimination in employment, public services, public transportation and in telecommunications. Disabled persons have come a long way in being mainstreamed into normal life. However, there is still a long way to go to change public perceptions and personal discrimination.

Films and books have at times depicted disabled people as dangerous monsters, such as in *The Hunchback of Notre Dame*. In modern times, disabled people are portrayed with much more sensitivity, as in films like *Forrest Gump*, *Rain Man*, *The Miracle Worker*, *My Left Foot*, and *The Elephant Man*.

In the past, were used as "poster children" to summon pity and raise money, usually by well-intentioned persons. Or they were thought of as sick, and in need of some cure or possibly a miracle. Sometimes disabled people are made to feel that they are "burdens" to society who cost a great deal of taxpayer money. The Nazis of Germany decided to ease the State of these burdens by sending handicapped people to concentration camps where they were usually killed. Sometimes adults and children are made fun of by "jokesters" who imitate their slurred speech or their "funny" way of walking. At times they are viewed as simple-minded children or even as freaks who belong in the circus.[53]

One disabled young woman points out that pity is not appropriate. She says "A great many people with disabilities like their lives a lot. I happen to be one of them. We tend to repudiate the medical model of disability, which views us as sick and in need of a cure, and the mechanical model, in which we are broken and require repair."[54] Rather than sympathy or pity, disabled individuals crave equality, independence, respect and inclusion in all facets of life. They advocate more public funding and services. Too many of them are without jobs, homes, friends, a church to attend, or access to public facilities.[55]

The same applies for many educational institutions. For many disabled people, it is extremely difficult to them to negotiate campus classrooms and other facilities. Professors are often not trained to provide for those who are impaired in hearing or sight. Their lectures, assignments and exams are usually geared only for those who do not have disabilities. It is true that many universities have special facilities for students with learning disabilities, but they do not have personnel trained or experienced in serving those with serious physical or mental challenges. More often, the elementary and high schools are much better equipped to serve the disabled than are the institutions of higher learning.

Disabled people want to be treated as any other human being with full human rights, and as persons with human dignity who deserve the same respect as everybody else. Most don't want to be placed in some other category as "special," or "objects of service." They want access, opportunity to live well, socialize, play and participate in as many activities as they are able.

We have seen how the Special Olympics have given so many disabled people the opportunity to demonstrate their athletic abilities and be proud of their accomplishments. It is common today to see disabled participate in marathons, triathlons, mountain climbing and other athletic events where they achieve remarkable performances.

Christians and the Disabled

Christians have had their own caricatures of the disabled. In the gospels, mentally and physically challenged individuals were thought to be possessed by demons or be receiving punishment for their sins. Gospel attitudes toward disabled people reflect popular views that they were punished by God for some sin committed by themselves or their parents. Jesus stands against this view. The sick and "possessed" are always cured in the gospels and restored to "normalcy." Unfortunately, they often lived in poverty; the handicapped are placed in the category of "the least of the brethren," and at times used as a derogatory term.

The disabled received a wide array of reactions from religious people. They might be told that they are special in the eyes of God and therefore have been blessed with this disability. Or they are advised that although they might suffer now, they will be made whole in heaven. Some tell them that God is giving them a test of their character. People even imply that they might have done something to deserve this or that they should be thankful they weren't given something worse. Others tell them to offer up their sufferings for others, just as Jesus did. Try to imagine how such statements are received by those with difficult challenges.[56]

Christians need to be reminded that all humans have been created in the image and likeness of God. Disabled people are no exception. As a matter of fact, one out of every five persons has some kind of disability. Some people point out that a disability is a limitation, and that we are all handicapped in some manner or other. Moreover, as we grow older, most of us will experience mental or physical challenges as part of the aging process. Just as Jesus was able to find his true mission and his love for all in his brokenness and suffering, each person can in fact discover God within his or her brokenness. As the great spiritual writer, Henri Nouwen, has pointed out—we are all wounded healers. And as the tenets of liberation theology explain, Jesus is uniquely on the side of those who are oppressed, invisible, on the periphery of society- in this case, persons with disabilities. From this perspective, Christians are called to liberate the disabled from their isolation and marginalization through friendship and love.

Churches can be notorious for their lack of sensitivity. Often they are not accessible, have no handicap accessible bathroom facilities and no seating spaces suitable for wheelchairs. For those whose hearing is impaired, signing is not provided; there are no guides for those whose seeing is impaired. Next time you are in church, observe how a blind or physically handicapped person could manage. In addition to those difficulties, with the shortage of priests in the Catholic Church, it is extremely difficult for the disabled to receive the sacraments of penance or the anointing in hospitals, nursing facilities or in their homes.

The disabled don't seem to want pity or pious sayings from their churches. Instead they look for access, consideration of their problems, and the ability to fully participate in the activities of the community. Church congregations can be a tremendous support for disabled people and for those who find themselves in "perpetual" or recurring crisis because of the complexity of their situation. Many Christians believe that this support is their responsibility as disciples of Jesus and seek out a ministry of care and assistance. As one Minister has commented: "During his earthly ministry, Jesus exemplified love for those who were sick, poor, and living with disabilities. He did not condemn them but restored them to wholeness."[57] Congregations can reach out to parents who are often overwhelmed by caring for a disabled child and also offer the child opportunities for making friends and worshipping in a caring community. More religious communities are beginning to realize that they can play an important role in providing lifelong support, care and nurturing to persons with disabilities- persons who up until this time have been "invisible" in their congregations.[58]

Certainly the work of Jean Vanier must be mentioned here. Vanier has spent most of his adult life dedicated to serving the mentally disabled, taking them out of institutions and providing them with comfortable homes supervised by professionals. His movement, called L'Arche, began in France and now is operating in many parts of the world. In working with the mentally handicapped, he has found they are a sign that peace, joy and happiness need not be gained from work or wealth. He writes: "The mentally handicapped do not have a consciousness of power. Because of this, perhaps their capacity for love is more immediate, lively and developed that that of other people. They cannot be people of ambition and action in society and so develop a capacity for friendship rather that efficiency."[59]

Diversity of Religions

Views on religion have changed considerably in the Americas since the arrival of Europeans. Christopher Columbus was on a journey to India to spread the Christian faith and to possibly discover treasures to support the Crusades. Instead he encountered a tall, noble people who fascinated him. Given the remoteness of their area, he concluded that they could not possibly descend from Adam and Eve and were therefore a somewhat different species of humanity. Columbus thought that the native people had no religion, and their openness to Christian symbols moved him to think that they could be easily converted to Christianity. Little did he realize that there were hundreds of native observances.

When the first English colonies were established in the 17th century, it became evident that the natives did practice their own religions. The pilgrims came to realize that there was a vast number of natives in this new land, and that they would have to learn to live with them, trade, make treaties, and fight side-by-side them against hostile tribes. Still, many Europeans believed that natives were "heathens" who worshipped false gods or even the devil. Other colonists assumed that the natives could eventually be converted to Christianity.[60] In time, the hostility toward the native people grew and moves were made to conquer, send them into slavery, and entirely displace rather than convert the American Indians.

The Spanish explorers were more aggressive. They had come for gold and encountered magnificent civilizations in Mexico and Peru. They were horrified by the native religious practices, especially with human sacrifice in Aztec and Inca religions, and set out to conquer, enslave and plunder these indigenous people, to destroy their temples and to crush their religions.

During the time of the establishment of the United States in the late 18th century, there was a diversity of Christian churches. Many of the Founding Fathers were children of the Enlightenment and approached religion from a more rational and deist point of view, committed to religious freedom. Jefferson, Adams and Franklin all challenged the divinity of Christ and approached a distant God through virtue and reason. They were more committed to the morality of Christianity than to its doctrinal positions, and they held firmly to religious freedom as the way to bind a new and fragile nation. In Virginia, Jefferson established a model of tolerance of diverse Christian groups, as well as "the Jew, Mahometan and the Hindoo."[61]

In spite of this country's commitment to religious tolerance and freedom, the United States was still thought of by many to be a white Protestant country until 50 years ago. Catholics and Jews frequently experienced deep prejudice. Hindus, Moslems and Buddhists were either ignored or looked upon as outsiders or foreigners. People of different national or religious persuasion lived in their own "ghettos," or neighborhood enclaves. Even among Catholics there was a strong distinction among national parishes: German, Polish, Italian and others.

Twentieth century wars were instrumental in bringing religions into contact with each other. In WWI, the British fought side by side with Muslims and Hindus. In WWII, Americans came into contact with the religions of the Orient; the Koreans and Vietnamese familiarized Americans with Buddhism and other religions of that region, and the recent wars in Iraq and Afghanistan put Americans in contact with Islam.

Today, America is becoming a different land. Americans are beginning to get used to the reality that the so-called "minorities" will soon be the majority. They are facing the fact that America in many ways is no longer #1 as they see the looming dominance of China and India and learn of the enormous resources of Russia, which is nearly twice the size of the United States. The growing reality of globalization places this country as simply one among many, as "part of" rather than "greater than."

Many Americans are not disturbed by the seismic shifts going on around them or by the growing diversity of religions. Rather, they welcome the latter as a challenge to not only get acquainted with the religions of others, but to actually learn from others' religious beliefs. Many feel that such diversity will help Americans live more free and open lives, a "freedom of choice to go and see what they are really looking for."[62]

Encountering People of Various Religions

The major religions come from only two sources, India and Semitic Middle East. From India, first came Hinduism, then Buddhism, then Jain and Sikh religions. From the Semitic Middle East came Judaism, Christianity and Islam. While there are many other religions, including Taoism, Confucianism in China, Shintoism in Japan, and indigenous religions such as the many Native American religions and the many religions of Africa, here we will consider the perception of the "thou" in major world religions.

The Hindu Thou

The oldest of the major religions is Hinduism. It began perhaps 7,000 years ago in what was then the northern reaches of India and today it has more than a billion followers worldwide. Hinduism is a Western title and this religion is better known by its followers as Sanatana Dharma (the Eternal Law). Hinduism is unique in that it has no known founder, and no single set of doctrines or scriptures. It is an extremely complicated and diverse religion, composed of many differing traditions and the worship of countless gods and goddesses.

A significant part of the evolution of Hinduism was the appearance of nomadic Aryans in northern India around 2,000 BCE. The Aryans brought Sanskrit as well as rich religious traditions including priesthood, fire ceremonies and chants, all of which remain part of Hinduism today.

The oldest Hindu scriptures are the Vedas, which is an ancient collection of hymns of divine praise and petition. From the famous Rig Veda, we have: "I pray to the God of Fire [Agni], the God of sacrifice, the one whose chants and hymns bring blessings. (Rig Veda, 1/1). Another sacred collection of Hindu scripture is the Upanishads, wherein ultimate questions about God, creation, the soul and afterlife are addressed. Then there are the magnificent epics like the Bhagavad Gita, which tells about the amazing Krishna, a skilled warrior, trickster and lover.

Often, Hindus are mistakenly thought to worship many gods and goddesses. On the contrary, Most Hindus maintain that they worship only one God and that the many gods and goddesses are but the manifestations of this one God. Brahman is the one God, the supreme universal Spirit, the foundation and source of all creation, and that which is in every living creature, the reality beyond comprehension, the ultimate truth for which we all search, the Savior of all. Brahman is manifested in Brahma, the Creator God, Vishnu, the Preserver God and Shiva, and the Destroyer God. Thus, all aspects of reality, creation, preservation and destruction are held to be within the divinity.

Temple communities often focus on one or the other of the gods. Shivaites focus on Shiva, the god who conquers ego and ignorance, helps in meditation and wards off disasters and death. Others are dedicated to Vishnu, the supreme Soul, the essence of all beings, past, present and future; the divinity who sustains the universe and protects against negative forces. His "avatars," or incarnations, are Rama and Krishna, great heroes for the Hindus.

Among the many goddesses are Mother Durga, who represents feminine energy, courage and strength in difficult times and the power to meditate; Sita the wife of Rama, who is a source of peace; and Kali, the wife of Shiva, who is a conqueror of evil, a protective mother, and one who can deal with the dark side of life.

Among the other more popular male gods are Ganesha, the elephant-headed one who is clever and can assist with exams or the job search, and the popular Hanuman, the monkey-faced god who can assist in becoming a leader and in overcoming obstacles.

There are a number of central beliefs that you could discuss with Hindus. The "Soul" is an important belief for most Hindus. The Soul is the vital entity, the Spirit of all life, the Truth. The Soul is beyond gender. Those who understand and love the Soul live in the divinity and the divinity lives in them.

The Soul is freedom from desire and evil, it is the source of immortality. For many Hindus the Soul is God. The traditional Hindu greeting is "Namaste" (the divine in me greets the divine in you!)

Another central Hindu belief is "karma," or Actions. It is held that all actions have consequences: good actions bring about good; bad actions bring about evil. In many ways, we become what we do, and for the Hindu, one's actions determine our rebirths after death. Presumed here is the belief in reincarnation, or that individuals after death pass through numerous rebirths, up and down the scale of creatures, depending on the quality of life and the need for purification. Hindus believe that all souls are evolving toward "moksha" or "liberation." They believe that all life is sacred and therefore are committed to "ahimso," or non-violence. For them "no particular religion teaches the only way to salvation above all others, but all genuine paths are deserving of tolerance and understanding." [63]

For the Hindu, there are three paths of liberation (Moksha). The first is knowledge, which can be gained from Gurus (derived from "Gu" (light) and "Ru" (darkness) – thus one who brings light to darkness. Knowledge can also be gained through reading the scriptures, practicing Yoga and through meditation. The second path to liberation is Works, which includes honesty in one's business transactions, gaining a good education, leading a virtuous life, following the rites of passage, and performing devotions (puja) in temples, at home altars and on religious feasts and pilgrimages.

There is still a strong caste system operating in Hindu society. Originally, the castes from top down consisted of: priests, warriors, farmers/ merchants/ craftsmen, and laborers/servants. On the very bottom were the untouchables or outcasts (individuals who have no caste). Though discrimination against outcasts has been ruled out since the time of the great Indian leader, Gandhi, many in that caste (the Delits) are still oppressed. It is estimated that there are over 300 million Delits in India today. A caste system based on language, birth, family roots, occupation and other factors is still operative and affects arranged marriages and many social structures.

Discuss these and other ideas with your Hindu acquaintances and friends, and if possible attend a Hindu ceremony, where you will experience inspirational singing and dancing, colorful sacrifices of fruit, tributes to the representation of gods and goddesses, and warm hospitality. There is a temple in most large communities.

The Buddhist Thou

Buddhism also began in India, but eventually all but disappeared there as it spread to Tibet, Sri Lanka, Thailand, Cambodia, China, Korea, Vietnam and Japan. Today, it has spread through Europe and the United States. Its founder was Siddhartha Guatama, who was born around 450 BCE. Siddhartha was born a prince and was raised in luxury, protected from the harsh realities outside the palace. He was given a beautiful wife who bore him a son. On several excursions outside the palace, Siddhartha encountered the realities of old age, sickness and death. He was moved to seek true enlightenment about the suffering he had seen, so he left home and became an ascetic, living in the forest for six years. Siddhartha was reduced to skin and bone, but gained no insight. Leaving that life, he sat down under a Bodhi tree, determined to find enlightenment. Siddhartha suffered many temptations and frightening images, but eventually he "woke up," and from that time on was referred to as the Buddha or "the enlightened one." He went back to some of his former ascetic friends and preached to them about his new awareness of how to eliminate suffering.

The teachings of the Buddha have been formalized into the Four Noble Truths and the Eightfold Path. The Four Noble Truths are as follows:

- Suffering is universal. All things are impermanent and must come to an end.
- Suffering is brought about by clinging to negative feelings or desires.
- The cessation of suffering can be brought about by detaching oneself from negative feelings and by the ceasing of desires.
- Freedom from suffering comes from this detachment, this letting go and by following the 8-fold path.

The 8-fold path consists in being right and just in every aspect of our lives:

1. Right vision (knowing the causes of suffering and how to address these causes)
2. Right purpose (doing no harm to others)
3. Right speech (avoiding lies, cruel or foolish talk)
4. Right action (avoiding stealing, anger, violence and lust)
5. Right livelihood (choosing professions that do no harm)
6. Right effort (mindfulness or constant monitoring of your mind to prevent toxic thoughts)
7. Right awareness (constant monitoring your body, feelings and attitudes)

8. Right concentration (the seclusion and quiet needed for meditation)

The goal of the Buddhist way is to develop a life that is loving, kind and compassionate. One key belief is that each person can be the architect of their own consciousness. Through regular meditation one confronts the toxic thoughts and actions that are poisoning our consciousness, works to let go of these, and develops a life for others (where there is the "no self").

Today there are well-known Buddhists: the Dalai Lama, Thich Nhat Hanh, and Pema Chodron, whose writings and teachings on YouTube can help you understand Buddhism and better prepare you to befriend the followers of Buddha whom you encounter. You will find a number of Buddhist chants are available on the internet.

The Jewish Thou

Jews are both an ethnic group and a religious people. Some prefer Judaism to be referred to as a way of life rather than a religion. Not all Jews observant religious practices or even believe in God. And since Judaism takes in converts, not all those who practice Judaism are ethnically Jews.

Judaism is a religious movement that identifies with the biblical Israel, going back to the founding father and mother: Abraham and Sarah. Jews are a people who accept the holy books of the Torah (the first five books of the Bible) and the Talmud (an extensive commentary), and whose lives are guided by belief in a covenant with the one God and the acceptance of Jewish laws of Sabbath, rituals, the celebration of feasts and the honoring of life cycles.

Judaism begins with the biblical account of Abraham being called to leave his home and migrate into a foreign land where God promised to make a great nation and through him bless all communities on earth. Abraham answered the call and God established a sacred covenant with him. Abraham's sons migrated to Egypt after the famine and eventually the Jews were enslaved there. They are brought out of slavery by Moses and given God's commandments on Mt. Sinai. Finally, the Hebrews settled in Canaan and by the 11th century BCE, established a kingdom there that was ruled by Kings Saul, David and Solomon. Jerusalem was established as the capital and a Temple was built there for worship and sacrifice. After a series of conquests by various empires, the Romans destroyed Jerusalem and the dispersed Jews formed rabbinic Judaism, which is the basis for Judaism today.

Two events in modern history have shaped Judaism: the Holocaust and the establishment of the nation of Israel. The Holocaust in many ways follows the consistent persecution of the Jewish people. Throughout the centuries, they have been subjected to expulsion, torture and execution. In Nazi Germany, Jews became Hitler's scapegoats and were at first driven out of their homes, then forced into ghettos and killed. Eventually The Final Solution was decided: every Jew in Europe was to be rounded up, shipped to extermination camps, systematically gassed and cremated in ovens. All told, over 6 million Jews met this horrible fate.

The second key event in modern Jewish history is the establishment of the State of Israel. In the 19th century, the Zionist movement began to demand a homeland for the Jews. After World War II, in 1948, the United Nations established the State of Israel. Ever since there has been violence and tension between the Jews and the Palestinians in that area. Today efforts are being made to establish two separate States.

Currently, 80% of Jews live in Israel and the United States. Nearly 6 million Jews are citizens of the United States. Small in numbers, the Jews are for the most part well-educated, successful and influential.Some notable Jews are Elie Weisel, holocaust survivor, writer and Nobel Peace Prize winner; Yehudi Menuhin (d. 1999) and Itzhak Perlman, both brilliant violinists; Albert Einstein, noted scientist; and Henry Kissinger and Yitzhak Rabin, both famous statesmen. Currently there are three Jewish Supreme Court Justices in the United States: Stephen Breyer, Ruth Bader Ginsberg and Elena Kagan.

Most Jews are proud to be Americans and consider themselves to be Jewish Americans rather than American Jews. Noted Jewish scholar Jacob Neusner says that the Jews in this country are "deeply American in their loyalties and commitments, but each has a distinctive theory of what it means to be an American. In the climate of a country open to difference but united in political institutions and loyalties to "one nation, under God, indivisible, American Judaism flourishes in diverse form... because America accepts and even nurtures diversity."[64] You will find many inspiring Jewish celebrations on the internet.

The Muslim Thou

Since the terrorist attack on the World Trade Center on 9/11/01, there has been much focus on Islam. The event engendered prejudice and suspicion upon Muslims, the United States engaged in wars in Iraq and Afghanistan, and worldwide anti-terrorist precautions have been established, especially in airports. The majority of Muslims want the world to know that they are peaceful people and want nothing to do with "holy war" or violence.

Islam is the second largest religion in the world, with over one billion people living in 56 countries. Only 20% of this Muslim population is Arab. The largest Muslim country is Indonesia, where 12% of the world's Muslims live. There are also Chinese, Indian and African Muslims. Islam is the second largest religion in Europe, and is growing rapidly. Soon, Islam will be the second largest religion in the United States. It is clear why people should be well informed about this religion.

The word "Islam" is translated to mean "peace" and "submission to God," and Muslims are taught to believe in peace and compassion and to live lives characterized by these qualities. They are also committed to justice for themselves and for others.

Islam was founded by Muhammad, who was born in Mecca around 570 CE. Mecca was a center for trade and pilgrimage to the Kaba, where images of the gods and goddesses were placed. Orphaned early on, Muhammad was raised by an uncle who he worked for, running camel caravans. When he was 25, he was hired by Khadijah, a widow who was successful in the caravan business. They eventually married and had six children of whom only the four girls survived.

Muhammad was often troubled by the tribal wars and violence around him, as well as by the corruption of the Arab religions. He was devoted to his spiritual life and traveled to the mountains each year to make a retreat in a cave. On one of these occasions, he was overpowered by a spiritual force and received a revelation. The experience terrified him and he fled to the top of the mountain, where he learned that his revealer was the Angel Gabriel. He returned home, where his wife reassured and comforted him. Later, he was grabbed by this mysterious force and received more revelations about Allah, the true God, and about Muhammad's calling to be Allah's privileged prophet. He began to tell family and friends of his revelation and his followers called themselves "Muslims," or those who submit to God. As the revelations began to condemn pagan idols in the Kaba and the wayward ways of the tribes, Muhammad became offensive and was ostracized and abused. He and some of his followers eventually migrated to Yahthrib (Medina), where he continued to receive revelations and became a reformer of that area. Now alienated from Mecca, Muhammad fought with its residents, and after several defeats took over that city, cleared out the Kaba and proclaimed it to be the house of the one God, Allah. He then returned to Medina, where he died in 632 CE.

Muhammad received his revelations for over 20 years over which time they were memorized and written down. After his death, all the revelations where gathered into one book in Arabic, called the Qur'an. This record is viewed by Muslims as the final revelation which corrects the corruptions of Judaism and Christianity. The Qur'an is honored by Muslims as "the words of God," and is at the center of the Muslim faith and way of life. This book and the Hadith are accounts of Muhammad's own teachings. There are many teaching in the Hadith, of which some are considered to be more authentic than others.

There are five pillars of Islam that are the foundation of this religion's practice. The first is the Shahada, the prayer recited daily by Muslims: "I testify that there is no God but God. I testify that Muhammad is the messenger of God." The second pillar is ritual prayer, which is to be recited five times a day. The third is the giving of alms to the poor (2.5% of one's possessions). The fourth is the month-long fast each year during the month of Ramada (usually late summer or early fall). Ramadan is a time for spiritual reflection and a heightened awareness of God's blessings. The fifth pillar is "hajj," or a pilgrimage to Mecca required once in one's lifetime.

There are two main groups of Muslims. The Sunnis represent 80% of Muslims and are those that hold that the leader of the Muslim community must be a learned man, but need not be a descendent of Muhammad. The Shia, however, hold that Islamic leadership can only be held by those who descend from Muhammad. Both groups have their own sets of Hadith and thus approach Sharia (Islamic laws) differently. Sunnis prevail in Saudi Arabia, Egypt, Turkey, Syria, Northern African countries, Pakistan and Afghanistan. The Shia are the majority in Iraq and Iran (which is Persian). The Sufis are a movement in Islam dedicated to asceticism and mysticism. Rumi (d. 1273) is a renowned Sufi poet who is still popular today.

The so-called "Arab Spring" indicates that many Muslims in the Middle East are tired of being ruled by wealthy dictators and require freedom and some form of democracy whereby they can choose their own leaders. The term "Islamic fundamentalism" can have a number of connotations. For some, such as the Taliban in Afghanistan, it means a return to a rigid and often violent enforcement of Islamic law (*sharia*), where a strict interpretation of the Qur'an controls life and especially the lives of women. For others, this fundamentalism means becoming more religiously observant, deepening the faith and spirituality of Islamic life. In this latter case, there is no place for violence or terrorism. The vast majority of Muslims are committed to this latter form of spiritual renewal. Realistically, this can place Muslims in America in an awkward position, given our culture's penchant for alcohol and sexual freedom, which are both forbidden by Islam.

American Muslims are eager for the world to see that most of them are peaceful people. They point out that "jihad" for most Muslims means the "struggle" to live a good and just life and not to be violent. They want nothing more than to demonstrate that they live normal lives in society, enjoying their families, their children and their work.

Summary

The challenge to be able to encounter a diversity of "thous" becomes increasingly more complicated. We travel more and work in businesses where both employees and customers are diverse. Our churches are now neighbors to mosques, temples and shrines of other religions. Social media can connect us to people all over the world. In our colleges and universities, we encounter more and more cultural variety as these institutions encourage diversity.

Here, we have looked at the Thou in just some of the categories that we meet: racial and ethnic minorities (Blacks, Hispanics and Asians); gay-lesbian-transgendered-bisexual persons; the disabled; and diverse religious persons. We have seen how religion touches each group and we have suggested that healthy and mature religion needs to be able to accommodate, understand and reach out to all these others. The Thou is the neighbor which most religions call us to love as we love ourselves.

◻️◼️ VIDEOS ONLINE

Racial prejudice: Imagine a World Without Hate
    http://www.youtube.com/watch?v=3KyvlMJefR4

Martin Luther King: *I Have A Dream* speech, August 23 1963
    http://www.youtube.com/watch?v=1UV1fs8lAbg

The Gay Rights Movement
    http://www.youtube.com/watch?v=u62OtM_vt5k

American disability rights activist Judith Heumann
    http://www.youtube.com/watch?v=-Crf44pj2Gg

Jean Vanier *Lecture, Part 1: Introduction and Fear*
    http://www.youtube.com/watch?v=PD60kaOo62Q

Religious Diversity and the Building Blocks of 'American Grace'
    http://www.youtube.com/watch?v=aM4WMjHQN44

▨ NOTES

1. New Strategist editors, *Who We Are: Blacks* (Ithaca, NY: New Strategist Publications, 2011), 1.

2. Valerie Martinez-Ebers and Manocher Dorraj, *Perspectives on Race, Ethnicity, and Religion* (NY: Oxford University Press, 2010), 3.

3. Nell Irvin Painter, *Creating Black Americans* (New York: Oxford University Press, 2007), 249ff.

4. *Who We Are: Blacks*, 91.

5. Ibid., 117.

6. Ibid., 59.

7. Utz Mcknight, *The Everyday Practice of Race in America* (New York: Routledge, 2010), 21.

8. Michelle Alexander, *The New Jim Crow: Mass Incarceration in the Age of Colorblindness* New York: The New Press, 2012,) 23.

9. Chester Hartman, *Poverty And Race In America* (New York: Lexington Books, 2006), 396.

10. Brennan Hill, *Jesus the Christ: Contemporary Perspectives* (Mystic, CT: Twenty-Third Publications, 2004), 196ff.

11. Ibid., 218.

12. Karen Teel, *Racism and the Image of God* (New York: Palgrave Macmillan, 2010), 124.

13. Shawn Copeland, *Enfleshing Freedom* (Minneapolis, MN: Fortress, 2010), 84.

14. Hill, 199.

15. Alexander, 170-71.

16. As late as the 1950s Catholic churches had separate lines for Blacks who wished to go to confession!

17. Peter J. Paris, "The Religious World of African Americans," in *World Religions in America*, ed. Jacob Neusner (Louisville, KY: Westminster John Knox Press, 2009), 60.

18. Alphonso Pinkney, *Black Americans* (Upper Saddle River, NJ: Prentice Hall, 2000), 120.

19. *Who We Are: Blacks*, 28ff.

20. This overview was taken from *Who We Are: Hispanics* (Ithaca, NY: New Strategist Publications, 2011).

21. Laura M. Padilla, "Latinas and Religion," in *The Latino/a Condition*, eds. Richard Delgado and Jean Stefancic (New York: New York University Press, 2010), 503-508.

22. See Justo L. Gonzalez and Carlos F. Cardoza-Orlandi, "The Religious World of Latino/a-Hispanic Americans," in *World Religions in America*, ed. Jacob Neusner (Louisville, KY: Westminster John Knox Press, 2009), 88-101.

23. Philip Yang, *Asian Immigration to the United States* (New York: Polity Press, 2011), 176-180.

24. Ibid., 188-190.

25. Most of this overview has been taken from *Who We Are: Asians* (Ithaca, NY: New Strategist Publications, 2011).

26. Jeffrey S. Siker, ed., *Homosexuality and Religion: An Encyclopedia* (Westport CT: Greenwood Press, 2007), 20.

27. Siker, 19.

28. Ibid., 21.

29. Stuart Biegel, *The Right to be Out* (Minneapolis, MN: University of Minneapolis Press, 2010), 47

30. Ibid., xiii.

31. Ibid., 76.

32. Ibid., xvii.

33. Siker, 5.

34. Ibid., 4.

35. Ibid., 11.

36. *Romans* 1:26-27.

37. Siker, 64ff.

38. See Paul Marshall, *Same Sex Unions* (New York: Church Publications, 2004), 66ff.

39. Dag Oistein Endsjo, *Sex and Religion: Teachings and Taboos in the History of World Faiths* (London: Reaktion Books, 2011), 167.

40. See Troy Perry, *The Lord Is My Shepherd And He Knows That I'm Gay* (Los Angeles: Universals Fellowship, 1997), 5ff.

41. Siker, 191 ff.

42. Catholic Church, *Catechism of the Catholic Church* (New York: Catholic Book, 1994), 2358.

43. Noah Berlatsky, ed., *Homosexuality* (New York: Greenhaven Press, 2011), 55ff.

44. Endsjo, 171.

45. Ibid., 172.

46. Ibid., 153ff.

47. Ibid., 170.

48. Siker, 8-9.

49. Deborah Beth Creamer, *Disability and Christian Theology* (New York: Oxford University Press, 2009), 14.

50. Ibid., 31.

51. Jennie Weiss Block, *Copious Hosting: A Theology of Access for People with Disabilities* (New York: Continuum, 2002), 48.

52. Ibid., 63.

53. Ibid., 49-50.

54. Nancy Mairs, "Learning from Suffering" *Christian Century*, May 6, 1998): 481.

55. Block, 14.

56. Creamer, 35.

57.   Dean Preheim-Bartel and Aldred Nuefeldt, *Supportive Care in the Congregation* (Goshen, IN: Mennonite Publishing Network, 2011), 29.

58.   Ibid., 42.

59.   Jean Vanier, *Eruption to Hope* (New York: Paulist Press, 1971), 42.

60.   Robert Wuthnow, *America and the Challenges of Religious Diversity* (Princeton, NJ: Princeton University Press, 2007).

61.   Ibid., 17.

62.   Ibid., 75.

63.   Gerald J. Larson, "Hinduism in India and America," in *World Religions in America*, ed. Jacob Neusner, 193-194.

64.   Neusner, *World Religions in America*, 140.

5

The "We"

Culture and Religion

In politics as in religion, my tenets are few and simple. The leading one of which, and indeed that which embraces most others, is to be honest and just ourselves and to exact it from others, meddling as little as possible in their affairs where our own are not involved. If this maxim was generally adopted, wars would cease and our swords would soon be converted into reap hooks and our harvests be more peaceful, abundant, and happy.
— George Washington

Using our integral approach, we have looked at religion from the point of view of the "I" through the stages of personal development, gender characteristics and personality types. We have also considered the perspective of the "Thou" by examining how the religious person interacts with people of different ethnic, racial and religious backgrounds, as well with gays, lesbians and people with disabilities. Now we turn to the communal "We." We will examine how religions, each "embedded in a particular 'we' with its distinctive perspective," relate to culture through the lens of political interaction and globalization.[1]

The Meaning of Culture

Culture is complicated in that it involves so many varied aspects, such as language, local traits, beliefs, customs, behaviors, art, music, and mindsets. The word comes from the Latin word "cultura," which means "cultivation." The modern usage began in Europe when referring to a person's cultivation of improvement. A "cultivated" person was one who was well educated and refined. Later, it was applied to the beliefs, values and customs common to one area or one group of people.

Cultures reflect what people wish to cultivate or develop, which in turn reflects what they value. Families, neighborhoods, cities, states and nations each have their own "cultures." A rural culture cares about the soil, animals, crops, weather and often neighborliness. An urban culture usually cares about housing, work, social life, safety and transportation. It might be said that religions have their own cultures. Judaism often values tradition, loyalty to identity, education and security. Islam cares about identity and fidelity to revelation. Christianity cherishes tradition, community and mission.

Each nation has its own culture, even though each nationality may include a diversity of citizens. In the United States, there is a New England, Midwest, Western, West Coast and Southern culture. Some states such as Vermont, Maine, Texas and California pride themselves on having particularly unique and independent cultures.

Today, we see cultures becoming more pluralistic, struggling for unity amidst differences. The United States includes African Americans, Native Americans, Latinos, Asians and some European cultures, each struggling to sustain their own cultures and at the same time assimilate into the mainstream American culture.

Cultural Shifts in the U.S.

The American culture has experienced a number of cultural shifts in recent times. The Great Depression in the late 1920s was catastrophic for the American economy and many people were reduced to poverty or at least a simpler life. World War II had significant effects on the American way of life. American industry boomed, men were drafted into military service, women replaced them in the factories, and American lost over 500, 000 military personnel in the war effort. All of this brought profound changes to American family life. After the war, veterans received free college expenses, which significantly raised the educational levels of American citizens and contributed to the emergence of a strong middle class.

The American culture in the late 1950s and early 1960s also reflected changing patterns. Society was often much more homogenous during that time and even though there were both wealthy and poor people, most Americans described themselves as either working class or middle class. The poor did not want to identify themselves with the "lower class" and many rich people were reluctant to describe themselves as "upper class." By the mid 50's, TV became common in households although there were a limited number of programs to watch on only a few channels. In the early 60's, music was limited to early rock, country and the music of the 50's. There were no DVDs, TiVo, computers or cell phones. Most consumers drove American-made cars; there were few restaurants to choose from and fast-food chains were just getting started.

The moral standards of the early 60's were quite different as a result of the more consistent, conservative culture. Abortion was illegal and rare and there was no birth control pill. When a woman got pregnant, the man was expected to marry her. Marriage was rather universal and unmarried couples living together was rare; divorce was unusual and parents and churches strongly objected to pre-marital sex or cohabitation. Films were not permitted to use profanity or to portray nudity, sexual scenes or even married couples sleeping in the same bed. The crime rate was low, a low percentage of the population was in prison and drug abuse was rare.

From the mid 19th to the early 20th century, the women's movement gained momentum, largely in an attempt to obtain the right to vote. Once the vote was obtained in 1920, the movement quieted. In the early 60's, the only two professions generally open to women were nursing and teaching; sexual harassment usually went unpunished.[2]

1963 and the years following seem to mark a division for the American culture. In 1963, Martin Luther King Jr. delivered his "I have a dream" speech in front of the Lincoln Memorial and the nation was traumatized by President Kennedy's assassination. Betty Friedan published *The Feminine Mystique*, which helped ignite a new women's movement, and oral contraceptive went on the market. The Beatles played for the Queen of England. A year earlier, Rachel Carson wrote *Silent Spring*, which awakened many Americans to the existence of environmental problems. In the same year, the Catholic Church opened the Second Vatican Council, which would hold meetings until 1965 and then publish documents that would revolutionize the Church worldwide. The so-called post-war Baby-Boomers were teenagers and America was beginning a new era.

A great many changes have taken place in the American culture since the 1960s. First of all, the work force has shifted from physical work in manufacturing to "mind work" for computer experts, managers, engineers, attorneys, scientists, professors, executives, financial analysts, writers and consultants. America has developed a new intellectual elite who are attracted to high-paying jobs.[3]

There seems to be an emerging pecking order among the privileged in this country. The privileged make up a small group of perhaps 100,000 people, in top executive levels in military or business. The next group is composed of a new upper class, which includes those who run the economic, political and cultural institutions. That group is followed by the upper-middle class and then the middle class, which shrank rapidly after the 2010 financial collapse. Finally, there are the growing lower classes that struggle with job loss, housing foreclosures, credit card debt and inadequate healthcare.

The magazine *Mother Jones* breaks all this down in an article called "It's the Inequality, Stupid." It is astounding that such a large share of the nation's money belongs to the top 100th of 1%, who make $27 million per household. The top 1% earns more than $1 million per household. The top 10% average over $115,000 per household and the bottom 90% average $35,000 per household. To look at this another way, the top 1% control 35% of the nation's net worth, the top 10% control 38.5% of the net and the bottom 90% control only 30% of the net. In the last 10 years, the growth of wealth at the top has almost doubled. Additionally, the wealthy hold most of their money in investments so they rebounded from the stimulus and pay less tax. The members of the bottom group who own houses had 60% of their assets tied up there and had extensive losses in the housing collapse. (http://www.motherjones.com/politics/2011/02/income-inequality-in-america-chart-graph)

The cultural shifts of the last decade have led many social scientists to believe that we are in the process of developing two mutually exclusive cultures in this country. One culture consists of people with money and education from elite private schools and the best universities. They send their children to prestigious schools, and carefully monitor their children's education as well as the performance of the teachers (helicopter parents). They drive expensive foreign cars, and own large and expensive houses that are luxuriously furnished. They exercise, take care of their health and usually belong to sports or fitness clubs. This group often travels abroad (first class) and vacations at expensive resorts. All of this tends to segregate this growing class of elite. Seldom do they socialize with or even meet members of the other classes.

There are many factors that have produced this class shift. First, there has been a major change in jobs. In 1960, 40% of the jobs in Manhattan, New York, were industrial. Today, that percentage has shrunk to less than 5%, with most jobs now belonging to the areas of professional, scientific, technical or information services. Most of these jobs require a college degree and specialized training, which means that people from the lower classes have little access to such jobs. This pattern exists across the nation.[4] The young adults who are skilled with their hands and who perhaps do not have the cognitive abilities or the financial means for higher education have fewer opportunities to make a good living. As a result, they are often relegated to low-paying service jobs or manual labor. Chances are that their children will also have few opportunities for advancement.

Besides these class developments, there have been other shifts in the American culture. Since the mid 80s, the personal computer has dominated the culture. The internet now offers access to unlimited information, films and ebooks. Technological devices such as iPads, smart phones, GPSs, and e-readers offer a multitude of services including email, texting and face-to-face communication.

Changes in Religious Morality

These many cultural shifts have brought with them changes in religious morality.

Abortion has become legal, accessible and often morally acceptable. For most, artificial birth control is permissible. Studies show that many young people have determined that pre-marital sex is also morally acceptable and "living together" has become much more common. At least from college age on, many parents and their children follow a "don't ask, don't tell" policy. As we saw in chapter 3, there is a developing sexual morality among young adults that is quite different from that of their parents.

Even among young adults that are "religious," sexual pleasure is often is taken more casually and can be easily separated from religious beliefs. Gay and lesbian relationships are accepted more commonly, as well as same-sex marriage. Even though many of the churches and religions might oppose such unions, they are becoming more acceptable throughout the States. The Supreme Court recently ruled that married same-sex couples were entitled to federal benefits and, at the same time declined to decide a case from California, effectively allowing same-sex marriages there.

Effects of the Women's Movement on Morality

The woman's movement has made great headway in the United States. Women participate in all types of professions and are beginning to gain wage parity. Unfortunately, the growing incidents of sexual harassment and affairs in the workplace reflect the deterioration of moral standards. Women have also made great advances in the military, but the shocking number of incidents of sexual assaults in the military reflects a breakdown in sexual morality among males.

Women have also made advances in gender equality in religion. There are female rabbis, female priests and bishops in the Episcopal Church, and female ministers in a variety of denominations. Even though the Catholic Church officially opposes the ordination of women, a number of women have become ordained even though they face excommunication for doing so. Catholic Nuns have become extraordinarily well-educated and are leaders in theology, education, social service and care for the needy and the poor. Recent investigations of American nuns by the Vatican would indicate that much of this success is threatening to the Catholic hierarchy.

Frameworks for Approaching Religion and Culture

As we have seen, some people consider religion a mere cultural creation derived from a human sense of weakness and need, and they think that religion was created to appease imaginary and angry gods or to explain the reason for death and the purpose of life. From this point of view, religion is a cultural production and is no longer needed in an advanced intelligent and scientific age.

Other thinkers view religion differently and point out that for most of the history of humankind, religion and culture have intertwined as two legitimate realities. Christopher Dawson, a renowned historian, describes these cultures: "Every moment of life, every social occasion, every gesture and form of expression is consecrated by religious tradition and invested with religious significance. From the peasant in the field and craftsman in his workshop to the priest in his temple and Pharaoh on his throne, the whole society obeys the same laws, moves with the same rhythm, breathes the same spirit. The gods are the life of the land, and human life follows the pattern of the divine ritual."[5] Dawson points out that in these ancient societies, cultures influenced religions and religions in turn shaped culture. Cultural institutions, literature and life were all influenced by religion.

Religion purports to relate to transcendence, the supernatural, sacredness, the holy, and ultimacy. This is the dimension of culture that religion claims to perceive and wants to nurture.[6] There are differing views on how successful religion is today in its mission. George Weigel thinks the world is becoming more religious.[7] Others opine that religion is merely getting more publicity by the media, especially since 9/11, and that the link between politics and religion in this country results in more emphasis on religion. It is important to make a distinction between the growth of religion's role in world affairs, and religiosity, which refers to the actual practice of religion. The latter seems to be on the decline, especially in Europe and among the mainline churches in the United States.

In some cases, religion and culture are still intimately related. This dynamism exists in the interaction between Hinduism and the Indian culture or between Islam and the Arab cultures. We know how non-conformist Protestants shaped the early American culture. We see how religious freedom is now re-shaping the Chinese and Russian cultures. Through the recent history of China and Russia, we have learned how nearly impossible it is to eradicate religion from culture. In both Stalin's Soviet Union and Mao's China, there were brutal efforts to persecute, imprison and kill followers of religion, but today religions are once again beginning to flourish in those areas.

Tillich's Theology of Culture

Paul Tillich (1886-1965) described himself as a theologian of culture and wrote extensively on the relationship between religion and culture. Although his perspectives with regard to religion and culture were originally shaped by his European experience, he later applied them beyond Europe and even beyond Christianity.

Tillich establishes a "method of correlation" in which culture and religion remain separate but at the same time have a means to relate. He maintains that culture raises the questions and religions offer the answers. One of the problems with his system is that there is really no consistent religious authority that answers these questions. Many of answers that Tillich suggests are provided by religion seem to come more from philosophers than from church tradition. Alternatively, Tillich proposes that theologians can sometimes offer the answers, which makes matters considerably more relative. Despite the problems with Tillich's views, they are still important to understand and they remain relevant to today's global society.

Tillich himself witnessed a major cultural shift in his native Germany during the beginning of the Nazi era. A once highly cultured Germany had been reduced to poverty and degradation by a worldwide depression and by having to pay financial retribution after its humiliating defeat in WWI. The dishonored but proud Germans allowed themselves to be wholly taken over by Adolf Hitler, a self-proclaimed dictator who promised that their culture would once again be successful and indeed dominant. The German culture recaptured its old sense of dignity, productivity and happiness at the price of a loss of democracy and millions of lives. As we know, the "Nazi vision" ultimately brought destruction to Germany. This once noble nation had to rebuild its culture once more and then, after the collapse of the Soviet Union, had to re-integrate the people of Eastern Germany that had been shaped for many years by Russian Communism.

Tillich, a successful university professor, theologian and Socialist, was forced to leave his native Germany forever and become an American professor. The lessons he learned are included in his theology of culture, which is a scholarly landmark in the study of religion's relation to culture.

Tillich observed a Hegelian dynamic occurring in different cultures, swinging from one extreme to the other and eventually achieving a synthesis.[8] On the one hand, he observed that certain cultures attempt to be autonomous but at the other side of the spectrum, cultures can rely on exterior authority.

Autonomous Culture

Autonomous cultures can be so bent on freedom that they can lose touch with substantial meaning, ultimacy or spirituality. Here, reason dominates and is cut off from mystery and faith. Personal and social needs take precedence over ultimacy. Religion becomes isolated to the realm of emotion and piety, irrelevant for everyday life.[9]

Tillich observes that autonomous cultures often emerge during times of uprisings like the French Revolution, when the government set out to destroy the Church. Likewise, in periods of great production and trade such as the industrial revolution, greed and the oppression of workers prevailed. Tillich also shows how technology and industry in modern times have led cultures to become autonomous and self-destructive.

In such cultures, the independent individual is the model for culture. These cultures are characterized by less government, fewer laws, a dominance of reason, increased secularization, and exaggerated humanism. Autonomous cultures tend to lose common goals and a moral compass, and can drift into chaos.

Tillich explains that extreme capitalism can lead to a state of self-sufficiency and freedom from all restraints, both secular and religious. Natural resources become mere things to buy and sell for profit. Consumption becomes the norm.[10]

For Tillich, the seeds of destruction are already sown into these cultures because they lack meaning, authority and genuine ultimacy. Think of the culture that existed in the American financial institutions before the collapse in 2008. With a motto "greed is good," and most restraints removed, the banks and markets enjoyed a period of unlimited profits. Meaning was often limited to accumulating things, buying houses and luxuries on credit and enjoying the "good life." Collapse was inevitable and has now spread through parts of Europe where such autonomy was also increasingly more common.

Heteronomous culture

The Greek word "heteros" means "other," so a heteronomous culture is one where a law or authority "other" than the self dominates. The "other" can be the Church, the State or some other authority. Here, a law outside of the people dominates, and absolutism and coercion can prevail. Tillich says these laws are often people in authority who maintain that they speak for the Ultimate, whether it be in the form of "the divine right of Kings" or the divine authority given the Pontiff in Rome. Tillich maintains that when the Church claims absolute authority or identifies itself with the "Kingdom of God" it is going in the heteronomous direction.[11]

When cultures collapse from extreme autonomy, they often turn to absolute authority instead. It times of anxiety, restlessness or even despair, ultimate authority can step in and promise "immortality, spirituality and perfection." Heteronomy does not recognize the God-given rights to personal freedom and conscience. Here, laws that are merely conditional are presented as absolute and unconditional.

There are examples in church history when the church moved in the direction of absolute authority. Tillich cites Vatican I, when the infallibility of the Pope was defined. At the same time, Tillich applauds the Church when it uses strong authority to preserve its central beliefs or to struggle against extreme governments or economic systems. He was encouraged by Vatican II's moves toward collegiality and the development doctrine.

Tilllich cites Nazism as a "demonic" example of heteronomy. Hitler assumed absolute authority and demanded that his people give their hearts, minds and strength to him and to the State. Blood, soil, power, race and nation were all raised to the level of the sacred. The Nazi government exercised absolute authority over all spheres of culture: education, the economy, the media, even the arts. Tillich, who was expelled from his professorship at the University of Berlin because of his views on the Nazi regime, wrote: "I would say that it is a misplaced ultimate concern. I might say this of the Nazis who made people believe in Hitler as the voice of God for the Germans. And they believed that the German people and the Nordic race were the elect, selected by God. This is a bad cause, a demonic cause."[12]

Theonomous Culture

Tillich views the theonomous culture as the ideal; it's a culture where God is basis for human existence and the ultimate that underlies all cultural forms. This culture reflects the eternal, encourages genuine autonomy, and follows laws and forms inspired by the Ultimate. Such a culture communicates "holiness...something ultimate in being and meaning in all its cultural creations."[13] Here, reason remains attached to depth and ultimacy. The laws of a theonomous culture are based on justice; its art points to authentic beauty. This type of culture is grounded in the transcendent, the basis of everything is God. Here, faith is integrated with reason in what Tillich calls a "belief-ful realism." At the same time, Tillich supports personal autonomy in matters of faith because he leaves room for doubt as integral to faith and separates the believer from any ultimate human authority.

For Tillich, the theonomous culture represents the synthesis of genuine autonomy and authentic authority, both of which are rooted in the divine. He gives examples of such cultural movements in the medieval period as well as during the Renaissance, periods where human autonomy was maintained but where both religion and culture maintained their uniqueness. He writes: "If a person who had been deeply moved by the mosaics of Ravenna, the ceiling paintings of the Sistine Chapel or the portraits of the older Rembrandt were asked whether this experience had been religious or cultural, he would find the question difficult to answer. It might be correct to say that the experience is cultural in form and religious in substance. It is cultural because it is not attached to a specific ritual act; but it is religious because it touches on the question of the Absolute and the limits of the human experience."[14] At one point, Tillich sees religion and culture so integrated that he says "The form of religion is culture."[15]

In a theonomous culture, religion speaks a "transcending and therefore a judging and transforming word" to culture.[16] The secular and sacred become integrated, although each attends to its proper spheres. The secular is held independent but still is related to the "holy," although is distinct from it.

Tracy's Revisionist Model

David Tracy (b. 1939), in *Blessed Rage for Order*, developed a new model for relating religion and culture. This model goes beyond the dynamic where culture raises the questions and religion offers answers. In Tracy's model, which I favor, culture and religion are integrated and each can raise questions and offer answers. In the revisionist model, Christian theology has two sources: the Christian texts as well as the common human experience and language. In this model, the religious thinker must listen to the tradition as well as to many questions of culture, and must accept that cultures have their own valid answers to important issues. Here, religion and culture can both raise important questions and offer valid answers; this model can be applied to all religions and cultures. This is made possible by the "religious dimension" that is present in everyday experience, language and culture. Tracy suggests that there is a cultural dimension to religion as well as a religious dimension to culture, so there are always grounds for the two being correlated. The religious person can confidently search within religious tradition as well as culture for the many existential questions as well as possible answers to them. Does this mean, as many young people maintain today, that one can enjoy the music, dance, celebrations of one's culture and hope to find transcendence as well as answers to ultimate questions in the celebration? Conversely, can one find in one's religious traditions offer relevant answers to the many burning cultural questions of today?

Megachurches often connect religion with everyday life. They have listened to their culture's need for socialization, informality, technology, music and teachings about relevant issues. At the same time, these churches flourish because they present a clear set of gospel values that are relevant to people's lives, no matter their age.

Secularization: An Opponent of Religion

One of the strongest opponents to religion in any given culture is the process of secularization. As we shall see, secularization can arise from a number of causes, ranging from culture's turn reason and science for truth to the embracing of atheistic ideologies; from reaction to religion's dominance in culture to religions rejection of culture. In the following we will briefly discuss some of these causes of secularization.

The secularization of culture is a modern phenomenon, beginning with 17th and 18th century philosophers and the development of the Enlightenment. At that time, the culture turned to reason and science, and as a result, the Christian churches that had been dominant lost much of their authority. The churches found that many people no longer turned to them for answers to important questions. Older biblical myths were replaced with "the power of reason" and "unlimited progress." This same dynamic applied in non-Western culture where other religions flourished. Reinhold Niebuhr (1892-1971) once described modern secularism as follows: "The secular culture of today turns out upon close examination to be either a pantheistic religion which identifies existence in its totality with holiness, or a rationalistic humanism for which human reason is essentially god, or a vitalistic humanism which worships some unique or particular vital force in the individual or the community as its god.[17]

Sometimes the separation of religion and culture comes from religion itself. Throughout history, religions have rejected cultures perceived to be "pagan" and have withdrawn from them. The early Buddhist monks lived in forests where they could meditate unsullied by worldly matters. Jews like John the Baptist and communities like the Essenes departed from their cultures to the desert so they could live according to their religious beliefs. The early Christian Fathers and Mothers of the Church withdrew into the desert in order to avoid being corrupted by their culture. From the early centuries, Christians have had monastic and convent communities who abandoned "worldly" culture and lived their own religious styles in seclusion. One thinks of some of the more traditional monasteries throughout the world today.

At times, religion itself can provoke secularization as a reaction to the dominance of a particular religion. This rebellion was seen during the time of the French revolution, as well as during the *Kulturkampf* in 19th century Germany. Daniel DiDomizio provides a brilliant study of the process of secularization in modern day Czech Republic. One would think that secularization in the Czech Republic would have resulted from the oppression of religion by the Nazi and Communist regimes that dominated this country during World War II, but in fact, DiDomizio traces the secularization process in that country to the burning at the stake of a local hero, John Hus, in 1415 by the Catholic authorities. Hus was a much beloved professor, theologian and biblical scholar. Rome rejected his views and invited him to come and discuss them. Hus went in good faith to participate, but was instead burned at the stake. His followers, the Hussites, rebelled and several crusades were launched to overcome them. Ultimately, the Hussites became part of the Protestant Reformation. During the 30 years war, the Protestants in that area, then called Bohemia, were defeated by the Catholics, who forced their faith upon them. Thus, modern day secularization in the Czech Republic goes back to bad memories of Catholic persecution and the Church's alliance with its enemies, in addition to the horrible disruptions by the Nazi and Communist regimes and other modern factors. This demonstrates that each separation of a culture from religion has its own unique history.

Rejection of religion can also come from forces outside the religious community. The powerful theories of Freud, Darwin and Marx in the 19th century contributed to secularization. They aimed to answer the ultimate questions about human nature, the origins of life and the purpose of the human struggle. Freud rejected religion as a primitive and childish neurosis and profoundly affected the secular mindset of modern psychology. Darwin's theory of evolution challenged the notion of there being a Creator and set science on a secular trajectory of its own. Marx rejected religion as a narcotic that comforted and deadened the downtrodden and kept them from revolting against their oppressors. His theories deemed religion to be irrelevant, and he precipitated revolutions and produced cultures where the main goal was to destroy religion. Those who espoused religious faith often faced imprisonment and death..

The focus on reason and science as well as the separation of church from state led to a strong trend toward secularization in the United States. Religious education was not allowed in the public educational system. Eventually, laws were passed against prayer in schools and there was pressure to remove religious symbols from Christmas. Opposition was also voiced when states began to give vouchers that could be used to attend private schools in areas where the public system was below standard. This was good news to church-related schools in the U.S., which serve over 4 million elementary and secondary students. Christian groups now tend to have their own media, which allows secular stations and channels to avoid religious topics. Currently, the vast majority of magazines and best-sellers are secular in content. Corporations, universities, government offices, companies and retail stores usually follow secular values.

At times, religious people themselves call for the separation of religion from culture. Many do not want their religious leaders to get involved in such issues as abortion, birth control, gay and lesbian rights, women's issues and the environment. They see these topics as personal and resist commentary from the pulpit. For many religious followers, religion has become compartmentalized and remains a Sabbath or Sunday matter. Today, religion has become more privatized and personal, affording little connection with social or cultural life. At the same time, there is a serious drop-off of church attendance in the Catholic and mainline Protestant churches. Overall, it is estimated that in the United States, only 29% of the population attends church once a week and 21% never go to church. [18] Many Catholics have left their church, turned off by the sex abuse scandals and cover-ups or by the official church's views on women, birth control, divorce, sexual morality and other issues. Many young Catholics simply drift off, thinking the church is not relevant to their lives. Similarly, many Jews, Muslims, Hindus, Buddhists and those connected with other traditions are no longer are active in their religions, finding them to be irrelevant to contemporary experience. The increasing diversity in this country has moved some people to set aside their own personal religious beliefs when it comes to cultural decisions. With the differing beliefs and values in each religion, it seems impossible to reach a consensus on complicated issues such as abortion, birth control, same-sex marriage, gun control or the death penalty. Some believers maintain their own religious beliefs in these matters but do not want to impose them on others in a free country.

The development of capitalism in the U.S. also contributed to secularization. Capitalism operates under its own rules and does not turn to religion for advice on how to produce goods, sell them for a profit, invest money, manage businesses, compete in the marketplace or accumulate wealth. Capitalism is the engine that drives this country, and it is often based on individualism, self-interest and corporate success rather than the common good. Capitalism can treat employees as a means rather than end. It is fueled by consumerism as well as materialism and it has a high tolerance for greed and injustice. [19]

The mobility of Americans has also contributed to secularization. Many have moved out of their "old neighborhoods" and "religious ghettos" and have set aside the religious formation they received there. The migration to the suburbs as well as the recent return to urban areas has left many people with little sense of community or religious identity.

The eviction of religion from the public forum has been gradual. There was a time when religion dominated the public sphere. The next stage occurred when religion became a rival to reason and science and it had to be pushed out completely. Some people think that the sense of meaninglessness, of feeling rootless and without values, might draw people back to religion. Rowan Williams, the former Archbishop of Canterbury of the Anglican Church, questions: "Are we at the point where as the public sphere becomes more value-free, the very survival of the idea of public sphere, a realm of political argument about vision and education, is going to demand that we take religion a good deal more seriously?"[20]

Post-modernism

The post-modernist mindset has also contributed to the secularization of the American culture. Post-modernism is a slippery term with many different interpretations. In general, post-modernism is a perspective that resists absolutes, reduces everything to relativity and views all ideas as locked in language that is temporary and cultural. Post-modern thinkers are often engaged in radical reconstruction of history, philosophy, even science. They disdain meta-narratives, such as that of the modern Enlightenment that reason would solve all problems and establish unlimited progress, or the modern "American Dream" that envisions that if one works hard one will succeed and have all that is needed for happiness. They also often reject the narratives of religion with regard to salvation and the establishment of a "kingdom of God." Post-modernism rejects centers of power, regardless of whether they be religious or secular. It rejects systems that attempt to control our lives, challenges the smugness of science and the academy and churches in their assumption that they alone have the truth. It both destabilizes thought and offers new ways of thinking. The post-modern perspective has been described as "turbulent, traumatic and dislocating, yet it is also one that is potentially creative."[21] The instability, skepticism, and resistance to authority in today's culture have given post-modernism a great deal of credibility.

Some people suggest that post-modernism is indeed the cause of today's instability; others propose that it is a term that merely describes our present dilemmas about truth and understanding.

Other Causes of Opposition to Religion

In the United States, there are other movements which resist traditional religious traditions: new forms of atheism and agnosticism and the strengthening of so-called civil religion. Today, religion receives serious opposition from non-believers. Atheists like Richard Dawkins and Christopher Hitchens have argued that religion is a danger to society. Hitchens believed that children are being brainwashed in religions and encouraged to be intolerant, righteous, and blindly obedient. Dawkins declared that religious faith is evil because it does not question, demands no proof and allows for no criticism.[22]

Others in today's society describe themselves as "agnostic," that is, they just don't know what to believe about religious matters and often would rather not discuss the topic. Another group maintains that they are "spiritual but not religious," and choose to separate altogether from whatever gives them frustration and aggravation, while another group accepts neither designation. Still others say that is it sufficient for them to be "humanists," and stay distant from talk of transcendence or religious practice.

Civil Religion

Underlying the formal religions in the United States, there seems to be what is often referred to as a "civil religion." Here, the nation tries to understand its history and purpose in religious terms. In this civil religion, Christian fundamentalist values on sexuality are sometimes imposed and religious fervor is invoked with sayings like "God's chosen people" and "the people of God". The words "one nation under God" is used in the pledge of allegiance and "In God We Trust," which appears on coins, invokes a national image rooted in divine providence.[23]

A kind of civil religion seemed to prevail as Americans moved west, confiscating territory from the Native Americans and justifying it with the notion of "Manifest Destiny." President Abraham Lincoln, who kept his distance from formal religion, seemed to believe that this country had a divine mission. At Gettysburg, he praised the "devotion" of those who sacrificed their lives for the Union's mission. He saw the violence of the Civil War as God's punishment for those, both in North and South, who supported "the great national sin" of slavery. Throughout WWI, President Woodrow Wilson called up American citizens to a mission "to make the world safe for democracy." President Ronald Reagan referred to America as the "city on the hill" and referred to the Soviet Union as "the evil empire." During the Cold War, the term "nexus of evil" was given to Communist regimes and many Americans thought the United States was on a mission to defend "the good." More recently, President George W. Bush spoke of his "crusade" against terrorism and this notion colored the invasions of Iraq and Afghanistan. Bush referred to Iraq, Iran and North Korea as "the axis of evil." At sporting events, a kind of religious patriotism is invoked as God, nation and flag are celebrated in the singing of "God Bless America."

This notion that Americans are God's chosen ones has been used to extend goods and services to the needy in other countries, come to their aid when there are natural catastrophes or horrible refugee situations. It has been used as we send our young people into the Peace Corps to serve around the world or to supply education to the developing countries. Unfortunately, such lofty self-imaging has also been used to justify the invasions of other countries, the bombing of innocent civilians, and even the vaporizing of hundreds of thousands of people with atomic bombs.

The Staying Power of Religion

All this being said about secularization, objections to state involvement in religion, and the substitution of civil religion, genuine religiosity is still alive and well in this country. In spite of the lack of church attendance, commitment to religious beliefs seems to be holding up. 90% of Americans say they identify with some religious tradition, 70% believe in God, and 50% pray daily.[24] Religious beliefs seem to be durable, even in the face of a developing secularism in our culture. People still "wonder about the meaning of life, the reality of death, the basis of ethical behavior and human cooperation. They ask, among other questions, why some people commit evil; why the good and innocent should suffer from it; and how, apart from instinct, they can even think to know what is good and what is evil. To answer these questions about life... they develop systems of belief that include religion."[25] Indeed we might say that "the United States is a confusing mix of both the religious and secular."[26]

For many, religion is part of the American Dream—going to church, giving religious values to their children, and wanting these same values to be at least implicitly included in the school curriculum. Americans belong to many church-related organizations, and half of their donations and their volunteer work are related to religion.[27] Americans as a whole are people-oriented, which might be one reason they turn to religion. Reinhold Niebuhr writes: "Whatever might be said about specific religion and religious forms, it is difficult to imagine people without religion; for religion is the champion of personality in a seemingly impersonal world."[28] At the same time, Niebuhr points out that we can drift away from religion because we become independent and impersonal.[29] Today, people can become so stressed with their finances and personal problems, as well as so pre-occupied with work, that they simply lose sight of what religion can offer them.

The United States, although diverse, is still a country where the majority of citizens who belong to a religion are Christian (74%). Among Christians, 51% are Protestant (although many of these belong to "non-denominational" churches) and 23% are Catholic. All other religions comprise 1% or below of the population. Some patterns: 44% of followers have switched their religious affiliation (changed churches or dropped out altogether) and 16% of our citizens are not affiliated with any religion. In fact, one in four young people (18-29) are not affiliated with any religion.

Recent studies reveal that religion is still important in the lives of Americans. 79% of Evangelicals, 52% of mainline Protestants, and 56% of Roman Catholics say that religion is very important in their lives. Church is attended once a week by 58% of Evangelicals, 34% of mainline Protestants, and 42% of Roman Catholics.[30]

Religion has been called part of America's "social capital." Church, synagogue or mosque is where many Americans meet friends and make new acquaintances. Religious people are more likely to be socially active, and involved in politics and service of others. Studies indicate that religious people often enjoy more satisfaction with their lives, are more dedicated to their work, and are even healthier than non religious people.[31]

There is a great diversity among Christians in this country today. They seem to be divided into three categories: conservative, moderate and progressive, with the moderates being the majority.[32] Generally, the traditionalists are the most eager to get involved in public affairs. As people become more traditional in their beliefs, they often become more conservative on social issues such as abortion, same sex marriage and the death penalty. All three groups share common ground when it comes to helping the disadvantaged, although many conservatives object to government assistance for the poor.[33]

Religious Freedom in the United States

The United States' unique position on the relation of Church and State has enabled it to be a leader on the question of religious freedom. The early pilgrims sought freedom from the religious persecution they experienced in England for their Puritan views. They wanted to establish a system of government where they could practice religion as they saw fit. The early settlers envisioned themselves as a "City on a Hill," far superior to the "heathen" Native Americans, and missionaries worked to convert the natives. The founding fathers were of one mind in establishing an early government with no ties to an official religion: neither government nor religion would meddle in each other's affairs.

Religious diversity is recognized in the United States Constitution, and this country is committed to religious freedom. Most of the founding fathers were Christians of a sort, although many of them including Jefferson, Franklin and Madison were Deists, who believed in a Creator God who has little to do with revealing truths or interfering with everyday life. They created civic space that would not be ruled by any religion, and God was not mentioned in the Constitution. Jefferson was adamant that civil rights should have no dependence on religious beliefs. Madison insisted that the state was not in a position to judge religious truth and should not interfere in religious matters. He wrote: "Whilst we assert for ourselves a freedom to embrace, to profess, and to observe the religion which we believe to be of divine origin, we cannot deny an equal freedom to those whose minds have not yet yielded to the evidence which has convinced us."[34]

In spite of this clarity, there have been serious efforts by some groups to have this country declared "Christian," or even to proclaim that it be governed by Jesus Christ. All of these efforts have failed, yet this country is still sometimes described as a "Christian" country. In the 1980s, Christian fundamentalists under the leadership of Jerry Falwell (1933-2007) organized the Moral Majority, a movement that achieved considerable influence on American politics, insisting that their views against evolution, abortion and other issues were followed by American politicians.

In the 2012 presidential campaign, some Christian fundamentalists opposed Mitt Romney's candidacy because they feared that his election would open the door to control by his Mormon church. Others thought that President Barack Obama was a Muslim who would be influenced in his decisions by Islamic law.

The Catholic Church has been wary, if not supportive, of the separation of church and state. Before Vatican II, if the Catholic Church was in the majority it wished to dominate other religions, maintaining that error had no right to exist. On the other hand, when the Church was in the minority it sought protection. Consequently, there was resistance to a document on religious freedom early on at the Vatican Council. Eventually, Fr. John Courtney Murray S.J., an American expert on religious freedom, led the way to a breakthrough document. The Declaration on Religious Freedom stated that all humans have the right to seek the truth as they perceive it in conscience and cannot be coerced in the area of religion.[35]

In recent times, there have been some objections to government being unduly influenced by religious involvement. During George W. Bush's administration, there were objections that he was being unduly influenced by religious fundamentalists and by a biblical notion of "Armageddon" in his approach to the situation in Iraq and its supposed possession of weapons of mass destruction. Some people feared that the White House was being turned into a cathedral that distributed money to faith-based groups and engaged in "crusades" against enemies. There were fears that America was becoming a theocracy, where Christian values were being imposed in a manner similar to the way Islamic values are imposed in governments led by the Sharia Muslim law.[36] There was also much discomfort with the bishops and priests who wanted to withhold Communion from politicians who were pro-choice with regard to abortion in the so-called "Communion wars" in 2008. More recently, the American bishops and many American nuns took a strong political position and opposed the Ryan budget of 2012.

Religion and Political Action

The great Black abolitionist, Frederick Douglas once asserted: "I prayed for twenty years but received not answer until I prayed with my legs."[37] Although Americans are often cautious about mixing religion and politics in their church services, they are usually willing to participate in public affairs.

In recent history, we have seen some extraordinary examples of the blend of religion and political action. Martin Luther King Jr. was a devout Baptist minister and it was obvious from the beginning that his Christian faith and theology were part and parcel of his mission to eliminate segregation and gain constitutional civil rights for his people in this country. In his famous "Letter from Birmingham Jail" he wrote:

> *"I am in Birmingham because injustice is here. Just as the prophets of the 8th century B.C. left their villages and carried*

their 'thus said the Lord' far beyond the boundaries of their hometowns, and just as the Apostle Paul left his village of Tarsus and carried the gospel of Jesus Christ to the far corners of the Greco-Roman world, so I am compelled to carry the gospel of freedom beyond my own hometown."[38]

Similarly, Cesar Chavez, who led the migrant farm workers in their efforts to receive just treatment, was motivated by his Catholic faith to sacrifice himself for his people. He wrote: "All my life, I have been driven by one dream, one goal, one vision: to overthrow a system that treats farm workers in that way, as if they are not important human beings. I think Christ really taught us to go and do something. We can look at his sermons, and it's very plain what he wants us to do: clothe the naked, feed the hungry and give water to the thirsty. It's very simple stuff."[39]

Presently, Jim Wallis (b. 1948), a powerful Christian writer and political activist, also brings his Christian faith to the table as he lobbies Washington for peace and justice. He founded the Sojourners Movement and *Sojourner Magazine* and has for many years been a leader of the "evangelical left," in their efforts to achieve peace and justice in this country. He maintains that: "The Right is comfortable with the language of religion, values, God talk. So much so, that they sometimes claim to own that territory. They own God. But then they narrow everything down to one or two issues: abortion and gay marriage. I am an evangelical Christian and I can't ignore thousands of verses in the Bible on [another] subject, which is poverty. I say at every stop, 'Fighting poverty's a moral value, too.' There's a whole generation of young Christians who care about the environment. That's their big issue. Protecting God's creation, they would say, is a moral value, too. And, for a growing number of Christians, the ethics of war—how and when we go to war, whether we tell the truth about going to war—is a religious and moral issue as well."[40]

Religious Lobby Groups

One way in which Americans accept mixing religion and politics is with religious lobby groups. There are a growing number of religious organizations whose mission statements include a commitment to lobby for just legislation. There are now over 100 of these non-profit groups, including The Christian Coalition, the U.S. Catholic Conference, the Union of American Hebrew Congregations, the National Council of Churches, the National Association of Evangelicals and Network. Each of these organizations has its own identity, beliefs, values and hopes to add their voice to the pluralistic American culture. Most groups lobby not only for their own agenda but also for the common good. The Jewish lobby has been most effective in promoting the State of Israel and securing funds for Israel since its inception in 1948.

One of these groups, Network, received considerable publicity during the 2012 presidential campaign. Network was founded over 40 years ago by 47 Catholic Sisters and has been a strong voice in Washington ever since, lobbying to close the gap between rich and poor and opposing policies that are rooted in racism, greed and violence. In the 2012 campaign, some of the members organized "Nuns on the Bus," a tour of depressed areas and service groups in order to counter Republican moves to cut food stamps and other governmental aid to the poor.

These groups seem to contradict the Freudian position that religion is childish as well as the Marxist view that religion is an opiate that dulls the masses to their suffering. Instead these movements demonstrate that religion can transform humans and their cultures and can inspire people to give everything, even their lives, for the causes of peace and justice.

Faith based initiatives

Religiously affiliated organizations provide public service in this country and have been supported by government grants. This includes large organizations such as the Lutheran Services in America, Catholic Charities, the YMCA and the Salvation Army.

When federal welfare reform was passed in 1996, funds were extended to many faith-based organizations through the Charitable Choice provision in the bill. Government funds for faith-based organizations were increased under President George W. Bush and continued in the Obama administration.[41]

Religion and presidential campaigns

Religion can play a prominent role in political campaigns, but winds can shift quickly. In 2004, when George Bush took over the presidency and the Republicans took over the House and the Senate, religious conservatives were elated and felt their influence would prevail for some time. Four years later, the Democrats swept into office, led by Barack Obama. The well-known-religious conservative, James Dobson, told his followers that this was the "most discouraging period" in their long struggle. Almost immediately, an economic crash ensued and the religious right became hopeful to once again lead the Republicans back to victory. Many conservative Bishops and Catholics aligned with the religious right, not because they shared their biblical literalism, but because of their allegiance to the absolute moral positions of the Roman Catholic "Magisterium." Obama's ultimate victory in the election might indicate that conservative religious views have lost much of their political influence.

Religious Fundamentalism and Politics

The term "fundamentalist" became popular in politics in the late 1970s and was used to describe conservative Christians who sought to return to the fundamentals contained in the Bible and apply these to their politics. As mentioned earlier, this group organized and soon became a political force under the leadership of ministers like Jerry Falwell and Pat Robertson. After 9/11, fundamentalism took on broader applications toward Islamic fundamentalists and became associated with extremists and terrorists. Here, we limit its use to Christian fundamentalists who reject Western secular norms and want to go back to what they perceive to be the fundamentals of biblical teachings. They have become a militant, non-violent movement with a strong group identity, and their goal is to purify the public sphere of its moral failures. Generally, members are family-centered, champion "family values," and are often culturally patriarchal.

Fundamentalists often fear that their religious values are under attack so they may become rigid in their morality and defensive toward modern culture and politics. They fight to change any laws or policies, domestic or foreign, that conflict with their beliefs. Thus, they are suspicious of such movements as women's liberation or gay rights, seeing them aimed at moral license.[42] The 2012 Republican convention produced slogans like "A Great Awakening" and "political power comes from God" which are all good examples of how many try to integrate religion into the political arena.

Catholics and Politics

Catholics have seen periods of opposition and discrimination the political arena. Al Smith, the Catholic candidate for President in 1928, lost the election in part because of his Catholicism and the fear of many Americans that this country would have been managed from Rome. The same fears emerged when John F. Kennedy ran for president in 1960. Kennedy was able to convince Protestants that his Catholicism would not influence his national decisions and he was chosen to be the first Catholic elected to the office of U.S. President. (There have been 35 Protestant Presidents.) Joseph Biden and Paul Ryan, both Catholics, opposed each other as Vice-Presidential candidates in the election of 2012.

While Catholics have not been very successful gaining the highest office in the land, they have done well in other key national positions. In recent history, about 1/3 of those serving in Congress have been Catholics. In 2011-2013 Nancy Pelosi and John Boehner, both Catholics, were respectively Minority and Majority Leaders of the House of Representatives. Other prominent Catholics politicians include: John Kerry, Rick Santorum, Newt Gingrich, Jerry Brown, Jeb Bush, Andrew Cuomo, Bobby Jindal and Rudy Giuliani. The 2012 Supreme Court was comprised of six Catholics out of the nine justices: Samuel Alito, Anthony Kennedy, John Roberts (Chief Justice), Antonin Scalia, Sonia Sotomayor, and Clarence Thomas. Three Jewish Justices occupied the three remaining seats.

Today, it has become more difficult to speak of "the Catholic vote" because there is such a broad spectrum of political views and party affiliation among Catholics. The Catholic Church in the U.S. is split among progressives and the conservatives who object to many of the liberal reforms of Vatican Council II and remain loyal to Rome in their beliefs and moral values. This latter group would usually oppose birth control, the pro-choice position on abortion, same-sex marriage and the ordination of women. On the other side, there are many progressive Catholics who accept the moral authority of conscience, a variety of interpretations of Christian beliefs, and religious freedom for everyone in this country. Most progressives would have no problem with the use of artificial birth control for themselves or others. They might also be pro-choice with regard to abortion. Even though they might oppose it themselves, they would honor the consciences of other citizens of this country. Progressive Catholics would usually approve same-sex marriage as well as the ordination of women. The majority of Catholics might describe themselves as moderates and would be open to change in some areas and might differ from the official church in one area or another. The so-called "Catholic vote" is well divided among Democrats, Republicans and Independents. Many conservative Catholics followed the lead of their bishops and voted for Romney, while many liberal Catholics voted for Obama. Latino(a) Catholics for most part voted for Obama.

Globalized Culture and Religion

It is only since the 1980s that globalization has become a buzzword. While globalization does seem to be a unique reality today, it has existed in many ways for millennia. At some point, the original humans seem to have migrated from Africa, and perhaps other areas, to gradually spread across the globe. Humans spread across Europe and Asia and then moved on to the Americas.

History of Globalization

Commonly there have been efforts to unite the world by domination. Powerful imperial forces developed (Babylonian, Assyrian, Greek, Roman) who attempted to extend their influence. In the 8th century, the Muslims conquered much of the known world, including parts of Europe, and gained control of the age-old trade routes from the orient and the Middle East for the exchange of products. The Vikings, Scandinavian seamen, merchants and pirates from the 8th to the 11th centuries, raided and plundered wide areas of Europe, Asia and the North Atlantic islands. In the 13th century, Genghis Khan established a great Empire. The medieval crusades sought control of the Middle East, along with its trade routes. In the age of exploration, Spain, Portugal, France and England extended their influence westward. Magellan circled the globe from 1515-27. The Spanish often controlled the seas until the English finally destroyed the Spanish Armada in 1588. During the colonial period, a number of countries used their power to take over Asia, Africa, and the Americas. In the early 19th century, Napoleon conquered most of Western Europe, Poland, and Northern Africa and attempted to take over Russia. The British Empire was so extensive in the 19th century that it was said: "On her dominions the sun never sets." During that period, there were great migrations from Europe and the Orient. In the 1930s, Adolf Hitler, the leader of Germany, set out to eventually dominate the world with a Nazi Reich that was to last for a millennium. At the same time, Japan set out to include most of the Orient in its Empire. Early Communist leaders hoped for the eventual domination of the globe by Communism.

Since the devastating destruction and loss of life in World War II (40 million died, including 12 million in the concentration camps), global leaders have been on guard against imperial intentions, the use of nuclear weapons and the abuse of human rights, and have often prevented military expansions. Today, organizations such as the United Nations seek world unity and abuses to justice and world peace are scrutinized by the World Court, the International Court of Justice and the International Criminal Court. Such organizations have not always been successful, as we have seen in the genocides in places like Rwanda, Bosnia and Darfur, the anarchy in Sudan,

Somalia and the Congo. Nevertheless, there seems to be enough influence in these organizations to stand in the way of any attempt of global takeover.

Today's globalization is unique and often so complex that it is difficult to grasp. As Ted Turner comments, "Globalization is in fast-forward, and the world's ability to understand it and react to it is in slow motion."[43] Globalization has a range of meanings: the interconnection of nations; the linking of economies; the westernization of the world; social relations through the Internet; or aid to areas that suffer famines or catastrophes. It has been said that in one way the world is getting smaller but in another it is getting larger, more complicated and difficult to understand.[44]

Globalization links money, markets, economies, education, cultures and religions. Rapid travel, the Internet and other factors have made visiting or contacting another country just a click of an electronic device or a plane trip away. Cameras on smart phones have made it possible to view uprisings, catastrophes and many other events on the news instantaneously. Any occasions where people are oppressed and any efforts to dominate them can be observed almost as they happen. One thinks of the global dramatization of the fall of Mubarak in Egypt and of Gaddafi in Libya in 2011. These connections present a challenging situation for anyone with imperial designs! In addition, the United Nations constantly monitors the globe, and the World Court stands ready to prosecute those who order atrocities. Since 1949, the International Red Cross and Red Crescent have stood ready to assist in wars and disasters. World interconnectedness is also celebrated bi-annually with the Olympics and annually with the World Cup in soccer. Green Peace stands ready to oppose nations and organizations that endanger the environment, and Amnesty International is a strong organization that acts as a watchdog over human rights abuses. The Global Health Council monitors health, Interpol pays attention to criminal activity, and strategic military and naval bases keep a watchful eye out for aggression. NATO, an alliance of 28 member states from North America and Europe, also guards global safety.

Global Citizens

Part of developing a "We" consciousness involves developing an identity as a "global citizen" or "citizen of the world." This entails being concerned about human rights, gender equality, ecology, and the plight of refugees, as well as doing what one can to participate in some of these issues. A global citizen today is a person who understands what is going on in the world and, with compassion and generosity, attempts to assist those in need. A global citizen uses his or her power, prestige and funds to advocate for the less fortunate. The motivations here are: the value of human life, a respect for other cultures and traditions, a desire for justice, harmony and peace, and a practical sense of what can be realistically done to help others without creating a dependency.[45]

Early on, prophetic thinkers spoke of a coming together of the world as a unified whole. In the 1920s, Pierre Teilhard de Chardin wrote about a stage of evolution where human minds would converge (the noosphere).[46] During that same period, the great English philosopher, Alfred North Whitehead, wrote of a process within the universe, a "Planning beyond planning," that is bringing the universe to a wholeness.[47]

In the 1940s, the renowned Reinhold Niebuhr wrote: "Perhaps the most significant development in our day is that the cumulative effects of history's unity in length is daily increasing its unity in breadth. Modern technical civilization is bringing all civilizations and cultures, all empires and nations into closer juxtaposition to each other."[48] Of course, Niebuhr notes how two world wars tragically threatened this process of unification.

There have been more recent indications of world unity. In 1960, Marshall McLuhan coined the well-known phrase "the global village." This phenomenon occurred when President John F. Kennedy was assassinated on Nov. 22, 1963 and the event was profoundly experienced across the globe, as well as in 1991 when the Soviet Union collapsed and there was talk of "a new world order." In 1985, many famous artists gathered to sing "We are the World" to call attention to the famine in Ethiopia and again in 2010 to bring assistance to those suffering from the earthquake in Haiti. People worldwide will always remember 9/11/2001, when terrorists flew planes into the World Trade Buildings and the Pentagon! In 2008, people reached out to the victims of a devastating earthquake in China and the again to those who suffered from the horrific earthquake and 2010 tsunami in Japan, as well as to the victims of the earthquake in Haiti during the same year. Today, there seems to be a new world-consciousness that never existed in the same way before!

More recently, Ken Wilber, whose models are adapted in this text, has developed an integral approach to human consciousness. It is his position that we are now moving into an integral age, an age of synthesis. He sees the movement from intra-cultural to trans-cultural, from ethnocentric pluralism to global integralism, from relativism to global integralism.[49]

Some see other forces than unity in the cultural process today. Besides the global dynamic, which points to the inter-connectedness of world economies, markets and ecologies, there is a process of disintegration. The failing economies of countries like Greece significantly affect those of the Euro-zone, as well as economies in other countries throughout the world. Political chaos in countries like Syria, Somalia and Afghanistan reverberate around the globe. The rapid growth of manufacturing in India and China deeply affect employment in the United States and other countries. Pollution in the United States, India and China increases global warming and contributes to extreme weather conditions throughout the world.

Another dynamic is emerging globally, perhaps as a reaction to globalization. These are the strong movements toward individualization, national identity and cultural uniqueness. After the collapse of the Soviet Union, many countries like Poland, Ukraine and Estonia emerged from that dissolution quite excited about their freedom and independence and proud of their national cultural, language and religion, as well as their links with Europe. Russia, on the other hand seems to be withdrawing, showing little interest in European culture or in learning other languages, and has once again begun to build up its military. Many countries in Asia, Africa and South America are strongly developing their national identities and reviving past cultures and religions. James Rubenstein observes: "People are taking deliberate steps to retain distinctive cultural identities. They are preserving little-used languages, fighting fiercely to protect their religions, and carving out distinctive economic roles."[50] In addition, in some countries in Europe and in the United States, there is a resistance to immigration. "Undocumented aliens" is a brand given those who come here illegally to do the harvesting and menial jobs that few Americans are willing to do.

Experts point to both the advantages and disadvantages of globalization. On the plus side, globalization offers a wide diversity of food, clothing and products of all kinds. It can provide security, give aid to needy nations, and increase the opportunity for cultural enrichment through travel and exchange of films, music and art. Globalization has led to variety of educational opportunities for students, as well as a valuable exchange of technologies.

At the same time, a consequence of globalization in some indigenous cultures has been the loss of identity. The so-called "macdonaldization" or "walmartization" of the globe can result in the loss of diversity of foods and even cause poor nutrition. A certain western homogenization can occur as local cultures lose their customs and traditions. Furthermore, the economies of the Northern hemisphere can overwhelm those of the South, and the developed countries can dominate the developing countries. The shoemaker in the Nicaraguan market who can expertly measure a foot and make a fine pair of shoes on the spot loses his life's work when the American shoe companies move into the market with their cheap machine-made shoes. The expert weaver of carpets in India fails to be able to meet the export taxes and falls victim to the factory that makes mass quantities of machine-made carpets. There is also concern that the global thrust will overwhelm the development of individuality in nations and people, threaten equality among peoples, and result in a boring uniformity of cultures.[51]

Many young people preparing to enter the job market complain that the complexity and fast innovation of global industries makes it difficult for them to prepare for the future. It becomes increasingly more difficult for colleges and universities to provide the proper skills needed for a job market that is in such constant flux. At times, a student can prepare for a career that has radically changed or disappeared by the time the preparation is finished.

Religion and World Unity

Niebuhr was convinced that in spite of the horrific world wars and all the opposition to religion from Nazism and Communism, religion would ultimately bring the world together. "The world is also one; and man is a creature who must achieve a spiritual unity... Since man's spiritual freedom rises to a height where he surveys the whole world, he must always seek to achieve that unity in terms of the 'meaning of the whole.' Religion is always the search for the meaning of life; and the meaning of life must be found in man's relationship to his total world."[52]

Nels Ferre maintains that every culture is in a way a venture in faith. This faith can be *supranatural*, which is dualistic and views the spiritual as a different realm cut off from the natural. The supranatural perspective isolates religion from culture or at best sees it as standing in judgment of culture. Religion here has little relevance to or power over everyday life or social change. *Natural* faith, on the other hand, precludes faith in a transcendent reality. It is limited to the human for its power and vision within culture. Ferre holds that it is *supernatural* faith that relates the spiritual to the natural and can be a creative force in the world. It is a faith that is free, but works within God's power and providence. For Ferre, human purpose and action are not enough on their own. He says: "Man's life is too short, too powerless, and too shut-in for these to suffice. Man needs to do more than work with God. He needs to rest in God and see God's fulfilling action beyond his own achievement."[53] For Christians wanting to be active in creating the culture,

Ferre has three presuppositions: 1. A world beyond culture that explains the origins of human history and the standards and power for making creative change; 2. God, the personal Spirit of Agape, who creates the conditions for freedom, providence, trust and prayer; 3. Life everlasting as a permanent direction for life and culture.[54]

Religions have the numbers to make an impact on global issues. Islam has over 1.3 billion followers world-wide, the Protestant and Orthodox churches together number over 1 billion; there are also over 1 billion Roman Catholics, 800 million Hindus, 400 million Buddhists, and 15 million Jews. We can only imagine the impact these and the other religions could have if they joined in unison for peace and justice in the world.

Most of these religions have their own worldwide organization that has a voice in world affairs. The Muslim Organization of the Islamic Conference represents 57 countries. The Christian World Council of Churches represents 340 different denominations. The Vatican represents nearly 8000 archdioceses and dioceses around the world. The Parliament of World Religions, which convenes every four years, invites over 10,000 civil and religious leaders from more than 80 countries to engage in dialogue on national and global issues.

Some religious scholars admit these are impressive numbers but point to the fact that Christianity faces a crisis in Europe and possibly in the United States, especially in mainline Protestantism and liberal Catholicism. Many Christians are "believing without belonging" and hold onto remnants of the tradition, but do not attend church. Others are "belonging without believing," that is, they attend church at times but really don't adhere to many of the beliefs of their church. Europeans often drop out but stay identified with the religion of their nation. Americans don't have a national religion, so they might drop out and become "spiritual but not religious."[55]

Only recently has such global discourse turned its attention to religion. One reason for this is the concern about the so-called "clash of civilizations" between the West and Islamic extremists. Terrorism is now a global concern, and the facility of Al-Qaeda to disperse to various parts of the world just as the military moves against them has distressed many on-lookers. Another reason is that some are worried about the tensions among religions themselves (e.g. Jews vs. Muslims in Israel, Hindus vs. Muslims in India, Buddhists vs. Hindus in Sri Lanka). Many people are concerned that these local conflicts could lead to larger conflagrations. A third reason for this global discourse is the growing awareness that it is often a mistake to simplistically blame world-wide struggles on religion and neglect the political, social and economic issues that might solve them. Finally, there is concern about the conflicts within the religions themselves; Sunni vs. Shia in Islam; Protestant vs. Catholics in Ireland; the clash of Evangelicals with liberal Catholics and Protestants in the so-called "culture wars" in the U.S. Some are concerned that this clash of values will influence American foreign policy and possibly lead to international blunders, like "nuking" a hostile country.[56]

The Contribution of World Religions to Culture

The followers of the various world religions bring a great deal to the globalized table. Their people offer experience with drought and extreme weather, poverty, refugee camps, violence, injustice, discrimination and so many other sources of suffering. They bring their sacred beliefs, values and commitment to mission. Many inspire a growing awareness that religions can play an important role in making the world a better place.

Hinduism

Hindus cherish their ancient faith in the sacredness of all life and the importance of sustaining good karma in their lives. The Hindu "eternal law" teaches that "Thou art that," meaning that the deepest inner self of each person is identified with ultimate reality. They bring their commitment to "ahimsa," (do not harm) as well as to their awareness that inner peace and happiness come from detachment and liberation from desire. One of their gifts to the world is yoga, which helps develop self–control of the mind, will, senses and spirit and ultimately can assist the practitioner in becoming one with the divine.

Mahatma Gandhi (1869-1948), the greatest Hindu figure in modern times, spent most of his life struggling for peace and justice; first for twenty years in South Africa and then in his native India. He was beaten, jailed and berated, but continued to hold onto his Hindu/Jain belief in the power of non-violence. His teaching inspired Martin Luther King, Jr., Cesar Chavez and many others who gave themselves to the cause of justice.

Hindus also point with pride to Anuradha Koirala, who won the CNN Hero Award in 2010 for her dedication to the rescue and rehabilitation of thousands of young women victimized by sex trafficking in Nepal. They also dearly love another woman, Amma, their "Mother" who comforts millions with her presence and hugs, while at the same time raising funds to build homes for the poor, hospitals, schools, shelters and soup kitchens for the poor around the world.

Buddhism

Buddhists are important to global culture because of their deep sense of love and compassion for all human beings. Buddhists value meditation to help let go of negative thoughts and actions, and they advocate a life of rightness on all levels. Buddhists are committed to the alleviation of suffering from all people and believe that letting go of desires and evils can liberate people from suffering. Selflessness and the achievement of a pure heart are strong Buddhist goals. At the same time, they encourage self-reliance and a constant striving for enlightenment. Buddhists also have a keen sense of community, realizing the value of spiritual strength in numbers.

The well-known Tibetan Buddhist, the Dalai Lama, has toured the world for fifty years (since his exile from his country), inspiring millions with his humility, gentleness and wisdom. He has championed non-violence, justice and freedom for his own Tibetans as well as for people throughout the world. Another Buddhist monk, Thich Nhat Hanh, started his personally dangerous advocacy for peace during the Vietnam war and has continued this mission ever since in his teachings, many books and on-going advocacy for non-violence. He has been a strong advocate of "engaged Buddhism," and urges all Buddhists to become more aware of world problems and more proactive in work for peace and justice.

Judaism

The Jewish community brings its ancient tradition of valuing God's creation, respecting life because it comes from God. It also contributes to global unity with its prophetic commitment to peace and justice. Jews have suffered perhaps more than followers of any other religion, notably during the Holocaust of WWII. They know how to survive and help others survive the worst through enduring hope and courage. Jews have an undying commitment and faith in the One God and believe that this God offers covenant, protection and liberation. They know that from the beginning, sin comes from humans, not God and their experience of the Exodus has taught them that their God is one who ultimately frees his people from their bondage and suffering.

Dartmouth Professor Susannah Heschel, daughter of the great Rabbi Heschel, has been an effective advocate against anti-Semitism and a champion for women's liberation world-wide. Justice Ruth Ginsburg, a member of the United States Supreme Court, has also been an impressive advocate for women's rights. She has been an outspoken supporter of abortion rights and the equality of women. Elie Wiesel, a survivor of the Nazi death camps, promoted justice in the world as well as the dignity of each human being in his many writings and lectures. In 1983 he was awarded the Nobel Peace Prize for his work towards peace, human dignity and atonement.

Islam

Islam brings a strong tradition on the sacredness of Allah's creation, including human life. Muslims have great devotion to God and the need for a life of obedience to divine laws. They believe that Allah's unity is reflected in the oneness of humanity and creation, and that humans have a responsibility to maintain balance and harmony in the world. Muslims believe that they are trustees of creation and are accountable for how they treat people and the earth. They are committed to serving the poor and working for justice in the world. They are engaged in "jihad," which in the Qur'an generally means the struggle against the dark side of human nature, the side that oppresses, grabs with greed or violates others' rights.

Tawakkul Karman's name appeared in the news when she won the Nobel Peace Prize in 2011. For years, Karman has been a human rights activist in Yemen and been arrested for demonstrating for a free press and against human rights abuses by the government in Yemen. In 2002, a young Pakistani activist for the education of women was shot in the head and neck by members of the Taliban and gained international notoriety for her courage.

Amina Wadud is a courageous advocate for women. She is a Qur'an scholar who teaches in Indonesia and has led controversial all-women mosque services. Her books, which include *Inside the Gender Jihad*, although extremely controversial among male Imams, have been influential globally.

Others

Many other religions bring valuable beliefs and actions to the global struggle. Baha'i is an effective and courageous advocate for peace throughout the world, Jainism advocates strongly for non-violence, Sikhs are dedicated to service and feed countless people in the kitchens attached to their temples, and Confucianism champions firm family values and respect for human dignity. Taoism teaches engagement in the creative process within the world, Shinto honors the spirits that exist within all of creation, and the Native American religions honor the spirits within all things and call for respect for nature and peaceful agreements among people.

The Contribution of Christianity to Culture

The Mission of the Churches

The human fallout from globalization presents tremendous challenges to the Christian churches. Poverty continues to grow at a distressing pace. In 1820, the difference in income between the richest and poorest countries was 3-1. In 1973, it was 44-1 and is now above 80-1. 48% of the world's population earns less than $2 per day. Half of the world's wealth is held by only 2% of the world's adults. Three of the richest people in the world hold more assets than that of 48 nations or ¼ of the world's nations.[57] Nelson Mandela has commented on this: "Massive poverty and obscene inequality are such terrible scourges of our times—times in which the world boasts breathtaking advances in science, technology, industry and wealth accumulation—that they have to rank alongside slavery and apartheid as social evils."[58] Every hour more than 3,000 children die of preventable diseases or hunger related causes. It has been estimated that two days of military spending by the U.S. could provide the health care services necessary to prevent the deaths of 3 million infants a year.[59]

Churches struggling to assist people in need recognize that the whole system is so complicated that it is hard know where to begin. There are many nations involved, but also numerous corporations. In fact, of the world's 100 top economic entities, 51 are corporations and 49 are countries. Corporations like Exxon-Mobil and Walmart have annual sales figures larger than a number of nations combined. [60] Moreover, the whole system gives the impression that no one can be held responsible. As Thomas Friedman has pointed out: "In the globalization system, we reach for the internet, which is a symbol that we are connected but nobody is quite in charge."[61]

At the beginning of the new millennium, the United Nations listed the enormous challenges that face the process of globalization: extreme hunger and poverty (10 million children die each year before the age of 5); lack of primary education (in Sub-Saharan Africa and South Asia less that 60% of children are enrolled in school); gender inequality (women have much less access to education, jobs or fair salaries); child mortality; lack of maternal care (530,000 women die each year during pregnancy and childbirth); spread of HIV/AIDS, malaria and other diseases; lack of safe drinking water and sanitation (1 billion lack access to safe water and 2.6 billion have poor sanitation); and a need for development and trade assistance to poorer countries.[62]

Catholic Social Teaching

Christians have from the beginning been concerned with carrying out Jesus' mission to the poor and needy. Acts recounts how the early Christians held all things in common and shared among themselves. The early bishops often served as the dispensers of funds and goods to the needy. Many religious orders were founded for the purpose of serving, educating and providing health care for the needy. Modern Catholic social teaching reclaims that social mission and begins with the writings of Pope Leo XIII (1810-1903). Leo lived in trying times of revolution, industrialism and colonialism. He was astutely aware of the dangers of extreme secular individualism on the one side, and the movement toward anti-religious and collectivism on the part of Marxist communism on the other. He denounced the extremes in both capitalism and communism and he stood up for private property, just wages, collective bargaining, and State assistance for the needy. Pope Pius XI (1857-1939) faced many new world threats: the devastating effects of WWI, the economic collapse of the Great Depression, a Soviet Union dominated by the ruthless Joseph Stalin and the rise of Nazism under the brutal leadership of Adolf Hitler, who seemed to be eager to start another world war. In 1931, Pius proposed a new social order based on Christian principles and advocated cooperation, concern for the poor and attention to the common good. He also urged Catholic laity to lead social reform movements.

Pope John XXIII (1881-1963) wrote significant papal letters on peace and justice that gained worldwide attention. He also initiated Vatican II, which brought the Church into the modern world. Vatican Council II announced, in a classic statement on solidarity, "The joys and hopes, the grief and anguish of our time, especially of those who are poor and afflicted, are the joys and hope, the grief and anguish of the followers of Christ." Pope Paul VI (1897-1978) continued this work, writing brilliantly on just progress and development and appearing in the U.N. to urge that there be "No more war." Pope John Paul II (1920-2005) was indefatigable in his efforts to stress the dignity of work, critique both the rigid systems of capitalism and communism, and to work directly for the defeat of the latter. He was indeed a global pope who traveled widely to condemn injustice and oppression. Pope Benedict XVI also traveled considerably and has been a strong advocate for human dignity, human rights, peace and justice. Pope Francis has provided fresh perspective to the papacy and is known for living a simple life and serving the poor.

The prominent Catholic theologian, Hans Kung, has been an effective advocate for development of a world ethic for decades. From his perspective, there will be "no survival without a world ethic No peace without peace between the religions. No peace between the religions without dialogue between religions."[63] Kung recognizes the ethical treasures within the world religions and the valuable insights of social and political ethicists, as well as the important contributions that non-believers have to make. Kung urges intense dialogue among all of these agents and the gradual formation of a global ethic that can lead the way toward peace and justice in a world that contains so much potential for its own destruction.

For a time, some of the Catholic and Protestant churches in Central and South America were committed to a liberation theology, which applied the gospels to the struggle of the poor and a militant resistance to their oppression. Archbishop Oscar Romero, who was assassinated for confronting his oppressive government in El Salvador, has become the icon in that movement. The movement still exists and its influence has spread to parts of Africa and Asia.

Justice in other Christian churches

Protestants also turned to social justice in the 19th century, led by the writings of Walter Rauschenbusch (1861-1918). These concerns have now reached the mainstream, and even some of the evangelical churches have become involved in social justice, led by ministers like Jim Wallis, an evangelical writer and political activist mentioned earlier and John Yoder, a Mennonite theologian and pacifist. It would seem that many evangelicals have turned their attention from "the end of the world" to service to the world.

A significant number of Christian churches, including the megachurches, have returned to the radical and prophetic teaching of the scriptures that are concerned with justice and defense of the vulnerable and poor. Many Christians now perceive the historical Jesus as one who grew up and worked in poverty and carried out a ministry that focused on serving the disabled, diseased and poor. He preached a kingdom of God, which was within the individual, as well as the loving, saving presence of God in the world and in all people. He summed up his mission in a synagogue one Sabbath after he had read the passage for the day from Isaiah 61: "The Spirit of the Lord is upon me, because he has anointed me to bring the good news to the poor. He has sent me to proclaim release to the captives and recovery of sight to the blind, to let the oppressed go free, to proclaim the year of the Lord's favor." (Luke 4:18-19)

Committed to carrying forth Jesus' mission

All Christians now face some unique questions that arise from globalization. Am I willing to face responsibilities during the present ecological crisis? How can I personally respond to the desperate needs of those in my own country and abroad? In purchasing, am I willing to be thoughtful of where things are made and whether they are made by people who are exploited? Am I open to become better informed about human rights abuses and become actively involved in protesting them?[64]

A noted Christian activist, Neil Ormerod suggests that the Christian who wants to become active in social justice must develop a faith that goes beyond beliefs to a deep relationship with God and Jesus, as well as a commitment to action for others in need. He adds that this entails the development of hope that has confidence in God's providence and grace; that works in the present, and looks forward to a better future. It means cultivating love that is universal and can embrace not only those near but those unseen and afar. Christians are called to be attentive to the truth of the situations going on around them and in solidarity with others who work for peace and justice as well as with those who struggle.[65]

Summary

We have looked at religion from the point of view of the "We." We have seen how religions have been shaped by human culture, in particular how past and present cultural movements have shaped religion is the U.S. This religious influence has brought forth both critics as well as advocates.

We looked at Tillich's theology of culture and saw the results when culture rejects religion (autonomy), asserts absolute authority over it (heteronomy), or integrates with religion (theonomy). We looked at Tracy's revisionist model, where culture and religion maintain a healthy mutual influence. We examined modern secularization, which seeks to exclude religion, and we looked at the critiques of religion by post-modernism, atheism and agnosticism. We examined the construction of civil religion in this country, as well as how the principles of separation of church and state and religious freedom are upheld in this country. We have shown that in spite of the many resistances to religion today, religion is still seems to be alive and well in the United States.

On a broader scale, religion today has to deal with globalization. The world has moved beyond older efforts at colonialism and global domination and now sees the people of the globe linked economically and through technology. Travel, media and the internet have linked the people of the world in ways never before experienced. Many religious people have become "global citizens" and seek to help people locally as well in other parts of the world with funds or direct assistance. World religions have joined hands in projects to assist refugees, the rights of women, in health care, peace and environmental issues. And many local religious "heroes" have emerged who put their religious values to work for others.

SUGGESTED READINGS

Thomas Banchoff, ed., *Democracy and the New Religious Pluralism* (New York: Oxford University Press, 2007), 259.

Hecht, Richard D. and Vincent F Biondo III, eds. *Religion and Culture: Contemporary Practices and Perspectives*. Minneapolis, MN: Fortress Press, 2012.

Kenneth D. Wald and Allison Calhoun-Brown, *Religion and Politics in the United States* (New York: Rowman & Littlefield Pub. Inc., 2011),

Michael Ryan and Les Switzer, *God in the Corridors of Power* (Denver, CO: Praeger, 2009),

Jan Aart Scholte, *Globalization* (New York: Palgrave, 2005), 20.

Jurgen Osterhammel and Niels P. Peterson, *Globalization: A Short History* (Princeton, NJ: Princeton University Press, 2005), 3.

Nigen Dower and John Williams, eds., *Global Citizenship* (New York: Routledge, 2002), 173.

See Ken Wilber, *The Integral Vision* (Boston: Shambhala, 2007).

James Rubenstein, *An Introduction to Human Geography* (Upper Saddle River,NJ: Pearson Prentice Hall, 2008), xv.

Peter Beyer and Lori Beaman, *Religion, Globalization and Culture*, (Boston: Brill, 2007), 38.

J. De Gruchy, *Christianity and Democracy* (Cambridge: Cambridge University Press, 1995)

Daniel G. Goody, *Globalization, Spirituality, and Justice* (Maryknoll, NY: Orbis Books, 2007), 4-5.

◻▣ VIDEOS ONLINE

What is American Culture? Part 1

   http://www.youtube.com/watch?v=PoG97ge66tA

On Common Ground: America's Religious Diversity

   http://www.youtube.com/watch?v=jU9fCwsuFFU

A Conversation with Dr. Paul Tillich - Part 1

   http://www.youtube.com/watch?v=oXoHORtc7OQ

Rev. Dr. David Tracy

   http://www.youtube.com/watch?v=7qTtCR2chNY

Secularization and the Transformation of Faiths

   http://www.youtube.com/watch?v=pC27eoWf-wI

Let's Talk Post-Modernism and the Emergent Church...

   http://www.youtube.com/watch?v=gv6uxCch7oc

An Evening with Brian McLaren 2009

   http://www.youtube.com/watch?v=EvVwvLkeJNI

Brian McLaren: Rediscovering Christian Faith

   http://www.youtube.com/watch?v=A5zZOPfrVxU

Rick Warren on Religious Freedom - A Conversation

   http://www.youtube.com/watch?v=1tbEnuGImI0

The Faith Debate: The Role of Religion in Politics

   http://www.youtube.com/watch?v=iNEB45GxFYo

Thomas Friedman: The World is Flat (Globalization)

   http://www.youtube.com/watch?v=UcK3b9qlBfk

Integral Operating System 1.0: Kenneth Wilber

   http://www.youtube.com/watch?v=2MKf-MsGEs8

Conflicting Philosophies of World Religions

   http://www.youtube.com/watch?v=9yQud-ckpJM

◼ NOTES

1. Thomas Banchoff, ed. (New York: Oxford University Press, Inc., 2008), 257.

2. Much of this overview is taken from Charles Murray, *Coming Apart: The State of White America 1960-2010* (New York: Random House, 2012), 2ff. See Gail Collins, *When Everything Changed: The Amazing Journey of American Women from 1960 to the Present* (New York: Little, Brown and Company, 2009).

3. Richard Florida, *The Rise of the Creative Class* (New York: Basic Books, 2002), xxviii.

4. Murray, 73.

5. Christopher Dawson, *Religion and Culture* (New York: Sheed and Ward, 1948), 197.)

6. Jeffrey Haynes, *Religion, Politics and International Relations* (New York: Routledge, 2011), 4.

7. Ibid., 4-5.

8. The Hegelian dialectic refers to a process of development whereby a thesis gives way to its opposite, an antithesis, and then the tension is resolved in a synthesis.

9. Paul Tillich, "The Conquest Of Religion in the Philosophy of Everyday Life," in *What is Religion?* ed. James Luther Adams (New York: Harper and Row, 1969), 14.

10. See Robert E. Fitch, "The Social Philosophy of Paul Tillich," in *Religion in Life* Vol. XXVII, No. 2, Spring 1958, 258ff.

11. Paul Tillich, *Church and Culture* (New York: Charles Scribner's Sons, 1948), 228.

12. D. Mackenzie Brown, ed., *Ultimate Concern: Tillich in Dialogue* (New York: Harper and Row, 1965), 21.

13. Paul Tillich, *Systematic Theology* Vol. 3, (Chicago, IL: University of Chicago Press, 1976), 250.

14. Paul Tillich, *On the Boundary* (New York: Charles Scribner's Sons, 1966), 68.

15. Paul Tillich, *Theology of Culture* (New York: Oxford University Press, 1959), 47.

16. Paul Tillich, Ch. 12 "The Word of Religion" in *The Protestant Era* (Chicago, IL: University of Chicago Press, 1957), 185.

17. Robert McAfee Brown, ed., *The Essential Reinhold Niebuhr* (New Haven, CT: Yale University Press, 1986), 80.

18. Kenneth D. Wald and Allison Calhoun-Brown, *Religion and Politics in the United States* (New York: Rowman & Littlefield Pub. Inc., 2011), 11.

19. Gordon Lynch and Jolyon Mitchell, eds., *Religion, Media and Culture* (New York: Routlege, 2012), 68.

20. Ibid., 63.

21. J. De Gruchy, *Christianity and Democracy* (Cambridge: Cambridge University Press, 1995), 5.

22. Richard Dawkins, *The God Delusion* (Boston: Houghton Mifflin, 2006), 304-308. See also Christopher Hitchens, *God is Not Great: How Religion Poisons Everything* (New York: Twelve, 2007).

23. Russell E. Richey and Donald G. Jones, eds., *American Civil Religion* (New York: Harper and Row, 1974), 14-18; See Robert N. Bellah, *The Broken Covenant* (New York:

Seabury, 1975).

24. Wald and Calhoun-Brown, 11.

25. Ibid., 17.

26. Ibid. 23.

27. Robert Putnam, *Bowling Alone* (New York: Putnam, 2000), 66.

28. Reinhold Niebuhr, *Does Civilization Need Religion?* (New York: The MacMillan Co., 1929), 4.

29. Ibid, 15.

30. Ryan and Switzer, 5-7.

31. Wald and Calhoun-Brown, xii.

32. Ryan and Switzer, 15.

33. Ibid., 19.

34. Thomas Banchoff, ed., *Democracy and the New Religious Pluralism* (New York: Oxford University Press, 2007), 259.

35. Vatican II, *Declaration on religious freedom* (2).

36. Michael Ryan and Les Switzer, *God in the Corridors of Power* (Denver, CO: Praeger, 2009), 456.

37. Wald and Calhoun-Brown, 139.

38. Martin Luther King Jr., *Why We Can't Wait* (New York: New American Library, 1963), 77.

39. Quoted in Brennan Hill, *Eight Freedom Heroes* (Cincinnati, OH: St. Anthony Messenger Press, 2007), 58.

40. Mical Lumsden, "God's Politics: An Interview With Jim Wallis" in *Mother Jones*, March 10, 2005.

41. See the website: http://www.motherjones.com/politics/2012/02/what-war-religion-obama-catholic-charities.

42. Haynes, 33-34.

43. Jan Aart Scholte, *Globalization* (New York: Palgrave, 2005), 20.

44. Jurgen Osterhammel and Niels P. Peterson, *Globalization: A Short History* (Princeton, NJ: Princeton University Press, 2005), 3.

45. Nigen Dower and John Williams, eds., *Global Citizenship* (New York: Routledge, 2002), 173.

46. Pierre Teilhard de Chardin, *The Vision of the Past* (New York: Harper and Row, 1966), 71, 230.

47. See Alfred North Whitehead, *Process and Reality* (Cambridge: University Press, 1929).

48. Reinhold Niebuhr, *The Nature and Destiny of Man* (New York: Charles Scribner's Sons, 1953), 314.

49. See Ken Wilber, *The Integral Vision* (Boston: Shambhala, 2007).

50. James Rubenstein, *An Introduction to Human Geography* (Upper Saddle River, NJ: Pearson Prentice Hall, 2008), xv.

51.   Peter Beyer and Lori Beaman, *Religion, Globalization and Culture* (Boston: Brill, 2007), 38.

52.   Reinhold Niebuhr, *The Contribution of Religion to Cultural Unity* (New Haven, CT: The Edward Hazen Foundation, 1935), 3.

53.   Nels F.S. Ferre, "Christian Presupposition for a Creative Culture," in *Religion and Culture*, ed. Walter Leibrecht (New York: Arno Press, 1979), 83.

54.   Ibid, 85-86.

55.   See Beyer and Beaman, 111.

56.   Ibid., 21-22.

57.   Daniel G. Goody, *Globalization, Spirituality, and Justice* (Maryknoll, NY: Orbis Books, 2007), 4-5.

58.   Ibid., 5.

59.   Ibid., 8.

60.   Ibid., 240.

61.   Thomas Friedman, *Longitudes and Latitudes* (New York: Anchor Books, 2003), 4.

62.   See Neil J. Ormerod and Shane Clifton, *Globalization and the Mission of the Church* (New York: T&T Clark, 2009), 50-51; See the website: http://www.millenniumproject.org.

63.   Hans Kung, *Global Responsibility: In Search of a New World Ethic* (Eugene, OR: Wipf and Stock Publishers, 1991).

64.   Ormerod, 146-470.

65.   Ibid., 156-57.

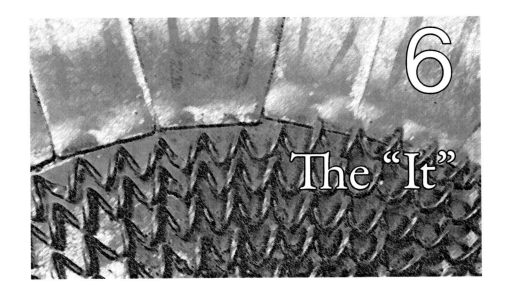

6

The "It"

Religion and Science

My religion consists of a humble admiration of the illimitable superior spirit who reveals himself in the slight details we are able to perceive with our frail and feeble mind.
— Albert Einstein

My paten and my chalice are the depths of a soul laid widely open to all the forces which in a moment will rise up from every corner of the earth and converge upon the Spirit.
— Pierre Teilhard de Chardin

The fourth and final quadrant is the "It," which refers to the material world—the object of scientific studies. In this chapter we will deal with religion's relationship with science, especially with scientific discoveries regarding the universe and Earth. We will focus mainly on the Christian response to science and evolution, but we will include other religious perspectives regarding ecology.

Science and Religion: Contrasting Methodologies

Science and religion are two powerful movements that attempt to understand and find meaning in the world in which humans live. Science focuses on discovery, primarily using human reason which Aquinas taught was ordered to know the world outside of our minds. It began with philosophy, exemplified in Greek thinkers like Socrates and Aristotle, who were ingeniously able to reason about the nature of things. Modern science is the maturation of that process "which goes beyond common experience to critically control objectification by means of experimentation and mathematization of results."[1]

Modern science examines the material world, a reality that can be measured and analyzed. Science uses evidence, proof and demonstration. Science has been recently defined by the National Academy of Sciences as "the use of evidence to construct testable explanations and predictions of natural phenomena, as well as the knowledge generated through this process."[2] Each branch of science has its own methodology. Biologists collect, analyze, dissect, test and organize while physicists often rely on mathematics to construct theories. Chemists use microscopes and test tubes and other measuring devices; astronomers use telescopes; and geologists perform digs, collect rocks and use radiometric dating. Each science has its own way of moving from trial and error, hypothesis and theories to factual positions.

Michael Barnes explains four main aspects of the methods of modern science. First, scientists gather and organize data in order to ascertain patterns and establish "fact claims." These are assertions about the reality under examination. Second, scientists make a hypothesis regarding the matter at hand. For instance, an archeologist begins a dig and collects the artifacts from the area, organizes, examines, and "dates" them. Then the expert begins to make hypothesis about the lifestyle during the period under question. The next step in the scientific method involves the scientists testing their hypotheses by gathering more materials from the site and perhaps comparing them to other sites. More evidence is gathered that either confirms or puts into question some of the earlier hypotheses. Perhaps similar findings from other areas are matched to these for points of comparison. Fourth, the fact claims and hypotheses are presented to the scientists' peers for scrutiny. Other scholars are able to see the evidence or at least read about it in a recognized journal. The findings of these critics are important in determining whether or not the finding is valid. Examination by other experts is crucial to the truth claim.[3]

An interesting example of the scientific method is an event in 2002 when it was announced that an ossuary (burial box) had been discovered with an inscription "James, son of Joseph, brother of Jesus." Experts were consulted, the box was verified to be authentic, and journal articles were published. There was a great deal of excitement and a lot of expense went into preparing a display room for the box in a Toronto museum. In the following weeks, enthusiastic crowds lined up to see the ossuary. Not all scholars were convinced and some found the inscription to be questionable. After more careful examination by experts, it was concluded that the inscription was a forgery and the box a fake. (Even scientists can make mistakes!)

On the other hand, religion is not concerned with collecting facts, making hypotheses, attempting to prove the hypotheses and or submitting the findings to experts. Religion is not concerned with measurable reality, but with transcendent or ultimate reality. Religion is not concerned with evidence or proof; rather religion is based on faith. In the case of the Christian religion, specific beliefs such as the incarnation or the resurrection are taken on faith and faith is believed to be a gift from God. Similarly, the object of the Jewish faith is the One God and the revelation manifested by that One God, while the object of Christian faith is God, the incarnation of God in Jesus Christ, and the revelation that comes from this Son of God. Religion deals with revelation, symbols, spiritual experience, teachings, rituals; all to put believers in touch with the divine and holy. Religion deals with mystery and a reality beyond the comprehension of the finite mind.

For Islam, Allah is beyond all comprehension, but at the same time Allah has revealed much about his mystery to the prophet Muhammad. For Hindus, the eternal truth is contained in Brahman, and at the same time is revealed through the many gods and goddesses that manifest Brahman.

Both science and religion deal with mysteries. Science attempts to explain the mysteries of the universe, the earth, the micro and macrocosm. Science works within its own limitations in that human reason is limited. The scientific process of revising theories shows that science's truth claims are not perfect or all-knowing. Even the exactness of Einstein's theory of relativity ($E=mc^2$) has recently been challenged.[4] Modern physics seems to have confronted those limits. Richard Feynman, 1965 Nobel Laureate in Physics, puts it this way with regards to physics' search for the fundamental laws of nature: "What I am going to tell you about is what we teach our physics students in the third or fourth year of graduate school... It is my task to convince you not to turn away because you don't understand it. You see my physics students don't understand it... That's because I don't understand it... Nobody does."[5]

Religion also works within limitations in that it relates to ultimate mysteries, the deepest and highest levels of reality which are beyond evidence and proof. In addition, religious traditions evolve and change; an indication of their relativity. Moreover, the wide diversity among religious traditions suggests that each tradition has only a partial grasp of ultimate truth.

It is easy to see why the relationship between science and religion can be contentious. Science deals with the authority of proof on the authority of experts, while religion appeals to the authority of God and to the authority of religious leaders. Science gets excited about progress, newness, usefulness for the future, as well as profit while religion is often pre-occupied with preserving and protecting the past. Religions often advise detachment from material things and are protective of their moral values, especially when science challenges them. Novelty is not relished by religion and modernization is often threatening. Where science likes the accelerator, religion prefers the brakes. Science tends to look to the earth, while religion often looks to the heavens. Science can be materialistic and mechanistic, but religion tends toward the spiritual, even mystical. Science, though it can be dedicated and heartfelt, emphasizes reason. Religion, while it values reason, is more concerned with the heart.

Another similarity that these different methods share is that both science and religion rely on faith, although in different senses of the word. Scientists must have faith in the work that has gone on before them and trust in their field's traditional sources. They have to trust that the material world is real and intelligible and that the tools of analysis and mathematics are reliable. They require faith in the evidence they use and in their own findings. Even though religious faith is usually placed in God, followers of religion trust that their ultimate realities really exist and that the revelations they receive from this reality are reliable. They have trust in those who convey revelations and in the validity of the sources, both oral and written. Religious followers have to trust in those who pass on their traditions, rituals, symbols and values.

Christians often distinguish between faith and beliefs. Faith is often described as a trusting relationship with God which is a graced-gift from

God, while beliefs are more often described as the truths that are accepted within that relationship, as well as within each believing community. For example, the content of the Catechism of the Catholic Church would be an example of Catholic beliefs; the teachings of the Buddha stand as examples of Buddhist beliefs.

Religion and science have to realize that they are two distinct fields involving different aspects of life. As John Haught points out, "Responsible scientists will agree that it is not their job to answer theological questions, and good theologians will rightly point out that it is not the task of theology to provide scientific information." [6] Nevertheless, healthy dialogue can be profitable for both!

Relations Between Science and Religion

Religions often have built-in antitheses to science. At times, religion has rejected scientific findings. A classical example is the Vatican's rejection of Galileo's position that the sun, not the earth, is the center of the universe. There are other incidents where religion has rejected science such as the modern Creationism rejection of evolution. Historically, religious truths have been presented as science. Some of the ancient Hindu sources posited an immutable and neutral force that pervaded the entire universe and underlay the multiplicity of phenomenon. This eternal element within the universe was seen to be identical with the divine power that sustains all things, which led to the Hindu belief that all reality is caught up in a cycle of endless transformations. (This is the basis for their belief in reincarnation). This process is considered to be beyond understanding and measure. Given this perspective, and the common Hindu and Buddhist belief that the phenomena we experience are actually illusions, one can see the difficulty of relating these traditions to modern science.[7] In spite of this, many modern Hindus have embraced science. Gandhi, often portrayed as opposed to science, was in fact supportive of scientific advances, but wanted it kept in the hands of the people rather than the corporate elite or the government.[8] The well-known Tibetan Buddhist leader, the Dalai Lama, has given much attention to the advances of modern science.[9]

In ancient China, Taoism took the material world and human life seriously and in a sense anticipated evolutionary thought by viewing the Tao as the basis for seeing reality as an on-going, endless cycle of growth and decay. Taoism actually posited that the goal of life, especially human life, is survival, which was perhaps prophetic of Darwin's view. However, for Taoisim, the weak and submissive survive, rather than the "fittest."[10]

The ancient Greeks often moved away from religious myths and beliefs toward philosophy, observation and critical analysis to posit the basic elements of the cosmos; study organic history, anatomy and the processes of development. Thinkers like Thales, Xenophanes, Heraclitus and Aristotle are thought to have laid the very foundations of science.[11] Others, like the great medieval Muslim thinker Avicenna of Afghanistan (980-1037), developed a holistic view of nature and the human and attempted to integrate religion and science. He and other Islamic thinkers made great contributions to medicine, astronomy, physics, mathematics and many of the other sciences.[12]

Western Science and Religion

In the West there has often been a love-hate relationship between science and religion. For instance, Christian churches were resistance to the development of modern science because they considered themselves the source of healing. The modern scientific study of the scriptures was at first rejected by the Church because it challenged belief in miracles. Conversely, the Churches now support modern medicine's ability to heal and save lives because all this is a benefit to the common good. Likewise, the churches for the most part now accept modern biblical criticism since it enables believers to get to the core truths of these writings.

Ian Barbour (b. 1923), a major contributor to the relationship between science and religion, cites four types of relations between the two movements: conflict, independence, dialogue, and integration.[13]

Conflicts

Conflicts between science and religion have been ardent and enduring. For Christians, this conflict has often involved a clash between scientific materialism and biblical literalism. At the very beginning of the modern scientific age, Galileo (1564-1642) was condemned for his theory that the earth revolves around the sun. Up until that time, the Ptolemaic theory that the earth is the center of the universe prevailed and was confirmed by the scriptural account of the stability of the earth: "the Lord set the earth on its foundations; it can never be moved" (Psalm 104:5) and other similar biblical passages. (It was not until 1992 that Galileo was exonerated by the Vatican.)

In the early stages of the development of Western science, studies were done in the context of Christian thought. Galileo, Newton and other scientists of the time worked within the context that God was the designer and orderer of the universe. Newton (1642-1727) at times found inconsistencies in the universe and presumed that God intervened in these situations to maintain balance.

It was Cartesian philosophy, with its motto "I think therefore I am" alongside the rationalism of the Enlightenment, that began to separate science from religion. By the time of Laplace (1749-1827), this "God of the gaps" was no longer in place. In the well-known story of Napoleon's discussion with Laplace about the universe evolving from a primordial mass, Napoleon asked: "But what about God?" Laplace responded: "Sire. I have no need of this hypothesis."

It was Auguste Comte (1798-1857) who coined the term "positivism," referring to the human progression toward positive knowledge. He maintained that the earliest stage was that of "theology," where God was seen as the direct cause of physical phenomena. The second stage was "metaphysical," which was the philosophical interpretation of the physical world through forces that have unobservable metaphysical causes. Comte pointed to the final scientific stage of positive knowledge, which confines itself to the observable, empirical and measurable. This later stage looks at former "religious" knowledge as mere opinion and even nonsense. Here, science replaces religion as the means for making progress for humanity.[14]

In the 19th century, religion came under attack by philosophers and scientists of the psyche. Ludwig Feuerbach (1804-1872), an influential philosopher and anthropologist, maintained that God was nothing other than a projection that came from human needs. His views influenced Karl Marx's development of atheistic Communism. In the field of psychology, Sigmund Freud (1856-1939) maintained that religion was based on neurotic illusions and childish needs. His views on religion have had a marked influence on many psychoanalysts even today.

Another conflict between science and religion erupted over the publication of Darwin's treatise on natural selection in *The Origin of the Species* in 1859. At the time, people of faith were on both sides, but many churchmen were shocked at this viewpoint, as well as Darwin's later position that humans are linked to higher animals in evolution. As will be seen later, the struggle still goes on between "creationists" and those who accept evolution.

Today, it appears that science and religion are going their separate ways. A recent Gallup Poll shows that only 1/3 of the scientists in the National Academy of Science believe in God or some higher power.[15]

Besides scientists who don't believe in God, there are also atheists who adamantly attack religion. 1979 Nobel Laureate in Physics, Steven Weinberg, is researching a final theory for the first cause of the universe. He criticizes religion for not being able to say "why" there is a creator God. It is his conviction that religions offer no evidence for their positions. He writes, "Religious theories...seem to be infinitely flexible, with nothing to prevent the invention of deities of any conceivable sort."[16] Other antagonistic atheists are involved in science, such as Daniel Dennett, who maintains that religion is nothing other than a "natural phenomenon"; Richard Dawkins, who holds that God is a "delusion"; and Victor Stenger, who writes off God as a "failed hypothesis." Christopher Hitchens, a political writer, joins their chorus, maintaining that religion "poisons everything." Even Stephen Hawking, the renowned astrophysicist who ostensibly began his work looking "for the mind of God," has now concluded that the findings of science now seem to preclude any need for a creator.

The Postmodern Critique

The postmodern movement presents new and unique challenges to religion. This movement carries the conflict between science and religion to a new level in that it challenges the very premises of both. Those who embrace the fundamental positions of postmodernism often reject the rational explanations of reality as posited by science as well as the validity of religious truths. Often, postmodernists so relativize the truth claims of both science and religion that science and religion are not so much in conflict as they are strangers in a relativized world.

Postmodernism is a difficult term to pin down since it refers to a movement with many diverse views. However, the term does seem to be useful in that it describes some contemporary perspectives, most of which challenge religion. Many of those who espouse some form of postmodernism see themselves as having moved beyond the "modern." The "modern" is associated with the Enlightenment, the so-called Age of Reason, which accented the use of clear reason and critical inquiry. The modern era led to such movements as modern science, industrialization, and systems of democracy, capitalism and communism. Post-modernism holds that this whole modern mentality has certain "narratives" or "stories" that interpret reality, values, ideologies, patterns of behavior, mindsets, and truths. Post-modernism sets out to challenge the validity of all of these narratives as being culturally conditioned and therefore completely relative.

One of the tenets of postmodernism is that culture shapes all human beliefs and patterns of behavior. Culture shapes ideas, rules, and language, and gives form to all our notions of what makes up reality. Cultures also construct religions, their beliefs and their narratives (e.g. creation stories, divine birth and resurrection stories). Culture constructs religious beliefs, rituals, symbols and laws. Since cultures vary and are relative, postmodernists believe that there is no way to determine the truth claims of any religion or the validity of their traditions.[17]

From the postmodern perspective, science is produced by culture and is in effect a culture in itself. Since modern science is largely a creation of Western culture, it also has to be seen as relative and open to critique.

A common term used by postmodern thinkers is "deconstruction." Cultural narratives such as "Democracy for all," "the American Dream," and "Science leads to Progress" are deconstructed and their fallacies are exposed. "Democracy for all," for example, can be used as a way of disguising the desire to have power over other countries. "The American Dream" is one thing for millionaires and another for those locked into minimum wage. "Science leads to Progress" shields the fact that science has given us weapons that can destroy the earth.

One can see some value in postmodernism for critique. At the same time, postmodernism seems to have a superficial view of culture. From the postmodern perspective, culture seems to be superficial and unable to produce treasured and lasting traditions. This perspective ignores that cultures are created by human beings who have deep resources for wisdom and truth. Cultures have links with the transcendent and are thereby able to create permanent values regarding family, freedom, equality, human dignity and community.

Similarly, postmodernism usually sees religion as a mere cultural product. Religious narratives about a creator, savior, healer, providential spirit are deconstructed to be mere cultural creations. This, of course, is to deny the very core of most religions, which is that there is a transcendent reality that can reveal itself to humans and even relate to them.

The postmodern critique can be useful in that it can unmask false narratives and resist the absolutizing of religious beliefs. On the other hand, postmodernism seems to ignore the depths that exist in both culture and religion, which can reveal the transcendent to each other in what David Tracy calls a "correlative method."

Religious Independence from Science

In the modern era, both religion and science have declared independence from one another. Commonly, neither one wants to have interference from the other. Christian churches and theologian often stay aloof from science; seminaries generally offer little training in science and one rarely hears about the integration of science and doctrine from the pulpit. The great Swiss Reformed theologian Karl Barth (1886-1968) maintained that theology is based on divine revelation and the science of human observation, and that the two should keep to their own domains.[18] The prominent Catholic theologian Karl Rahner admitted that he was quite unfamiliar with the field of science and was intimidated by science. He wrote, "Each time I open some work of whatever modern science, I fall as a theologian into no slight panic. The greater part of what stands written there I do not know... And so I feel as a theologian that I am somehow repudiated."[19] Some separate the two disciplines by giving science the role of answering the "how" questions and letting religion deal with the "why." Others maintain that each field works in a different area of linguistics and maintains different truth claims. [20]

Dialogue

There has been considerable open dialogue between religion and science, such as between scholars like T. F. Torrance, Arthur Peacock, Wolfhart Pannenberg and John Haught. Recently published in *Light from Light: Scientists and Theologians in Dialogue*, scholars from the two fields carried on a fascinating discussion on the topic of "light."[21] The Over the last 25 years, John Templeton Foundation has been instrumental in fostering dialogue between science and other disciplines, including religion. As one scientist puts it: "Science shows how the universe works, and religions address the meaning and purpose of the universe."[22]

Science and religion are often in dialogue with regard to moral issues such as health care, abortion, surgical procedures, in vitro fertilization, end of life issues and birth control. Dr. John Rock (1890-1984), the developer of the birth control pill put on the market in 1957, was a Catholic who felt that in producing the pill he was following the natural processes of feminine reproduction. He was profoundly disappointed to see his own church condemn the use of the pill in 1968.

Pope John Paul II gave a number of addresses on the relation between science and Christianity and raised the bar for dialogue. He pointed out that science must not be used to prove the tenets of Christianity but must bear witness for its own truth. Each field offers distinct dimensions of culture and today there are great opportunities for learning from each other. Pope John Paul encouraged openness on the part of both science and the church since both are integral parts of our culture. The Pope encouraged dialogue for mutual benefit, "As dialogue and common searching continue, there will be growth towards mutual understanding and gradual uncovering of common concerns which will provide the basis for further research and discussion." He adopted a new position from Popes of the past in that there were no accusations that science is atheistic or antagonistic. He was not sure what the future of this dialogue would be, but he expected good things. The Pontiff invited both the Church and science on a common quest. [23]

Integration

It is encouraging to see that there are major efforts today to integrate science and religion through dialogue and cooperation. As we shall see, there have been serious efforts to integrate the findings of both disciplines in the areas of cosmology, evolution and ecology.

In one sense, modern science in the Western world grew out of theology. During the medieval period, "scientia" referred to knowledge that was derived from critical thinking. Theology was called the queen of sciences, and Aquinas produced his amazing *Summa Theologica* by applying the philosophical tools of Aristotle to Christian doctrine. Early scientists like Kepler, who discovered the laws of planetary motion, and Galileo, who demonstrated that the earth orbited the sun, were devoted to their Christian faith and integrated their beliefs into their studies. Some other well known religious scientists include Copernicus, influenced by Greek astronomer Aristarchus (310- 250 BCE), who preceded Galileo in proposing that the earth revolved around the sun; Lemaitre, who was an evolutionist before Darwin; and Mendel, who discovered the genetic laws of inheritance, were all Catholic priests.

Teilhard de Chardin, a Jesuit priest, profoundly integrated evolution with Christian doctrine, developing a theory whereby Christ is the force within the process of Christogenesis, acting as both the Alpha (starting point of creation) and the final point of fulfillment (the Omega). We will discuss Teilhard's synthesis in more detail in the section on the cosmos.

Albert Einstein, one of the greatest scientists of modern times, seems to have at least partly integrated a religious view into his work as he sought to discover the "Old Man's" plan for the universe. He once remarked that he was drawn to Spinoza's notion of God, a monistic view where God and the universe were merely two aspects of a single substantial reality."[24]

Process theologians, taking their lead from the philosophy of Alfred Whitehead, have proposed a "process theology" which applies notions of process to God and the universe creation. As we will see later, they propose "panentheism," whereby all things are in God, a cosmic force, which "lures" the universe into order, complexity, consciousness and beauty.

An enormous amount of attention on the part of religious thinkers has been given to integrate religious thinking with concerns about and actions on behalf of the environment. A notable example of this was the series of conferences organized by Dr. Mary Evelyn Tucker at Harvard in 1996-1998 where 800 scholars addressed environmental issues from the point of view of religion. Ten volumes were published from this conference. The same type of Forum has been established at Yale. In 1995 Prince Philip of England launched the Alliance of Religions and Conservation, which has challenged most religions to focus on the environment. More will be said about this in the section on ecology.

Religious Response to Modern Scientific Issues

Contemporary religion has a new context—a new story in which to place itself. Christians no longer struggle to think of themselves as descendents of a couple living in a garden in a newly created universe by an old man in the sky 5,000 years ago. Rather they strain to place themselves in a new story that began nearly 14 billion years ago with an incredible energy event that produced our universe, and then the gradual formation of our earth about 5 billion years ago. Christians have a new family tree—hominids that stood up on two feet around 6 million years ago and evolved into fully conscious human beings "just a moment ago" (around 50,000 years ago). In the next section, we are going to discuss the two epochs of this story—the birth of the cosmos and evolution—and consider how Christians are relating to this new family history with a new faith.

Discovering the Cosmos

Modern technology, especially the use of the orbiting Hubbard telescope, has enabled our generation to have a comprehensive understanding of the dimensions of our universe. The first scientist to propose a theory on the expansion of the universe was Abbe Georges Lemaitre (1894-1966), a Catholic priest who taught physics at the Catholic University at Louvain.

In 1927, he published an article on the "hypothesis of the primeval atom" which described the origin of our universe. During that same period, Edwin Hubble used his telescope in southern California to determine if our Milky Way was the only galaxy in the universe. His discovery amazed the world: the universe is filled with galaxies that are rushing away from each other. This led to the so-called "Big Bang" theory that our universe began from a colossal expansion of a tiny dot billions of years ago. Expansion from the energy and contraction from gravity shaped the stars and the galaxies. Connecting and separating, one might say the feminine and masculine forces brought forth the universe: expansion and contraction, the movements of life-giving breathing and the beating hearts.

With a burst of radiation, quarks, protons and neutrons combine to form bonded structures at the exact rate to later produce life. As one scientist said, "the universe in some sense must have known we were coming."[25] Atoms of hydrogen and helium, which form the foundation of the microcosm, were formed so that now the new structures of stars and galaxies could be formed.

A century ago we knew of but one galaxy, our own Milky Way. Now we know that there are a hundred billion galaxies, each containing several billion stars! All of these were formed through the fluctuation wave in the density of matter literally breaking the universe apart as it expanded. Many scientists propose that there are many universes in existence.

Amidst the vast gathering of galaxies in our universe there exists our own Milky Way, with a spiral structure the enables it to freshly bring forth new stars amidst the amazing creative process of creation. It is a process always expanding, always bringing forth new creations.

Stars are born out of this process. Stars are "fiery cauldrons of transformation... wombs of immense creativity. Humans have always stared at them in the night sky, as though intuiting what we now know, they are our ancestors and our bodies are formed from their elements."[26]

Stars implode and then explode into supernova. Five billion years ago, our solar system emerged out of this creative process, with a shining star, our sun and its eight planets that were produced from stellar dust amidst an ocean of energy. Some of these planets are gaseous, some rocky like our Earth. The earth's satellite, the Moon, was originally part of the earth and now shines with light from the sun and controls our tides.

Our sun is a massive burning star 93 million miles away. The earth receives but a tiny portion of light and energy from this star, but all life here depends on that gift. The sun's roaring energy affected human life so much that cultures in Egypt, the Orient, early England and the Americas saw it as a god.

Our planet, Earth, emerged about five billion year ago cooked and cooled in the midst of this cauldron of energy for millions of years. Volcanic processes released steam that became liquid. Back and forth, the process of water to steam to water eventually formed lakes and streams and then oceans. In the midst of this vast creative process, the first living cell was produced around 4 billion years ago. Around 2 billion years ago, more complex cells with nuclei appeared which provided the basis for all living forms on earth.

Scientists have come to realize that the universe is not a thing but rather "a mode of being of everything." It consists of a microphase and a macrophase, both of which are closely related. Science today shows that humans, rather than being separate from the universe, are part of it. Molecular biology demonstrates that the biological community on earth shares a common ancestry and DNA studies make clear that all living things are part of a single family tree. New studies have expanded the list of self-aware animals. Moreover, the diversity of microscopic and macroscopic life on earth has led many scientists to believe that life has evolved elsewhere in the universe.[27]

Religion and Science Look at the Cosmos

Some scientists maintain that modern cosmology eliminates the need for a Creator, renders human life rather insignificant, and even precludes any meaning from the whole process of cosmic activity. Steven Weinberg says that as we know more and more about the universe, the more it becomes "pointless."[28]

Others hold that given the vast scale of time and distances of the universe, humans represent but a moment in time and don't play much a role over the long haul. Still others see the whole system as mechanical and view humans as mere thinking machines or animals that can reflect. If this be so, there is no need for a God, no purpose to the process of life, and all of it comes about by chance. As a well-known atheist-scientist puts it, religious believers are those who are "scientifically illiterate."[29]

As science began to uncover the origin of the universe, there were efforts to align the creation story in Genesis 1 by saying that the "six days" represented millions of years. With the discovery of "deep time" in terms of billions of years, that explanation was no longer credible. With the advent of biblical criticism, it became evident that the creation stories were faith myths concerned with the "why" of creation and not with the "how" or the "when."

As the scientific explanations developed, many scientists took the position that "The cosmos appears to be self-explicative. There is no causal space left for any God."[30] At the same time, arguments for the "God of the gaps," where God's actions were used to fill in gaps that science could not explain were dropped. Science was just too quickly filling in the gaps itself!

Some religious thinkers have tried to sustain God's role in creation by maintaining that God is the original cause (e.g. God detonated the Big Bang). This tends to be a deist approach, which sees God as inaugurating creation and then standing back and no longer intervening. This seems to harken back to the "clockmaker" image offered by William Paley in 1902, which said that God designed the universe to run on its own. Science's discoveries of the chaos and the destructive forces in the universe easily made that argument untenable.

Modern theologians have adopted other approaches to God's role in creation. Some see creation as gift from God, which in the limitations of its materiality includes chaos and titanic changes. They engage the universe with faith, trust in its ultimate benevolence, and give thanks for its beauty and sustenance. Muslims, Jews, Christians and followers of other faiths can accept the on-going scientific findings and in faith stand in awe of God's creative power and energy. Religious faith often sees the mystery of the universe as symbolic of God's on-going incarnation of Self. From this perspective, the complexity, intricacy, magnitude and beauty of the cosmos becomes demonstrative of a creator God. This is captured in Gerard Manley Hopkin's poem, *God's Grandeur*

> *The world is charged with the grandeur of God.*
> *It will flame out, like shining from shook foil;*
> *It gathers to a greatness, like the ooze of oil*
> *Crushed. Why do men then now not reck his rod?*
> *Generations have trod, have trod, have trod;*
> *And all is seared with trade; bleared, smeared with toil;*
> *And wears man's smudge and shares man's smell: the soil*
> *Is bare now, nor can foot feel, being shod.*
> *And for all this, nature is never spent;*
> *There lives the dearest freshness deep down things;*
> *And though the last lights off the black West went*
> *Oh, morning, at the brown brink eastward, springs —*
> *Because the Holy Ghost over the bent*
> *World broods with warm breast and with ah! bright wings.*[31]

It was Dostoevsky who said: "Beauty will save you!" If salvation here means connecting us with the divine, which is the very purpose of religion, might we not assert the realization that the beauty of the universe can indeed put us in touch with the Creator? The brilliant luster of a full moon on a crisp fall night, a multicolored sunset at the end of a day at the beach, the grandeur of a mountaintop, the deep, dense darkness of a forest, the innocence of a new-born baby, the opening of a rose—all of these have the power to connect a person of faith to God.

John Polkinghorne, a physicist and Anglican priest who has written extensively on science and religion, points out that science can neither prove nor disprove the existence of God, but can provide some "nudge factors" to move in that direction. He agrees with those mentioned earlier that the "life principle" within the cosmos finds its most amazing climax in human life with all our capacities for thought, emotion, self-sacrifice and transcendence. Moreover, the complexity and design of the cosmic process seems to point to someone responsible. The unity, beauty and depth of the universe reflect One who is a source for all creation. Others maintain that the apparent infinity of universes, which appear to be without beginning or end, point to an infinite designer.[32]

There has been much discussion in recent times about whether there is directionality, goals or purpose to the universe. As opposed to scientists who deny any sense of design, meaning or purpose to the process of the universe, there are scientists that maintain that there is a "creative self-organization" and a "complex interrelatedness of entities" within the universe that provide theologians with the basis for a theology of creation. Brian Swimme is a well-known cosmologist who maintains that there is coherence and directionality in the process of the universe, whether that be in genetic mutation, the formation of galaxies, the nucleosynthesis of stars or the chemical reactions on planets. He maintains that the universe is "endowed with the potential to construct order. He writes that "The point I wish to make here, however, is that given our understanding of 15 billion years of cosmic evolution, including 4 billion years of biological evolution, we have begun to see the whole process as a seamless enterprise where particles become atoms that become galaxies with stars and planets and complexifying organisms."[33]

Traditionally, religions have explained the universe as an expression of divine wisdom (Hebrew) or as an expression of Logos, the creative aspect of God (Christian). Islam sees nature as the manifestation of Allah's infinite intelligence and compassion, while Hindus connect to the eternal truth of the dharma and Confucians see the universe as having a moral character. The universe was often thought of in terms of hierarchical structure produced and given meaning by divine intervention.

Science has challenged these notions of hierarchy and eternal purpose and has revealed a chaotic cosmic process with fits and starts where there is no need for divine intervention or presence of hierarchy of being or even a need for purpose.

John Haught, a professor of theology at Georgetown, maintains that a certain hierarchical ordering with regard the universe is necessary to preserve value and meaning, especially where humans are concerned. He points to the fact that science today acknowledges a certain "information" inherently in nature—a metaphor to indicate that "there is more to nature than just combinations of matter, or transformations of energy in time."[34] Science also recognizes that something in the universe gives pattern, order and form to the cosmic process even the midst of discontinuity. This element is most obvious in DNA sequences. Haught maintains that there can be links between this "information" and some religious notion. He cites the religious notion of Tao which Taoists believe to be the self-concealing power that shapes the universe. This might be described as the humble and "non-interfering effectiveness" associated with "information," the "quiet presence of cosmic meaning."[35] Haught notes a parallel in Paul's writings where he preaches that God's power can be made manifest in weakness and humiliation: "For the foolishness of God is wiser than human wisdom, and the weakness of God is stronger than human strength" (1Cor 1:17) Here, God's power in the universe might be found in divine kenosis (self-emptying), the power of a Creator that is self-effacing, loving and the source of all goodness; a God deep within the process with a benevolence that produces consciousness and freedom. Paul points out that this is the God that was incarnated in Jesus Christ.

Owen Gingerich, a Harvard professor of astronomy, has his own perspective on design and purpose in the cosmos. He recognizes that proposing a designer Creator can no longer be acceptable in view of modern cosmology. Science finds no evidence of a "blueprint" or rigid plan for the cosmos. Still, as a scientist, Gingerich finds there to be coherence in the universe, "a framework in which intelligent, rational, self-conscious life could emerge."[36] He recognizes an intention, a purpose in the process and a balance among the forces. It is as though there is a built-in "necessity for ultimate emergence of life."[37] He also mentions the many "contingencies," which allow for freedom as well as the element of "luck." He points out that "Seen with the eyes of faith, the world seems to be organized with purpose, direction, a pervasive sense of movement toward higher organization, but not necessarily with a total blueprint."[38]

As for the significance of human life, some follow the "strong" anthropic principle and see that the universe is so fine-tuned that it was designed to produce human life. From this perspective, the universe and earth is "just right" for human existence. The cosmic process is designed for and culminates in human consciousness as its most intricate product. Human awareness, reflection and creativity represent the goal of the cosmic process. Others follow what is called the "weak" anthropic principle, which says that the universe must be this way *because* we are here. If the universe turned out any other way, we would not be here to observe ourselves and figure out the process of the universe.

There are other approaches to religion and cosmology that are worth noting. Process theologians, inspired by the brilliant work of Alfred North Whitehead, view the universe as being made up of "energy-happenings." Here, the universe is viewed as constantly in a process that has active physical events and passive mental events. The process moves through levels of complexity, guided by an interiority that moves toward consciousness and beauty. According to many process theologians, God is a cosmic force that "lures" the universe toward these goals. Here, there are two aspects to God: one eternal and changeless, the other a cosmic self that is active in the world and changing. This is a God who is also in a sense "changing." This theological movement uses the term "panentheism" meaning that "all is in God."[39]

Paul Davies, an English physicist, has written extensively on science and religion. In *God and the New Physics* (1987), he maintains that science is more useful in answering God's role in creation than is religion. Cosmology points to basic answers as to the origin, nature and purpose of the universe, which can be related to a Creator. He suggests that the mathematical system in a way reflects the "mind of God." He concludes that a divine purpose for the universe lies hidden beneath nature, the same nature that physics investigates. Given the ambiguity of physics these days, that does not leave the religious person much to work with!

Understanding Evolution

During the 18th and 19th centuries a number of scientists proposed various theories of evolution, and Alfred Russell Wallace, a contemporary of Darwin's, developed a theory of natural selection very similar to Darwin's. Both theories were presented by the Linnean Society in 1858 and published, but little note was taken of these momentous theories. Only after Darwin published *On the Origin of Species* in 1859 did scientists and the public take notice of this sensational theory.

Darwin based his theory of natural selection on the vast amount of evidence he had garnered on a five-year voyage around South America and in the Galapagos Islands. On the voyage he gathered and sent back to England many fossils of extinct animals, and he observed a great deal from ancient rock formations. On the Galapagos he bagged many birds, which turned out to all be various species of finches. Once back in England, Darwin examined all the evidence, including many species of finches, all of which had evolved different forms of beaks. He proposed his theory of natural selection, using the model of a tree to illustrate the evolution of different species from a common ancestor. He continued his work and in 1871 published *The Descent of Man* which explains his position on the human evolution from lower species of animals.

150 years of further study of rock-formations and fossils, both in the sea and on land, as well as recent studies of DNA, have advanced our knowledge of the evolution of life on earth. Single-celled life seems to have appeared nearly 4 billion years ago, and the multi-cellular life appeared 1.2 billion years ago. 550 million years ago, life developed rapidly in the oceans; then came vertebrates, which 350 million years ago evolved into large predators. Around the same time, plants and vertebrates made the transition from water to land to begin the evolution of life on earth. 230 million years ago, the many forms of dinosaurs evolved and dominated the earth until 66 million years ago when they were rendered extinct.

After the demise of the dinosaurs, there was a massive development of other mammals and birds. Among the mammals were our closest relative, the chimpanzee. As the earth's climate changed several million years ago, the earth dried out in central Africa. Food became hard to come by for these ape-like creatures. Some responded by remaining in the trees, while others left the trees and begin walking on two feet. It was this group that developed over millions of years into hominids (pre-human figures). As these hominids adapted to the many challenges of their environment, their brains developed first the size of a lemon, then of an orange, a grapefruit, and finally the size of a melon. One type of tool-using hominid (homo-habilis) emerged several million years ago. The species that could fully walk and permanently remain upright (homo erectus) dates back 1.5 million years ago. Our human species (homo sapiens) perhaps goes back 200,000 years ago, but modern humans fully developed around 50,000 years ago. The pre-humans still "knew" as did their fellow animals, but these evolved individuals "knew that they knew." They could reflect, contemplate and figure things out like never before. They could plan shelters, make better tools and weapons, devise symbols and artifacts and develop language; humans could now tell stories about their beliefs, their memories, their hopes for the future. They could dream, plan, make promises and serve each other. They could outsmart the other animals and their enemies. Eventually, humans migrated out of Africa and began populating other parts of the world, moving across into the Middle East, then to Europe, onto the Orient and from their down through the Americas. By 7,000 years ago, they had reached the southern tip of South America. Humans began to establish elaborate cultures, often near rivers like the Nile in Africa, the Tigris and Euphrates in Mesopotamia, the Indus in India, the Yellow in China and the Mississippi in America. The first cities were established in the Middle East and then Southern Asia. Eventually elaborate civilizations were established in places as disparate as the Middle East, Mexico and Peru with advanced architecture, literature, weaponry, laws and agriculture, wheeled travel and sailing vessels. These humans were now prepared "to figure out" new ways to survive and advance. A conscious, self-aware human community was on the march.[40]

We now understand that the entire process is interconnected. It is a process that some think is actually "alive," moving forward with purpose and goal. As Brian Swimme writes: "When we today remember that the energy of our lives comes from the original flaring forth of the universe, and that the atoms of our bodies come from many ancestors over billions of years, we begin to appreciate the intricate manner in which life remembers the past and brings it into fresh form today. Life adapts. Life remembers. Life Learns."[41] We see because the process has produced sight. We hear because evolution developed hearing. We think because of a dynamic movement toward reflective consciousness.

Evolutionary Science and Religion

Once Darwin published his position on Natural Selection, there were vigorous reactions from Christians. At Oxford in 1860 there were vehement debates, including the notable one between Bishop Samuel Wilberforce and Thomas Huxley, who was often referred to as "Darwin's bulldog." Debates also proliferated in this country, the most famous being the Scopes "Monkey Trial" in Tennessee in 1925. John Scopes, a high school teacher, was charged with breaking the State law by teaching evolution in a public school. The case was argued by two famous figures: Clarence Darrow, who defended Scopes, and William Jennings Bryan, who served the prosecution. The trial turned out to be a struggle between biblical literalists and scientists. Darrow ridiculed Jennings' literal interpretation of Genesis. Scopes was declared guilty, but his verdict was overturned and he was set free. Catholics also got into the fray.

Pierre Teilhard de Chardin (d. 1955)

Teilhard is a classic example of a professionally qualified scientist who is also a qualified religious thinker. Teilhard was a French Jesuit and served as a medal-winning medic in World War I. After the war, Teilhard received his doctorate in science and served as professor of geology and paleontology at Institut Catholique in Paris. Teilhard's studies led him to accept evolution which got him in trouble with the Vatican. His scientific findings on the development of human cells seemed to call for a revision of the Church's teaching on original sin. Rome forced dismissal from his professorship, forbade him to publish on any religious topic and exiled him to China. In China, Teilhard continued his scientific work and played a role in the discovery of the "Peking Man." His extensive writing was at times circulated in mimeograph form and was published after his death. Teilhard's magnificent synthesis of modern cosmology with Christian faith has continued to influence theologians as well as scientists.

Teilhard maintained that there was "inwardness in all matter" and a consciousness within both animals and humans that is ignored by materialistic science. He perceived two movements in this dynamic process: complexity and convergence. One of his signature statements was: "Everything that rises must converge." For Teilhard, the cosmic process moves through a series of beginnings: *Cosmogenesis* (cosmos), *Geogenesis* (earth), *Biogenesis* (life), *Noogenesis* (mind). His Christian faith indicated to him that the final stage is Christogenesis (the fulfillment of all creation, where God is now incarnated in all; the Omega Point or Cosmic Christ). Teilhard proposed a spirituality that integrates science and Christianity: "To live the cosmic life is to live dominated by the consciousness that one is an atom in the body of the mystical and cosmic Christ."[42]

Teilhard insisted that our concept of God must be extended to the dimensions of the universe and viewed in the context of a universe whose creation is still ongoing. The Christian belief in the incarnation signals God's presence in all material things. Teilhard writes, 'Through your own incarnation, my God, all matter is henceforth incarnate."[43] *The Divine Milieu*, one of Teilhard's seminal books, describes a world that is "divinized created being."[44] Humans are able to perceive all this because God has given them an impulse for both wanting and being one with the divine.[45]

Teilhard envisioned a future convergence of Eastern and Western religions that would recognize this vision of God within the entire world. He sensed the development of "noosphere," (the thinking envelope of the earth) "multiplying its internal fibers and tightening its network." He saw a future convergence of nations, a "coming together of the human layer taking place in the form of the interpenetration of thoughts and interests." (No doubt Teilhard would have been quite pleased with the development of the internet!) Teilhard sums up the integration of his scientific beliefs and his Christian faith as follows:

> *I believe that the universe is an evolution.*
> *I believe that evolution proceeds toward spirit.*
> *I believe that spirit is fully realized in the form of a personality.*
> *I believe that the supremely personal is the Universal Christ.*[46]

Fr. John Zahm (1851-1921), a brilliant priest-scholar at Notre Dame University, is another example of someone who had a conflict with Catholic authorities over his acceptance of evolution. Zahm wrote extensively on the compatibility of evolution with Catholic dogma. Some critics called him a modernist and even an atheist and in 1898 the Vatican threatened to exile his works to the Index of Forbidden Books. Zahm turned away from writing on evolution, moved into administration in his Order and turned his research to other areas.

Eventually the Catholic authorities came to agree with the theory of evolution. In 1950 Pius XII wrote that there was no intrinsic contradiction between evolution and Catholic doctrine; in 1996 John Paul II strongly supported evolution and exonerated Teilhard. In 2004 the Vatican gave its approval to both the Big Bang Theory and Evolution.

In Evangelical circles, there is still an on-going conflict between Creationists, some of which have overflowed into the courts over the teaching of creationism in public school science classes. Some Catholic schools are still shy of teaching evolution in their science classes.

Scientific Creationism

One movement against evolution is scientific creationism. Biblical literalists who view the bible as a report of historical events lead this lobby. They reject the scientific view of the age of the universe and the earth, as well as the evolution of humans from pre-human figures. They deny the validity of fossil records as well as the dating of dinosaur bones that shows they lived hundreds of millions of years ago. From the creationist's perspective, the earth is just 6,000 years old—the age of the Bible. They follow the biblical story literally, where God made the world in 6 days and directly created all the planet's vegetation, animals and humans (Adam and Eve). The Bible describes how the great flood destroyed the earth with the exception of the people and animals on Noah's ark. People and animals today descended directly from the Ark survivors. For creationists, the biblical account is science and they want it to be taught as such in the schools. Their legal efforts to bring this about have not been successful, largely on the grounds that teaching creationism in science class would be bringing religion into the classroom of public schools. Creationists even deny the evidence of science for evolution that is now derived from DNA studies, and maintain that the authority of God's account in scripture trumps that of science. A good example of this approach is the Creation Museum in Northern Kentucky, where Bible scenes of creation have been recreated, including a life-size replica of Noah's ark.[47]

Intelligent Design

Intelligent design is another form of creationism. In an approach similar to past Deists, this view suggests that God designed and created the universe by direct interventions, but is no longer involved. This movement accepts the age of the cosmos and earth, but explains that an intelligent agent intervened at each stage to create the aspect in question, whether that be stars, planets, animals or humans. Obviously, those who propose this perspective reject the notion of cosmic development and natural selection, as evidenced by science. William Dembski, a mathematician and philosopher, is a strong proponent of intelligent design. It is his position that the mathematical odds are strongly against anything other than an intelligent designer of the world. The complexity of everything from the DNA molecule to the human brain demands that there be a designer intervening with a given plan. Dembski allows for some events in the universe to be products of the "laws of nature" and others the result of chance, but he insists that events like the beginnings of human life are by design. (Some Catholics hold a version of this when they declare: "I can accept human evolution, but at some point God had to infuse a soul into the body.") Many scientists think that Dembski's manner of sorting these events out is rather arbitrary and not accurate according to scientific analysis. Another version of intelligent design is proposed by Michael Behe, a biochemist. He deduced that biochemistry uncovers situations in genetic coding, blood clotting and mutation that would require a designer.

The immense distances in the universe as well as the immeasurable time lapses render the notion of divine intervention difficult to accept. Moreover, the gradual and complex development of the universe as well as the earth and living things, along with many chaotic breakdowns and extinctions, seem to preclude the intervention of a designer.

Surveys show that the vast majority of scientists support evolution and favor scientific teaching in the schools. The major proponents of both scientific creationism and intelligent design seem to come from religious perspectives or sometimes from politicians hoping to capture the fundamentalist vote. The general public often does not accept evolution, not only because they are biblical literalists, but also in reaction to the disregard or even hostility toward religion on the part of many scientists.

There have been many State lawsuits over the right to teach creationism in the public school systems. Surprisingly, in spite of all the scientific evidence to the contrary, the 2012 Gallup poll shows that 46% of American citizens accept the creationist view over that of evolution.[48]

A Contemporary Christian View of Creation

Christians today who accept science and its findings in astrophysics, astronomy, biology, physics and other fields have to revise their beliefs in God and creation. The context is no longer a span of 6,000 years, with an "old man in the sky" directly creating the world, or even a grand designer intervening within the processes of the universe and earth to shape stars and create human life. The context is now the vastness of an expanding macrocosm, a universe (possibly many universes), with the often chaotic explosions of stars and supernova over billions of years and light years in the distance. It is a complex microcosm of quarks and nuclear activity, intricate DNA patterns and cellular transformations. Although marvelous in beauty and design, the whole process includes much chaos, breakdown, death and extinction. It is a magnificent process but seemingly without discernible goal or purpose.

Creation stories

Many religions have their own creation stories which have often been interpreted literally and thus stand as challenged by modern theories of evolution. In the following, we limit our discussion to the tension between evolution and the creation stories in Genesis in the Hebrew Scriptures.

Two central questions emerge for a contemporary Christian who accepts both biblical and scientific truth: What are we to make of the creation stories in the Bible and how is this Creator God involved in the cosmic and evolutionary process? In the following, we will explore some interesting attempts to answer these questions.

The creation stories in Genesis have been part of the Christian tradition for over 2,000 years. We stay "stories," because there are two accounts of creation: Genesis 1: 1- 2, 4 and Genesis 2: 4-3, 24.

The second story (Gen 2) is actually the oldest, written around the tenth century BCE. It begins with a rural setting, bare earth and a stream. God first forms a human from the earth and breathes life into the creature. Then God creates a garden and sees that Adam is lonely so he creates animals and birds. None of these make suitable companions for Adam, so God then takes a rib from Adam, and makes a woman. The rest of the story concerns the eating of the forbidden fruit and the couple's expulsion from the garden.

The other story (Gen 1) is written around 400 years later and is more cosmic and poetic. It tells of God creating in 6 days, beginning with light (day and night); waters above and below; dry land, sea and plant life; sun, moon and stars in the dome-sky; fish, sea creatures and birds; land animals and humans made in God's image. They are given dominion over the creatures and are told to "increase and multiply."

Contemporary biblical scholars who ascribe to the methods of "biblical criticism," view these stories as "myths," i.e. religious stories that teach truths of faith. From this perspective, these stories tell us nothing about history or modern science. They are concerned with conveying the religious beliefs of the Hebrew people about "who" is the source of creation and creation's goodness, but not about "how" creation came about or "when" it took place. These "myths" are about faith, not fact; they describe the mystery of the divine source and presence in all things, not the process of the "Big Bang" or evolution.

This point of view obviously differs from those who reject biblical criticism, take the creation stories literally, and view the theory of evolution as contradictory to their religious beliefs in creation. Orthodox Jews, as well as many conservative Protestants and Evangelicals would be included in this category. This would apply also to those who follow intelligent design who accept the timeline of cosmic, living things and human development but insist that a divine designer intervened at certain key points of the process.

How is the Creator God Involved in Creation?

The religious believer who accepts evolution might now have to see the Creator's involvement in creation differently from the traditional view that God directly created everything at a particular point in time. Denis Edwards suggests that the Creator God can be linked to the modern scientific view is a "God of mutual relations," a God of love and friendship. In the gospel of John, this love is an "abiding in," "dwelling in." God's Spirit abides in Jesus as well as in those baptized into his Spirit. Jesus tells his disciples "who abides in me does His works. Believe me that I am in the Father and the Father is in me." (John 14, 10-11) In 1 John occurs that amazing identification of God with love: "God is love." (4:8,16) Elizabeth Johnson points to this God within creation as the power of love: "The creative love of Mother Wisdom reaches throughout the universe and all its embedded individuals for the well-being of the whole of her creation."[49]

Pierre Teilhard de Chardin, S.J. was a significant contributor to the question of how the divine can be integrated into evolution. Teilhard called our world "the divine milieu," the environment, if you will, where God, "the divine immensity," manifests self and charges the world with divine grace, the "true sap of the world." Teilhard proposed that that the entire process of evolution is headed for a oneness in God, and now is in an earthly phase. He wrote: "The divine milieu, which will ultimately be one... must begin to become one during the earthly phase of our existence." The future of the universe lies still ahead: The "divinization of the universe is still open to vast possibilities."[50] Teilhard also held that love, which has it source in the divine, is a major factor in the process of creation. He maintained that love is the most universal, tremendous and mysterious of the cosmic forces. It is a "primal and universal psychic energy."[51] For Teilhard, love is more than a sentiment; it is an energy, a natural dynamism. It is an affinity of being with being that exists within all matter and living things. Love is a cosmic energy, the withinness of all things that draws all things, especially humans, together. God both produces this energy and draws all reality toward the divine goal, which is the culmination of creation, the Omega Point.[52] In Teilhard's synthesis, love is the power that binds humans and God to each other. Here God is a personal and relational God and is the foundation of the interconnectedness that is so characteristic of creation. This God, a "God-within," is the presence that sustains what Teilhard calls the "withinness" of all material things. Yet this God is transcendent and accessible only through gifted faith, not through scientific investigation. This is a "Beyond-Within" that is the creative power of stability, beauty and goodness in the world.

Creation Views of Other World Religions

In other world religions there are a wide range of beliefs regarding the divine role in creation. The great teacher of Sikhism, Nanak (1469-1539), held that the One God "projected" self on all creatures and now is in the process of drawing all back to the original divine source. Sikhs are open to accept evolution, but see God as in charge of the whole process, sustaining it and directing it.[53] While Jains do not deny the spiritual or the divine, they also do not speak of God as a Supreme Being or as Creator the universe. Creation is an endless process with no beginning or end, and therefore most Jains are quite open to the findings of modern evolutionists and cosmologists.

For Taoists, the Tao is beyond definition and is associated with the formless, the perfect, the eternal energy that gives birth to and transforms all things. Many Taoists are open to evolution and interpret in terms of the movement of the Tao.[54]

The Problem of Evil in Creation

The problem of evil has been an enigma for many religions. If traditions such as Judaism and Christianity believe in a good God who is the source of all creation, how does one explain the presence of so much physical and moral evil in the world? While the universe manifests beauty, magnificence, order and complexity, it also includes massive extinctions, natural and moral evils, horrible crimes, suffering, pain and death. Is the Creator actually the cause or evil, or does he simply "allow" it. Or, is there some other source or evil in the world—perhaps evil demons? Is this Creator really as good as we think?

In the treasured drama, Job, the protagonist asks why God tries him every moment, destroys him and makes him suffer:

"Know now that God hath overthrown me, and hath compassed me with his net. Behold, I cry out of wrong, but I am not heard: I cry aloud, but *there is* no judgment. He hath fenced up my way that I cannot pass, and he hath set darkness in my paths. He hath stripped me of my glory, and taken the crown *from* my head. He hath destroyed me on every side, and I am gone: and mine hope hath he removed like a tree. He hath also kindled his wrath against me, and he counteth me unto him as *one of* his enemies. (Job 19:7-12)

After Job's friends present all their explanations for Job's misfortunes, Job stands before God himself for the answer. The much-awaited answer comes in which God in effect says that Job has not been privy to the mysteries of creation and will never understand its workings. Then God brings him blessings and restores what he has lost. The ancient Hebrew who wrote this play understood well that our limited minds will never understand the workings of God in our world. At the same time, many Jews, especially those who endured the Nazi camps, can say with Abraham Heschel : "God weeps with humans in their sufferings. God participates in our sufferings."[55] The God of evolution is a compassionate and empathetic God that somehow is within the breakdowns as well as the triumphs of creation.

Theologians can't explain the problem of evil, yet they do recognize that by its very nature the material world has limitations and breakdowns. If it did not, it would not be a material world. In addition, humans have been created with conscience and freedom and thereby can inflict evil on themselves and others. Existing as an eternal God, God chooses to create a limited world and give humanity freedom.

Some would say that in creating a limited world and giving both the world and humans freedom, God has put limits on the Divine self—limits that love sometimes demands. Perhaps only an infinite God could have the power to be so loving and so generous as to give independence to the cosmic and human process. Walter Kasper puts it this way: "It requires omnipotence to be able to surrender oneself and give oneself away; and it requires omnipotence to be able to take oneself back in the giving and to preserve the independence and freedom of the recipient."[56]

The incarnation itself, a central doctrine of Christianity, can perhaps assist in understanding God's role in creation. Is not the incarnation, wherein God becomes a human person, symbolic of how God has entered materiality and allowed self to be limited by its unpredictability, its chaos, randomness, its suffering and death? Does this not signal how "God so loved the world" that God mysteriously entered into its fragility in order to bring it into ultimate union with the divinity?

The question of the human soul is always a part of the discussion of Christianity and evolution. In the past, there was a Greek dualism between body and soul which led to the thinking that God put a soul into human beings. As mentioned earlier, intelligent design claimed that at one point in human evolution, God intervened with a soul that made the creature forever immortal.

Contemporary theologians seem to prefer to think of humans as "ensouled" bodies. This view is perhaps more compatible with evolution, in that the human spirit seems to have slowly developed over millions of years until it was conscious and capable of reflection. It is quite impossible to say at what stage of human development we acquired "soulness." Look at the development of the human being: first a tiny swimming figure, then an embryo, a fetus, a baby. At what point is that creature a human person? While both a five-year-old and a thirty-year-old are truly human, there is an enormous difference in the brain development and the power of reflection. Perhaps the same was true between the early hominids and *homo sapiens*.

The person of faith insists that God is somehow involved in the process of planetization and natural selection. The "how" is not easy to answer, but might it not be present with a kind of causality unfamiliar to science; with intentionality, creativity and benevolence that is beyond measure, even beyond intervention, or drawn-up design?

Placing a creator God in the midst of the process of natural selection, producing the infinitesimal variety can be challenging for the person of faith. The vast array of plants, insects, animals and sea life is beyond measure. Aquinas' explanation still bears notice. He proposed that the infinite majesty of God could never be exhausted by the variety of created things, so God keeps creating more diversity to reflect the infinity of the divine nature.[57]

It is difficult to place a divine creative power in an evolutionary process where there are so many dead ends and boundless extinctions; so many of these changes seem to us to be irrational and even random. Paul Tillich suggests that this can indicate God's infinite love that overflows in "holy waste." This is a God beyond the narrowness of our reason, a God who is self-wasting and self-surrendering, a Creator who can lovingly let nature be independent and free.[58] Haught incisively sums up this involvement of the Creator "as bringing into being a world that can in turn give rise spontaneously to new life and lush diversity, and eventually human beings. In that case, evolution is the unfolding of the world's original God-endowed resourcefulness. The divine maker of such a self-creative world is arguably much more impressive—hence worthier of human reverence and gratitude—than is a "designer" who molds and micro-manages everything directly."[59]

Another important question for Christians who are challenged by evolution is with regard the uniqueness and "superiority," if you will, of the human species. Science generally indicates that evolution is a process of "descent" from lower creatures. Humans then evolve in such continuity with animals that they are seen as nothing more than "thinking animals." This of course stands in stark contrast to the Christian belief that humans are made "in the image of likeness of God," called to a responsible morality (as opposed to animals) and destined to live on after death.

Teilhard turns the scientific argument on its head and proposes the cosmic process is an "ascent" of complexity that is drawn upward from cosmos to life to human consciousness, and ultimately to union with God (the cosmic Christ). It was his conviction that the cosmic process both came from and ascends to a reality that is already One. Rising and convergence is fundamental to Teilhard's experience of the universe.

For Teilhard, the human person is "something new," the thinker and planner who now both understands the evolutionary process and participates in its on-going progression. He accepts that humans emerge from nature and culminates from deep cosmic evolution. But once humans appear, "From this point onward humans cease to be a spark fallen by chance on earth and coming from another place. He is the flame of a general fermentation of the universe which breaks out suddenly on the earth. He is no longer a sterile enigma or discordant note in nature. He is the key of things and the final harmony. In him everything takes place and is explained."[60] For Teilhard, the cosmic process rises to "spirit," which is the indestructible part of the universe. He declared that without a realization of that truth, the universe is absurd.[61]

Religion and Ecology

Concern for the conservation of the environment was galvanized only in recent times. Since the industrial revolution of the 19th century, the West focused on production and consumption, accepted polluted air and water as necessary evils and assumed that raw materials such as oil and coal were limitless. Then in her 1962 book *Silent Spring*, Rachel Carson revealed how the use of DDT was killing life systems. In the same year, Aldo Leopold published *A Sand County Almanac* on the beauty and interconnection of living things and proposed a land ethic. In the 1970s, Wendell Berry and others elevated public awareness about the degradation of the environment.

The litany of environmental problems is well known: polluted air, contaminated lakes, rivers and oceans, climate change, extinction of species, degradation of the rain forests, ozone depletion that exposes plants as well as people to dangerous ultra-violet rays, nuclear waste disposal, the recent "disappearance" of winter and extreme heat in summer, drought, flooding, landslides, "frankenstorms" and other critical issues.

There is no doubt that advances have been made. There are stricter environmental laws for industry and many waterways have been cleaned up. Automobiles have improved their mileage per gallon and some use alternate fuels and battery systems. In the U.S., greenhouse gasses have been reduced by 10% over the last 5 years. Alternative forms of energy are utilized with the development of solar and wind turbines. Nevertheless, many authorities still warn that our environment is in crisis and that progress is too slow. Moreover, "fracking" of oil and natural gas is introducing new potential dangers to the environment. China and India, countries with enormous populations, are adding 5,000 new cars each day in major cities, which contributes mightily to CO_2 in the atmosphere.

Thomas Berry, a great visionary with regard to the relation of religion and ecology, reminds us that in earlier cultures, humans felt that they were in alliance with cosmic and spiritual processes. They recognized a spiritual presence in the cosmos and nature. Their terror in the face of natural catastrophes and their struggle to survive moved them to accept a "benign providence" at work in their world. Often they honored a deep sense of the sacred in nature, which in fact moved them to develop religious beliefs, symbols and rituals. Religions enabled these early peoples to connect with the holy and the sacred, and to join with that dimension of reality in cherishing and protecting the earth.

Berry points out that in the modern era there was a shift to regard nature as a material thing, which humans could use and control. With the advent of science and industry, many saw themselves as liberated from the spiritual dimensions of the earth and felt authorized to manipulate nature as they pleased. Berry cites four challenges that the human community faces towards reclaiming the spiritual aspects of reality. First, religions must return to their fundamentals regarding the spiritual presence in all things, especially the earth. Secondly, religions need to get in touch with their universal values— values that go beyond their traditional concerns and apply to the cosmos and the earth. Thirdly, religions must be more aware of what they have in common and how they complement each other; they in fact need each other to accomplish their universal mission. "None can be fully itself without the others," points out Berry, and "Each has a distinctive contribution to make to human development."[62] From this perspective, humans and their religions can realize that they all live in a global setting. And finally, religions are admonished to see themselves in the context of the new cosmological story of the birth of the universe and evolution. They must shift their focus from personal redemption to redemption in the context of the scientific vision of reality.

Berry, a master historian of culture and expert on world religions, maintained that there have been three "Mediations" during the last 3,000 years in the West. The first was concerned with bringing the divine into touch with the human. This began in ancient Israel, was continued by Jesus Christ and the Christian mission and then continued with Muhammad and the

Muslims.

The second mediation was an inter-human one, between classes and nation states. During this period, there developed a need to mediate between those in major conflicts both within and among nations, eventual world wars and the appearance of great political movements such as National Socialism, Communism and conflicts both within and among nations. In our own time, we have experienced conflicts in Africa, the Middle East and other areas throughout the world. This mediation has to deal with on-going violence and killing, along with the spending of billions of dollars each day for arms and military conflicts.

Finally there is now the need for a third mediation, between the human community and the earth, upon which humans depend for their survival. Berry writes, "I speak of the mediation between the human community and Earth, the planet that surrounds and supports us and upon which we depend in an absolute fashion for our nourishment and our breath... Our arts and our education, too, all proceed from the Earth. Even our knowledge of God comes to us from our acquaintance with earth, for the divine reveals itself first of all in the sky and in the waters, and in the wind, in the mountains and valleys, in the birds of the air and in all living forms that flower and move over the surface to the earth."[63]

Berry postulates that we are now closing what he calls a Cenozoic era, which commenced millions of years ago with the development of life forms and now closes with their endangerment. The present degradation of life and the environment began with the development of industry and consumerism. The devastation now, according to Berry, appears to be on a scale of what it was when the dinosaurs disappeared. He hopes that humans are now moving into a new Ecozoic period in which we will once more revere our intimate connection with the Earth and the urgent need to sustain it.

Sadly, we have abused this earth, marred its beauty, fouled its air and water, and squandered its resources. We now stand to pass on to our children an Earth that is degraded and endangered. Materialism has moved us to "thingify" nature and lose touch with its "spirit" and meaning. Our young often don't play outdoors and many children experience little of nature. Children who aren't acquainted with the workings and beauty of nature aren't aware of how much is at stake if nature is endangered. Urban sprawl has made nature increasingly unavailable to our young, and many have few opportunities for coming to the appreciation of the wonders of the woods, mountains, birds, animals or creatures of the sea. If education has not provided them with the knowledge of the universe or the earth, it is difficult for them to be concerned or to realize how the world around them is deteriorating at a rapid pace.

In the past, religions have not distinguished themselves by protecting nature. Christians in particular have often interpreted the "dominion over nature" as a license to use and abuse the earth. Instead of seeing "dominion" as partnership with the Creator in sustaining nature with care, Christians have interpreted dominion to mean the domination and manipulation of their environment. Instead of holding a responsibility for preserving and sustaining nature, humans have felt free to manipulate nature for their own profit. Berry strongly denounces such a position: "We have rejected the divinely established order of the universe and are attempting to establish a contrived human order in its place, under the assumption that we know better than nature how the universe and the planet Earth should function. No pathology ever invented could be so perverse and so devastating to the delicate balance of life and existence on this planet."[64]

Christianity has had a checkered career with regard to the earth. Christians have often followed a spirituality that was "unworldly," and joining religious life was seen as "leaving the world." The word "cosmos" in the gospels can have two meanings: "the world as the earth" or "the world of sin." Monastic life originated as an abandonment of the latter. It should be clear that no one can leave the "world as the earth." There is no way one can leave the cosmos, the earth, or abandon all cares about its beauty, its suffering, or its degradation. The great Dutch theologian, Edward Schillebeeckx, has revised the old statement "Outside the Church there is not salvation" to read "Outside the World there is no salvation." If the Church chooses to train its religious and clergy in seminary "hot houses," one wonders how effective these ministers can be in dealing with the many real problems that earthlings face today. That is the very reason why Vatican II encouraged the Church as "the people of God" to be actively concerned about and engaged in the realities of the modern world.

Christians also are inclined to make religion privatized, primarily concerned with the salvation of the individual rather than the salvation of the community and its environs. The "Me and God" approach to religion is still prevalent among religious people. Add to this, the situation where many individual parishes and congregations exist in their own little world; each religion can gather in its own synagogue, temple, mosque or church, closed off from serious local and global problems. With such cloistering, it is easy to see why so many religious people do not have deep concerns about their Earth. It is easy to create family, school or church "bubbles" where we can remain enclosed and oblivious to the needs and crises that surround us.

Of course, those Christian churches that take literal positions on the scripture and deny the findings of science are not likely to be concerned about environmental problems that are described by science. Moreover, Christian churches pre-occupied with the imminent "end of the world" are generally not concerned about sustaining the earth and its resources since none of it will be here for long anyway.

A New Awakening

In the last 20 years, religions have made tremendous progress in addressing environmental issues. Christians were stirred into action by Prof. Lynn White's charge that the Christian belief in "dominion over nature" was instrumental in causing the environmental crisis. Christian centers for environmental concern were established at Au Sable Institute in Michigan, St. John the Divine Cathedral in New York, and a Website of Creation was established on the Internet. The World Council of Churches published a significant statement on the environment in 1991. The Council took up the theme of liberation, and pointed out that our concern for the freedom of humans should be extended to animals, plants and the earth itself. Presbyterians published a document on ecology very early, in 1971, and then a more thorough document in 1991. They declared that the environmental crisis is also a human crisis, since many people, especially the poor, suffer from living in polluted areas and millions (most often children) die each year from diseases from polluted water. They point to a liberating God and to Christ as a redeemer who can teach us, inspire us and empower us to sustain the earth where we live and on which we depend for survival. They described the true "good life" as one of frugality and sharing.[65]

The Evangelical Lutherans adapted scripture and the accounts of creation and the covenant to show that God is near and is passionately involved with the earth. They emphasized that incarnation reveals that God is present in the material world.[66]

Speaking for Roman Catholics, Pope John Paul II made a substantial address on ecology in 1990. The pontiff proclaimed that disrespect for nature should be included in the threats to world peace alongside the arms race, injustice and local wars. He admonished Christians that this "crisis" is a seedbed for selfishness, dishonesty and disregard for others.[67] Pope Benedict XVI has voiced a number of key statements with regard the environment, was known as "The Green Pope" and rode in a plug-in Popemobile. The Jesuits have designated the environment one of their international priorities.

Throughout the late 80's and 90's, many national Bishops Conferences articulated strong concerns about the environment, especially in developing countries, Central America and the Pacific. The Bishops of the U.S. published an important statement in 1991, stressing that preserving the Earth was a matter of social justice and concern for the common good. One of the most impressive Catholic statements on ecology came from the Appalachian churches in a dozen states. For many years these citizens have had to witness their land being de-forested, strip-mined and used as dumps for out-of-state garbage and radioactive materials. Their moving document became an outcry over the abuse of their areas, a desire for freedom so they can restore and once again live freely and healthily on their lands. The Appalachian people pleaded that the gospel message of justice and love of neighbor be applied to their desperate situation. Overall, Christians bring many gospel values to the table when discussing ecology: recognizing the goodness of a creation that comes from the hand of God; being part of a mission to be co-creators along with God; and maintain a concern for the poor who are so often victims of the mistreated environment. The medieval St. Francis is their role model along with Sr. Dorothy Stang, who in 2005 was assassinated for her efforts to save the rain forests and their inhabitants in Brazil. The ARC is an example of the partnership that is being established among world religions to improve the environment. It was founded in 1995 by Prince Philip, the husband of Queen Elizabeth. Philip invited representatives from world religions to Windsor Castle to discuss ecology. Eleven religions decided to establish seven year plans for improving the environment in their regions. Over the last ten years, there have been reports of the success of these plans at well-attended meetings.[68]

Other Religions' Views on the Environment

The contemporary partnership among world religions with regard to the environment is encouraging indeed. This partnership has moved individual religions to examine their beliefs and values in order to see how they can be motivated to find ways to improve the environment. In addition, religions have been able to compare their traditions and see how their different views on God, creation, religious way of life and afterlife can enrich their partnership rather than divide them. Religions are beginning to see that their differences can offer new perspectives and considerations to each other. In the following section we will look at several religions and how they are becoming more concerned about the earth and its resources.

Hinduism

In their efforts to restore their mountains, forests and sacred rivers as well as better control pollution, Hindus have identified the religious values that drive them; the sacredness of all living things, the interconnection of all aspects of creation, "ahimsa," which means non-violence or "do no harm." Noteworthy are the so-called "tree-huggers," the Chipko Movement founded by Gaura Devi (1925-1991). Originally, this was a group of 27 women and girls who risked their lives holding trees about to be cut down near their village. They saved 2,500 trees and started an environmental movement throughout India that still flourishes.

Buddhism

Many Buddhist monks and nuns are active in the environmental movements in their countries, especially in Mongolia, Cambodia, Thailand and Tibet. They have applied ancient Buddhist values to their mission to care for the earth: 1) Interdependence or the belief that all in the cosmos and on Earth act on cause and effect and are linked together as whole; 2) All actions have consequences, so wasteful use of resources and degradation of the earth will rebound to punish; 3) The universe is a web that must remain connected and cared for with compassion; and 4) Mindfulness, which is a central Buddhist value and here means to be enlightened and aware of the surrounding beauty, and the human tendency to destroy nature wantonly.

A dedicated activist is Sulak Sivaraksa, a Buddhist monk in Thailand who has been an influential leader in the country's environmental movement. He has been imprisoned and exiled for his criticism of his government and their policies. Sulak uses the Buddhist principle of "continual questioning" and has applied that principle to seriously question those who abuse the earth.

Jiyul Sunim is a Buddhist nun in South Korea who has protested the destruction of ecosystems to build high-speed trains and has resisted the development along the Nakdong River. She has also been an advocate for Thai women's involvement in ecology.

Judaism

The people of Judaism have also become more involved in ecology. The Torah not only links them to God, but also to God's creation and its preservation. There is a flourishing environmental movement in Israel itself.

The citizens there now realize that years of development have produced serious pollution and health problems. Jews believe that the "earth is the Lord's," that humans are caretakers of the earth, all people are our neighbors and we have an obligation to love them. This emphasis has moved many Jews to become better stewards and to reclaim areas that have become degraded.

A notable example of this is Alon Tal, a professor at Ben-Gurion University in Israel who has been an effective leader in ecology and who has assisted Palestinians with water management, air quality, nature preservation and the proper disposal of solid waste.

Islam

In the last few decades, Muslims have adopted new attitudes regarding ecology. Instead of seeing this as a Western problem, many Muslims confess that they have been part of the problem. Large environmental conferences have been held in Iran, Saudi Arabia and throughout the Middle East. Muslim organizations in Turkey and Pakistan have combined with governments to protect local ecosystems and limit pollution. The Islamic belief in the unity between Allah and all creation has provided Muslims with motivation to better cherish the earth and its resources. Their belief in "trusteeship" (*khalifa*) teaches that creation belongs to Allah and that Allah created humans and entrusted them to act as trusted protectors or guardians of creation. Belief in accountability now moves many more Muslims toward acting more responsibly toward the earth and its resources. A key player here is Fazlun Khalid, the founder of the Islamic Foundation for Ecological and Environmental Sciences. He travels the Muslim world to teach Muslims how to apply their beliefs to sustaining the natural world and its resources.

Summary

The "It" quadrant refers the material world, which is measured and analyzed by science. Today the findings of astronomy, evolutionary studies and environmental science in particular are challenging to religion.

Science and religion have different approaches to reality. Science measures and analyzes material reality, while religion deals with the transcendent dimension of reality. Science has its proofs while religion generally deals with faith, which from the Christian perspective is a graced gift from God. Both science and religion work within their unique limitations.

The relationship between religion and science has always been contentious, especially in the periods of major scientific breakthroughs such as those of Galileo and Darwin. Today many scientists, as well as those of the postmodern persuasion, fail to take religion very seriously. For some religions, the feeling is mutual.

On the other hand, many religious leaders and scientists respect each other's endeavors and are in close dialogue, hoping to mutually enhance their understanding of reality. Prominent religious thinkers accept scientific discoveries and attempt to adapt religious beliefs to them. They accept the new story of the cosmos and have attempted to reinterpret beliefs about God and creation to this new narrative. Likewise, serious efforts have been made by religious thinkers to adapt religious beliefs to the discovery of evolution. And finally, most religions have come to accept the environmental crisis and have joined together to seek practical solutions.

SUGGESTED READINGS

Allen, Peter and Paul Allen. *Catholicism and Science*. London: Greenwood Press, 2008.

Barbour, Ian. *Religion and Science*. New York: HarperCollins, 1997.

Barnes, Michael H. *Understanding Religion and Science*. New York: Continuum, 2010.

Clayton, Philip and Zachary Simpson, eds., *The Oxford Handbook of Religion and Science*. New York: Oxford University Press, 2009.

Haag, James W. and others (eds), *The Routledge Companion to Religion and Science*, New York: Routledge, 2012.

Haught, John, *Making Sense of Evolution*. Louisville, KY: Westminster John Knox Press, 2010.

Holder, R. *God, the Multiverse and Everything*. Aldershot: Ashgate, 2004.

McCalla, Arthur, *The Creationist Debate*. New York: T.T. Clark, 2006.

Swimme, Brian T and Mary E. Tucker, *Journey of the Universe* (New Haven: Yale University Press, 2011

Taylor, Victor E. *Religion After Postmodernism*. Charlottesville: University of Virginia Press, 2008.

◄📹 VIDEOS ONLINE

Science's 10 Inventions that Could Have Changed the World
    http://www.youtube.com/watch?v=U-eJoWXVmys

the Dalai Lama, *Religion and Science*
    http://www.youtube.com/watch?v=HGtACJBTX4M

Christopher Hitchens, *Science vs Religion*
    http://www.youtube.com/watch?v=Hv6U2BtdFGc

Postmodernism: *Chomsky on Science and Postmodernism*
    https://www.youtube.com/watch?v=OzrHwDOlTt8

Science, Religion & Human Nature: *The Chomsky Sessions*
    https://www.youtube.com/watch?v=f02gcRrdK2I

Rediscovering Fire: The Evolution of Teilhard de Chardin (trailer)
    http://www.youtube.com/watch?v=TObSQFGUNEo

Ecology and religion: *Religion and a new environmental ethic*
    https://www.youtube.com/watch?v=BG0bQ3SwDI8

BBC The Cosmos- A Beginner's Guide (1 of 6) *Life in the Cosmos*
    http://www.youtube.com/watch?v=m0NGabKD2DY

John Haught, *God After Darwin*
    https://www.youtube.com/watch?v=wgu4OkZ0brY

Origin of Species by Charles Darwin
    https://www.youtube.com/watch?v=vfmOaAz371M

Vatican Sponsors Conference On Evolution
    https://www.youtube.com/watch?v=ekngxTBIO6o

A Scientist Visits A Creationist Museum
    https://www.youtube.com/watch?v=z1xUiuZvUuw

Taoism, Christianity, and Evolution
    https://www.youtube.com/watch?v=noPBSgE8NGQ

CS Lewis on Free Will & The Problem of Evil
    https://www.youtube.com/watch?v=rH2DEOxvaWk3

Rachel Carson Introduction
    https://www.youtube.com/watch?v=T_Njv5Ygg0g

Thomas Berry, *The Dream of the Earth*
    https://www.youtube.com/watch?v=POomCHT6hNE

⬛ NOTES

1. Benedict M. Ashley and John Deely, *How Science Enriches Theology* (South Bend, IN: St. Augustine's Press, 2012), ix.

2. Carl Zimmer, *The Tangled Bank* (Greenwood Village, CO: Roberts and Company Publishers, 2010), 20.

3. Michael H. Barnes, *Understanding Religion and Science* (New York: Continuum, 2010), 80ff.

4. See the Gemini website at http://www.ip-192.com/2012/10/10/speed-of-light-einsteins-theory-of-relativity/

5. Ashley and Deely, 13.

6. John Haught, *Making Sense of Evolution* (Louisville, KY: Westminster John Knox Press, 2010), 27.

7. H. James Birx, *Interpreting Evolution* (Buffalo, NY: Prometheus Books, 1991), 41.

8. See "*Gandhi Did Not Oppose Science*" at the Rediff India Abroad website at http://www.rediff.com/news/2007/feb/26inter.htm.

9. See Tenzin Gyatso, "*Science at the Crossroads*" at the website of His Holiness the 14th Dalai Lama of Tibet at http://www.dalailama.com/messages/buddhism/science-at-the-crossroads.

10. Birx, 41.

11. See G.S. Kirk and J.E. Raven, *The Presocratic Philosophers* (Cambridge: Cambridge University Press, 1962).

12. Birx, 44.

13. Ian Barbour, *Religion and Science* (New York: HarperCollins, 1997), 24ff.

14. Geoffery Cantor, "Science and Religion" in *The Routledge Companion to Religion and Science*, eds. James W. Haag and others (New York: Routledge, 2012), 24.

15. Barnes, 90.

16. Ashley and Deely,16.

17. See Victor E. Taylor, *Religion After Postmodernism* (Charlottesville: University of Virginia Press, 2008), 56ff.

18. F. Leron Shults, "Religion and Science in Christian Theology" in *The Routledge Companion to Religion and Science*, eds. James W. Haag and others (New York: Routledge, 2012), 8.

19. Karl Rahner, "The Experience of a Catholic Theologian" Communio 11, 4 (1984) 412.

20. Shults, 8.

21. Gerald O'Collins and Mary Ann Meyers, eds., *Light from Light* (Grand Rapids, MI: Wm. B. Eerdmans Publishing Co., 2012); See Philip Clayton and Zachary Simpson, eds., *The Oxford Handbook of Religion and Science* (New York: Oxford University Press, 2009).

22. See the John Templeton Foundation website at http://www.templeton.org.

23. See George V. Coyne, S.J., "John Paul II on the Relationship Between the Natural Sciences and Religious Belief: Five Key Discourses" at the website of INTERS - Interdisciplinary Encyclopedia of Religion and Science at http://www.disf.org/en/OtherTexts/Coyne.asp.

24. Ashley and Deely, 27.

25. Brian T. Swimme and Mary E. Tucker, *Journey of the Universe* (New Haven: Yale University Press, 2011), 12.

26. Ibid., 28.

27. Grace Wolf-Chase, "Astronomy" in *Routledge Companion*, eds. Haag and others, 110.

28. Clayton and Simpson, *Oxford Handbook*, 145.

29. Ibid., 147.

30. Antije Jackelin, "Cosmology and Theology" in *Routledge Companion*, ed. Haag and others, 139.

31. See Gerald Manley Hopkins, *God's Grandeur* at The Poetry Foundation website at http://www.poetryfoundation.org/poem/173660.

32. See R. Holder, *God, the Multiverse and Everything* (Aldershot: Ashgate, 2004).

33. Brian Swimme, "Cosmic Directionality and the Wisdom of Science," in *Science and Religion in Search of Cosmic Purpose*, ed. John F. Haught (Washington, D.C.: Georgetown University Press, 2000), 94.

34. Haught, *Cosmic Purpose*, 113.

35. Ibid., 116.

36. Owen Gingerich, "Is There Design And Purpose In The Universe?" in Haught, 124.

37. Haught, *Cosmic Purpose*, 125.

38. Ibid., 129.

39. See Norman W. Pittenger, *God in Process* (London: S.C.M. Press, 1967).

40. Swimme, 84ff

41. Ibid., 61.

42. "Cosmic Life," quoted in Ursula King, *Spirit of Fire* (Maryknoll, NY: Orbis Books, 1996), 55.

43. Pierre Teilhard, *Hymn of the Universe* (New York: Harper and Row, 1965), 24.

44. King, 62.

45. Ibid., 62ff.

46. "How I Believe," King, 158.

47. See Arthur McCalla, *The Creationist Debate* (New York: T.T. Clark, 2006).

48. See "The Latest Gallop Poll on Evolution" at the website of The National Center for Science Education, June 1, 2012 at http://ncse.com/news/2012/06/latest-gallup-poll-evolution-007431.

49. Elizabeth Johnson, *She Who Is* (New York: Crossroad,1992), 217.

50. Pierre Teilhard de Chardin, The Divine Milieu (New York: Harper and Row, 1957), 121, 143.

51. ——, Human Energy (New York: Harcourt Brace, 1969), 32.

52. ——, The Phenomenon of Man (New York: Harper and Row, 1959), 264ff.

53. W. Owen Cole and Piara Singh Sambhi, The Sikhs (Boston: Routledge, 1978), 70.

54. Martin Palmer, The Elements of Taoism (New York; Barnes and Noble, 1991), 14ff; P.C. Nahar, ed., An Encyclopedia of Jainism (Delhi: Sri Satguru Pub. 1988), 264ff.

55. See "Abraham Joshua Heschel" on Religion and Ethics Newsweekly at the website of PBS, January 18, 2008, at http://www.pbs.org/wnet/religionandethics/episodes/january-18-2008/abraham-joshua-heschel/1789/ .

56. Walter Kasper, The God of Jesus Christ (London: SCM, 1983), 194-195.

57. See Haught, Making Sense of Evolution, 36.

58. Paul Tillich, The New Being (New York: Charles Scribner's Sons, 1955), 48.

59. Haught, Making Sense of Evolution, 42.

60. Teilhard de Chardin, Human Energy, 23-24.

61. Ibid., 41.

62. Thomas Berry, The Christian Future and the Fate of the Earth (Maryknoll, NY: Orbis Books, 2009), 4-5.

63. Ibid., 9.

64. Ibid., 470.

65. Roger Gottlieb, ed., This Sacred Earth (New York: Routledge, 1996), 251-270.

66. Ibid., 243-251.

67. Drew Christiansen and Walter Grazer, eds., Catholic Theology and the Environment (Washington, DC: USCC, 1996), 215- 223.

68. See the website of the Alliance of Religions and Conservation at http://www.arcworld.org/about_ARC.asp.

7

Spirituality

We are moving towards a completely religionless time; people as they are now simply cannot be religious anymore. Even those who honestly describe themselves as 'religious' do not in the least act up to it, and so they presumably mean something quite different by 'religious'?.... Do people not know that one can get on as well, even better, without 'religion'?
— Dietrich Bonhoeffer

For human beings, the most daunting challenge is to become fully human. For to become fully human is to become fully divine.
— Thomas Keating

Sarah was raised in a Catholic family and attended Catholic schools. As a child, she enjoyed Sunday Mass with her family, but in high school she lost interest. When Sarah entered a Jesuit college, she stopped going to Church. A course on Catholic doctrine was required but Sarah began to wonder if she really believed "all this stuff." When Sarah was a senior, her parents got divorced, remarried and learned that since they hadn't received an annulment they could not any longer receive Communion. They felt shunned by their church and it hurt Sarah to see how they were treated. She decided that Catholicism was no longer relevant to her life and drifted away. Sarah maintains that she still has faith and prays regularly. She "reads" weekly to a blind shut-in woman. She feels that she is a good person, but no longer discerns a need for belonging to a church.

Sarah is typical of many people today who declare that they are "spiritual but not religious." In the last five years the numbers of U.S. citizens who are not affiliated with religion has increased to 20%. At the same time, about 65% of the unaffiliated say they believe in God, 37% say they are "spiritual," and 21% report that they pray everyday. Mainline Protestants and Roman Catholics have lost the most members, (although the increase of Latinos has kept the Catholic numbers up). There has also has been a migration of Catholics to the megachurches. A good percentage of people unaffiliated with a religion are young adults.[1] The numbers of unaffiliated have increased even more drastically in Europe, especially in Germany, Austria, France, the Czech Republic, the Scandinavian countries, Britain and Ireland.[2]

In this chapter, we are going to explore some meanings for spirituality and then focus on Christian spirituality, since that is where most tension exists between spirituality and religion ("I am spiritual but not religious"). We will examine the history of Christian spirituality and then investigate how some of the most valuable aspects of this tradition are being recovered in today's Christian spirituality. We will close by looking at what it might mean to be spiritual but not religious.

What is Spirituality?

Let's start with the word "spirit," which in Latin is "spiritus" or "breath." Spirit refers to an invisible, intangible reality like breath. We might note that a child already has a determined "spirit," or that a school has a certain "spirit." Sometimes young people tour colleges trying to decide where to attend and they might make their choice based on a certain spirit they find there. The way they are treated, the energy of the students, the concern of the faculty all contribute to an invisible spirit that appeals to the prospective student.

The human spirit is the invisible aspect of the human person, and Christians believe that our spirits come from God and are intended to return to God. The spiritual life involves efforts to continually increase intimacy with the Ultimate and to one day achieve union with it. Spirituality involves the deepest capacities of human persons as they search for meaning purpose and oneness with the divine. Spirituality generally involves interiority, prayer, and some form of asceticism or personal discipline. While spirituality may be carried out within a community, it is profoundly personal.

From the beginning, Christian spirituality has referred to a way of life that seeks to be in union with transcendence, the beyond, the mysterious Spirit of God, as lived by Jesus Christ; "God is Spirit" (John 24:4). It is a lifestyle concerned about oneness with God and all God's creation. It is a way of life where one attempts to join one's own personal spirit with the Spirit of God, which exists in all things. Christian spirituality is being incorporated into and transformed by this Spirit of God "in whom we live and breathe and have our very being" (Acts 17:28). It is a spirituality that allows God's Spirit, the Spirit of Jesus Christ, to take over one's life. Paul describes the results, "the fruits of the Spirit: love, joy, peace, patience, kindness, generosity, faithfulness, gentleness and self-control" (Galatians 5:22–24). Christian spirituality is coming to God as we are, with our true selves, and allowing God to change us. Thomas Merton, one of the most enlightened spiritual writers of our time, put it this way: "The way of perfection is not a way of escape. We can only become saints by facing ourselves, by assuming full responsibility for our lives just as they are, with all our handicaps and limitations, and submitting ourselves to the purifying and transforming action of the Savior."[3]

This notion of "life in the Spirit," central to the life of all Christians, prevailed in the Church until the 12th century, when the word "spirituality" became more associated with the clergy. Eventually the term "spirituality" all but disappeared and was replaced by "asceticism" and "mysticism." Both of these areas applied to religious life and seminary training and, especially after the Reformation, became subordinated to doctrinal theology. Neither asceticism nor mysticism had much relevancy to the laity, who largely turned to devotions to nurture their spirit and at times participated in retreats, novenas or parish missions to energize their very private life of the soul.

Vatican II changed all that when it made a declaration that would cause a sea of change to the Christian life. The Council declared that "All the Christian faithful, of whatever state or rank, are called to the fullness of the Christian life and to the perfection of charity."[4] Old dualisms such as natural and supernatural, worldly and unworldly, body and soul were set aside. Rather than the church being equated with the clergy and hierarchy, the church was now described as "the people of God" and all members were called to holiness.

Since the 1970s, personal and communal spirituality has held center stage in Christian life. It has been opened to influences from other religions and been integrally linked with peace and social justice.[5]

Not everyone was prepared for this sea of change. Many of the clergy and hierarchy continued to be trained in doctrine and morals and did not have sufficient training or experience with spirituality to meet the needs of the community. The official church generally remained concerned with doctrinal and moral matters, as well as with scandals, and was not prepared to deal with the spiritual concerns of the community. In the United States, the charismatic movements and programs such as *Christ Renews His Parish* and *Renew* provided spiritual revitalization, but often lacked on-going follow-up or continuity. As a result, many in the community have discovered other sources for their spiritual growth. Some turned to the East, to the Hindu or Buddhist traditions. Gandhi's deep Hindu spirituality, which understands spirit as the "life of all things" or "the inner self" and is committed to a life of self-sacrifice and non-violence, was influential. Martin Luther King Jr. was profoundly disposed to that spirituality in his struggle for civil rights for Blacks. Others in the community turned to the Buddhist tradition, which focuses on the inner life and constant meditation that attempts to root out the causes of suffering by the development of loving, compassionate individuals. Spiritual guides like the Dalai Lama and Thich Nhat Hahn have become influential guides.

As mentioned earlier, a growing number of people in the religious community are leaving formal religion altogether and pursuing their own spiritualities in meditation and in small communities. They often describe themselves as "searchers," looking for God "in unexpected places." Sadly, others have just gone adrift and lost touch with both religion and spirituality altogether.

The History of Christian Spirituality

An overview of the history of Christian spirituality can help locate and restore the best of the tradition. Christian spirituality has a long history that spans over 2,000 years. For two millennia, Christians have searched and struggled within many different cultures and through challenging times to discern the Spirit of God in their lives. Each period developed its own spiritual emphasis, tailored to "the signs of the times." The struggles often fall off track, so each age has to somehow return to the center, sustain the living core, and develop spirituality for its own time.

Honoring the post-modern perspective that all narratives have to be accepted as relative and that our cultural resources from the past are conditioned and partial, I have still dared to order the history of Christian spirituality into six eras (focusing mainly on Catholic spirituality): 1. New Testament; 2. patristic; 3. monastic; 4. medieval; 5. post-Reformation; and 6. post-Vatican II. Granted that there is often scant interest in history by some today, background is still warranted to help us reclaim the best of the core of Christian spirituality in the NOW. In addition, only a clear picture of the history of spirituality will enable us to see how it has been traditionally related to religion and not practiced on its own.

New Testament Spirituality

The primary source for Christian spirituality is scripture, primarily the New Testament. From the time of the early urban communities and desert dwellers, people who desired to deepen their spirituality have gone to the well of the gospels and the other scriptures in the New Testament, which is why we will spend substantial time on New Testament spirituality.

Christian spirituality begins with a person, Jesus Christ, as he is described in the New Testament. The Christian scriptures were all written within 30-70 years after the death of Jesus and describe not so much his life as the spirituality lived by his followers. The gospels are not so much biographies as they are "faith proclamations" of the early churches, their life in Christ wrapped around memories of what Jesus said and did. Just as we, consciously or unconsciously, emulate the lives of our parents and grandparents, the early followers of Jesus imitated the life of their friend, brother and savior. For the early Christians, Jesus was the epitome of all that is human and divine, the perfect union of God and the human, the role model for joining their own lives with the divine. Discipleship is described as a call (Come follow me!) to internalize Jesus' teachings and example as found in the New Testament.

Early Christians did not so much see themselves as following a religion, but a "Way." Christian spirituality was the way of discipleship which involved a radical change in their personal lives, a commitment to share this way with others, and a willingness to lay down their lives for others just as the Master did.

Like Jesus, the disciples were to engage in a ministry of healing, teaching, serving, prayer and sacrifice for others. The earliest gospel, Mark, indicates that the disciple had but two laws: "You shall love the Lord your God with all your heart, with all your soul, with all your mind, and with all your strength. You shall love your neighbor as yourself" (Mark 12:30–32). The spiritual life is a life that is blessed by God, and for over 2,000 years disciples have endeavored to live this life of being poor in spirit, mournful for the losses of others, meek, hungering and thirsting for righteousness, merciful, clean of heart, peace-making and persecuted for the sake of righteousness (Matthew 5:3–20). People who cherish Christian spirituality conscientiously recognize this divine dimension of their lives, acknowledge their spiritual needs, and look to God to empower them to grow in holiness.

Christian spirituality is holistic in that it is not concerned with some mysterious "soul" within the body, but rather sees human persons as "embodied spirits" in the world, who reach out to the divine with mind, heart, feelings and will.

Sheldrake identifies four elements in the early discipleship. First, the disciples realized that following Jesus was not so much a choice as it was a call. In following Jesus, they were responding to God's grace to seek union with the divine (the very heart of spirituality). Secondly, this call was not to some special status or official position. It was an inclusive invitation that included women as well as men, outcasts, sinners—all were welcome! Thirdly, it was a call to repentance, to turn their lives around to face goodness rather than evil. It was a beckoning to recognize that the kingdom of God, the loving saving presence of God, was in their midst; it was not in the heavens somewhere, but right under their noses! The call involved carrying their everyday crosses, like Jesus, with the same faith, courage and love. It asked for detachment from all that was keeping them from being one with God, including all that is false in the self. Finally, it was a call to carry out Jesus' mission to spread the word about God's loving and saving presence (Kingdom) throughout the world. [6]

In the four gospels we pick up different elements of the spirituality of these early Christian communities.

Mark

In the gospel of Mark, which may have come from a community in Rome only several generations after Jesus, the members appear to be more doers than thinkers. Their spirituality is vibrant and practical. Jesus moves rapidly from place to place healing, driving out evil spirits, dealing with conflicts until his act of ultimate self-sacrifice on the cross. His disciples are with him every step of the way, struggling to understand him, yet they are cowardly and abandon him in weakness before his death. Ultimately they experience forgiveness and assurance that Jesus will always be with them. The gospel reflects a spirituality that attempts to follow Jesus' ministry, but is constantly aware of how human limitations make this so difficult.

In the community described by Mark, we see an early spirituality that struggles to understand Jesus and his message. It is a spirituality characterized by efforts to accept and bring healing into a world of suffering and evil. It faces setbacks, rejections and challenges. The disciples have their small mustard seed of faith. They will face violent storms, but they can count on Jesus for support. In their blindness they join Bartimaeus in his plea, "Master that I may see" (Mark 10:52). Jesus says to them: "Be opened" (Mark 7:34). They will face rivers and mountains to cross and in each challenge they will experience the confirmation that Jesus is their savior. As Jesus fed the 5,000, he feeds his disciples in amazing ways. Their lives must be centered on love of God and neighbor (Mark 12:30–32). They take up their crosses, at times reluctantly, but always with the knowledge that "whoever loses his life for my sake and that of the gospel will save it" (Mark 8:35). Jesus is there with them. They fall, they fail, and they stand with the women at the tomb, trembling and bewildered at the word of Jesus' resurrection. They are then called to spread the good news far and wide, always aware that "the Lord worked with them" (Mark 16:20).

Matthew's community

Matthew's community forms a sharp contrast to Mark's. This gathering of Jews and Gentiles probably lived in Antioch around 50 years after Jesus. Their spirituality recognizes that Jesus is a kingly messiah (son of David and Abraham) and was conceived of a virgin by power of the Spirit of God (Matthew 1:16–25). He is the "new Moses" that calls them out of Egypt (the Flight from Herod). These early Christians expect rejection from Jews (Herod is the symbol) and acceptance by Gentiles (the Magi). Jesus is the Savior who came "to save his people from their sins" (Matthew 1:21). Like Jesus, at their baptisms they were acknowledged as beloved sons and daughters of God (Matthew 3:13–17). Again, the spirituality of this young community has experienced God's call to have a change of heart. Like Jesus himself, they face temptations to be concerned about material things, to seek power and connive with evil.

The Matthean community understands Jesus' teaching more thoroughly and in a more orderly fashion. They put together the core of his message in the Sermon on the Mount which says to be "blessed" by the Spirit of God, they must be poor in spirit, mournful, meek, hungry and thirsty for righteousness, merciful, clean of heart, peacemakers and persecuted for the sake of righteousness (Matthew 5:3–10). They are committed to loving God and neighbor.

Luke's community

The author of the gospel of Luke seems to be a third generation Christian. He represents a community that has a much more cosmopolitan view of Christianity and he actually seems far removed from Jesus' homeland in Palestine. The community looks at the "big picture" and recognizes that the Spirit has guided their movement throughout Jewish history. They develop a spirituality of trust and hope which accepts that in the midst of rejection and failure, the divine plan moves inexorably along. Jesus is acknowledged in continuity with the Jewish prophets and recognized as anointed by God. In the synagogue, Jesus reads from the prophet Isaiah and declares that the prophecy is fulfilled in him. The reading was as follows: "The Spirit of the Lord is upon me, because he has anointed me to bring glad tidings to the poor" (Luke 4:18).

The Lucan community sees their mission as spreading the word to all people. Forgiveness is a central value for them as exemplified with Jesus' words from the cross: "Father forgive them, they know not what they do" (Luke 23:24). With no recriminations for their desertion, Jesus appears to the disciples after the resurrection and simply says: "Peace be with you" (Luke 24:26). This theme comes through strongly in the parables of the prodigal son and the lost sheep. In this community, the spirituality of the poor and oppressed rejoices in salvation by their God. The rich, on the other hand, resist salvation by clinging to their worldly possessions. Jesus tells the rich official to give all that he has to the poor, just as he does the rich young man in Mark's Gospel (Luke 18:22; Mark 10:17). Both go away sad, unable to be detached from their wealth. The strong commitment of the community to repentance comes through in the story of Zacchaeus, the corrupt tax collector who turns his life around at the mere sight of Jesus (Luke 19:1–10). The tension between contemplation and action comes through in the story of Martha and Mary, as the early Christians struggled to integrate their faith into their daily lives. In Luke's gospel, the meaning of resurrection has become much more developed than in Mark, as evidenced in the well-crafted resurrection stories.

Johannine Christians

The final gospel, after going through several additions around the end of the first century, seems to come from a robust and mobile community which had "the beloved disciple" in their midst to witness first-hand for Jesus' teaching. This community has a well-developed understanding of Jesus' divinity and expressed this in a sophisticated word theology. Jesus was and remains "God with them," and the Johannine Christian spirituality is one that accents a special intimacy with Jesus, the Son of God. At the very outset, Jesus is proclaimed to be the Word (the creative aspect of God): "In the beginning was the Word, and the Word was God... and the Word became Flesh and made his dwelling with us" (John 1:1–14). Faith in this Jesus, the Christ, is the key to eternal life, and he is surrounded by powerful symbols of light, life, water, bread, shepherd and vine. Jesus' teachings are extremely well developed in long discourses.

This community is known for their deep awareness of God's love for them and at the center of their life is Jesus' "new commandment": "Love one another. As I have loved you, so you also should love one another. This is how all will know you are my disciples, if you have love for one another" (John 13:34–35). Members are deeply aware that Jesus has called them "friends," has chosen them, and has promised to send them the Advocate, the Spirit of truth (John 15:26). The community realizes that there is no middle ground in their spirituality: one is either for the light or the darkness, for life or death. They follow a dynamic Savior whose divine power is dramatized by his ability to change water into wine, multiply loaves, walk on water and raise the dead. The Johannine Christians are devoted to Jesus, who is "the Light of the world," "the source of living water," "the Good Shepherd." Their spirits are enlightened, nourished and protected by Jesus.

We have seen some of the highlights of the early spirituality of the gospel communities. Many see John's gospel as uniquely spiritual: "What has attracted many people is this mystical dimension of New Testament spirituality that emphasizes God's presence, mutual indwelling, and a union of light and love rather than simply moral conversion."[7]

Now let us turn to some of the spiritual values of the early communities in Acts and Paul.

Acts of the Apostles

The Christian spirituality in Acts is one that is open to other cultures and to the world. It perceives God's providence directing Christian life to emerge from Judaism into the cultures of Gentiles and into a wider world. Paul, starting in the Antioch community and moving throughout Asia Minor, is the leader of this mission and works with Peter, the leading member of the Twelve and a miracle worker like Jesus. Christianity now recognizes leadership in the persons of Peter, Paul and James, the brother of Jesus, who leads the community in Jerusalem.

The Christians in Jerusalem are portrayed as having a spiritual life where they are "of one heart and mind, and no one claimed that any of his possessions was his own, but they had every thing in common" (Acts 4:32). No one was needy among them because of this sharing of resources. Their prayer was in common and "they were all filled with the Holy Spirit and continued to speak the word of God with boldness" (Acts 4:31). The sick and mentally disturbed are brought before the apostles and cured. This evokes jealousy among the Jewish leaders, and the apostles are arrested, but soon freed by an angel (Acts 5, 18–19). New ministries are developed (deacons) and the first martyr, Stephen, is stoned to death. Living the Christian "way" becomes risky, but the privilege of living close to God is well worth that risk. Many more conversions occur, most notably that of a Pharisee, Paul, who becomes a leading missionary and model for all to be committed to spreading the good news. Paul proclaims to the Christian leaders in Jerusalem, "We believe that we are saved through the grace of the Lord Jesus" (Acts 15:11). For Paul, grace is the very life of God and spirituality is a vibrant participation in that divine life.

Thessalonica

Paul established this fledgling community in Greece, just a generation away from the time of Jesus. The Thessalonians are dear to him and he reminds them that in their spirituality, they should remember that they are brothers and sisters loved by God and chosen "in power and in the Holy Spirit" (1 Thes 1:5). He exhorts them to "conduct yourselves as worthy of the God who calls you into his kingdom and glory" (1 Thes 1:110). He prays that they grow in love for one another and live in holiness before God and Jesus. He calls them to responsible sexual morality and mutual charity, and reminds them that they can hope for resurrection. Paul reminds them to stay alert and sober, to be peaceful and to "pray without ceasing" (1Thes 5:17).

Roman Christians

The Christian community in Rome was established very early on and when Paul wrote to them around 56 CE, they were a combination of Jews and Gentiles. They seem to be impoverished, persecuted by the Romans, and gathered in "house churches."

In this compelling and extensive letter, Paul tells the Roman Christians, that whether they are Jew or Gentiles, God has a plan of salvation for them through faith in Christ. Gentiles need not live as Jews in order to be Christians, for all "are called to belong to Jesus Christ" (Rom 1:6). Paul presents a perspective on spirituality wherein all are justified through their faith in Christ and are now graced to live lives of freedom from sin, death and the law. Even though all have sinned, they can be gifted with salvation from their God through Christ. God's will is to justify all God's children not through the law, but through the gift of Christ's life, death and resurrection (Rom 5:10.) Christians live in "peace," in a "newness of life," "freed from sin" and "in the newness of the Spirit" (Rom 6:4; 7:6). Christians are saved from their sins; they have been immersed in the death and resurrection through baptism and they are saved because they now "are in Christ Jesus" (Rom 8:1). "Nothing can separate us from the love of God in Jesus our Lord" (Rom 8:38ff).[8] Paul tells the Roman Christians that those "who are led by the Spirit of God are children of God" (Rom 8:14). They belong to Christ and nothing can separate them from Christ. "Who will separate us from the love of Christ? Will anguish, or distress, or persecution, or famine, or nakedness, or peril, or the sword?" (Rom 8:35). Paul emphasized the importance of community, telling the Romans that they are all part of Christ: "So we, though many, are one body in Christ and individually part of one another." For this reason they love their neighbor as they love themselves (Rom 14:9). They must live and die for Christ.

Corinthian Christians

Corinth was a Christian community founded by Paul himself in the 50's. Corinth was a hectic seaport and trading center, whose diverse population ranged from the very wealthy to the extreme poor and included Jews, Christians and pagans, sailors and merchants. It was a rough town! Though the Christian community was united, individual groups met in different homes. Paul had spent many months with them, but once separated, he apparently received some bad reports about immorality and conflict, so he writes about his concerns. Paul reminds the Corinthians, who are divided over leadership and issues of incest and sexual misconduct, that they are sanctified in Jesus Christ and called to spirituality that seeks holiness. Many thinking that the "end is near," have raised questions about whether they should marry. Paul's advice is "to remain as you are," but he prefers celibacy since it is "free of anxieties" (1Cor 7:22). He reminds them marriage is forever. Christians are at odds with one another and even over-imbibing at eucharistic meals, so Paul quotes the earliest words of consecration and informs them that in such conflicts they are bringing judgment upon themselves (1Cor 11:29). Paul reminds the Corinthian Christians that they are all one with Christ and that their spirituality must be characterized by unity with one another. At the same time, Paul teaches them that each is endowed with different gifts from the Spirit and called to use these gifts to serve the community.

Paul's section on love is classic, and teaches the core of Christian spirituality, the basis for kindness, patience, humility, forgiveness, truthfulness, belief and forbearance. Paul ends this section with a line that has reverberated throughout the ages; "So faith, hope, love remain, these three; but the greatest of these is love" (1Cor 13:13).

Paul reminds the Corinthian Christians of their central beliefs: Christ died for their sins and was raised from the dead. He leaves no doubt about the importance of the resurrection of Christ: "If Christ has not been raised, your faith is in vain" (1Cor 15:17).

Galatian Christians

There were a number of Christian communities in the cities of southern Asia Minor (now in Turkey). The converted populations were of Celtic origin and were brought from paganism to Christianity by a number of missionaries. Paul reminds the Galatians that there is only one true gospel approved by the Christian leaders in Jerusalem. This is the same gospel that he is now teaching them and their spirituality must be based on the belief that Christ lives in each one of them. Paul here pens a line which is central to Christian spirituality: "Yet I live, no longer I but Christ lives in me; insofar as I now live in the flesh, I live by faith in the Son of God who has loved me and given himself for me" (Gal2:20). He reminds the Galatians that they are all equal before God. Being a child of God trumps nationality, social standing and gender: "There is neither Jew nor Greek, there is neither slave nor free person, there is not male and female, for you are all one in Christ Jesus" (Gal 3:28). Paul exhorts the Galatians to cherish a spirituality that is free: "For freedom Christ set us free" (Gal 4:1). Yet, this freedom is not to be used for sin, but for love and service of others. They are to "bear one another's burdens, and so you will fulfill the law of Christ" (Gal 6:2).

The Patristic Period

This period is the time immediately after the deaths of the original apostles. In this period, the churches become more organized and develop a spirituality that is linked to sacraments and moral values. The Didache, or The Teaching of the Twelve Disciples, is a particularly valuable resource here. It dates back to around 130 CE and presents an excellent picture of Christian life, its moral values, organization and liturgy. Morality is divided into the Way of Life, which means love of God and neighbor, doing to others what you wish done to yourself and the Way of Death, which is the life of wickedness, including murder, adultery, lust, hypocrisy, fraud and pride. Those preparing for baptism are taught the nature of these two ways.

Baptism is central in bringing new members into the life of Christ and the Didache offers details of how this is to be done using running water if possible, "In the name of the Father, Son and Holy Spirit." As for ritual, the faithful are obligated to recite the Our Father three times a day and to attend Eucharist on Sunday. Here are given the earliest Eucharistic prayers and fine points for celebrating. The faithful give thanks by saying: "Thou, Lord Almighty, hast created all things for the sake of Thy name, and hast given food and drink for people to enjoy, that they may give thanks for Thee; but to us Thou hast vouchsafed spiritual food and drink and eternal life through Jesus your servant. Above all, we give Thee thanks because Thou art mighty. To Thee be the glory forevermore."[9]

Confession of one's sins is required prior to the reception of Eucharist. "In church confess your sins, and do not come to your prayer with a guilty conscience."[10] This was done with a simple confessional prayer, similar to what is recited before Mass today.

The notion of "church" during the patristic period is twofold: first, the local congregation of believers and secondly, the universal new race of Christians that one day will be established. Church leadership is simple and is carried out by elected bishops and deacons who serve as prophets (traveling preachers) and teachers. The local leaders seem to be the presiders over Eucharist. Quasten said "There are no indications whatever in the Didache which warrant the assumption of a monarchical episcopate."

This document shows that the early Christians expected the second coming of Jesus Christ to be imminent. In the Eucharistic prayer they say

"May Grace come, and this world pass away," and conclude with the Aramaic words Maran atha: "My Lord, come."[11]

Charity through almsgiving is important in these early communities, but is provided for those who can't work. All others have the duty to maintain a livelihood.

The so-called "Apostolic Fathers" are a group of Christian writers of the first and early second century. Their writings are extremely valuable in that they echo the teaching of the first Apostles, who did not leave us written documents. Here we will offer just a sampling of these Fathers to see what they have to say about early Christian spirituality.

Clement of Rome (d. c 101) seems to have been the third Bishop of Rome. His Epistle to the Corinthians addresses the discord that appears to be perennial among the Corinthian Christians. He urges them to develop a spirituality that stresses repentance, hospitality, piety and humility. A charming picture of Christian virtues!

Ignatius of Antioch (35- 117) was the second bishop of Antioch in Syria (in what is now Turkey). Ignatius was ordered to Rome to be executed and penned some extraordinary writings to the Christian communities on his journey. He knew he was to be thrown to wild beasts but he stood strong "like an anvil under the hammer" and associated his death with Eucharist. He wrote: "I am the wheat of God, and I must be ground by the teeth of wild beasts, that I may become the pure bread of Christ."[12] Ignatius firmly believes in the humanity of Jesus, but now sees Christ as "timeless and invisible." His writings reveal how central both Jesus and Eucharist are to early Christianity. The Eucharist is "the medicine of immortality, the antidote against death, and everlasting life in Jesus Christ."[13] He has a holistic view of spirituality and teaches that "even the things you do in the flesh are spiritual, for you do all things in union with Jesus Christ." He sees his bloody martyrdom as a way of emulating Jesus himself: "Permit me to be an imitator of my suffering God." Ignatius believes that God dwells in all humans and that Christ dwells within Christians and binds them altogether. He writes: "Union with Christ is the bond that encircles all Christians."[14]

Polycarp (69-155) was the bishop of Smyrna and another early martyr for the faith. At that time it was quite dangerous to be a Christian and martyrs viewed themselves as imitators of Jesus, who was sacrificed for preaching peace and love. Polycarp writes about the early ministers with a relevancy for many clergy today, who focus more on administration than on pastoral ministry. He observes that ministers must be "tenderhearted, merciful toward all, turning back all that have gone astray, visiting all the sick, not neglecting widow or orphan or poor man...respect all persons, unrighteous in judgment, being far from all love of money, not hastily believing anything against anyone, not stern in judgment, knowing that we are all debtors because of sin."[15] He encourages ministers to have a deep spirituality characterized by compassion and love for their people.

Clement of Alexandria (150-215) was an example of an urban, well-educated Christian. He believed that religion should be based on love and not fear. It was his position that as long as a Christian has an independent heart and is free from attachment to material things, there is no reason to withdraw from the world or culture. It was the Christian mission to see to it that culture be imbued with the spirit of Christ.[16]

Origen (182-254) has been described as "one of the most original thinkers the world has ever seen."[17] An expert in scripture and theology, his writings on prayer greatly influenced later monks. Origen maintained that prayer is a conversation with God and has a sanctifying effect on one's entire existence. Prayer "enables us to enter into a union with the spirit of the Lord, which fills heaven and earth. Its real purpose is not to influence God but to share His life, to communicate with heaven."[18] The Christian should engage in prayer at certain times every day and indeed make his or her entire life a prayer. Origen's model of the spiritual life being a journey of progress through stages of growth in recovering the image of God in the soul has been extremely influential throughout Christian history.

The Mothers and Fathers of the Desert

Another new shift in Christian spirituality came in 313 when the Emperor, Constantine, approved Christianity as a religion. Within a short time, Christianity became the official religion of the Empire and asceticism shifted from possible martyrdom to sacrificing the self in new ways (white martyrdom in contrast to the earlier red, bloody martyrdom). Christian monasticism was about to be born and was initiated in the desert.

The desert played a central role in the Bible as a meeting place with God. The Israelites wandered there for 40 years seeking the Promised Land. John the Baptist lived there, praying, fasting, baptizing and preparing for his mission of introducing Jesus to the world. Jesus himself entered the desert to fast, pray and face temptation before beginning his mission.

For the early Christians, the desert became a place for withdrawal from the world for solitude and prayer. It could be a place where one could live in harmony with nature; a desolate environment where they could face their "demons." There were influential precedents for this practice in other religions: the withdrawal to the desert by the Jewish Essenes, the movement to the forests and mountains by Buddhist monks, the isolation of Hindu recluses.

Perhaps reacting to the new influx of Christians who were drawn to conversion by the acceptability and the inwardness of this new faith, many decided to withdraw to practice more authentically. Possibly they were resisting the sensuality and materialism that characterized the dying Roman Empire and wanted to withdraw from society so that they could be more serious about their spiritual lives. Many admired Jesus as single, poor, homeless, sacrificing and prayerful, and they wanted to imitate his life as closely as possible. They would become hermits in the desert and early on a significant movement in this direction happened among lay people in the Egyptian desert.[19] In isolated arenas, hermits could experience the fragility of life, dependence on others for survival and the equality of all in such circumstances. (Much the same as people experience sudden solidarity with others in the stark devastation after storms, earthquakes and tsunamis.)[20]

St. Anthony of the desert (251-356) was one of the leaders of this movement, and seems to have been inspired by the story of the rich young man in the gospels whom Jesus invited to give all he had to the poor and come follow him. It is said the Anthony withdrew into the desert in the middle of the 3rd century and drew many after him. By the year 400, thousands had embraced this life. Some lived in pairs, others in small groups and still others in rather large communities. These communities consisted of both men and women and were led by spiritual fathers (Abbas) and mothers (Ammas). Silence, solitude and the spirit of prayer characterized the life of these early Christians. Removed from all comforts of life, limited in their food, deprived of pleasures, they saw themselves as spiritual athletes, in training for the Kingdom of God, seeking union with God. One is reminded of those who put themselves to severe training and tests and then attempt to climb Mt. Everest or seek an Olympic challenge. Only, here, the goal is to conquer self and be in union with God.

Anthony became influential through the powerful letters he wrote to many people about the spiritual life; he wrote to desert communities as well as to Emperors. Anthony taught that the first obligation of the monk is to know the self because only those who know the self are able to know God. Here self-knowledge includes an understanding of the Holy Spirit within us. Anthony points to three roads: 1. Answering the call of God; 2. Reading scripture; 3. Atonement for overindulgence in food and drink and giving into the passions.[21]

About the year 320 CE, another form of Christian life began to form among the Copts in southern Egypt. This was the kind of monasticism that we are more familiar with and it was founded by Pachomius (292-346). He wrote a rule for a highly organized form of monasticism and set up 8 foundations for men and 2 for women. These were communities led by abbots and vowed to poverty, obedience and chastity. The communities were dedicated to hard work in either farming or the trades and were to pray in common twice a day. This rule was extremely influential in the development of later monasteries.

In the magnificent and exotic area of Turkey known as Cappadocia, the "Fathers" in that area established other forms of monasticism where the spiritual life would take center stage. Following Basil's Rule, large communities were formed, where there was a balanced life of manual labor, liturgy and prayer as well as care for the poor and the education of children.

Benedict and his Rule, which was written in the 6th century in Italy came to have the most influence in the formation of monasticism in the West. Life in Benedictine communities was urbane, dedicated to hard manual labor, regular prayer, liturgy and obedience to God and the Abbot who stood for Christ. The central task or "work of God" was common prayer, which was complemented by personal meditation, spiritual reading and difficult manual work. Obedience and humility were stressed, as well as stability (staying in one monastery until death), and a commitment to deep conversion and spiritual development. These monasteries were strong until the invasions by the Vikings, which decimated many of them. The Cluny reform in the 10th century revived western monasticism and by end of the 11th century there were more than 1,000 monasteries in France, England and Italy. So much emphasis was placed on spirituality and liturgy that manual labor all but disappeared, which cut the monks off from the lifestyle of the everyday Christian. In the 12th century, the Cistercian Reform restored manual labor, allowed humanism into the monasteries and founded monasteries for women. These monasteries are also called Trappist and became well known through the writings of Thomas Merton (1915-1968).

The monastic tradition has deeply influenced Christian spirituality. It has kept focus on the scriptures as the primary resource for spirituality, liturgy as the source and summit for spirituality, asceticism (the disciplining of the appetites for food, drink, sex and other pleasures), and mental prayer or meditation. All of these have been seen as a preparation for contemplation, or the union of the person with God in mind, body and spirit. Such union is the very core of Christianity, and as we have learned in our time, is the goal for all disciples of Christ. As Vatican II put it: "All are called to holiness."

Celtic Spirituality

Today we tend to associate "Celtic" with Ireland, Scotland, Wales and Breton. Yet evidence of the ancient Celtic tribes has been found in many areas of Europe and possibly even in India. The Gauls of Roman times, as well as the Galatians who were converted by Paul, are said to have been Celts. Britain was Celtic before the invasion of the Angles and Saxons in the 5th century CE. The Romans pushed the European Celts into Scotland, Wales and Ireland. The latter did not experience a Roman invasion and were never a part of the Roman Empire, so they were able to sustain their Celtic traditions.

The Celts, and indeed the Irish still today, were known for their poetry, story-telling and verbal jousting. Their fighting spirit made them fierce warriors and there are many stories of their celebrated heroes like Finn MacCumhail. Celts were known for their love of nature and worshipped in sacred groves, led by their Druids, who were a combination of priest, scholar and counselor. Women always played a central role among the Celts, both in leadership and religion.

Patrick came to Ireland around 432. As a boy, he was kidnapped from the British Isles by Irish pirates and forced to work as a shepherd for six years. Eventually he escaped but felt a calling to return to convert the Celts.

This he did quite successfully, largely because Patrick allowed the Celts to integrate their indigenous ways to Christianity. Their poetic, musical, mystical talents, as well as their love of nature were transposed into Christian spirituality. "Thin places," where the supernatural could be experienced through the thin veil between the divine and human were established as shrines. Their strong sense of clan helped them form Christian communities. Their sense of equality allowed both women and men, both married and single to share religion in monastic communities and move about spreading the gospel together. The ancient goddess' name, Bridget, was given a saint of the same name. They established a "people's church," similar to that that of New Testament times. Their monasteries became places of great learning and they copied and preserved many of the great manuscripts of Europe.[22]

Over the following century, a number of factors overwhelmed the Celtic church. Many of its indigenous beliefs about the positive aspects of human nature, creation and women were not acceptable to Rome. In addition, the Norman Conquest in 1066, as well as the Protestant Reformation and subsequent Protestant control from England in the 16th century suppressed the Celtic tradition.

There have been many efforts in modern times to restore the values of Celtic spirituality in Ireland. Many today are disillusioned with the Roman Catholic tradition and are looking to their forbears for a model of church that values equality, freedom, love of nature, and dynamic small communities dedicated to gospel life.[23]

The Medieval Period

During the medieval period, new spiritualities emerged. The strong revival of cities brought about a different kind of Christian: urbane, better educated, more concerned with social needs and less with spirituality. The monastic cloisters were largely rural and removed from the world. Now the city became the new religious milieus, with the construction of magnificent cathedrals and universities for learning. These amazing churches, with their sweeping arches and stained-glass windows, were designed to give the faithful the experience of the upward movement toward heaven.

New religious communities began to emerge from the cities, which were concerned now with action as well as contemplation. There was a shift to the laity who wanted to remain in the world but live gospel simplicity, and who wanted to move about preaching the good news and serving the needy. Communities of men and of women formed who were dedicated to pastoral care and simultaneously committed to contemplation and mysticism. Francis of Assisi left his life of wealth and ease, divested himself of all things, and began a group of friars dedicated to following Jesus' life of poverty, simplicity, service of the poor and love of nature. He was joined by his friend Clare, who formed similar groups for women. Dominic founded communities dedicated to learning and preaching. These orders spread rapidly and had a tremendous impact on the development of Christian life in the Middle Ages and into modern times. Francis has been a Christ-like figure for both Catholics and Protestants.

Groups of women, the Beguines, were formed throughout northwestern Europe. They lived together in simple dwellings where they prayed together and dedicated themselves to running schools for girls and working with the poor and the homeless in the cities. In northern Europe, mostly in France and Germany, the Cathars gathered to live austere Christian lives. Some who held heretical beliefs about the humanity of Christ, his resurrection, the need for sacraments and the sanctity of marriage were condemned. They were tracked down in 1209 by a crusade and assassinated. Those that escaped were pursued throughout the next two centuries and were burned at the stake when discovered. Similarly, the Waldensians protested against the wealth of the church and attempted to live in poverty and focus on the scriptures, which they translated. Eventually they held many positions that were considered by Rome to be unorthodox and many of their groups merged with Protestants. All of these movements of the laity toward a biblical and pastoral spiritual life planted seeds that ultimately came to fruition during the Reformation.

The Reformers abandoned monasticism, the clerical life, and the emphasis on the sacraments and adopted a spirituality based on a strong faith rather than fear of punishment, good works, and the practice of devotions. Only the sacraments of baptism and Eucharist were acceptable, and the later reformers, Calvin and Zwingli denied the real presence of Christ in Eucharist. The sermon became the centerpiece of the Lord's Supper, the preaching of the Word which brings the knowledge of a faith, a faith that is ultimately a gift from God. "Reformation spiritually is characterized by the desire to make myself less in order that Christ can grow in me. Yet it is a communion with Christ and I keep my individuality. This communion with Christ and one's fellow Christians, as celebrated in the Lord's Supper, is characteristically Protestant."[24] For Protestants, the monastery is the world and God can be served in everyday life. Spirituality belongs in the trades, in commerce, in politics. Calvin wrote: "The beauty which the world displays is maintained by the invigorating power of the Spirit."[25] The Protestant leaders maintained that neither priests nor monks were needed as mediators for spirituality. Each disciple mattered before God and each individual's journey to faith was important.

Protestant spirituality diversified, ranging from the very strict Puritan spirituality to the non-doctrinal, non-ritual spirituality of the Quakers; from the mystical spirituality of Boehme (1575-1624) and the the inward and emotional spirituality of Schleiermacher (1768-1834) to the vigorous Methodist spirituality led by John Wesley (1703-1791) who urged that Christians return to the original gospel way of life, experience their sin, guilt and grace, and conversion and surrender their hearts and lives to Jesus Christ. The individual experience of conversion was to be shared with others in small communities dedicated to bible study, prayer and regular celebration of the Lord's Supper.[26]

Protestant spirituality, then, is lay-centered, focuses on faith and scripture. It tends to be individualistic and practical. Today, many in the evangelical churches are inclined to engage in politics and some are moving toward involvement in social justice and service of the poor.

Post-Reformation Catholic Spirituality

Many Catholics today were trained in one version or another of post-reformation spirituality. Some have sustained the often private devotional and formal prayer approach, but others, as we shall see later, moved in other diverse directions.

Post-Reformation spirituality began as a reaction to Protestantism. The strongest impetus occurred in Spain, with the igniting of Jesuit spirituality and the rekindling of mystical spirituality by the Carmelites, Teresa or Avila and John of the Cross.

Ignatius of Loyola

Ignatius (1491-1556) was a Basque nobleman and knight. He suffered a serious wound to the leg in battle and read the gospels and lives of the saints to pass the time away while he healed. During that period, he experienced a profound conversion and after several pilgrimages he decided to live the life of a poor Christian beggar who helped others. Realizing that he needed some education in order to be an effective minister, he commenced studies in Spain and France. In 1534, he and six friends decided to live a life of gospel poverty and serve others. The group grew to ten, were ordained, moved to Rome and as the Society of Jesus offered their services to the Pope.

The Jesuits adopted a new form of religious life. They did not live in monasteries or chant their prayers; rather they lived a simple life in houses, prayed and worked in the world, especially in the missions. Today the Jesuits are known as outstanding educators. Their spirituality is based on the *Spiritual Exercises*, which were written by Ignatius. It is a handbook for prayer, meditation and discernment of one's spiritual condition.[27] The exercises are still a popular guide for retreats, spiritual direction and personal spirituality.

The Mystical Tradition

Some are put off by the word mysticism, associating it with extraordinary phenomena such as visions or levitation. In fact, mysticism is simply an advanced stage in spirituality. The mystical tradition has always been integral to spirituality; up until the Middle Ages it was associated with intimately carrying on Jesus' mission and then the personal experience of the divine.

The great expert on mysticism Evelyn Underhill maintained that mysticism was a progression in spirituality and "is to be regarded as a matter of biology." She saw mysticism as part of all the higher experiences of the human race, comparable to those sustained by the great musicians and poets. Her mantra was that of Paul: "There are diversity of gifts, but the same Spirit."[28]

All humans seem to have a hunger for the transcendent and the ultimate. For the religious person, this ultimate might be described as God, Nirvana, Brahman or Allah. It would seem that meditation, contemplation and ultimately the mystical realm are all various stages of union with the Ultimate.

Underhill maintained that humans have an "instinct for God." She believed that all humans have a "titanic craving for a fuller life and love," which finds its proper fulfillment in life in the Spirit.[29] The experience of the eternal or holy gives humans a sense of security in the cosmos and in life, a certain apprehension of the divine through personal and emotional intimacy, and a joyful energy and invigorating life. Spiritual experience on all levels offers inner peace, a sense of surrender to goodness, and an impulse to action. She holds that the path toward such experience is through intuition, adoration, moral effort and love.[30]

Notable intimacy with God has been exemplified throughout religious history.

We see this in the Buddha, the great prophets of Israel, the Hindu followers of Rama or Brahma, Jesus, who for Christians was the epitome of union with God, Paul the apostle, the Sufis, the Jewish Hasidim and followers of the Kabbalah, Francis, Catherine of Siena and so many of the Christian saints. They were people who went up to the mountain, into the desert, into ghettos of cities and were gifted with extraordinary experiences of the divine. As we have seen, most religions indeed begin with some extraordinary experience of revelation from the Ultimate and historically join in communities, whether they be the ashrams, ummas, synagogues, sanghas or churches, where they could be nourished by leaders and fellow members in the life of the Spirit. The followers joined groups where they could learn detachment from what Kierkegaard called "the One Thing," and be free to open themselves to the Eternal through prayer and self-sacrifice.[31] To facilitate such experiences of the divine would seem to be "the business of religion." Religions' beliefs and rituals should provide a way to reach out for the Infinite. Tragically many are leaving religion because they don't think they are receiving such assistance or inspiration with regard the spiritual life. Too often religions focus on doctrinal defense, moral rigidity, control and rubrics, which causes them to miss their core goal of helping people experience the holy. Rather than seeing this as a failure on the part of those who leave religion, this should rather be reframed as a breakdown on the part of religion.

The mystical experience might be thus seen as the ultimate spiritual experience which is in continuity with all levels of the spiritual life. Where most climb hills, the mystics climb Everest; where most walk or jog, the mystics run marathons; where most work out, the mystics prepare for the Olympics. Underhill defines mysticism as "the expression of the innate tendency of the human spirit toward complete harmony with the transcendent order."[32]

In the mystical experience, "the will is united with the emotions in an impassioned desire to transcend the sense-world, in order that the self may be joined by love to the one eternal and ultimate Object of love, whose existence is intuitively perceived by that which we used to call the soul, but now find it easier to refer to as the 'cosmic' or 'transcendent' sense."[33] As the Buddha taught, it means giving up the "I," the Self, and surrendering to the Ultimate. Or, as Paul put it, "It is no longer I that live, but Christ lives in me" (Galatians 2:20). Many spiritual writers agree that it is in the true self that one finds God. As the brilliant writer Friedrich von Hugel put it for Christians at the opening of the 21st century, "For it is opening the shell in which Plato said we live as oysters; it is breaking out of the confines of our local "bubble" and looking deeply within as well as far beyond to find and be one with the Eternal Source and Goal. All that religious people do: their readings, prayers, devotions, services, sermons, teachings, service to others, etc, need to be facilitations for union with the Ultimate or Transcendent Reality, the Presence of the divine."

For von Hugel, an expert on Christian mysticism, the choice is crucial: "only through self-renunciation and suffering can the soul with its true self, its abiding joy in union with the Source of Life, with God who has left to us, human souls, the choice between two things alone: the pangs of spiritual child-birth of painful-joyous expansion and growth; and the shameful ache of spiritual death, of dreary contraction and decay."[34] Yet von Hugel also points out that even though there are choices made by us, it is God who is the originator and true end of spiritual experience. It is God who "touches our souls and awakens them...to that noblest, incurable discontent with our own petty self and to that sense of and thirst for the Infinite and Abiding."[35]

The mystical tradition has been within Christianity beginning with early disciples like Paul the apostle (ca. 5-67) and continuing with Ignatius of Antioch (ca. 35-105) and later greats like Augustine (354-430). During the medieval period there was an explosion of great mystics such as Bernard of Clairvaux (1090-1153), Hildegard of Bingen (1098-1179), the anonymous writer of *Cloud of Unknowing* (d. 1395) and Julian of Norwich (1342-1416). The post-Reformation period produced such outstanding mystics as the Carmelites, John of the Cross (1542-1591) and Teresa of Avila (1515-1582).

Teresa of Avila's famous work, *Interior Castle*, presents an excellent model for mystic prayer. She describes the human person as a castle with many rooms inside. The castle is crystal and its rooms are in concentric circles surrounding the central room where God dwells. The light of God's presence shines out of the center throughout the castle, but its brightness is impeded by human sin. The human journey is one that is inward and must include the elimination of sin and ultimately union with God in the center of one's being.

The journey begins in the first rooms with prayer. The second rooms involve facing our sinfulness, the third conventional church going, but not much commitment or depth. Many get stuck here, but others proceed to the fourth rooms, where they allow God to take over their lives, practice contemplative prayer and engage in a deeper love of God and others. In the fifth rooms the closeness to God increases as well as the love for neighbor. In the sixth rooms we begin to realize that following Jesus means joining in his suffering. It is a period in the journey where there is great joy mixed with desolate suffering. Finally, there are the seventh rooms, where one experience oneness with God, with the true self and with the neighbor. The contemplative and active lives combine as we love and serve the divine in others. Teresa notes that during the journey these stages need not be sequential and differ from person to person. At the same time, she does provide a schema that all Christians can use in their journey to be one with the God within.[36]

Spirituality Today

Many people both inside and outside religion are interested in spirituality today. People practice yoga, tai chi, Buddhist meditation, Sufi methods, healing touch, creation spirituality, meditation, contemplation, prayer beads, enneagram insight, chanting and journaling. They use mantras, make pilgrimages, take nature walks, attend retreats and pray in small faith groups.

In our time there have been many outstanding spiritual leaders, including Gandhi, Martin Luther King Jr., the Dalai Lama, Cynthia Bourgeault, Richard Rohr, Ken Wilber, Sandra Schneiders and Mother Teresa of Calcutta. In the following section, we are going to focus in some detail on two individuals that have been significant in promoting Christian spirituality in our time: Thomas Merton and Thomas Keating. Both represent a reclaiming of the best of Christian spiritual traditions and both have offered these traditions to the masses.

Thomas Merton

It is important to review Merton's life because it so important to his message. Merton was born in France in 1915. His father Owen was from New Zealand, his mother Ruth from the United States. Both were artists and met while studying art in Paris. When WWI broke out the family moved to the States, where Merton's mother died when he was only six. He traveled with his father, who also died when Tom was 16, leaving him an orphan. Tom commenced studies at Cambridge University when he was 18, but spent his time partying and fathered a child. He left Cambridge, went to the U.S. and attended Columbia, where he was a serious student and converted to Catholicism.

After a brief teaching stint, Tom entered Gethsemani, a Trappist monastery in Kentucky. His early biography, *The Seven Storey Mountain*, was an instant best seller. Merton became a celebrity and continued to write throughout his life. After decades in the monastery, Merton was granted permission to live as a hermit in a cabin near the monastery, where he wrote on controversial peace and justice issues. He became a warrior for civil rights for Blacks and condemned the Vietnam War.

During a stay in a hospital for back surgery, Merton and a young nurse fell in love and sustained a romantic relationship for some months. Merton struggled with the intense pull of human love against his religious vocation. The love affair ended in 1966, leaving Merton with many lessons about the depths of human love and passion. Two years later Merton was accidentally electrocuted at a conference in Thailand.

Merton brought spirituality and contemplation into the daily discussions of many ordinary people. It was his conviction that "monastic prayer should be of interest to all Christians, since every Christian is bound to be in some sense a person of prayer."[37] He pointed out that the early desert fathers and mothers that we mentioned earlier were not engaged in some esoteric religious practices, but were trying to purify their hearts and minds "so that they might altogether forget themselves and apply themselves entirely to the love and service of God."[38] In other words, what they were doing was just plain everyday gospel living. Like all Christians, the early desert fathers and mothers were soul-searching, trying to detach themselves from everything that kept them from God, staying close to Jesus. The early monks were not isolationists, cut off from humanity, but were instead deeply in touch with their humanity and fully aware that they were members of the people of God. Their prayer, reading of the scriptures, meditation and contemplation was to "rest in God" a God "who loves us, who is near to us, who comes to us to draw us to himself." Their silence and solitude was the emptiness they provided to be filled with God's presence.[39] Merton points to the prayer of the mystics of the Eastern Church, the "prayer of the heart," where Christians "seek God himself present in the depths of our being and meet him there by invoking the name of Jesus in faith, wonder and love."[40]

Merton taught that the spiritual life was not easy and that it required much effort and discipline over the long haul. As on any journey, there would be darkness, trials, challenges and hardships. This journey was in faith, so it would be "without seeing" and "unknowing." It would be awe-filled entering into the mysteries of the holy and eternal. As the Celtic saints teach us, the spiritual life also provides friendship in community, pleasure in working, and satisfaction in feeding the poor. Their monastic life was not an escape from life. It was a plunging deeply into life with its conflicts, torment and doubt. Their contemplation was not a flight, but a plunge that "awakens a tragic anguish and opens many questions in the depths of the heart like wounds that cannot stop bleeding."[41] Merton taught that the spiritual life can provide deep satisfaction and happiness because it acts out of the true self. The spiritual person is freed from masks, pretenses, consuming roles, and acts out the self as it was made from the hand and breath of the Creator. This is "a self beyond all ego." It is the self, stripped down where one is no longer free to kill, exploit or destroy. It is the self no longer afraid of death, evil, poverty or even failure.[42] It is a life that is always rooted in the real, rather than in pretence and illusion. It aims at a life that is "a total acceptance of ourselves and our situation as willed by him. It means renunciation of all deluded images of ourselves, all exaggerated estimates of our capacities, in order to obey God's will as it comes to us in the difficult demands of life in its exacting truth."[43] Merton described his prayer in this way: "I penetrate the inmost ground of my life, seek the full understanding of God's will for me, of God's mercy to me, of my absolute dependence upon him."[44]

For Merton, all Christians are called to contemplation. He believed that contemplation was the "highest expression of human intellectual and spiritual life." It is being fully awake, fully alive, and standing in awe of the sacredness of life.[45] One might say, contemplation is a couple looking at their newborn baby, a grandparent walking in the woods with a child, a young woman stepping out onto the campus on her first day in college, or a fireman carrying a senior citizen from a blazing fire.

For Merton, the spiritual life means entering into the life of God. This is not God as a "thing" or a "what," but God as a "who" with whom we rest in love. He writes that God "is the 'Thou' before whom our inmost "I" springs into awareness. He is the "I Am" before whom with our own most personal and inalienable voice we echo "I am."[46] This is brought about by Grace, which is not a thing or substance, but "God's very presence and action with us."[47]

Merton's spiritual life eventually brought him to a sense of oneness with the human race as he became more sensitive to their suffering and poverty. In the latter part of his life, he dedicated himself to issues of peace and justice and in doing so faced much opposition.

The year of his tragic death, Merton summed up his spirituality in his journal: "I am the utter poverty of God. I am His emptiness, littleness, nothingness, lostness. When this is understood, my life in His freedom, the self-emptying God in me is the fullness of grace... A love for God that knows no reason because He is God; a love without measure, a love for God as personal. Love for all, hatred of none, is the fruit and manifestation of love for God—peace and satisfaction."[48]

Thomas Keating

Keating is a Trappist monk and one of the architects of Centering Prayer, a significant method of prayer for many Christians today. He graduated from Fordham and Yale universities and entered the Trappists in 1944. Keating served as Abbot for St. Joseph's Abbey in Spencer, Mass. from 1961 to 1981, when he went to St. Benedict's Abbey in Snowmass, Colorado. Here, he established programs in Centering Prayer along with several other monks. In 1984 Keating founded Contemplative Outreach, which is an international and interfaith spiritual network that offers retreats and programs on Centering Prayer.

Contemplation

Centering prayer is a discipline that attempts to open the way for contemplation, or the experience of God's presence within us. Before centering prayer could be put in place, it was first necessary to restore the central role of contemplation in the Christian spiritual life.

In his book *Foundations for Centering Prayer and the Christian Contemplative Life*, Keating says that for the first 15 centuries of Christianity, contemplation was part of the normal Christian life and was thus open to all Christians. He offers an explanation why contemplation suddenly disappeared from Catholic life for several centuries. First, prayer was too often reserved for the monasteries and convents and following the Reformation, private prayer was usually limited to "mental prayer," or thinking holy thoughts. Keating observes that a narrow understanding of Ignatian prayer gave this approach to meditation a wide influence. Secondly, in the 17th century church, there was a widespread suspicion that contemplation led to mystical experience, which was considered to be extreme and even dangerous. The mystical tradition was then set aside for several centuries—and contemplation along with it. In addition, from the 17th century on, Jansenism achieved a foothold in the church with its negative view of humanity and its narrow asceticism focusing on overcoming sinfulness. This perspective was hardly inclined to see Christians, especially the laity, as being open to experience of the divine. Widespread regard for devotions, apparitions, miracles and private revelations prevailed and contemplation was viewed as being far beyond the average priest, religious or lay person, and was even thought to be hazardous to the faith.

It is only in recent history that contemplation has once again become mainstreamed into Christian spirituality. Vatican II made the historic pronouncement that "all are called to holiness," and summoned all the faithful to a more mature spirituality beyond sentimental devotions. Scholars restored the writing of the mystical tradition, and spiritual writers like Thomas Merton brought in influences from the East, insisted that all were called to a mature spirituality and contemplation and linked prayer with action for social justice. Women spiritual writers brought in the feminine perspective, historians restored the early monastic traditions, and the scriptures were brought front and center in spirituality.

Once contemplation becomes the "new normal" for Christianity, centering prayer can become a useful tool in preparing the way for fruitful contemplation or the experience of the divine.

Keating begins by saying that Centering Prayer can open a whole new world, one that is far removed from our private self-made worlds. From his perspective, Christian spirituality should be founded on faith in our own basic goodness and the belief that God has given us potential for the transcendent. We are gifted with our true selves, and Christ and the self can become one in our prayer. The Spirit of God is already within us, all that is needed is to be open to its power—this is the nature of contemplation.

Contemplative prayer is laying aside our thoughts and concerns and "opening the mind and heart, body and emotions—our whole being—to God. This Ultimate Mystery of God is beyond words, thoughts or feelings. This prayer is silent and acknowledges this Presence with all its love, compassion and creativity. We come with detachment from things, as well as from the false self that is loaded with habitual thinking, illusions and toxic emotions. We must come with an openness to the presence of Jesus, with a desire to become pleasing to God and therefore to follow God's law of love.

Centering Prayer

Centering prayer focuses on reviving the contemplative dimensions of the gospel. It sets down a method for going to the center of the self where God dwells in order to become more intimately acquainted with the divine presence. Centering prayer is grounded in the rich history of Christian spirituality and its treasured tradition of mysticism. It sets out to respond to the spiritual hunger of people everywhere. For Christians, it provides a means to practice spirituality and at the same time be part of institutional traditions. Keating remarks, "The Christian religion is primarily about a transformation of consciousness. This takes spiritual practice and the cultivation of wisdom... the main thing is to be transformed into God, what the early church called deification, *theosis*, divination."[49] Centering prayer restores Eastern Christianity's central belief that "God became human so that humans could become godly." Keating has been involved in interfaith dialogue for many years and teaches contemplation in this broad and universal context.

Centering prayer is a blend of the spiritual treasures from the Christian tradition: *The Cloud of Unknowing* (c. 1395), a medieval text on prayer; the Eastern Orthodox "Jesus Prayer," "lectio divina," readings from scriptures, being in God's presence and turning to "God is love" as described in John of the Cross, and other spiritual traditions from the past. Centering Prayer carefully selects the best teaching from the Christian spiritual legacy from the Desert Fathers, as well as the outstanding saints and teachers on gentleness, self denial, discernment, humility, love, mysticism, faith and freedom of the spirit. Keating points this out when he writes, "Centering prayer is a blending of the finest elements of the Christian contemplative tradition with an eye to reducing contemporary obstacles to contemplation."[50] He identifies some of the obstacles as over-activity, over-intellectualism and over-confidence in our own efforts. Centering prayer also puts these traditions into dialogue with modern discoveries by psychology about the unconscious and even insights from modern science about quantum mechanics and the "new physics." Centering prayer is ancient and yet contemporary at the same time!

Keating lists the important aspects of this prayer model: choosing a place of quiet and solitude; focusing on our breathing and the beating of our heart; centering on some symbol of God's presence within (a word like "Jesus," "Abba," "God," or "Peace") while not being annoyed by unwanted thoughts, gently and patiently moving them aside. The object is to bypass thinking, assure confidence in God's mercy and love for us, surrender to God's will for us, accept the darkness that comes with this search for Mystery, trust God's bringing us into oneness and the growth within us, awaken to the true self deeply within us and center on Christ's life, death and resurrection.

Centering prayer restores the basic elements of the spirituality of the early centuries in the church: solitude, silence, simplicity, prayer and action. It organizes a practice that is to be done twice a day in the midst of all the hustle and bustle of today's life. It adapts contemplation to the contemporary understanding of the human person and to the world in which we live. It looks to the unconscious with its hidden influences from culture and conditioning. It looks at the insecurities and esteem deficits of today, the anxieties and feeling of isolation that plague so many. Keating calls centering prayer "divine therapy" because it opens the self to healing through the divine Spirit.[51]

Centering prayer is taught in a global context which recognizes the need today for the world religions to "speak to the human family regarding its common source and the potential of every human being to be transformed into the divine."[52] Keating believes that at this point in time religions can speak with a powerful moral voice on behalf of the poor and oppressed.

The goal of centering prayer is to live from the center of ourselves, from the "true self." This is a common theme of all religions: to move beyond selfishness and self-centeredness. Buddhism calls it moving toward the "no self." The Hindus speak of the Absolute Self. Christians speak of the loving, giving self that is one with Jesus. It is a self that runs deeper than our thoughts, our feelings, our senses, or even the ego itself. It is a self that is made in the image and likeness of God; the self as we were born, uncontaminated by sin or limitations of family and culture.

Religion is a reaching out for the other, the Ultimate or Transcendent. Centering prayer opens the deepest level of self to Grace, "which steadily affirms the truth of one's being, one's basic human goodness, while at the same time Divine Mercy heals a lifetime of personal faults, wounds and failings."[53] Thus it is not so much trying to find God, but allowing God to find us. Centering prayer expresses the deep human desire to be one with God.

Centering prayer focuses on Jesus, his life, his teaching on prayer, his self-emptying (*kenosis*) in life and on the cross. It identifies with the Risen Lord who opens the doors to humanity to embrace abundant life, life with God. It is prayer without words, an opening of one's heart and life to the healing and transforming presence of God amid the joys and sorrows of everyday life.

Centering prayer is about transformation of the self into the life or Jesus. Paul speaks to the Colossians about this early Christian spirituality as rooting their lives in Jesus, coming to fullness in him, taking on his mind and his behavior through the power of the Spirit (Colossians 2:6–10). He tells the Ephesians that Jesus manifests the fullness of God and that if they let Jesus dwell in their hearts they will have the fullness of God (Ephesians 3:16–19). In his epistle, Peter goes so far as to say that through divine power we "may become participants in the divine nature" (2 Peter 1:3–4).

Centering prayer is a method of prayer that prepares the participants for contemplation, which is relating to God's presence. It is a way of clearing the mind of everyday concerns by quieting down, listening to one's breathing and impeding stray thoughts by reciting a mantra such as "Jesus" or "Abba" and moving to the interior of the self. It acknowledges that God is already within and that one needs only to pay attention and enjoy the Presence. Centering prayer quiets the individual, and says to God: "Here I am."[54] It is an opening to God, which can then result in experiencing God's presence as one goes about the business of the day.

There are also methods that bring the results of centering prayer into daily life. Keating recommends first of all an acceptance of the self with all its past history, successes, failures and mistakes, as well as a determination to learn from all of life's surprises. Then, one should choose some favorite passage from scripture that can be recited during the day. From the beginning of Christian spirituality, the New Testament has been the primary source and should be read prayerfully for at least 15 minutes. It is the Word of God "that speaks to the heart."[55] Also carry a small book of passages from one's favorite spiritual writers to read when there is a spare minute. Another part of the method is ridding the self of toxic emotions that disturb and upset. The daily life should be monitored so that one is able to handle whatever turns up peacefully, without being derailed. It is also recommended that one learns to accept others without judgment or pre-conditions, quieting fear, anger and hatred. Resisting the cultural conditioning of materialism, secularism and propaganda is also important. And finally, a regular celebration of the Eucharist and belonging to a faith group are key components of this spirituality.

Ken Wilber, a leader in the integral approach to religion and spirituality that we have followed in this book, gives his support to centering and contemplative prayer. He points out that until recently the contemplative experience was looked at by many as just "wishful thinking." He observes that now there has been much scientific research that demonstrates the positive value of contemplative methods on human development. We saw earlier the stages of human and moral development and how humans can move to higher stages. Wilbur cites some of these higher stages as being pluralistic, integral and super-integral. He observes that programs like psycho-therapy and gestalt therapy have not been able to raise individuals to the higher states of development. By way of contrast, scientific research has shown that regular contemplative practices have indeed been able to assist individuals in moving into these higher states of transcendence. Wilber holds that contemplation can definitely open individuals to the experience of the divine light within them.[56]

Spiritual but Not Religious

One often hears Christians remarking today that they are "spiritual but not religious." This seems to be especially common among mainline Protestants and progressive Catholics. In many European countries, as well as in the United States, many Christians have become disillusioned with their local churches as well as with their national and international church leadership. For the first time in history, the Protestant population in the U.S. has dipped significantly below 50%. In the last five years, the population of individuals in this country with no religious affiliation has risen from 15% to 20% (33 million people). This is particularly true among young adults, who view organized religion as "retro" and as being "judgmental, homophobic, hypocritical and too political." Others see organized religion as being too concerned with money and power.[57] For Catholics, both young and old in Europe and North America, the child-abuse scandals along with the cover-ups by bishops has become a significant alienating feature.

There is one other factor producing this move away from organized religion that is not often discussed. We have seen that religion's key task is to nurture faith and spirituality, to facilitate one's experience of the divine or ultimate. Quite often the hierarchy and clergy have not been able to provide this nourishment and their people feel let down and feel the need to proceed on their own.

There are trade-offs for deciding to be "spiritual but not religious." On the plus side, the individual becomes free from authority which may have been oppressive and used fear to control. For Catholics, bad experiences with a pastor, bishop or even the Vatican can cause them to leave the church. Many gays and lesbians, the divorced and remarried, and couples living together often don't feel welcomed by their churches. Many Catholic women are frustrated by the inequality in their Church and by the few opportunities available to them to use their gifts for leadership in the Church. A good number of Catholics were given great hopes for the renewal of their church after Vatican II, yet have watched the progressive agenda be dismantled over the last fifty years. Where these disaffected individuals land varies. Some find their God in family, nature, art, music, or in good reading. Others describe themselves as agnostics or atheists. Hopefully, wherever they end up, they pursue some form of spirituality or personal enrichment and offer service to others. Being free from religion can free individuals to pursue spirituality on their own, outside the legal controls of religion. This method can be free of the toxic emotions sometimes generated by religion and can allow the individual to pursue their own spirituality more peacefully.

Leaving religion for spirituality also has its downside. People can lose contact with the belief system, the tradition that shaped their lives. Outside of religion, they may lack community support and guidance. They no longer have a bond with others who can nurture their faith and enrich their spirituality. Without community, the spiritual life can become quite individualistic. Without religion, there is little access of meaningful symbolism or ritual. There can also be a loss of sacred texts and spiritual leadership, as well as fewer opportunities to be educated through the church and to meet others' needs for charity and justice.

Keating points out that it is not simple to "go it on one's own" spiritually. Doing spirituality without religion requires a movement toward some definite method of spirituality, a community of like-minded people, and opportunities for ritual, resources for learning, and opportunities for service.[58]

Summary

Spirituality is about the human spirit reaching out for and wanting to be one with the Ultimate Reality, the Divine Spirit. Christian spirituality comes to this Spirit through identifying with the Spirit of Jesus Christ. It is the task of Christian religion to help its members in this search.

After centuries of spirituality training being limited to clergy and religion being under methods of esoteric asceticism, spirituality has once again become mainstream in Christian life. At the same time, the institutional church often finds itself ill equipped to instruct and nurture the spiritual lives of its members.

We looked at the history of Christian spirituality as a useful means to rediscover its treasures. The New Testament period is a primary source for the example and spiritual teachings of Jesus and the ways practiced by the earliest communities. Each gospel, the Acts, Paul's letters and the other Christian scriptures present their own unique elements of Christian spirituality and remain a primary source today.

The desert fathers and mothers fled the urban areas to practice silence, solitude and prayer, and their lifestyle and values served as the foundation for Christian monasticism. This monastic spirituality was further enriched by the Coptic Christians in Egypt, the monks in beautiful Cappadocia and quite significantly with the Rule of Benedict. For centuries Celtic spirituality flourished in Ireland, with its love of nature, its strong social ties and its recognition of equality and inclusivity.

During the medieval period, the more active "Friars" appeared. As Dominicans took up preaching, the Franciscans and Carmelites set out to serve the poor. Lay movements such as the Beguines, Cathars and Waldensians attempted to bring Christianity back to its simple roots, but too often moved into doctrinal or lifestyle positions that were considered by the church hierarchy to be extreme and threatening.

The Protestant Reformation rejected Catholic religious life and monastic spirituality and developed its own religious traditions. These ranged from the mystical Quakers, to the strict and unworldly Puritans and the practical and stolid Lutherans and Presbyterians. In the post-Reformation, Catholic spirituality was profoundly influenced by Ignatius and his Spiritual Exercises, with its emphasis on meditation, mission and later on educational ministry. The Carmelites, Teresa of Avila and John of the Cross developed a powerful tradition on mysticism, but this was often deemed dangerous or only for the elite. Thankfully, this wisdom was reclaimed in the 20th century by such figures as Baron von Hugel and Evelyn Underhill, but still was considered suspicious by the institutional churches.

Among the many spiritual leaders in our time, we discussed two who have been key in restoring the contemplative tradition that had been so fundamental to Christian spirituality.

Thomas Merton was a pioneer in demonstrating that contemplation was appropriate for all Christians. His perspective was supported by Vatican II which called all the people of God to a deep spiritual life and holiness. Merton also bridged Christian spirituality with the religions of the East and with action for peace and social justice. Thomas Keating and several others reached into the traditional treasures of Christian contemplation and developed the method of centering prayer. Centering prayer returns to the gospel tradition of silence, solitude, prayer, simple living, unselfishness, and service to others. It stands as a preparation for contemplation and the union of the disciple with the divine, which should be the primary purpose of all religion. We ended with a discussion of the trade-offs when one decides "to be spiritual but not religious."

◨ VIDEOS ONLINE

Roger S. Gottlieb, *Spirituality: What It is and Why It Matters*
https://www.youtube.com/watch?v=BORt53UWyeY

Gregory C. Wolfe, *Spirituality of the Gospels*
https://www.youtube.com/watch?v=skXLhHTcBlI

N. T. Wright, *Simply Christian*
https://www.youtube.com/watch?v=_hlVhiuOAqg

Apostle Paul (Part 2/4)
https://www.youtube.com/watch?v=KIrorT_aqsQ

The Light of the Desert (Documentary on St Macarius Monastery, Egypt)
https://www.youtube.com/watch?v=o3eJrvW9MF8

Thomas Merton, *What Is Contemplation?*
https://www.youtube.com/watch?v=U8h3Hbf9wik

Celtic Spirituality
https://www.youtube.com/watch?v=R-tMeprN7Tg

Called to The Monastic Life
https://www.youtube.com/watch?v=wMo8Dcc9k10

Mark Mossa, *Elements of Ignatian Spirituality*
https://www.youtube.com/watch?v=kYex4Ux04zA

Underhill, *Mysticism Explained-What is a Mystic?*
https://www.youtube.com/watch?v=jean9sr7Eps

Fr. Peter, *What is Christian Mysticism?*
https://www.youtube.com/watch?v=Pg4ZJUHNP48

Fr. Keating and Ken Wilber, *Tomorrow's Spirituality*
https://www.youtube.com/watch?v=SUNlpyfT2LU

Martin E. Marty, *Mapping American Spiritualities*
https://www.youtube.com/watch?v=E--V3NhoAig

Thomas Merton, *Renunciation contemplation*
https://www.youtube.com/watch?v=LMY68vNcLT8

Thomas Keating, *Centering Prayer Guidelines Intro*
https://www.youtube.com/watch?v=3IKpFHfNdnE

Father Thomas Keating, *Spiritual, But Not Religious?*
https://www.youtube.com/watch?v=04gdsFt_zDY

▚▞ NOTES

1.	*National Catholic Reporter*, 17. October 26-November 8, 2012.

2.	See http://www.economist.com/node/16767758.

3.	Thomas Merton, *Life and Holiness* (New York: Herder and Herder, 1963), 60.

4.	*Lumen Gentium* (November 21, 1964), 40.

5.	Philip Sheldrake, *A Brief History of Spirituality* (Malden, MA: Blackwell, 2007), 3-4.

6.	See Sheldrake, 15-16.

7.	Sheldrake, 20. See Sandra Schneiders, *Written That You May Believe: Encountering Jesus in the Fourth Gospel* (New York: Crossroad Publishing, 1999).

8.	For an overview of Paul's writings, see Donald Senior and others, eds., *The Catholic Study Bible* (New York: Oxford, 1986), RG 470-529.

9.	Johannes Quasten, *Patrology* (Westminster, MD: The Newman Press, 1951) I, 32-33.

10.	Ibid., 33

11.	Ibid., 35.

12.	Ibid., 64.

13.	Ibid., 66.

14.	Ibid., 71-72.

15.	Ibid., I, 81.

16.	Ibid., II, 11.

17.	Ibid., II, 37.

18.	Ibid., II 67.

19.	Sheldrake, 43-44.

20.	David B. Perrin, *Studying Christian Spirituality* (New York: Routledge, 2007), 66.

21.	Anthony Louth, *The Wilderness of God* (London: Darton Longman and Todd, 1991), Chapter 3.

22.	See Timothy J. Joyce, *Celtic Christianity* (Maryknoll, NY: Orbis Books, 1998), 18 ff.

23.	Joyce, 149ff.

24.	Gordon Mursell, ed., *The Story of Christian Spirituality* (Minneapolis, MN: Fortress Press, 2001), 68.

25.	Ibid., 174.

26.	Ibid., 198-200.

27.	See Arthur Holder, ed., *Christian Spirituality* (New York: Routledge, 2010), 197ff.

28.	Evelyn Underhill, *The Life of the Spirit and Life of Today* (New York: Harper and Row, 1986), 1ff.

29.	Ibid., 21.

30.	Ibid., 11-12.

31.	Soren Kierkegaard, *Purity of Heart* (New York: Harper and Row, 1956), 33ff.

32.   Evelyn Underhill, *Mysticism* (London: Methuen and Co., 1926), xiv.

33.   Ibid., 71.

34.   Baron Friedrich von Hugel, *The mystical element of religion as studied in Saint Catherine of Genoa and her friends* (New York, E. P. Dutton & co., 1923), 395.

35.   Ibid.

36.   Mursell, 206-207.

37.   Thomas Merton, *Contemplative Prayer* (New York: Herder and Herder, 1969), 19-20.

38.   Ibid., 21.

39.   Ibid., 32.

40.   Ibid., 34.

41.   Thomas Merton, *New Seeds of Contemplation* (New York: Penguin Books, 1962) 12.

42.   Thomas Merton, *Love and Living* (New York: Harcourt Brace, 1979), 5ff.

43.   Ibid., 83.

44.   Ibid., 83-84.

45.   Merton, *New Seeds of Contemplation*, 1.

46.   Ibid., 13.

47.   Thomas Merton, *Life and Holiness* (New York: Herder and Herder, 1963), 30.

48.   Patrick Hart and Jonathan Montaldo, *The Intimate Merton: His Life from His Journals* (New York: HarperCollins, 1999), 328.

49.   Thomas Keating and others, *Spirituality, Contemplation and Transformation* (New York: Lantern Books, 2008), xii.

50.   Ibid., 3.

51.   Ibid., 32.

52.   Thomas Keating, *Intimacy with God* (New York: Crossroad, 1994), 124.

53.   Keating, Spirituality, *Contemplation and Transformation*, 65.

54.   Thomas Keating, *The Foundations for Centering Prayer and the Christian Contemplative Life: Open Mind, Open Heart; Invitation to Love; The Mystery of Christ* (New York: Continuum, 2006), 33.

55.   Ibid., 106.

56.   See Thomas Keating, Video: *Spiritual But Not Religious?* at http://www.youtube.com/watch?v=04gdsFt_zDY.

57.   See *National Catholic Reporter*, Oct 26-Nov. 8, 2012, 17.

58.   See Thomas Keating, Video: *Spiritual But Not Religious?* at http://www.youtube.com/watch?v=04gdsFt_zDY.

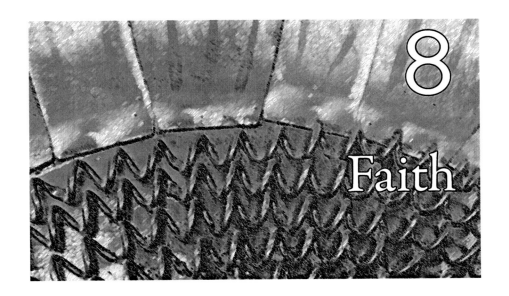

8

Faith

Faith is the belief that there is an unseen order, and that our supreme good lies in harmoniously adjusting ourselves thereto.
— William James

Faith is to believe what you do not see; the reward of this faith is to see what you believe.
— Saint Augustine

Faith is a word with many meanings. From one perspective, faith refers to a collection of beliefs ("guard the faith"); from another, faith can refer to a developmental process (the stages of faith) or to a relationship with the Ultimate (is your faith in God strong?). Faith involves trust, an extension of all the human capacities and a commitment to relationship. In this chapter, we will begin with a discussion of human faith and religious faith, focusing in particular on Christian faith, after which we will look at faith as it is understood in other religions and as it is studied by some modern students of the human brain.

What is Human Faith?

Human faith is not exactly the same as religious faith, but there are similarities between the two that are worth exploring. Humans have a unique capacity to be faithful. Of course, pets, especially dogs, are known to be extraordinarily faithful but that comes through instinct, not with deliberate reflection. Only a human person can reflect, deliberately place trust in someone else, make a commitment to that person, and decide to live in a caring and serving relationship.

A marriage tragically broken by an affair can demonstrate the nature of human faith. Mary and Bill were married ten years ago in Mary's parish, where before the altar they took vows to love and cherish each other "until death do us part." Each expected that the other would be "faithful" and trusted that sexual intimacy would be only shared between the two of them. Last month, Mary discovered that for many months Bill had been carrying on an affair with a woman in his office. The mysterious disappearance of money, the late evenings "at work" and the breakdown in their communication now had an explanation.

Mary was devastated and yelled out as she threw her wedding ring across the room at Bill, "I trusted you. I gave my life to you and loved you and was committed to you. And all these months you have betrayed me, lied to me, cheated on me. As far as I am concerned, it is over between us. You have been unfaithful and I no longer trust you. Get out of my life!"

Human faith is about trust, commitment and choosing to be together. It includes decisions carefully considered in our minds, deep emotions in our heart, and deliberate and free choices by our will. Such faith bonds us with parents, friends and lovers. When there is infidelity or betrayal, the bond can collapse, often irrevocably.

Human Faith and Trust

We put our trust in many things. We may trust our car, our bank, our church or our friends. Trust implies confidence and reliance. We put trust in a teacher who is friendly, well-qualified and fair. We trust that what he or she says has been carefully studied, and is well nuanced and truthful. We put trust in a doctor who is well-trained, experienced and dedicated. There may even be occasions when we put our very lives in a doctor's hands. If we choose to eat a certain restaurant, we trust that the food is safe to eat and that careful rules of cleanliness are followed. Getting on a plane, we have placed our trust in the mechanics, air controllers and pilots. There is little room for error when one is flying 30,000 feet in the air at 600 miles per hour! Often, without even consciously thinking about it, we place our trust in people and things around us.

Erik Erikson, a well-known psychologist, pointed out that the very first task in human development is to gain trust. Early on, we learn such trust if our parents or care-givers are there for us, responding to our cries and meeting our needs for drink, food, comfort, security and love. People who experience abandonment in those early years have a much more difficult time establishing trust.

There is a story out of a Boston hospital that confirms Erikson's observation. An infant who had been severely beaten and tossed in a dumpster was brought in the children's ward in critical condition. He baby was stabilized but remained in the fetal position and was completely unresponsive to any medical care. Then, one of the nurses suggested that the baby be given a name, Kevin, and placed at the entrance of the nurses' station. Every doctor and nurse that passed by greeted Kevin or patted him affectionately; some picked him up and cuddled him. No response. One morning, when a nurse picked up Kevin, he opened his eyes, uncurled his little arms and legs and smiled. Kevin had at last gained trust; he began to take nourishment and could begin his life. Kevin's story shows us that trust begins with ourselves. Somehow we have to come to believe that we matter, that we are capable and lovable. Only then can we step out and take risks, allow ourselves to be vulnerable and allow ourselves to be loved.

Self trust is required to achieve goals and be productive, which include a risk of failure. Brian Williams, the newscaster, has said that he would never hire anyone who has not experienced failure because that person has not been tested. We all have our battle scars; times when we were defeated, insulted, abandoned or abused. Most of us at have at times that nagging feeling within us that we won't succeed or won't measure up. A sustained trust in the self enables us to get through these times and go forward with our hopes and our dreams. Such trust offers us a lifeline to hold onto during trying times.

Think of the self-trust it takes to start college and face all the challenges required socially, academically and possibly in athletics. Fortunately, most young people seem to be given a good dose of optimism and self-confidence, but there are some who lack that trust in themselves and back away from the challenges.

We also can put trust in others: our family, church community, or country. When we are young we want to trust that our family will attend to our needs, keep us safe and be there for us when we are having difficulties. We always want to trust that our families will have our backs when we run into trouble. We expect that our church communities will support us in troubling times. (Catholics all know what a break in trust it was when it was discovered that some priests were abusing children.) Think of the trust a marine must put in his government to be confident that he or she is being properly prepared, being sent on a legitimate mission and that all precautions are being made for his safety. That trust can be broken when our troops are sent into harm's way in a senseless war.

The ultimate trust is trust in human nature itself. It is said the Gandhi extended trust even to his enemies and was thus often able to win them over. It was his conviction that to practice his *satyagraha* (truth force) and *ahimsa* (non-violence) one had to abandon fear of other and trust in their better instincts. He said that his followers "were never afraid of trusting the opponent. Even if the opponent plays him false twenty times, he is ready to trust him for the twenty-first time, for an implicit trust in human nature is the very essence of his creed."[1]

Human Faith and Reason

There is always some risk when we put our faith in another or a group. Our commitment needs to be reasonable but it cannot be certain. Thus, we are careful where we place our faith. It is never smart to put faith in a stranger we have just met. Our faith has to be developed; our trust has to be earned. Faith is based on an accumulation of perceptions and experiences that build up our confidence. For instance, our faith in a teacher develops as we observe the teacher's knowledge, competency and dedication. Most of us remember a teacher whom we trusted because they believed in us. H. Richard Niebuhr once wrote, "When student and teacher are related to each other as mature beings who trust each other and keep faith with each other, they are at the same time acknowledging each other as selves who are bound to serve a cause that transcends both."[2] Similarly, our faith in a friend progresses as we find that he or she is loyal, keeps confidences and truly cares about us. In other words, in human faith there is always a certain degree of certainty, but at the same time such faith is always risky and requires a kind of a "leap of faith."

Human Faith and the Heart

Human faith involves more that reasonableness and evidence; it also draws on a whole range of feelings. Pascal (1623-1662), a French mathematician and philosopher, wrote: "The heart has its reasons which reason does not understand." Faith can include such feelings as security, confidence, peace, pleasure, joy, peace and hope. It might be said that faith is a "knowing in our hearts" that our friends or loved ones are faithful. A happy marriage is one where both spouses can rest in the confidence that neither will be unfaithful nor do harm to the other.

Human Faith and Free Will

Human faith is always a choice, a commitment, a pledge to carry out certain responsibilities. If we decide to enter into a friendship or an intimate relationship, begin studies in a college or take a job, there are decisions and choices involved. Faith is involved in any intention to somehow alter our lives, take on new responsibilities, or go in new directions. Such decisions are usually not made lightly because it involves putting our faith in another person, institution or company.

Freedom of choice is an important dimension of faith. Force, manipulation, or deception diminish our free choice to be faithful. The sign over the concentration camp Auschwitz read "Work makes Freedom" but most people entering the camp put no faith in that sign for they knew that in this camp they would be worked to death and then incinerated.

Sometimes it is difficult to freely extend our faith because of our lack of freedom. Bernard Lonergan, the great Catholic philosopher and theologian, made the distinction between essential freedom and effective freedom. He taught that a person is created with essential freedom, that is, freedom to make choices, but that many of us are limited in the choices we can effectively make. A child born into the ghetto often finds his or her choices limited by lack of parenting, poor schools, poverty, race and crime. A person just out of prison finds that his felony limits him in housing, employment, socialization, and government aid. A contemporary theologian, Terrence Tilley sums up the ambiguity about freedom this way, "We can say that it seems to us that we are, at least sometimes, including very important junctures of our lives, free to believe, feel, or act in certain ways—even though we recognize that most of the time we may not have any effective freedom to think, feel, or act other than as we do."[3]

Human Faith is Holistic

Faith is a commitment of the whole person: reason, emotions, will. Faith also includes our imagination, which generates our dreams for our future. Many people in this country put their faith in "The American Dream," which to them may include prosperity, ownership of their own home and vehicles, and the ability to send their kids to good schools. In addition, faith includes our aesthetic sense whereby the beauty of nature, art, music, dance, literature and art can inspire us to continue our search and make new commitments. Note the popularity of talent shows today, where so many have a dream of being a celebrity.

Faith in Action

Human faith is also about doing. If someone has faith in a political party, he or she may promote that party and vote for its candidates. Faith in a team generally involves attending or watching its games, cheering the team on and celebrating its victories. Faith in a friend means keeping in touch, being with that friend when possible, and showing up when the friend is hurting. Faith without action can be merely theoretical or abstract. Genuine faith is vibrant, interested, involved and serving. Many of our young have such faith in their country that they have been willing to give their lives for its security and freedom. That's faith in action!

Faith and Beliefs

Faith and beliefs are closely related, but in fact are distinct. Faith is a trusting commitment, whereas beliefs are ideas and truths—the cognitive content that is integral to our faith. When we decide to purchase a new car, we want to believe that the car is worth the price and is reliable and safe. If after driving the car for a while, our beliefs are confirmed, we can now have faith in the car. For a time, many Americans did not believe that cars made in this country were reliable and they turned to cars made in Japan or

Germany. Now American car companies have brought many consumers to believe in the quality, affordability and safety of cars made in this country, and are gaining their share of the market.

Faith and beliefs are also closely related yet distinct with regards to specifically religious faith. At its core, religious faith is trust in God and in God's revelation; faith is made possible by God's grace and enables the person to related to God. Beliefs, however, are the object of faith—the tradition that is believed in. For Catholics, that tradition is contained in the scriptures and the teachings of the official church.

Beliefs tend to multiply. The very first gospel, the Gospel of Mark, goes on for about 20 pages, the first modern Catholic catechism (1885) came to 64 pages and the latest Catechism of the Catholic Church (1994) contains 688 pages.

The Second Vatican Council pointed out that within Catholic teaching there is a "hierarchy of truths." This means that Catholic beliefs range from defined dogmas to theological opinions. Dogmas contain the fullness of Christian teaching and the bedrock of the tradition: Jesus is both divine and human, Jesus died for us and was raised from the dead, the scriptures are the inspired word of God, and Jesus is really present in the Eucharist. Such teachings as these are central to the Catholic tradition. On the lower end are beliefs such as "limbo" (unbaptized babies don't go to heaven) and that you have to be Catholic to be saved. Both of these have been quietly dropped!

Beliefs can change and this might either weaken or strengthen the faith. A person might believe that God is an old man in the sky who sends people to hell for missing Mass. Changing that belief to one where God is loving and forgiving might enrich the faith. On the other hand, for a Catholic to no longer believe that the gospels are the inspired word of God might well be detrimental to that person's faith. To begin to make material things, success seeking or self-indulgence our focus is no doubt going to have a negative impact on faith.

The Value of Beliefs

Having beliefs are essential to human life. Beliefs help us get a sense of ourselves and our world, help us organize meaning, and move us to take action and accomplish our goals. Beliefs affect our emotions; they help us socialize and guide us in our morals and lifestyle. Without positive beliefs in ourselves and others, we would not be productive persons. Beliefs give us inspiration and hope.[4]

On downside, distorted beliefs can move us to oppress others or even enact violence toward them. One thinks of the distorted beliefs of such demagogues as Hitler, Stalin or Osama bin Laden and the horrors their beliefs unleashed on the world.

Five Ways to Come to Believe

H. Richard Niebuhr, a student of faith, proposes that there are five ways in which we arrive at our beliefs. The first way includes things that are just taken for granted: the sun rises in the east and sets in west. The second way is on the authority of others. People tell us that is healthy to eat vegetables, that too much sugar will make us put on weight and that it is safer to wear a seat belt. The third way we arrive at our beliefs involves matters that become evident through experience. Experience teaches us that study is necessary to do well in exams or that practice is essential to succeed in sports. Fourthly we come to beliefs through persuasive means such as advertising. Ads convince us that it is more cool to drink a certain beer or that a certain deodorant is more dependable. Finally we come to our beliefs through reasoning. A professor, along with our reading, convinces us about the leading causes of the Civil War. Our research and observation of extreme weather brings us to believe that climate change is a factor in causing severe weather changes.[5] Beliefs are truths that are products of searching, listening and using critical thinking. As Archbishop Desmond Tutu, a courageous leader South Africa put it, "I am a traditionalist. Yet I'm also awes-struck when I hear new ideas from brilliant scholars that help clarify my framework of truth. Truth has a self-authenticating quality about it. When someone resonates truth, we respond. In the end, you discover truth has a certain ring about it."[6]

We All Have Doubts

Human faith usually includes some doubts. College students can have doubts whether they will make it through their maze of courses or whether they will be successful in their chosen profession. Lovers can have doubts whether their relationship will last or develop permanence and commitment. Doctors can enter into surgery with some doubts as to its success. Teachers can have doubts as to whether a class or even an entire course will be productive. We can have doubts about our safety on a trip, about our investments, and about our job security.

Doubt seems to be a normal aspect of human faith. Given the limitations of our reason and choices, our lack of knowledge of the future and our natural drive to want things to go right, there is always room for doubt. Faith is always risky and, as theologian Paul Tillich always insisted, requires "the courage to be." Doubts can be a normal part of faith, perhaps mere passing thoughts with no basis in reality. They need not paralyze faith or move the believer to despair. Human faith has to stand strong as long as there is no reason to give into doubt. Faith stands on the evidence as it exists now and need not give into unsubstantiated fears or uncertainty.

Doubt seems to be a companion to religious faith. At one time it was thought that doubt was sinful, but now a certain kind of doubt is thought to be healthy. Doubt can mean we are searching, questioning, trying to better understand our religion. Theologian Monika Hellwig said that a health doubt can actually lead us to new insights and discoveries. She distinguished between destructive and constructive doubt. Destructive doubt goes the way of cynicism and rebellion. It has an "I don't know and I don't care" attitude. Beliefs are simply pitched aside with little or no effort to reevaluate or better understand them. This often leaves the faith in wreckage because of the negative and toxic attitudes. Constructive faith, on the other hand, sincerely searches for a better understanding and is open to new insights and interpretations. The religious search here has doubts that are accompanied by respect for the tradition, an honest inquiry and a willingness to take a new direction in thinking. The questioning here proceeds with a desire to grow in a deeper faith.[7]

Religious Faith

Religious faith as a whole parallels human faith in that it also entails a trusting commitment that holistically includes all the human faculties, including reason, emotions, and the will whereby a given set of beliefs are accepted within a relationship with the Ultimate. Generally a person who is deficient in human faith also has difficulty with religious faith. Religious faith differs from human faith in that the former is often concerned with ultimate mysteries that are beyond understanding or rational proofs. Human faith comes from human nature, while religious faith transcends human nature. In the Christian tradition, religious faith is viewed as a gift from God, a divine grace which enables the believer to accept religious beliefs and relate to the divine.

We will first focus on Christian faith, looking at scripture, patristics, some key theologians past and present, the Catechism of the Catholic Church as well as the joint declaration by Catholics and Lutherans on faith and justification. Then we will discuss how Christian faith parallels human faith. We will close with a discussion of the notion of faith in some other world religions and how scientists today are addressing the question of faith.

Faith is central to the Christian tradition. In the New Testament the word "faith" (*pistis*) occurs 243 times and the word "believe" (*pisteuo*) the same number of times. St. Anselm put faith at the very center of Christian theology when he defined theology as "faith seeking understanding." During the Reformation, Luther put all his eggs in the faith basket. He took the position of "justification by faith alone," and for centuries there was a dispute over "faith and good works."

Biblical Foundations of Religious Faith

If we examine the Christian Bible, which includes both the Hebrew and Christian scriptures, we find a wide range of meanings attached to faith. In the Hebrew Scriptures, the word "faith" is usually a verb, referring to "he believed" or "he trusted." When used as a noun, faith means truth, honesty or loyalty and is characteristically attributed to God, who faithfully carries out his promises. Many times God is portrayed as being faithful to His people! From the human side, faith is trust in God. Abraham is presented as the father of faith in that he trusted in God's promises and was faithful to what was asked of him. In the Exodus story, the Israelites are brought back to faith in God and his messenger Moses by their rescue at the Red Sea. In the case of the later prophets, faith in God gives security from the fear of enemies. The prophets call their people to trust in God's saving action. In the Psalms, faith is described mainly as trust in the mercy and goodness of God. In post-exilic Judaism, the notion of faith shifts to fidelity to God's law rather than a personal relationship with God.[8]

In the New Testament, the meaning of faith shifts toward meaning conviction or persuasion and is presented in such a variety of ways as to set up vigorous debates throughout the history of the tradition. In the miracle stories, faith varies from being the result of a miracle to its cause, and at times the lack of faith prevents miracles from happening (Matt 5:3, Mark 6:5). Faith can be a hopeful expectation of a God who is all-powerful. Faith can also be a powerful force that can move mountains and yet be as small as a mustard seed. (Matthew 17:20, Mark 9:23). People cry out for their unbelief to be helped, and Jesus often rebukes his disciples for their "little faith." (Mark 9:24, Matthew 14:31). On one hand, faith implies belief in the presence of God in Jesus and in his message of the kingdom. On another, faith is a gift given by God to accept Jesus as messiah and savior (Matthew 11:25).

In Acts, the apostles have a mission to proclaim the message, awaken faith in the risen Lord, call for repentance and baptize converts into the community of the faithful. At one point, the apostle Paul writes that faith is the response to the Christian message that the Risen Jesus is the Lord (Romans 3:22). Believers are those who accept Jesus as their Savior and such faith can only be achieved with the help of God's grace. They are called to "walk by faith, not by sight" (2 Corinthians 5:7). Paul writes about justification by faith (Romans 1:17) but also refers to the need for faith, hope and love, with the latter being the most important. (1 Corinthians 13:13). For Paul, this means that living with the Spirit in Christ and faith in Jesus is the key to salvation: "...if you confess with your lips that Jesus is the Lord, and believe in your heart that God raised him from the dead, you will be saved" (Romans 10:9).

The Gospel of John has its own unique tradition on faith. Here, faith is a personal process, an intimate union with Jesus whereby one receives the Word and accepts confessional statements. Faith justifies, saves and bestows eternal life here and now (John 5:24). Faith, though supported by miracles, relies on the word of Jesus (John 2:22). It is the resurrection of Jesus that confirms the faith and works of love that are its sign. Empowered by God's love, we can overcome the evil in the world (1 John 5:4-19).[9]

This overview of the biblical views on faith points to how rich and diverse its understanding can be. Faith is God's fidelity to his promises and faith is our trust in his word, saving action, mercy and love. Faith is the acceptance of Jesus as savior, belief in the saving power of his life, death and resurrection. Faith is a personal union lived with Jesus that gives his followers eternal life now and forever. Faith has many facets: it is a gift of God, a free response, a system of beliefs and a way of life.

Christian Theology of Faith

The Christian theology of faith has a vast range of perspectives. All we can do here is point to mountaintops: the early Fathers, Augustine, Aquinas and several Catholic and Protestant theologians. By way of contrast, we will later discuss the notion of faith in some world religions.

In the Patristic period (2nd to 8th centuries), there is a gradual evolution of the notion of faith. Saint Justin the Martyr (105-165) speaks of faith in the subjective case as an assent given to revealed truths. Irenaeus (130-202) speaks more objectively of faith, describing it as the truth proposed by the Church. For Clement of Alexandria (150-215), faith is more of a process of passing from darkness to light; he stressed that faith and reason are always in harmony. Clement also taught that faith is only made possible by the grace of God, "It remains that we understand then the Unknown by the grace and by the Word alone that precedes Him."[10] Origen (182-254) also stressed the necessity of grace for faith. He pointed out that preachers, no matter how talented, cannot reach the hearts of others "unless a certain power be imparted to the speaker from God and a grace appear upon his works.[11] Athanasius of Alexandria (296-373) was a staunch defender of the divinity of Jesus and insisted that faith always has a priority over reason, which has enough difficulty explaining natural matters, much less those supernatural.[12]

During the golden age of Greek patristic theology, the limits of reason with regard faith are addressed. Basil (330-379) defined faith as "a whole-hearted assent to aural doctrine with full conviction of what is publicly taught by the grace of God." Gregory of Nyssa presents a rather mystical view of faith, pointing out that God is essentially incomprehensible and can only be approached through faith. This mystical view of faith prevailed through the next few centuries of Greek patristic thinking.[13]

The climax of this development of reflections on faith came with Augustine (354-430), whose thought had a profound effect on later Catholic and Protestant thought. Augustine wrote about the act of faith as an assent to revelation, a progression of wisdom about the mysteries of faith, which, though real, always remain obscure in this life. For Augustine, faith was a free gift of God and although he thought faith cannot be demonstrated by reason, certain signs like miracles and prophecies can give the faith support and credibility.[14] Augustine wrote of coming to God with a clean and humble heart, obediently open to God's light that comes to save us. Faith allows us to allow God's love to take possession of our hearts, moving us to serve and love. At the same time, Augustine valued reason's role in faith for reason persuades and helps us understand that which we accept in faith. Ultimately, faith is a work of God, whereby one is enabled to lovingly submit to Christ and thereby become one with God.[15]

Thomas Aquinas (1225-1274) viewed faith as a "habit of the mind" whereby eternal life begins in the believer. It is "an assent of the mind to things that are not manifest." For Aquinas, God is the formal object of faith, the "first truth," and God is then witness to the truth of revelation. The veracity of faith comes from God and surpasses other forms of knowledge. This faith lacks certainty and yet has an intellectual character. Aquinas writes, "To believe is an act of the intellect assenting to the divine truth by virtue of the command of the will as this is moved by God through grace." Mind, will,

God's grace are all important factors in the act of faith.[16]

During the Reformation, Martin Luther's notion of faith was pivotal in the debates. Luther was strongly critical of those who allowed too much of a role for human reason and works with regard faith and justification. For Luther both faith and justification had their origins in God, who brings about faith in believers through the preaching of the word and then justifies them when we accept the free gift of salvation. Such faith is twofold: first an acceptance of what God says as true, and secondly an act of trust and surrender to God. Luther's position was that "faith alone saves," which opened the classic debate about faith and good works. Luther maintained that good works follow from faith and can be meritorious, but do not play a role in obtaining forgiveness, grace or justification.[17] (Later in the chapter we will discuss recent developments in this debate.)

Hans Urs von Balthasar (1905-1988) was a Swiss Catholic theologian who attempted to go beyond reason's role in faith to the fullness of human experience. He follows Augustine's lead in describing the human heart as restless and searching, and links all this with faith. He shows how the believer is attracted by the splendor and beauty of the divine and how all this all is reflected in Jesus. He shows how the aesthetic sense is also related to faith. Faith, then, is much more than reasonableness or obedience; it involves the whole person, including the human attraction to harmony, beauty and form.[18]

Karl Rahner (1904-1984) discusses his theology of faith in the context of his understanding of the human person. Early on, Rahner described the human person as a "spirit in the world," a reality present to itself in knowledge, freedom and love. The human spirit has a given capacity that is ordered to God and can connect with God. For Rahner, God is the horizon for human knowledge and love, the goal toward which the human reaches out to. In other words, union with God is the only ultimate that can genuinely bring satisfaction to the human person. For Rahner, God always offers the grace necessary for the human dynamism to be united with the divine. It is his position that faith is the acceptance of the offer of the divine for union: it is offered to all and all are capable of responding by the very fact that they are human.[19]

H. Richard Niebuhr on Faith

Niebuhr has been chosen as our Protestant theologian because in his book on faith he not only offers his own views, but he does this in the valuable context of other Christian theologians.

Niebuhr (1894-1962) developed some of his ideas in the 1940s and 50s, a time when the great educational leader John Dewey was encouraging a "common faith" in democracy divorced from religion, and when the renowned mathematician Bertrand Russell was associating religious faith with "superstition and the faithless power-seeking ecclesiastical groups."[20] Niebuhr wrote at a time similar to ours when many people observed the many horrors around the world and questioned whether there is a benevolent God. In his book, Niebuhr points to the bewilderment of many who are so filled with anxieties that they are not able to believe. He relates to the many people in this scientific age who feel the tension between reasoning and faith and points to the wide diversity of religions in his world and wonders if they indeed have anything in common. Niebuhr points to the spreading to civil religion in this country, with its nationalistic and materialistic "American Creed" and its "Manifest Destiny" that drives Americans to dominate. He cites Nietzsche's view, which sees faith as a cloak over our instinctive selfishness and our inclinations toward violence. Niebuhr charged that religious faith today is often dead and is dedicated to belief in propositions, but without action or love.

Niebuhr took his cue from the Catholic English thinker, John Henry Newman (1801-1890), who humorously cites the limits of a faith in mere propositions. Newman wrote that "Many a man will live and die upon a dogma; no man will be a martyr for a conclusion." For Newman, beliefs can't be simply statements. They must convey a message, a history, a vision. They are can't be mere written assertions, but must be realities that enliven, empower and move to action.[21]

Niebuhr distinguished between having faith "concerning God," which is faith in statements and actually is more knowledge than faith, and faith "in God." In the latter, faith is both holding to be true what is said about God and putting "trust in him in such a way as to enter into personal relations with him." He considered this to be a living faith.[22]

Niebuhr opts for a notion of faith that goes beyond propositions to attitudes and behavior. He refers to both Kierkegaard and Nietzsche who strongly criticize the hypocrisy of those who have a faith that makes life easy and those whose faith is challenging and related to real life with all its suffering.

Niebuhr also addressed the contemporary need for evidence in faith. He faced modern challenges of the scientifically-minded who say that there is no evidence for religious faith. He referred back to the New Testament

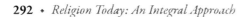

notion of faith which is "assurance of things hoped for, the conviction of things not seen," (Hebrews 11:1) and "we walk by faith, not by sight" (2 Corinthians 5:7). For Niebuhr, faith was "conviction of the reality of the unseen," "a relation to the unseen," indeed a new "kind of seeing" of what is hidden in the divine mystery. It was seeing with the "light of faith" and "through the grace of the Spirit."[23]

Niebuhr put his finger on one of the most central contentions about faith: the relationship between the subject (the person who has faith) and the object of faith (God). How can a limited subject connect with an object that unlimited? How can a finite being relate to an infinite Being? Those who emphasize the subject, the "I," tend to end in relativity or in the extreme in a theology of illusion. Ludwig Feuerbach (1804-1872), one of the founders of modern atheism, maintained that the gods of faith were mere "wish beings" created out of the human longing for someone on whom we can rely on for meaning. To him, God was nothing other than man projecting his needs into the sky.

Conversely, those who place their emphasis on the object of faith, God, can lose touch with the freedom of the human person who responds in faith. In his book, Niebuhr points to Karl Barth, who insisted that God is the source of all knowledge of Himself and wills to be known only through Himself. Niebuhr pointed out that in that perspective the interpersonal dynamic of faith between God and humans can be lost. Taking his lead from Buber's notion of the I-Thou, he views faith as a relationship of trust and communication. Faith is a two-way street, a "keeping faith with," a mutual fidelity and a covenant sealed by love. He uses as an example a teacher-student relationship, wherein both are committed to the search for truth.[24]

For Niebuhr, faith is relational, between the person and God, between the person and community. He points to Christian faith: "Faith, as we have seen, is not something which exists in a person. It is an interpersonal relation... The community of faith which rises into view as the great possibility with the restoration of faith in the Creator by Jesus Christ is the community of every self with God and all God's creatures. It is the community of selves who trust God in his loyalty to all that he has made, to all the companions of the self; it is the community of fidelity in which all selves bind themselves and are faithful to all their companions as those to whom God is faithful. It is the community in which Christ is the companion."[25]

Paul Tillich on Faith

Paul Tillich (1886-1965) was a German Protestant theologian who was forced out of his native Germany by the Nazis and spent the rest of his life teaching in the United States. During the 1950s he was very popular with college students, especially with his definition of faith as "the courage to be."

Tillich began with faith in general and defined it as "the state of being ultimately concerned." He pointed out that every living being has concerns about living, food and shelter, but that humans are unique in that they have spiritual concerns that are cognitive, aesthetic, social and political. Some of these concerns have ultimacy in that they promise total fulfillment and surrender. These concerns can often be misplaced in such things as wealth, success, national pride. People can turn their minds, hearts and wills to false ultimates.

True faith for Tillich is concern for what is truly ultimate, the Holy, the Divine. He wrote, "An act of faith is an act of a finite being who is grasped by and turned to the infinite."[26] Faith for Tillich is an act of ultimate risk and courage. It is an act that faces its doubts and yet is able to accept ultimacy as mystery; it is both personal and communal. As for the creedal statements of the community, Tillich maintained that such statements in themselves are not ultimate but that they point to the ultimate that is always beyond such statements. Thus, doctrines stand before the criticism and prophetic judgment. Here Tillich asserted what he called "the Protestant principle," which maintains that some finite doctrinal statement or ecclesiastical authority should not be allowed to take the place of the Ultimate. Tillich cautioned that one should not even give ultimacy to one's own religion, lest the way be open to intolerance of other religions. That which is finite should point to the Ultimate and not take the place of it.[27]

For Tillich, faith is a centered act of the whole personality and not be limited to an act of knowledge, emotion or will. It is a human act whereby God's grace moves the person to accept the truth. Faith is an "obedience," a "commitment" of the whole person.[28] Faith, for Tillich, is being grasped by the Holy, whether that be through nature, scripture, laws or sacramental symbols.

As for the relationship between reason and faith, Tillich maintained that reason is the "precondition of faith," in that faith is an act where "reason reaches ecstatically beyond itself." Faith is an act whereby reason becomes open to infinity and ultimacy. It is an act which intrinsically includes love, which is "the power in the ground of everything that is, driving it beyond itself toward reunion with the other one and ultimately with the ground itself."[29]

Faith in the Catechism of the Catholic Church

The recent Catechism offers a detailed description of Christian faith. The process begins with God addressing his people as friends and inviting them into his company. Faith is a submission of intellect and will to this invitation; an assent, an obedience of the whole person. The traditional models are given: Abraham and Mary, the mother of Jesus. Hebrews 11:1 is used for a definition: "Faith is the assurance of things hoped for, the conviction of things not seen." Faith is "a free assent to the whole truth that God has revealed."[30] Christian faith is described as belief in Jesus Christ "because he is himself God," "the Word made flesh." It is the Holy Spirit who reveals who Jesus is, so faith is Trinitarian.

The Catechism lists the characteristics of faith. First, faith is a grace, a free gift of God. Grace moves the mind and heart to be open to God and his truth. Secondly, faith is a human act, an act of trust and freedom, a cooperation with God's grace. Thirdly, the truths of faith are understandable. The truths of faith are intelligible, in accordance with reason, indeed more certain than human knowledge in that God sheds divine light on this truth. Moreover, the truths of faith do not conflict with science since the things of the world and the things of faith derive from the same God. Next, faith is a free act and should never be coerced. Faith is an invitation. Finally, faith is necessary for salvation and requires perseverance, endurance and constant hope and love. Faith is the beginning of eternal life, a taste of what is to come when we will see God "face to face."

The Catechism notes that faith is both individual and communal. The latter implies that faith is received from others and handed on to others. The Christian faith is the faith of the Church, which nourishes and sustains the faith.[31]

Joint Declaration on Justification

The question of the relation of faith and good works was central at the time of the tumultuous division of Catholics and Protestants during the time of the Reformation. Luther maintained that faith alone saves and charged the Church with teaching that Christians could bring about salvation through good works. Condemnations were exchanged and to controversy continued into modern times. In 1999, this age-old controversy was openly addressed and a peaceful compromise was reached. At that time, the Lutheran World

Federation and the Catholic Church made a historic joint declaration on justification. This joint declaration is of great significance because it represents a consensus on basic truths about justification.

It is important to note that the declaration admits that there have been new insights in both churches that make such a consensus possible. Both sides now agree that justification is the work of the triune God. The Father sent his Son to save sinners and Christ's incarnation, death and resurrection provides the foundation for justification, which we share through the Holy Spirit. Both churches confess that "By grace alone, in faith in Christ' saving work and not because of any merit on our part, we are accepted by God and receive the Holy Spirit who renews our hearts while equipping and calling us to good works."[32] Faith is a gift, and all that becomes possible in our living out of the faith, including our good works, is gift and the work of grace. Justification is solely due to God's grace, so when Catholics say the "cooperate" they mean they consent to God's justifying action. When Lutherans say that we cannot cooperate in justification, they "exclude any possibility of contributing to one's own justification, but do not deny that believers are fully involved personally in their faith, which is effected by God's Word."[33] Both faith and good works are the works of God in Jesus Christ. Therefore, both Lutherans and Catholics can confess "that persons are justified by faith in the gospel apart from works prescribed by the law" (Romans 3:28). "Christ has fulfilled the law and by his death and resurrection has overcome it as a way to salvation.... a Christian life lived in faith, hope and love - follow justification and are its fruits. When the justified live in Christ and act in the grace they receive, they bring forth, in biblical terms, good fruit."[34]

After centuries of separation, both Catholics and Lutherans have come to agree that faith, the good works that flow from it, as well as justification are the work of God and his grace and mercy. They are all gifts, freely given and freely received.

Dynamics of Christian Faith

Although Christian faith is only possible through the gift of divine grace, it is built upon the human capability to have faith and follows the lines of human faith in that is activated through the all the human capacities, including trust, reason, emotion and will.

Christian Faith and Trust

At its core, Christian faith is trust in God and in God's incarnation, Jesus Christ. Faith is trust in God's revelation and saving power, in God's love, compassion and forgiveness. Faith is a trusting acknowledgment of the divine offer of covenant and eternal life. Bernard Haring, one of the great moralists of our time, defined faith as the "joyous and grateful acceptance of him who is the Way, the Truth and the Life: a grateful acceptance of our Father's free gift to us."[35] Faith is a confident expectation that God, through Jesus Christ, will be with us in good times and bad and surround us with divine benevolence.

Christian Faith and Reason

Thomas More (1478-1535) wrote that humans are unique in that they must work things out "in the tangle of their minds." Humans are unique in that they not only "know" as other animals do, they go further and "know that they know." We humans are searchers, questioners who bring all considerations to the bar of reason. Good education develops critical thinking, so naturally young adults today want to seriously consider what they put their faith in, including in religious matters.

As we have seen, the Catholic tradition has always said that its tradition can be reasonably accepted. Catholics have always treasured "theology," which is thinking about the dynamic interpretation and critical consideration about the truths of faith. Thomas Aquinas, perhaps the greatest of all Christian theologians, used Aristotelian philosophy to analyze and interpret the Christian tradition. Both before and after him, countless theologians have analyzed and interpreted God's revelation.

At the same time, Catholics view revelation as a mystery that is neither measurable nor provable. Spiritual reality cannot be seen, heard, touched or subjected to scientific investigation. When all is said and done, faith must make a "leap" beyond observable phenomenon.

Christian Faith and the Heart

If Christian faith is limited only to the mind it will, by necessity, become abstract and sterile. Humans reach out in relationships with their hearts, their feeling and intuition, and the Christian faith commitment is not exception. Christian faith extends the self in trust and love to a God who reveals "Self" in the person of Jesus Christ. Christian faith takes Jesus on his word when he said his followers could call him "friend," and recognizes that he loved his friends so much he was willing to die for them and seal that promise of love and forgiveness with resurrection. Humans are usually quite cautious about "letting go" of their hearts. Christian faith is "letting go" of the heart to God, putting the self in God's hands and giving in to the spirit within. The prophet Ezekiel wrote of God's promise to the faithful: "I will give you a new heart and place a new spirit with you, taking from you bodies your stony hearts and giving you natural hearts. I will put my spirit within you" (Ezekiel 36:26-27). Jesus taught within this same Jewish framework when he said, "Whoever loves me will keep my word and my Father will love him, and we will come to him and make our dwelling in him" (John 14:21). The apostle Paul spoke of the faith as actually being within this God "in whom we live and move and have our very being" (Acts 17:28).

Christian Faith and Free Will

To be authentic, Christian faith must be a free choice, made deeply in ones' conscience. Christian faith is abandoning oneself to this Jesus, the Son of God. As Walter Kasper, a contemporary theologian, puts it, "What is faith here other than a total self-abandonment to God's promise and call, a letting go of all human security, a holding to and standing fast in God's world alone. Faith here is a ... conversion from one's normal attitude of one's normal security, a standing fast independent of all human security, a trust and a confidence in God alone."[36]

Christian Faith in Action

Faith, though a gift, must be a free choice of the will and rightfully culminates in action. Christian faith moves beyond understanding and feeling to a way of life. The early Christians referred to their movement as "the Way." For them, faith was much more than a private set of beliefs or devotions, it was a commitment to radically turn the lives around (repent) which involved a fundamental option or choice to love, forgive, extend compassion and serve the needy of the world. For them, a private faith was a stunted faith. A genuine faith is a "doing" faith, a faith that is active in imitating Jesus life of healing and serving.

There is story out of the time of the revolution in El Salvador in the 80's of a young woman named Maria. She was a person of deep faith who followed the example of her Archbishop, Oscar Romero, who gave his life for his people. Maria decided to reach out to the many refugee families of that time, bringing them food and clothing and registering them to vote for a better government. Maria's actions marked her as a "subversive." One night she was taken from her bed by soldiers, tortured and raped, and her tongue was cut out. Maria was taken to the garbage dump to be executed and told to kneel down and beg for mercy. Instead, she stood with courageous defiance until she was cut down in a burst of bullets. The local peasants gathered up her broken body, washed her and took her to the local church for burial. Maria is still remembered for her courage and strong faith and, during processions, her name is chanted and the people sing "*Presente*, she is still present with us."

As we will see in a later chapter, many Christians as well as many in other religions, have moved beyond a privatized faith to an active faith. They are vigorously involved in service in their communities and in such issues poverty, violence, women's rights and ecology. If you have followed the CNN Heroes movement, you have heard many inspiring stories of people all over the world who profess a "faith that does justice."

"Faith" in World Religions

The word "faith" is not used as commonly in world religions other than Christianity, yet there are notions that are similar to some of those we have been discussing so far.

Hinduism

The Hindu notion of faith is best described in its tradition of bhakti, or devotion. In many of the Hindu schools, bhakti entails "having a strong faith in the protection of the Lord; praying to the Lord; discarding all false pride and egotism; completely entrusting oneself and whatever belongs to oneself to the Lord, being convinced that such complete resignation earns God's grace and mercy."[37]

Since there are so many diverse traditions of Hinduism, it is most useful to singularly focus our discussion of Hindu faith on Mahatma Gandhi (1869-1948), one of the most influential Hindus of modern times.

Gandhi seems to have viewed faith as the "central experience of life," a pervasive awareness wherein he could relate all that he did to God. For Gandhi, God was not a distant reality but an indwelling presence that witnessed everything he said and did. Faith was an awareness that deepened over years of prayerful living. Gandhi often pined for a fuller faith, believing that as faith deepened he would be more able to act and suffer for others "in a godward way."[38]

Gandhi writes about faith as the context for prayer, which for him was "longing of the heart," "the soul turning to God" "longing of the heart of merge myself in the Master." Faith was also the context in which he carried out his fasting and commitment to "ahimsa," or non-violence.[39] Faith for Gandhi was intimately related to his passionate search for Truth. For him, truth-force was the foundation of our very being. Indeed he believed that Truth was the best name for God and could be in part realized through study, prayer, fasting and ahimsa. He believed that if God is Truth then God is the highest good for one and all. Gandhi saw truth as the wisdom of all religions. If he was to commit to God as Truth he would have to listen to other religions. In his personal life, Gandhi felt a deep obligation to be truthful with himself and others and he avoided all situations which required lying as a cover.

Gandhi's Hindu faith led him to believe that God was always near at hand and would never let him down. He wrote, "The more I live the more I realize how much I owe to faith and prayer. I am quoting an experience extending over 40 years. I have never found Him lacking in response. I have found him nearest at hand when the horizon seemed darkest. I cannot recall a moment in my life when I had a sense of desertion by God."[40]

Gandhi believed that faith was dependence on the Highest power and a sense of self-effacement in the face of God's immense power. He wrote: "Faith is nothing but a living, wide-awake consciousness of God within, whose eye misses nothing and with whom I strive to keep in tune. God is in my heart 24 hours. He has been my savior. He alone can claim to have faith who in life ceaselessly endeavors to observe the law of God."[41]

Living faith for Gandhi meant belief in God's governance of the world and the rejection of all that was contrary to Truth and Love. He insisted the underlying all the suffering and pain in the world was a divine benevolent plan that ultimately prevails.[42] His unbreakable commitment to ahimsa was based on the belief in soul-force of the power of God within us, enabling us to love and forgive.

Buddhism

In Buddhism, there is generally no God-talk or description of faith as a relationship with God. Buddhists do not rely on the help of divine grace, but stress that each person "be a light unto yourself." At the same time, Buddhists take refuge in the Buddha, which means they discover their meaning and salvation in the Buddha. "Buddha's body is enlightenment itself. Being formless and without substance, it always has been and always will be. It is an eternal body whose substance if Wisdom. Buddha, therefore, has neither fear nor disease; He is eternally changeless... Buddha awakens faith in them who are deceived by ignorance and cannot see their own Buddha-nature, leads them away from illusions."[43] Buddhists take refuge in the Dharma (teaching), believing that "there is no falsity in the Eternal Dharma which Buddha taught for He knows all things in the world as they, He teaches them to all people."[44] They take refuge in in the Sangha (the community). "The rain of the sacred teaching falls on all people alike without regard to their conditions or circumstances. Those who accept it gather into small groups, then into organizations, then into communities and, finally, find themselves in the great Ocean of Enlightenment."[45]

In addition, Buddhists place their faith in the four noble truths and the eightfold path of the Buddha's enlightenment. The four noble truths include the teaching that suffering is universal and is connected with clinging to desires, that liberation is brought about by ceasing to cling, and that letting go is achieved by following the path of righteous living.

Buddhists believe that each person has within the self, Buddhahood, whereby they can reach Nirvana by following these teachings. So there is a faith-bond with the Buddha, his teachings and their community, as well a commitment to the Buddhist teachings. Peter Harvey sums it up this way, "Most traditions of Buddhism consider *saddha*, 'trustful confidence' or faith, as a quality that must be balanced by wisdom, and as a preparation for, or accompaniment of, meditation."[46] The Buddha opposed blind faith and encouraged his followers to test the teaching themselves. *Saddha* at first is a listening and then a deeper *saddha* leads to a deeper practice, an uplifted inspiration that leads to a calm and joyful faith (*pasada*).[47]

Islam

The centerpiece of the Muslim faith is that there is but one God, Allah, and that Muhammad is His prophet. Early on, Muhammad's disciples identified themselves during his life by saying "All of us accept that God reveals himself to Muhammad at all times of night and day."[48] Muhammad's own faith is quoted in the Qur'an: "I take refuge in the light that shines from your face; your light penetrates even the darkest recesses of my existence. All things in this world and the next are ordered and governed by you. My only wish is that you approve my thoughts and actions, and your wrath never descends on me. Your pleasure is my happiness. Your power alone can shield me from harm."[49]

It is the Qur'an, the collection of God's revelation to Muhammad over 23 years, that is the vessel of Muslim faith. The Qur'an says "This book should not be doubted. It is a guide to the righteous, who believe in the unseen mysteries and are steadfast in prayer, who give generously from what we have given them; who trust what has been revealed to Muhammad and others before him; and who firmly believe in the life to come."[50]

For Muslims, piety is the exercise of faith. True piety consists in believing in God and his final judgment, believing in angels, the Book, the prophets, sharing their wealth, attending prayers and giving to the poor. It means being faithful to your promises and being steadfast in times of distress, adversity and war. The Qur'an says: "Those who show true poverty are genuine in their faith; they honor God."[51]

Biological Studies on the Human Capacity for Religious Faith

Some scientists who specialize in brain studies have asked this question: Are humans wired for religion and faith? A great deal of work has been done in genetics and neurology to see if there is a connection between the human make-up and religions. Some of this study has attempted to show that that religion can be reduced to genes or neurons. From this perspective, religion and faith then are explained away by certain human "wiring," but in fact there is no Ultimate Reality involved as either cause or response to such capacities. Some "materialist" scientists see humans as mere products of natural selection, simply a higher form of animal. They point out how other animals can learn, trust and feel, and that humans simply have the same capacities on a more complicated level and express these in their formations of religions. In other words, they believe that humans are "hard-wired" for religion, made so that we can carry out religious practices, but this does not indicate that there are such things as spiritual realities. In fact, some scientists propose that these religious capacities arose out of the fear of death as a survival mechanism.[52] Some materialists go so far as to propose that the great spiritual leaders actually suffered from temporal lobe epilepsy. Others, echoing Freud, claim that spiritual experiences are illusions. Other materialists have even gone to genetics and tried to identify some "God gene" that explains religion.[53] The explanation goes like this: "Cave dwellers in the remote past who believe in a supernatural reality were more likely to pass on their genes than cave dwellers who didn't."[54] Another individual in Canada, Michael Persinger, has devised a "God helmet" which can stimulate the temporal lobes with electromagnetic waves, causing them to experience a sensed presence. Persinger maintains that this can be used to explain what religious people have described as "God" and can also be used to explain how people have "spiritual" experiences. Some scientists maintain that this can also be used to explain the experience of aliens, visions and near death experiences.[55] Unfortunately, Persinger's tests offer no imaging data, only subjective reports and is considered by many to be "pop science."[56]

Other scientists perform studies to demonstrate that humans actually do have built-in capacities for religion and faith, and to explain how we can indeed be linked to the holy and transcendent.

Several observations about the human brain are relevant to the reception of beliefs. First of all, we are prone to believe what we hear—people often take as true what they read in the paper or what they see on TV. Secondly, we tend to resist beliefs that are not in accord with what we have been taught. For instance, Christians often have a difficult time even considering the beliefs of other religions. Even those who share the Christian tradition such as Catholics and Protestants are resistant to each others' beliefs. In addition, we are creatures of habit and we get used to our ways of eating, driving, etc. and come to think that we are doing things correctly. And finally, we carry so many prejudices that make it difficult to embrace different beliefs.

Andrew Newberg, M.D. is a radiologist and psychiatrist and is a good guide in this area because he remains neutral, neither pushing religion nor denying it. Rather, he objectively presents the findings of his and his associates' work to show the biological connection between human nature and spirituality. Newberg studies how the brain creates memories, thoughts, behavior and emotions and attempts to understand how beliefs emerge from the brain and are shaped by relationships, culture, education and spiritual searching. He maintains that all beliefs, whether they be natural or supernatural, are processed by the brain. Biology and neurology have shown that our beliefs are products of our brains. They are "neural representations of experiences that seem to be meaningful and true."[57]

Science tells us that beliefs are a combination of perception, cognition and emotion, and all of that relates to different areas of the brain. Belief also includes social consensus. Let's say a neighbor who bought a lottery ticket with you comes over and says: "We are rich. We won the lottery." You have an initial emotional excitement, but your cognition tells you that you need to check the number on your ticket with your neighbor's number and the number on the television. Once you have checked that many times you have to take your tickets down to the lottery office and make sure there is no mistake. Only when you have verified that you have the winning ticket and have the check in hand, do you now celebrate and believe that you are rich

You heard the news from your neighbor and the TV and the lottery office (perception), your mind has gone through the proof process (cognition), you have experienced the initial and then final thrill of winning, and everyone accepts that you and your neighbor are winners. Your final belief comes from the evidence.

However, even observable evidence is not always convincing. At one time it was thought that the sun revolved around the earth because it appeared to come up in the morning and set at night. Galileo observed with his telescope that instead, the earth revolved around the sun (and as a result he was condemned by the church, put under house arrest, and was not officially exonerated by the Vatican until 1979). There are other scientific findings that are still not believed by many people. Since the 19th century, the scientific world has accepted evolution, and yet possibly ½ of Americans do not accept evolution. Today there is much evidence for climate change and its destructive effects of weather and the environment, yet many people do not believe this to be true.

There are other areas where even the scientists themselves are puzzled and have to admit their limitations. With regard the microcosm, science has not been able to ascertain the elemental particles of the universe. As for the microcosm, science continually observes the presence of many new universes and has not been able to ascertain as to whether the cosmos had a beginning or will have an end.

With regard to religious beliefs, even though there are many written propositions, none of these can be proven with evidence to be true. Beliefs in God, creation, eternity, and life after death cannot be proven. They may be reasonable in that they can be partially understood, but there is no proof or evidence where these areas are concerned. These areas remain mysteries, and ultimately can be only known through divine revelation and accepted in faith. The renowned spiritual writer, Evelyn Underhill put it this way; "Since perfect proof of the supersensual is beyond the span of human consciousness, the element of risk can never be eliminated; we are obliged in the end to trust in the universe and live by faith."[58]

Brain experts tell us that our capacity to accept beliefs, religious or otherwise, is located in the frontal lobe of the brain where we have the capacity to analyze and understand beliefs. This part of the brain is also the seat of the will where we choose to accept beliefs. The whole process is described as follows: "The flow of external data, and the sensation and actions triggered by them, feed into the ordering framework of our brains and create an ever more elaborate, and ever more idiosyncratic, internal conceptual universe. It forms the dislikes, habits of thought, dispositions, beliefs and memories that in time we come to think of as our "selves"[59]

Our beliefs are usually able to be expressed in language. Within our consciousness there is a microscopic molecule that gives us our capacity for language and communication. This is the way that beliefs are given to others concretely and beyond mere intentional propositions. It should be noted that there is often dissonance among these neurological capacities to think, feel and express and this "static" might explain the our tendency for doubt or even disbelief.

As we have seen, emotions move us to reason we accept and get attached to beliefs. The limbic system of the brain finds these emotions are positive and the beliefs follow suit. When love moves us to beliefs, our beliefs are usually healthy. However, when we are moved to belief out of toxic emotions, the outcome is usually negative. If for instance, if a child is taught to obey out of fear of punishment, that child will probably be rebellious later on. Similarly, when religious beliefs are forced on people through fear, these beliefs might well be dropped later on because of the tension they cause. Many times, Catholics who were taught that they had to go to Mass or they would go to hell decide when they are older to withdraw altogether just to get rid themselves of that tension. Rejection can also last in the memory part of the brain. A person who has been rejected by his or her father might have difficulty with authority figures later in life. A faithful person feeling rejected by the church over his or her divorce might find it difficult to remain a member of the church.

When anger and hatred are stimulated in our brain and attached to beliefs, people can be moved to violence. In some Muslim countries, young terrorists are groomed by being taught to hate their enemies and are promised that they will go directly to heaven if they serve as suicide bombers. In the middle ages, some Christians who differed with the church were condemned as heretics and burned at the stake. This was all a result to the development of the belief shaped by self-righteous anger that those who refused to believe the doctrines of the faith were worthy of death. Despair after World War I drove the German people to turn over all their rights and be blindly obedient to the dictatorship of Hitler, believing that he would restore their pride and prosperity. Even many of the church leaders fell under the spell of Hitler's vision and some theologians reinterpreted Christian hopes in terms of the Reich (Kingdom) that would last for 1000 years.

Our neuron circuits hold onto beliefs in ways as to affect later behavior. Children who are raised by nurturing parents tend to see the world in a loving and trusting way and treat others accordingly. On the other hand, children who have been abused often find it difficult to trust and may be inclined to abuse others.[60]

Humans are unique in their ability to believe, as several scientists have attempted to show. Newberg has been studying the spiritual capacities of the human brain. He was originally inspired by the extraordinary experience of enlightenment by a 19th century physician, Dr. Richard Bucke. The doctor attempted to summarize his experience as follows: "I saw and knew the cosmos is not dead matter but a living Presence, that the soul of man is immortal, that the universe is so ordered that without any peradventure all thing work together for the good of each and all; that the foundation principle of the world is what we call love and that the happiness of every one in the long run is absolutely certain."[61]

First, Newberg studied the meditation of Tibetan monks through brain imaging. He concluded that the altered states of consciousness of these monks as well as other mystics and saints, was not delusional fantasies or the misfiring of damaged brains as some critics would have it, but instead were genuine experiences brought on when the person focused on some sacred image or thought. Such practices over years, he maintains, alters the brain's neurological processes in significant ways, and he believes that these changes can be studied in the lab. It is Newberg's conviction that "transcendent, mystical, and spiritual experiences have a real biological component."[62] In these religious experiences, the normal processes of the brain are disrupted and the person has an experience that is "indescribable, awe-inspiring, unifying and indelibly real."[63] It is Newberg's position that in turn, these experiences are interpreted by the subject in terms of their own religious beliefs, whether that be the Christian experience of the presence of God or the Buddhist experience of absolute awareness of the universe.

Newberg performed experiments on cloistered nuns who practiced "centering prayer." This is a form of prayer which brings one into the presence of God and prepares the person for contemplation. In his experiments, Newberg wanted to show the effects that meditation and prayer had on the brain. Before prayer the nuns agreed to be hooked up to a catheter in their arms and injected with a radioactive tracer into their blood stream. The purpose of this was to track and measure the blood flow to various parts of the brain during prayer and then photograph the tracer to determine how the prayer affects the brain. While the nuns practiced their centering prayer, the effects of this prayer on various parts of the brain were scanned. It was revealed that during the nuns' prayer, there was considerable neural activity in the frontal lobe as well as in the language center of the brain. The frontal lobes showed significant alertness. As in his other studies, Newberg learned that the frontal lobe of the brain plays a vital role in processing religious beliefs and spiritual activities. He also found that in the parietal lobes were affected, as he nuns experienced a loss to time and space. It is this part of the brain that seems to be most affected when we experience rapture in prayer, nature or sexual experiences.[64]

Similar studies were carried out by Mario Beauregard with Carmelite nuns in Canada. The nuns were asked to recall and attempt to relive their most intense mystical experiences. While they were doing this, the nuns' brains were scanned. One nun described her experience as follows, "I don't know how much time had passed. It is like a treasure, and intimacy. It is very, very personal. It was in the center of my being, but even deeper. It was a feeling of fullness, fullness, fullness."[65] Others described their experiences as "an experience of what I knew to be sacred," "an experience in which something greater than myself seemed to absorb me," or "I have experienced profound joy."[66]

The scanning revealed that there were a number of areas of the brain affected by mystical experiences, ranging from the frontal lobe to the parietal lobule, and the visual cortex to the left brain stem. Such experiences appear to be quite complicated and linked to many capacities of the brain.

It is clear that though science cannot prove the existence of the holy or of God, it can demonstrate that those who claim to have such spiritual experiences are not having illusions or are victims of some kind of neurological disorders. Scientists can't prove that God exists, but they can demonstrate that humans have normal capacities to transcend themselves and that such spiritual experiences are in line with normal human capacities.

The Near-death Experience

Other studies concerning the human capacity for spirituality focus on the so-called "near death experience." This is a rather common phenomenon experienced by those who have been clinically dead for a time but who have been revived. This NDE became well-known through the work of George Ritchie, a physician who described his own experience of near death in Return From Tomorrow. Since that time, there have been many studies examining this occurrence, which involves such things as an out-of-body experience, a review of the person's life, encounters with a Being of Light, meeting deceased relatives and friends, and a call to return to life, which is often accepted reluctantly by the person. The after-effects of this experience are often the disappearance of the fear of death and growth in compassion for others.

Some explain this phenomenon as a mere result of prescribed drugs, as fragments of consciousness, a lack of oxygen to the brain, or even the activation of special brain function that serves as a survival mechanism by those who face death.

Others view the near-death experience as an authentic spiritual and conversion experience of the soul: "The purpose of life, most NDEers agree, is divine knowledge and love. Studies on the transformative effect of the NDE show that the cultural values of wealth, status, and material possessions become much less important, and the perennial religious values of love, caring for others, an acquiring knowledge about the divine ascend to greater importance."[67]

Summary

We have seen how complicated the notion of faith is. Humans have a unique capacity to trust, reflect, feel, choose and indeed holistically reach out in faithful relationships. Human faith includes the acceptance of beliefs and is often challenged by doubts. It also has an inclination toward action.

Religious faith follows these same lines as human faith, but for Christians is seen as made possible only by divinely gifted grace. Christian faith is explored in the scriptures, early patristic writings, in the works of theologians, in the Catholic Catechism and in the joint statement by Catholics and Lutherans on justification and faith. Christian faith has its own dynamics, which include trust, reason, feelings and action. Beliefs are integral to this faith but also distinct from faith and include healthy doubt. Faith plays a role in other religions, often similar to Christian faith. And finally, contemporary studies of the brain have thrown light on the human capacity to believe and have faith.

◼◼ VIDEOS ONLINE

Daniel Berrigan, Sharing Faith
> https://www.youtube.com/watch?v=Fw7SYM35Gnk

Daniel Berrigan, truth and differences
> https://www.youtube.com/watch?v=Fw7SYM35Gnk

Pope Francis on his faith journey
> www.youtube.com/watch?v=bk3Ex24R_Tg

Martin Luther, The True Meaning of Faith
> https://www.youtube.com/watch?v=R4KX8mtTHyU

Karen Kilby, Why study Karl Rahner?
> https://www.youtube.com/watch?v=ZWeqGTaxJFM

Joint Declaration on the Doctrine of Justification
> https://www.youtube.com/watch?v=JOtfVgY2AVU

Faith vs. Belief
> https://www.youtube.com/watch?v=Mg3MY4LEXCc

Crisis of Faith (2008) (movie clip)
> https://www.youtube.com/watch?v=KSc0srYx9-4

human capacity for faith
> https://www.youtube.com/watch?v=2J2ToJfQ9Cs

Andrew Newberg, Is The Human Brain Hardwired for God?
> https://www.youtube.com/watch?v=uxREBlWvxfk

Near death experiences:

Pam Reynolds (BBC)
> https://www.youtube.com/watch?v=WNbdUEqDB-k

George Ritchie's Near-Death Experience
> https://www.youtube.com/watch?v=ruKjIrejDCk

◼◼ NOTES

1.   James A. Douglas, *Gandhi and the Unspeakable* (Maryknoll, NY: Orbis Books, 2012), 11.

2.   H. Richard Niebuhr, *Faith on Earth: An Inquiry into Human Faith*, ed. Richard R. Niebuhr (New Haven: Yale University Press, 1989), 51.

3.   Terrence W. Tilley, *Faith: What it is and What It Isn't* (Maryknoll, NY: Orbis Books, 2010), 55.)

4.   Andrew Newberg, *Why We Believe What We Believe* (New York: Free Press 2006), 5.

5. Niebuhr, 75.

6. Dolly K. Patterson, ed., *Questions of Faith* (Philadelphia: Trinity Press International, 1990), 70.

7. Monika K. Hellwig, *Understanding Catholicism* (New York: Paulist Press, 1981), 4ff.

8. See Avery Dulles, S.J., *The Assurance of Things Hoped For* (New York: Oxford University Press, 1993), 7ff.

9. Ibid., 10ff.

10. Johannes Quasten, *Patrology* (Westminster, MD: The Newman Press, 1953), 20.

11. Ibid., 55.

12. Quasten, III, 56.

13. Dulles, 23ff.

14. Richard P. McBrien, *Catholicism* Vol. I (Oak Grove, MN, Winston Press, 1980), 39.

15. Dulles, 26.

16. Ibid., 33ff.

17. Ibid., 44ff.

18. Hans Urs von Balthasar, The Glory of God Vol. I (San Francisco: Ignatius, 1982), 151ff, 460ff.

19. See Karl Rahner, "On the Situation of Faith," *Theological Investigations* Vol. 20 (New York: Crossroad, 1981), 20, 13-32.

20. Richard R. Niebuhr, ed., *Faith on Earth* (New Haven: Yale University Press, 1989), 2.

21. Niebuhr, *Faith on Earth*, 8.

22. Niebuhr quoting Luther in Niebuhr, *Faith on Earth*, 9.

23. Niebuhr, *Faith on Earth*, 16.

24. Ibid., 47ff.

25. Ibid., 109.

26. Paul Tillich, *Dynamics of Faith* (New York: Harper and Row, 1957), 16.

27. Ibid., 29.

28. Ibid., 37ff.

29. Ibid., 112ff.

30. *Catechism of the Catholic Church*, http://www.vatican.va/archive/catechism/ccc_toc.htm, §150.

31. Ibid., §151-175.

32. Ibid., §15.

33. Ibid., §21.

34. Ibid., §37.

35. Bernard Haring, *Free and Faithful in Christ* Vol. I (New York: Crossroad, 1984), 120.

36. Walter Kasper, *Transcending All Understanding* (San Francisco: Ignatius Press, 1989), 52.

37.   Klaus K. Klostermaier, *A Survey of Hinduism* (Albany: State University of New York Press, 2007), 193.

38.   Sushil Kumar Saxena, *Ever Unto God: Essays on Gandhi and Religion* (Calcutta: Indian Council of Philosophical Research, 1988), 50.

39.   Saxena, 113.

40.   M.K. Gandhi, *Prayer* (Ahmedabad: Navajivan, 1977), 115.

41.   Saxena, 121.

42.   Ibid., 139.

43.   Bukkyo Dendo Kyokai, *The Teaching of Buddha* (Tokyo: Kosaido Printing Co., 1966), 50, 146.

44.   Ibid., 50.

45.   Ibid., 480.

46.   Peter Harvey, *An Introduction to Buddhism* (New York: Cambridge University Press, 1990), 170.

47.   Ibid., 31.

48.   Robert Van De Weyer, *366 Readings from Islam* (Delhi: Jaico Pub. House, 2010), 2:2.

49.   Ibid., 2:7.

50.   Ibid., 4:4.

51.   Ibid., 4:8.

52.   Matthew Alper, *The God Part of the Brain* (New York: Rogue, 2001), 140.

53.   Dean Hamer, *The God Gene* (New York: Doubleday, 2004).

54.   Mario Beauregard and Denyse O'Leary, *The Spiritual Brain* (New York: HarperOne, 2007), xiv.

55.   Ibid.

56.   Ibid., 90ff.

57.   Andrew Newberg and Mark R. Waldman, *Born to Believe* (New York: Free Press, 2006), 18.

58.   Evelyn Underhill, *The Life in the Spirit and the Life of Today* (New York: Harper and Row, 1986), 168.

59.   Newberg and Waldman, 69.

60.   Ibid., 66.

61.   Ibid., 168.

62.   Ibid., 169.

63.   Ibid.

64.   Ibid,, 175ff.

65.   Beauregard and O'Leary, 270.

66.   Ibid., 271.

67.   Neal Grossman, "Whose Afraid of Life After Death?" *Journal of Near Death Studies* 21, No. 1 Fall (2001): 21.

Dealing with Diversity

9

I came to the conclusion long ago that all religions were true and that also that all had some error in them, and while I hold by my own religion, I should hold other religions as dear as Hinduism. So we can only pray, if we were Hindus, not that a Christian should become a Hindu; but our innermost prayer should be that a Hindu should become a better Hindu, a Muslim a better Muslim, and a Christian a better Christian.

— Mahatma Gandhi

It follows that though there are many nations there is but one people of God, which takes its citizens from every race, making them citizens of a kingdom which is of a heavenly rather than of an earthly nature.

— Vatican II, *Lumen Gentium*

December 14th, 2012, Newtown, Connecticut. Americans, and indeed many around the world, will never forget that day just before Christmas when a deranged young man shot his way into an elementary school and slaughtered six administrators and teachers as well as twenty first-graders. Newtown is a small idyllic New England town, and many religions are represented there. On the Sunday evening following the horrific killings, many of the parents and relatives of the deceased gathered for a painful memorial service in the high school auditorium. A Jewish rabbi sang a moving prayer in Hebrew, a young Muslim chanted prayers for the Koran in Arabic, Protestant ministers and a Catholic priest recited prayers, a Pentecostal leader prayed spontaneously and a Native American connected the event to nature. Finally, President Barack Obama brought the consolation and compassion of the nation to these heart-broken people. The world had witnessed a snapshot of today's world, a world with many religions seeking unity and meaning amidst much division and violence.

One of the most challenging aspects of dealing with the religions of the world is their diversity. Engaging diversity in religions properly is central to peace and unity and there have been many efforts to explain these differences. Some have said that religions are like different fingers pointing at the same moon. Others have said the religions are like many paths up the same mountain. These metaphors have been challenged by those who suggest we are in fact pointing at different moons or perhaps climbing different mountains!

Gandhi held that there is one Truth (which he believed was in fact God) and that each religion offers some insights into the one Truth. It was his conviction that to gain even a glimpse of truth, one must learn from all religions.

Some people take a narrower view, claiming that only one religion (usually theirs) is true and that the others are false. Others explain the differences between religions by maintaining that there is one revelation that is received differently by different cultures. Some suggest that religious differences reflect the ways people hear the same thing differently (the proverbial telephone game).

Whatever the approach to the diversity of religions, it is clear to anyone who has studied religions that there exists differing and even seemingly contradictory beliefs, as well as a wide variety of rituals, laws and positions on moral and social questions.

In this chapter we are going to examine some of these differences. We will begin with a discussion of the different approaches to God in various religions. Then we will compare religious beliefs regarding ritual and the afterlife. Next will be a discussion of some of the different approaches to the diversity of religions: the exclusive, inclusive and pluralistic and others. Finally, we will discuss interfaith dialogue as a way of dealing with religious diversity and perhaps even benefiting from it.

Diverse Approaches to God

As we have discussed, the purpose of religion seems intent on putting humans in touch with some kind of ultimate reality. This ultimate reality has been described in manifold ways and metaphors. Some religions describe the divine as spirits that dwell in nature, as in Japanese Shinto and in the Native American religions. For others, the ultimate is a state of freedom and enlightenment as in Buddhism and Jainism. Some religions speak in terms of personalities and refer to gods and goddesses, as in Hinduism, Taoism and the ancient Roman and Greek religions. And then there are the religions of Judaism, Christianity and Islam that hold that God is One, a creator and all-powerful personal Being. Some religions accent the "beyondness" or transcendence of God, while others stress the "withinness" or immanence of God. Some stress that God is within all, others believe that all is within God. And even though religions can be placed in various categories with regard their approach to God, each religion has its own unique characterization of the ultimate. The recurring question, of course, is: do all these depictions somehow refer to the same ultimate reality, or are there in fact a number of contrasting ultimates competing for human attention?

Religions Emerge

Scholars appear to have moved beyond trying to discover the origins of religions. The 19th century approach (often carried on from armchairs) of seeing early religions as "primitive" expressions of inferior humans has been abandoned. Limiting such early religion to "animism" (attributing spirits to animals) or "totemism" (religion as a binding force in early societies) has also been largely set aside.

Most scholars today recognize that religion is a universal phenomenon in the history of humankind. Karen Armstrong, a leading authority on religion, points out that "The desire to cultivate a sense of the transcendent may be the defining human characteristic."[1] At the same time, scholars admit that we in fact know very little about the beginnings of religion, largely because most the earliest evidence of religion has been swallowed by the sands of time.

Some of the earliest indications that "homo sapiens" might also have been "homo religiosus" are the hundreds of decorated caves in Southern France and Northern Spain. Some of these cave date back to 30,000 BCE and depict images of the humans trying to relate to animals. Many of these caves seem to be sacred places where rituals were celebrated by shamans. Similar sites have been discovered from the Stone Age in Siberia, Australia and the Americas. We can only speculate about what the many images mean at these sites, but they do seem to indicate a religious inclination in the first humans. From the beginning, humans seem to have struggled to reach beyond themselves to a power or energy that links them to nature and animals, as well as to the phenomena in the heavens, the stars, moon and sun.

By 4,500 BCE the evidence of religion becomes more specific. At this time, the ancient Indo-Aryan migrating tribes honored a force within themselves and all other reality—a pervasive "Spirit." Eventually, "Beings" were recognized that were spiritual and superior and these were called gods. When the Aryans settled into India, their traditions united with that culture and the notion of Brahman emerged, an unseen principle that transcended all and held all together.[2] This marked the beginning of the "Sanatana Dharma," the Eternal Law, whereby the impersonal Brahman is manifested through countless gods and goddesses. Technically, Brahman is not really a god. "Unlike the gods, who have personalities and ways of operating on their own, Brahman is better thought of as a unifying principle, a principle that animates the entire universe with its power."[3] Brahman is the source and foundation of all that exists and is present in everything. Brahman transcends all, is within all and liberates all.[4] Through intercession of the manifold deities, the faithful are able to commune with Brahman and receive blessings. A trinity of gods represents Brahman and the three dynamic forces in reality: Brahma is the Creator, Vishnu the Preserver, and Shiva is the Destroyer. There are also favorite "avatars" (incarnations of the gods) among the Hindus: Krishna, an avatar of Vishnu and Ganesha, an avatar of Shiva.

Buddhism, which seems to be in part a reaction to the countless gods and goddesses of the Hindu tradition, bypassed all god-talk. In the earliest Buddhism, Theravada, there is such a strong belief in causality that it is impossible to think of an uncaused God. Moreover, Buddhists reject the notion of a divinity who creates and controls the universe, since this would interfere with individual freedom and well as personal responsibility for one's own Karma.[5] Buddhists believe that all suffering comes from human clinging to impermanent things as though they were enduring. One can be liberated from suffering through living a righteous life and through meditation. Here there is no need for divine intervention of grace in order to be enlightened and liberated. The ultimate goal, then, is not for the individual to be united with God, but rather the elimination of the self and its desires. It is only in the later Mahayana Buddhism that the Buddha comes to be viewed as a divine being. In some traditions, Buddha is looked upon as divine and there are many Buddhas.[6]

Jainism, which began in India around the same time as Buddhism, similarly does not concern itself with God. While not atheistic, Jains believe that since the universe is an eternal and endless process there is no need to posit a God who is a creator or sustainer. For Jains, the "divine" has more to do with the liberation of the self and recovery of the "supreme self," which entails uniting with the divine essence that is in all things.[7] The ultimate here, rather than being some transcendent reality, becomes Nirvana, a state of peace, freedom and truth.

The Jewish God

As we move from the Indic world of gods, goddesses and the no-self to the Semitic World, notions of the divine change. The story of the people of Israel is that of a group of people who at one point see God as many but constantly struggle to answering to see God a as One. In Genesis, we see the Hebrews struggling with the image of a benign God who creates and walks with them in the cool of the evening, and yet one who casts them out for their sins. At the time of the flood, this benign creator god becomes a vindictive god of mass destruction. At one point, the divine includes images such as the golden calf, Baal and the feminine Ishtar.[8] The Hebrews see their god as one who ruthlessly destroys their enemies and saves them from captivity and harm. God nourishes his people, with whom he made a covenant, in the desert and accompanies them in their suffering. God harshly punishes them for their return to other gods and for their infidelity and lack of trust. At one point, this God is one who lives in a Temple and is appeased by sacrifice. At another, this God is one who cannot be confined to Temple or manipulated by sacrifices. He is a god who cannot be seen, and yet can be felt as a presence. At times He supports violence and vindication; conversely He supports justice, non-violence and toleration.

What ultimately emerges in Judaism is not a god that can be understood by facts or human reason. As the great Jewish thinker Jacob Neusner points out, "The knowledge of God that Judaism sets forth derives not from humanity's reasoning about what it knows, but from God's making manifest what only God knows—and wants us to know too. And for Judaism, God's self-manifestation takes place in the Torah."[9] Ultimately this God is one, a divine Creator, a divine presence, a personal being who can be addressed in prayer, a divinity who can be known and imitated. This Oneness, which seems to have gelled during the Babylonian Captivity, has prevailed in Judaism.[10] This is the Divine One, whose divinity cannot be shared by anyone or anything.

The Christian God

The God of Israel is also the Christian God, but with one radical difference. The Christian God is a trinity of persons, the Father Creator, the Son who becomes incarnated in Jesus Christ and the Spirit who enlivens, inspires and transforms.

The God of Christianity can become human, incarnated, and walks the earth as Jesus the Christ. The God of Christianity can share the life of grace and holiness with human beings and be a presence in nature as well as in holy writings and sacraments.

The Christian God has been described through conciliar and papal announcements and is often a God of orthodoxy and cognition. This God has been pursued through the great theological work of giants like Augustine, Aquinas and Bonaventure, each presenting varying theologies of God. Mystics have pursued God in the realms of contemplation, in the experience of "nothingness," "unknowing" and "centering." The great Francis searched for God in poverty; Anselm decided that God was the greatest thought that could be conceived; and Aquinas decided that next to his personal experience of God, all his research and writing about God was as so much "straw." The Deists put God high in the heavens, unconcerned and uninvolved. Devotees of the Enlightenment held that their God could be discovered through clear reason and science. Romantics were convinced that God could only be encountered in nature.

Christians have had a checkered history with their God. In his name, they have set out on Crusades to slaughter thousands of Jews and Muslims to regain the "Holyland." For His sake, they have fought wars among themselves, burned and excommunicated those believed to be in error. They have attempted to enclose his voice and authority in the Vatican. At the same time, Christians have served the poor and the helpless in the name of Jesus and given themselves for social justice and peace. In his name, they have empowered the laity and raised women to be priests and bishops. Quakers have listened for his voice in the silence of their meetings. Pentecostals have awaited his gifts and movement in their singing and praise. Missionaries have spread His word to the far corners of the world.

The God of Islam

Muslims believe that God (Allah) revealed himself for the final time to the Prophet Muhammad over a period of 23 years. These revelations have been collected in the Qur'an and are believed to be the exact words of God in Arabic.

The final self-revelation of God stands as a corrective to the divine revelations which supposedly were corrupted by Judaism and Christianity. Allah is the creator-God, the sustainer of the universe who can be known through the natural world. The Qur'an says: "Is not He who created the heaven and the earth, able to create the like of them [humans]? Yes, indeed; He is the All-Creator, the All-knowing. His command, when he desires a thing, is to say to it 'Be,' and it is. So glory be to Him, in whose hand is the dominion of everything and unto whom you shall be returned."[11]

For a time, Muhammad's mission to spread his revelation was successful because he had not yet insisted the Quraysh tribe stop worshipping the other Arabian deities. Once the prophet began to insist that his people worship only one God, Allah, and stop worshipping other gods, he lost many of his supporters and the tribe began to split over this teaching. The leaders of the city of Mecca saw this monotheism as a major threat to their ancient traditions, as well as to the important of their shrine at the Kaba.[12]

Muhammad was trying to convert his people from polytheism to monotheism in just a few decades, whereas it had taken the Jews many centuries after Moses to come to a conclusive monotheism.[13] Allah, and Allah alone, was the head the tribe and was the only God who could provide the protection and help that the people needed. The other gods and goddesses had no power to rely on. The famous Sura of Sincerity (Sura 112), still used in the Muslim daily prayers, says this clearly: "Say: 'He is God, One God, the Everlasting Refuge, who had not begotten, and has not been begotten, and equal to Him is not anyone." Muhammad's mission was no easy matter and he was looked upon as a heretic and an outcast. His life and the lives of his followers were in jeopardy and they would have to move to Medina.

Muhammad sees the revelation he received about God as a final reforming of the God revealed in Judaism and Christianity. This conclusive revelation stands as a corrective to the Judaic tradition which relapsed into polytheism for centuries before it became secure with monotheism. Islam also claims to hold up a God who is knowable only through symbols and does not come across with the personal vindictiveness or even cruelty of the Hebrew God. Islam also believes that their notion of Allah excludes any Christian notion of Trinity or the Incarnation of the Son of God who is thus divine. Both of these beliefs are regarded by the Muslims to be in opposition to the Oneness of God.

The God of Islam is One to be experienced in nature, in the reading of the Qur'an and in mystical experience.[14] The fact that Allah is all-knowing and all-powerful has raised challenging questions for Muslim theologians with regard the problem of evil and the notion of human freedom. There is no original sin in Islam, which makes the explanation of evil even more problematic. Allah is completely in charge and His infinite power and actions are completely beyond human understanding. At the same time, no matter what the human predicament, humans can count on God being compassionate and forgiving. Their responsibility is to live good and faithful lives, always in obedient submission and service to Allah. The Qur'an says, "And remember God's blessing upon you, and his compact which He made with you when you said: 'We have heard and we obey.' And fear you God, surely God knows the secrets of your heart."[15] Allah created all at the beginning of time, continues to create and at the end of time will gather the world and all human souls back to Himself. This God had 99 beautiful names, including The Holy, Pure and Perfect; The Peace, the Source of Peace and Safety, the Savior; The Utterly Just: The Gentle, the Subtly Kind; The Destroyer, Bringer of Death and The Avenger. Above all, Allah is known for his basic characteristics of Justice, power and mercy.

Many Gods

In early religions it was more common to believe in many gods and goddesses. Caves from the Neolithic period in France and Turkey display drawings and small statues that may have represented rituals to gods and goddesses. During the 19th and 20th centuries, scholars thought these were products of primitive and inferior cultures, but today much more human sophistication is attributed to these cultures.[16] The 16th century works of Catholic missionaries reveal extremely advanced cultures and religions among the "primitive" Aztec, Mayan and Inca people. Magnificent temples, elaborate rituals and complicated hierarchies of gods and goddesses existed in these cultures.19th century scholarship about the aboriginal Australians maintained that these cultures were elemental and godless, but modern scholarship reveals that these people had quite sophisticated beliefs in deities and a Supreme being.[17]

A great scholar of religion, Mircea Eliade (1907-1986) maintained that the original Australians believed that the world, man and animals were created by Supreme Beings. He also identified well-developed beliefs in High Gods in South America and Africa. Beliefs in such High Gods have also been discovered among the religions of the North American tribes.[18]

The many thousands of tablets in cuneiform script have revealed a great deal about religion in the ancient culture of Sumer from 3,000 BCE. Like the ancient cultures of Mexico and South America, this was a well-advanced temple culture with a priesthood, advanced rituals and well-defined festivals. In all of these cultures there was a well-developed hierarchy of gods and goddesses. In Sumer, the three main gods were An, Enlil and Enki. An's consort was Ninmah, the Mother Goddess. There were gods of Storms, Wind and Sun. Ishtar, the goddess of War, Rain and Carnal love played a role in the Semitic pantheon but was set aside as the Israelites became committed to monotheism.

The ancient religion of Sumer bore influence on the religions of Egypt, Greece and even Israel. In Egypt, the Creator God was called Ra and he was the father of all the gods, who came to be associated with the Sun. Thoth was the moon God and Amun the patron God of the pharaohs. Over time, an immense pantheon of gods and goddesses evolved in Egypt and became the models for many of the Greek gods.

In Greece, Zeus, the son of Cronus and Rhea was the High God. Other children of Cronus ruled the universe: Hades and wife Persephone ruled the underworld, and Poseidon ruled the oceans.

Eliade points out that the high divinities were often pushed into the background and replaced with gods that were more like humans—gods with foibles who could be more easily persuaded to give favors through sacrifices. Such gods tend to be more involved in human life than the One God who can remain distant and, while all-powerful, not seem to intervene to save people from evil. Still, one or another version of monotheism has prevailed in Judaism, Christianity, Islam and Sikhism.

The oriental religions have also preferred to believe in many gods. Shinto, which is of Japanese origin, has the myths of Kojiki which are creation myths telling how Japan was created by the deities as a sacred land. The imperial families are supposedly descendants of these deities and thus rule by divine right. Kamis are heavenly deities that descended from the eternal universe and created Japan and its people. The kamis now dwell as spirits in the sea, the wind, trees, flowers and rain.

Shinto is indeed the "way of the kamis." Kami is difficult to define, but it has been well-described by the great Shinto scholar, Motoori Norinaga: "Kami signifies in the first place deities of heaven and earth that appear in the ancient records and also spirits of the shrines where they are worshipped.... Eminence here does not refer merely to objects as birds, beasts, trees, plants, seas, mountains and so forth. In ancient usage anything whatsoever which is outside the ordinary, which possesses superior power or which is awe-inspiring is called kami."[19] One thinks here of the emphasis on "indwelling spirits" that has been made in so many of the Native American religions.

Another oriental religion is Taoism, which is still quite influential in China. "Tao" means "path" or "way" and has several connotations. It can mean the "path" of proper living or the path to immortality. More broadly it refers to the mysterious power that links the entire universe. The true path for humans is to be linked with this power which is perfect and eternal, flowing in every person and indeed in all things. It is the very energy that transforms the world as it cycles back and forth between the yin and yang. The power of this energy of all things is described as follows: "The Way gives birth to them, nourishes them, matures them, completes them, rests them, supports them and protects them. It gives birth to them, but doesn't try to own them; it acts on their behalf but doesn't make them dependent; it matures them but doesn't rule them."[20]

Taoism also recognized many deities. The three highest are The Three Purities, who emanate from the Tao and are omnipresent. There are also heavenly Emperors and Goddesses who rule the universe, bless, pardon sins and protect from disasters. Certain rivers and mountains have their own deities.

Differing Views of the Afterlife

Humans seem to be driven to seek immortality, through world records, championships, publications, inventions, buildings, one's children and even in life eternal. Religions differ widely in their beliefs regarding life after death, ranging from the Hindu-Buddhist traditions of rebirth and the Christian belief in individual resurrection, to the common Jewish belief in survival in memory and descendants.

Burial of the dead is limited to humans alone. There is evidence from the Stone Age that ritual food and materials were buried with individuals, a possible indication of some belief in afterlife. Practices of mummification in Egypt as well as among the Incas of Peru indicate an effort to preserve the individual for some future journey. The Incas often treated mummies as though they were alive, offering them food and drink and even bringing them to council meetings for consultation.[21]

In many of the traditions that began in India, there is a belief in rebirth after death. In some of the Hindu traditions, the atman, or the inner self of all humans, is linked with the Ultimate, Brahman. Depending on karma, one moves backwards or forwards toward oneness with the Ultimate. As the Upanishads puts it, "As one acts and as one behaves, so one becomes."[22] The ultimate goal is to be united with Brahman, no longer caught up in the endless cycle of deaths and rebirths. A virtuous life free from desires leads to moksha, or liberation and union with the Absolute.

Buddha's enlightened way moves away from Hindu entanglement with gods and goddesses and the endless cycle of rebirths. Buddha teaches that each person is the architect of his or her own consciousness. Through rigorous meditation and a life dedicated to right living characterized by love and compassion, a person can achieve liberation from rebirth and the nirvana of happiness. In some Buddhist traditions, there are various hells that one might experience between rebirths, but these are temporary.

Beliefs in afterlife are diverse in the Jewish tradition. The earliest tradition taught that the dead live in a kind of shadowy existence beneath the earth (sheol). Later there is evidence of praying for the dead and the belief in resurrection of the dead in the endtime. Today, many Orthodox Jews believe in bodily resurrection in the endtime. The beliefs of Reform Jews range from a living-on of the spirit to humans continuing on in memory of their accomplishments or through their children.

Christians base their belief in afterlife on the resurrection of their founder Jesus. Mainly, this is a belief in bodily resurrection, albeit a "spiritual body." There is ambiguity as to whether final resurrection is immediately after death on in the endtime. Christians posit a hell for those who die unrepentant. Traditionally this has been a result of condemnation by God, but more recently this is described as depending on human choice.

Beliefs in afterlife differ even among Christians. Some see the resurrection of Jesus as the resuscitation and expect the same for themselves, if not immediately after death, at the endtime, or the time of the "final judgment." Others view his resurrection to be a spiritual event, which they too can expect after death if they have been faithful. Some see hell as God's punishment for all eternity. Others view hell as a choice and one that is perhaps not irrevocable.

Shinto varies in its beliefs with regards to afterlife. In some traditions, life after death is nothing more than existence in a dark underworld. Other traditions, influenced by Buddhism, hold for rewards after death depending on one's karma. During WWII, the so-called suicide pilots on Japan (kamikaze) believed that they would share in divinity by dying for the Emperor.

The Taoism funeral is interesting and indicates their mindset with regards to afterlife. A priest is engaged to pray, offer sacrifices, and plead for forgiveness of the deceased. Here the priest hopes to light the way of the dead person through "the Land of Darkness" to the light where the spirit might flourish.

A Diversity of Rituals

Ritual is integral to religion, an essential religious "work" for gathering the community, expressing beliefs in symbols, and celebrating events. Each religion has a wide variety of rituals and the diversity among the rituals of religions is another way of getting in touch with the differences among religions.

As prehistoric caves and archeological digs reveal, ritual has always been integral of to religion. The many Stone Age caves at Lascaux, France, dating back 17,000 years ago, with their hundreds of wall drawings and over a thousand engravings indicate early ritualistic activities. In addition, Shaman ritualistic activity has been detected in the Paleolithic period in Africa and Europe, and during later periods in America and Australia.

The early Hindu Vedas seem to have their origin in ritual; these are songs and melodies. In this tradition the gods and goddesses were quite active. Those devoted to the eternal tradition believed that through ritual sacrifices they could participate in the work of the deities. Early rituals were around blazing fires, honoring Agni, the god of fire, and sacrificing hundreds of valuable animals to the gods, praying for protection and prosperity.

Today, visitors to Varanasi, India, can witness once again these fire ceremonies (without animal sacrifices) honoring Mother Ganges. In Hindu temples throughout the world there are colorful ceremonies with songs and dance honoring the various gods and goddesses. Simpler rituals are celebrated at home altars. Yoga exercises are also common among Hindus and are practiced as a meditation and a means of coming close to god.

The Jains, since they do not honor a god, gather for devotional services where they honor those who have become deified by reaching nirvana. They make offerings of flowers, rice, incense, sweets, fruit and water to statues of these individuals, praying for blessings on their own lives. Jains also value reciting mantras—words and phrases that are charged with power to pay homage and even obtain cures. These mantras are often addressed to great teachers, souls who have been liberated, and monks and nuns who have been inspiring spiritual leaders.

Sikhism, a religion of India that was founded by the visionary Nanak in 15th century Punjab, has unique rituals in their temples. The gathering around their scriptures (Guru Granth Sahib) which is a collection of the revelations to Nanak and others, to listen to the singing of these sacred writings and be in touch with the name of their God. The book is solemnly carried from its special room, where it resides as though it were a person. Adjoining the temple is a large kitchen and dining area where all are welcome to be fed. In the Golden Temple in Amritsar, India, nearly 40,000 people are fed each day; all part of the Sikh vow to serve others.

Since Buddhists do not worship gods or goddesses, their rituals take other forms, such as pilgrimages to holy places like Buddha's birthplace, Lumbini, or the place where he was enlightened, Bodh Gaya. They also visit immense stupas which contain relics of the Buddha and large statues of the Buddha, where they can be inspired to follow his teachings. Of course, the central ritual for Buddhists is meditation, wherein they construct their own consciousnesses and root out toxic thoughts and attachments.

Judaism's ritual became formalized with the building of the first temple by Solomon around 950 BCE. Temple became the place for the sacrifice of animals as a means of praising the Creator. The Temple of Judah was destroyed in 586 BCE by the Babylonians and rebuilt in 515 BCE after the Babylonian Captivity, only to be destroyed again in 70 CE by the Romans. After that destruction, Judaism moved into its rabbinic period. The synagogue model of learning and prayer that had developed among dispersed Jews would prevail. No longer would there be priests or altar sacrifices. Self-sacrifice for others would now replace the sacrifice of animals and the praise and blessing of God in his sacred presence would be central for Jews. Jacob Neusner puts it this way: "To be a Jew in the classical tradition, one lives his or her life constantly aware of the presence of God and always ready to praise and bless God."[23]

Today Sabbath (sunset Friday to sunset Saturday) is the sacred time for Jews to worship and home and synagogue. Key feasts are also celebrated: Passover, commemorating the exodus from slavery in Egypt, and the High Holy Days of Rosh Hashanah, the Jewish New Year, and Yom Kippur, the Day of Atonement.

Christians began with simple rituals: water baptism as an initiation rite, and the "breaking of the bread" to commemorate Jesus' last supper with his disciples. Eventually a number of other sacraments evolved: Confirmation to later confirm those baptized as infants, Penance for forgiveness of sin, Marriage for the bonding of couples, Orders for the ordination of ministers, and the Anointing for the sick and dying. During the Reformation in the 16th century, Protestants opted for only two sacraments, baptism and eucharist, while Catholics maintained the seven.

For Catholics, the Mass is the central ritual. It is a service which features reading from scripture, a sermon, prayers, an offering of bread and wine, consecration and then communion. For many Protestants the service primarily consists of the readings of scripture, preaching and prayers, with communion on occasion. Significant feasts for Christians are Christmas, the celebration of Jesus' birth, and Easter, the commemoration of his resurrection.

One of the five pillars of Islam is ritual prayer (*salat*). Muslims are required to pray in mosques or on their own five times a day to praise their God, Allah, and listen to the words of the Qur'an, their sacred book. They are also required to celebrate Ramadan, a month-long time for fasting and penance designed to help them become more aware of their blessings and move them to share with the needy. Once during their lifetime, Muslims are expected to make a 12 day pilgrimage to Mecca, the center of Islam.

Oriental religions also have unique rituals. There is a saying in Japan that a person is born a Shinto and dies as a Buddhist. By this is meant that the elaborate Shinto ceremonies around birth are highly valued, but the funeral rites of the Buddhists are preferred to those of Shinto. The Shinto birth ritual involves the community gathering at the local shrine to wash and welcome the newborn and to celebrate with a special meal. Shinto shrines are often in natural settings, where the kami (spirits) are thought to dwell and each shrine honors its one particular deity. The ritual begins with a purification of the hands and mouth with water. (Cleanliness is a key value for the Shinto religion.) Then a bell is rung to ask the local deity for favors and give thanks for blessings, followed by dropping coins in an offering box. One then bows twice, claps twice to alert the spirit, and then bows once more. Prayers are then led by the Shinto priests. At the end, one signs the register and takes home some small item for remembrance.

There are a number of magnificent Taoist temples on mountain tops or even carved into the sides of mountains in China, many of them restored after religious freedom was granted. The followers of Taoism usually precede their temple ceremonies with a month-long purification period for fasting, meditation and cleansing from sin. Then the people gather at the local temple, where the priest summons the gods as well as the much-revered ancestors. Texts are read and offerings are made for sins, and prayers are recited for forgiveness and healing. A large community banquet follows to celebrate the blessings of the cosmos.

Among the Native American tribes, especially the Plains tribes, the Sun Dance was a common ritual. This was an elaborate summer ritual of prayers and dances for the renewal of the tribe, successful future plans, fertility of the land and protection of the people from dangers and diseases. This was a key time for the clans to unite, renew old relationships and catch up on tribal news.

This wide array of rituals further exemplifies the diversity of religions. In a sense, "by their rituals you shall know them." Rituals indicate whether a religion recognizes many gods, one god or no god at all. Rituals indicate the mindset of the practitioners whether it be to appease, petition, praise, give thanks or ask forgiveness and healing. In cases where there is no gods involved (Jainism, Buddhism), the rituals are more for self-purification, enlightenment or the honoring of those who have been liberated. Rituals are outward signs of inward dispositions and their study tells us a great deal about the beliefs and intentions of each religion's followers. Much of the "truth" of each religion can be learned by studying and, more importantly, participating in its rituals.

Religious Approaches to Diversity

There are a number of approaches today to deal with the diversity of religions. The exclusive approaches generally views one's own religion or one's own division of a religion as true to the exclusion of others. Inclusive approaches attempt to include other religions as being true and salvific. Pluralistic approaches tend to view all religions on the same level with regard to truth and salvation claims. As you read the explanation of each of these approaches, you might reflect which one is the closest to the one you learned with your family and its religious community, and which approach you'd most like to follow.

Exclusive Approach

Those following the exclusive approach to other religions might say:

"My religion is the one true religion and the others are simply false." From early on, Romans rejected Christians for their refusal to accept the imperial gods while Jews rejected Christians for the deification of Jesus. Early

Christians referred to those who believed in other religions as "heathens" or "pagans" and called those who held false beliefs within the Christian tradition "heretics"; they often excommunicated such believers, excluding them from the true community. The Christian pilgrims in America and later the European Christians viewed the Native Americans as pagans.

Exclusivists can even take a hostile attitude toward those who believe in other religions. The Israelites came to reject the Canaanites, the Philistines, the followers of Baal and other groups as pagans believing in of false and idolatrous religions. Conflicts arose among Israelites themselves over the worship of "other gods." Christians were persecuted and even executed by the Romans in part because Christians did not recognize the divinity of the Emperor or the legitimacy of the Roman gods. Once Christianity became the official religion of the Empire in the 4th century, Christians began their own systematic destruction of "pagan" religions and persecuted pagan believers. When Islam came into its ascendency in the 8th and 9th centuries, it overran the territories that had been Christian and dominated and at times persecuted them. In the medieval period, Christians carried out brutal Crusades against the Muslims and Jews in the Holy Land. During the same period, Inquisitions were established to imprison or burn heretics at the stake. After the Protestant Reformation in the 16th century, brutal wars were fought between Catholics and Protestants. During that same period, the Spanish Conquistadors fought to destroy the Aztec, Mayan and Inca religions. For centuries, Europeans felt justified in annihilating the Native American "heathens" and confiscating their lands.

Today conflicts still erupt between religions; Catholics and Protestants fight in Ireland, Muslims and Christians fight in Sudan and Egypt and Bosnia, Jews and Muslims fight in Israel. Since 9/11 there has been antipathy in the United States toward Muslims and even Sikhs, who are often mistaken for Muslims.

Within religions themselves there is often an exclusive tendency. There is an on-going tension among the many sects within Hinduism. Shiite and Shia Muslims regularly clash over the legitimacy of their leadership and the Sufis struggle for recognition within Islam. Theravada and Mahayana Buddhists clash over the legitimacy of their individual teachings of the Buddha. Followers of Confucius debate whether their tradition is a set of ethics or actually a religion. Legitimacy has been debated by Jews; early on, the northern and southern kingdoms were in conflict, the Essenes rejected Jerusalem's tradition, and there were factions in Jerusalem itself between the Pharisees, Sadducees and Zealots. Today, legitimacy is highly debated among

Orthodox, Conservative, Reform and Reconstructionist Jews.

Exclusivity has also been a characteristic of the Christian tradition. Early on Christians remained part of the Jewish faith, but with the work of Paul the apostle and the destruction of Jerusalem by the Romans, Christianity became largely a Gentile (non-Jew) movement. From that time on, part of the Christian mission was to convert everyone possible to Christianity, the religion that "saved." In the early centuries, communities that were designated as Arian, Gnostic, Nestorian, etc. were condemned as heretical. The Celtic tradition was rejected by the Roman tradition; the Eastern and Western churches separated in the 11th century; Protestant, Anglican and Catholic churches separated during the Reformation; and in the following centuries there has been many divisions among the Protestant traditions, ranging from mainline churches (Lutheran, Presbyterian, Methodist, Baptist, Congregational and others) to the Quakers, Evangelicals, Pentecostals, Amish and Mennonites, to mention only a few.

An expression, "Outside the Church there is no salvation," became part of the Catholic Church's tradition. The necessity of baptism into the church for salvation had been taught by such greats as Augustine and Aquinas. No salvation outside the church was proclaimed by Pope Innocent in 1208 and taught by the Fourth Lateran Council in 1215, the Council of Florence in 1442 and by other Popes as late as Pius IX in 1863.[24]

The only hope for those outside the church was "baptism of desire," which meant that those who did not know about the truth of the church and who led good lives could be saved. Many Catholics living in the United States, where so-called "mixed marriages" existed between Protestants and Catholics remember being challenged by this belief. How could their Protestant parent or grandparent, who were devout believers and even more dedicated to the Bible than their Catholic parent not be saved? Something had to be wrong about this belief!

This whole issue came to a head in the United States when a charismatic Jesuit, Father Leonard Feeney, who worked with zealous young Catholics in Cambridge, Massachusetts at St. Benedict Center, took all this teaching very seriously. Fr. Feeney took the position that he believed that most people would not be saved, and that most certainly those outside the Roman Catholic Church had no chance for salvation. He said: "Saying first that there is no salvation outside the Church, and then adding that sincerity outside the Church is salvation within the Church, is the most diabolical double-talk ever to be uttered in the name of religious teaching."[25] It was Feeney's conviction that those who disagreed with him, including Archbishop

Cushing of Boston, were heretics.

Another exclusivist approach to "other" religions is to simply ignore them as false and irrelevant. Generally, Christians know little about other religions or even about other denominations in their own religion. Ask most Christians what they know about other religions, and you will often hear only vague notions and stereotypes. Even those studying at Christian universities rarely learn about world religions or have opportunities to worship in the temples, mosques or synagogues of other religions. This same lack of understanding of other religions exists throughout the world. In visiting other countries one finds that most Buddhists, Muslims, Jews, Hindus, Jains, Sikhs, etc. know little or nothing about any religions other than their own.

Exclusive religions often take a mission approach to the followers of other religions. Christians attempt to convert others to the true faith so that they will be "saved" from their false faith and brought into the true fold. Evangelicals often use the media or "crusades" to make converts to Christianity. Buddhism has spread their truth to Japan, China, South Asia and many other areas. Early on, Muslims established an enormous empire, hoping to spread the truth that is Islam to the world.

Inclusive Approach

The Christian churches took an important step toward inclusivity in 1948 when the World Council of Churches was established. The WCC is a world-wide fellowship of 349 churches in more than 110 countries and seeks Christian unity in faith and worship, and the promotion of peace, justice, and ecology around the world.

The Parliament of World Religions has made a major contribution to unity among the different faiths around the globe. The Parliament held its first meeting Chicago in 1893 and in recent times has met in Capetown, South Africa (1999), Barcelona, Spain (2004), Monterrey Mexico (2007) and in Melbourne, Australia (2009), where over 10,000 people representing most of the world's religions gathered. The Parliament's vision includes respect, understanding and harmony among the religions of the world, to promote the common good and concern for the earth.

The Alliance of Religions for Conservation was established in 1995 by Prince Philip of England. The Alliance includes 11 different religions and each has committed to put together a 7 year plan that links its most treasured beliefs with efforts to conserve the earth and its resources. The vitality and efforts of the Alliance have been most impressive. For instance, in October

2012 eleven holy towns and cities in India came together to launch the India chapter of the international Green Pilgrimage Network. In September of the same year, the ARC held a major celebration in Nairobi, Kenya to launch 26 eco commitments by Christian, Muslim and Hindu traditions. It was said to have been the biggest civil society movement on climate change the Continent has seen.

Catholics and Inclusivity

The Catholic Church attempted to be more inclusive in 1949 when Pope XII answered the position cited earlier by Fr. Feeney that those outside the church could not be saved. The Pontiff pointed out that while Jesus established the church as a means of salvation that does not mean that all must belong to the church. Those outside the church can desire the means that the church has for salvation and therefore can be saved, even when this desire is implicit. In the same letter, Pius XII' s teaching on the mystical body of Christ were reiterated: even though only Catholics belonged to the mystical body of Christ and thereby had access to salvation, those who are even unconsciously ordained to the mystical body could also be saved. Pius also taught that while is not true that one can be saved "equally well in any religion," an implicit desire for the means of salvation, along with charity and faith, is sufficient for salvation.[26]

Vatican II made considerable advances on the issue of the salvation of those outside the Church. Protestant communities were recognized to be ecclesial communities and those in schism, such as the Orthodox faiths, were considered to be churches. The latter are joined with the Catholic Church "in the Holy Spirit," and receive God's gifts and graces and are "by no means deprived of significance and importance in the mystery of salvation." These other Christian communities were also thought to be used by Christ as a means of salvation.[27] Vatican II no longer exclusively identified the Roman Catholic Church with the Church, but instead taught that the "the Church of Christ subsisted in the Roman Catholic Church" (*Lumen Gentium*, §8). This seems to open the way for the Church of Christ to exist in other Christian communities as well. It was no longer maintained that non-Catholics must have an implicit desire to belong to the Catholic Church to be saved. Rather they belonged to communities with their own truth as well as the means for salvation.

Vatican II also attempted to include religions outside of Christianity in its vision of salvation. The Council pointed out that all people are indeed related to the Church (the People of God) by virtue of their being children of God. Jews are related to the Church in that they were the first to be given the covenant from God and are dear to God. Muslims share in salvation in that they acknowledge God the Creator, profess the faith of Abraham and adore the one and merciful God.

Finally, the Council opened its arms to all people, in that God wills all to be saved. It acknowledges that God is near to those who seek the unknown God, people both in and outside of religion. God's truth and goodness exists everywhere. In the most inclusive statement yet made by the Church, it proclaimed: "Those also can attain salvation who through no fault of their own do not know the gospel of Jesus Christ or his church, yet sincerely seek God and, moved by grace, strive by their deeds to do His will as it is known to them through the dictates of conscience."[28]

There has been much theological discussion since the Council about the salvation of those in other religions. Even though many religions such Hinduism, Buddhism, Jainism, Shinto, Taoism, as well as the religions of Africa and the Native Americans don't seem to be explicitly concerned about "salvation," Catholics are concerned about saving them. It is doubtful whether these religions are impressed by the Church's statement that they have truth and goodness (albeit not in the fullness that the Church has) and that God loves them and wants to save them. As we have seen, they are more often concerned with liberation or with being in union with the ultimate principle, energy or spirit. One also must wonder how other religions react to statements by the Church that it has the Truth while they have a ray of that truth. It must seem quizzical to them when they hear the Church say that it possesses the Word, while other religions have a "seed of the Word," or that their religions have serve as a "preparation for the gospel."[29]

Many members of other religions and indeed Catholics also were distressed at the Karl Rahner's proposal regarding "the anonymous Christian." Rahner, perhaps the greatest theologian of the 20th century, took the position that the grace for salvation is only the grace of Christ, of which the Church of Christ is the mediator. For Rahner, Jesus Christ is the only mediator of salvation. At the same time, he insists that God wants all to be saved. The way to salvation is to freely in faith respond to God's offer of salvation. Rahner concludes that each person's response to that offer is in fact a response to the grace of Jesus Christ, whether he or she knows it or not. They are in fact, then, in their response, "anonymous Christians."[30] Needless to say, the phrase was considered by many to be an unfortunate, kind of patronizing comment to those in other religions, as well as deflating to missionaries and their mission to convert others to the true faith.

In the years following the Vatican Council, ecumenical and interfaith dialogue was encouraged and there was a new closeness among religions. Paul VI reached out to many churches and religions, including those of India and Africa. Still, he largely looked at other religions as "man-made" and did not seem to acknowledge that they had saving power of their own.[31]

John Paul II was extremely dedicated to dialogue with other churches and religions and was widely respected by Jewish leaders. He acknowledged the truth and goodness in other religions, as well as the work of the Spirit in them.[32] In 1986, he organized a historic Day of Prayer for Peace in Assisi, which included representatives of most churches and religions. Still, in his official writings, John Paul II insisted that Jesus Christ is "at the center of God's plan for salvation," and maintained that at best other religions have "participated forms of mediation." The latter, of course, only find meaning and value through the mediation of Jesus Christ.[33]

In 2000 the Vatican published a document on "the unicity and salvific universality of Jesus Christ and the Church,"[34] which received a great deal of attention both inside and outside Catholicism. This document made it quite clear the revelation of Jesus Christ is both full and definitive, and not complementary to the truths of other religions. Only the Old and New Testaments are inspired, while the goodness and grace in the texts of other religions are gained "from the mystery of Christ." Jesus alone is the mediator and universal redeemer and his significance and value for the human race is "unique and singular, proper to him alone, exclusive, universal and absolute." There is only one Church of Christ and therefore the "ecclesial communities" that have not preserved the valid episcopate or the genuine eucharist and not churches in the proper sense. Nor, as some have suggested, is the "kingdom of God" be detached from Christ or the Church. Equality in dialogue is personal equality, not equality of doctrine or the equality of other religious founders with Jesus.[35]

The reactions were many, and at times heated. Of course, Protestant and Anglican churches were upset that they were not considered to be churches. Some felt that the tone was arrogant and condescending. Others, especially Jews, were stunned to read that the major objective for Catholics for dialoging was their mission to convert. Others felt that the "kingdom of God" most certainly extends beyond the Catholic Church. Many Catholic leaders, on the other hand, were pleased that the Vatican had made a definitive statement on the Catholic position, a clear presentation of Catholicism unique identity, and a strong position with regard other Christian professions and religions.

It was hoped by some that the current debates about the uniqueness of Jesus Christ and the Catholic Church would be settled. The presence of God and truth in other religious communities were acknowledged, but it was still made clear that Jesus Christ and his Church has God and the fullness of His presence in Jesus Christ and that Christ is the only source of salvation.

Pluralistic Approach

Religious pluralism is largely a product of Western Christian "theologians of religion." The followers of this movement have concluded that the absolutist positions of many, even in the inclusive model, sets up obstacles to interfaith dialogue. Pluralist thinkers are diverse in their thinking and generally place Christianity of an equal footing with other religions while viewing Jesus as one among many religious founders. John Hick, one of the main leaders of this movement, maintains that religion has come to a new "Copernican revolution," which places God or Ultimate Reality at the center of religious truth and salvation rather than Jesus Christ. From this perspective, being a Christian involves believing in the teachings and example of Jesus, but at the same time acknowledging that the Jesus' way is not the "only" way. His message is universal and should be shared with others, but it is neither final nor superior to others. Here Jesus might be considered the "Jesus of the Beatitudes" (Gandhi's view) or as a great guru or even an avatar (Hindu views).[36] If the word "best" is to be used at all it is in the sense that "my wife is the best" or "my family is the best," always conscious that this is a subjective view. Pluralists apply the same thinking to the New Testament about Jesus being "the only begotten Son of God," and about being saved in "no other name." They see this as subjective "love language" from the enthusiasm of the early church, which was caught up in the enthusiasm of the Spirit and a new faith. Or perhaps it is "performative language" designed to invite disciples to follow Jesus.[37] Here, Paul's language about the uniqueness of Jesus and his incarnation are interpreted as poetry and mythology, which must not be taken literally.[38]

Pluralists take the position that no religion should consider itself superior to others, think that its way is the only way to salvation, or hold that its truth is the one with any validity. Pluralists want a level playing field in religious dialogue which means that Christians have to give up belief in any real incarnation or resurrection, any centrality of the Church in salvation and the divine inspiration of their scriptures. Since pluralism is usually from the point of view of Christians, it is not clear if Buddhists have to concede that the Buddha's enlightenment was utterly unique or that Muslims must give up on Muhammad being the final prophet.

Pluralists generally accept that there is but one ultimate goal and that religions are different paths to that one goal. Some counter that perhaps religions have separate goals and unique ways to achieve these goal.[39]

Since Jains do not believe in a Creator God and the source of all, they do not share in wanting to be united with God as do so many other religions. Since neither Jews nor Muslims believe in a "fall," they do not share the Christian goal of being saved from sin.

The challenge seems to be to move beyond exclusivism, which rules out the validity of other religions and puts limits on God's power to reveal and save. For some, even the option for inclusivism falls short because it often holds that truth and salvation are mediated fully through only one religion.

Some in this approach suggest that a move must be made even beyond pluralism, where truth and salvation is mediated equally by all religions. They suggest that pluralism homogenizes religions, requiring that each forfeit their uniqueness in order to honor equality and respect. Catholic objections to pluralism were strongly stated in *Dominus Iesus*: "The Church's constant missionary proclamation is endangered today by relativistic theories which seek to justify religious pluralism… It is held that certain truths have been superseded; for example, the definitive and complete character of the revelation of Jesus Christ."[40]

Some Protestant theologians also have their criticisms of pluralism. Wolfhart Pannenberg writes that "such a situation is taken seriously within the discussions of Christian theology and is felt by many theologians to challenge the foundations of what Christian doctrine has been through the centuries." He sees this as a "process of erosion of the confidence of theologians in the truth of the Christian faith…a symptom of crisis within the modern Christian mind, especially in the West."[41]

Many advocates of interfaith dialogue maintain that each religion can hold on to its treasured traditions without coming to the table with an air of superiority. Truly for Muslims their tradition is "the best" for them, much as one's family or nation might be the "the best" for the individuals within that group. Generally a person commits to a religious tradition because they believe that tradition to be true. Therefore some question what is to be gained by watering down the truth of that tradition so the dialogue will be "friendly"?

One must ask if it really objectionable to maintain that in certain areas, one religion or another has a unique strength. Is it not possible to say that the

Catholicism is better at sacramentality, while Protestantism is superior where faithfulness to the scriptures is concerned and is it not possible to come to the conclusion that the Muslims have a superior dedication to prayer than do many Christians? In dialogue can we not truly learn from other religious traditions and thus enrich our own position with regard religion? Shouldn't the truth claims of the Hindus and Buddhist on rebirth be a challenge to the Christian belief in individual resurrection? Can't the Sikh's deep and daily honoring of their inspired scriptures be an inspiration to Christians who often take little interest in their Bible?

Keith Ward puts his critique of pluralism clearly: "would I accept the pluralistic hypothesis? I would not feel quite comfortable with that, for I do not think that all religious paths are intended to reach the same goal, however vague the goal is. Yet I would want strongly to encourage the study of religions in a global perspective, because I believe that such a study would deepen and enlarge one's own religious understanding, and place one's own religious beliefs in a wider and more illuminating context."[42]

It is interesting to examine the results of a recent study of how students at Amherst College in Massachusetts are dealing with religious diversity. Statistics show that on campus, Protestants (35%) and Catholics (33%) were in the majority. 18% were Jews, 4% Hindus, Buddhists and Muslim, and 1-2% were agnostics and atheists. As for religious involvement, around 50% of the students were active in their religion. The Christian and Jewish students were the highest on the influence that their religion had on their lives and on their personal identity. Many seemed interested in learning more about other religions and enjoyed one-on-one discussion on such matters, rather than group discussions. 80% in focus groups that were set up said that such discussions strengthened their faith while 67% felt that they their faith was challenged. Some felt that it clarified their own position. One student said: "Having these long discussions with my friend who is a devout atheist made me realize I am not an atheist. That is something I hadn't figured out before." Learning about the faith of others was clearly the benefit of dialogue that was mentioned the most often. The majority felt discomfort attending interfaith services, reporting that they felt more like observers rather than participants. Many saw such study, discussion and participation in services as a valuable way to get into deep topics, prepare for the future diverse society, a means to overcome stereotypes and misconceptions, and a way to grow close to others on a new personal level.[43]

Interfaith Dialogue

Many religious leaders and scholars stress that interfaith dialogue must be a crucial activity in today's global world. Ewert Cousins believes that we are moving into new consciousness which includes serious concern about dangerous political, social and ecological issues. It is his conviction that interfaith dialogue must be an important feature of today's world so the human community can work together for solutions to our many crises and avoid conflicts that could be calamitous. The noted Catholic theologian, Hans Kung asserts that "There will be no peace among nations among nations without peace among religions; and there will be no peace among religions without greater dialogue among them."[44]

Since the early 19th century, considerable progress has been made in interfaith relations. At that time, Christian missionary groups began to consider the legitimacy of other religions and then, during the two World Wars, people from differing religions fought side by side and became familiar with each other's faith. In 1893, The Parliament of World Religions held their first meeting. In recent times they have met every five years in some major city. The last meeting, in 2009, was held in Melbourne, Australia, where 5,000 religious leaders from 80 nations gathered to discuss important world issues. The Christian movement, the World Council of Churches, was formed in 1948 and has been a strong voice for unity as well as for active involvement in political and social issues.

As mentioned earlier, Catholic leaders at Vatican II recognized the truth and goodness in all faiths and strongly advocated dialogue among all traditions. The recent Popes have made serious efforts to reach out to other religions. Paul VI established the Secretariat for Non Christian Religions in Rome and warmly met with the Orthodox Patriarch Athanagoras at the Jordan River in 1964. John Paul II preached in a Lutheran church, accompanied the Archbishop of Canterbury as an equal down to the aisle of the Canterbury Cathedral, prayed at the Jewish Western Wall in Jerusalem and condemned anti-Semitism. In 1986 he invited 120 religious leaders (including an African Voodoo priest) to Assisi for joint sharing and prayer. Benedict XVI has made significant efforts to meet with religious leaders, the most notable a gathering with Muslim leaders in the Blue Mosque in Turkey.

Many other notable religious leaders have been dedicated to interfaith dialogue. The Hindu leader, Gandhi, gathered people of different faiths in his ashram in India and dedicated himself to peace between Muslims and Hindus (which ultimately cost him his life). The Tibetan Buddhist leader,

Dalai Lama has dedicated his life to touring the world, advocating peace with leaders of all religions. Abraham Heschel (1907-1972), the great Jewish scholar, marched with Martin Luther King Jr. and often participated in dialogues with other faiths. The World Jewish Congress has promoted such interfaith dialogues. Buddhist leaders such as Thich Nhat Hanh and Ghosananda have built many bridges among religions.

What is Interfaith Dialogue?

Productive interfaith dialogue is a process of careful listening and sharing of religious beliefs, values and rituals. It is a sincere and respectful exchange among individuals about their religious journeying and searching. It should a time for honest exchange and mutual learning, a time wherein trusting relationships can be established. It can also be an occasion for sharing concern about tensions among religions and talking about world issues and how religions can join together to improve matters.

Such dialogue should recognize the diversity among religions and attempt to explain individual commitments to these diverse views. Gandhi once said, "Truth is one!" No religion should assume that it has figured out the mysteries that surround ultimate questions. Each religion has its own unique revelations and insights into ultimacy. While differing, religions can also be complementary and assist each other in understanding ultimate Mystery. One scholar suggests that the sharing in religious dialogue is like different photographers taking pictures of the sun after different times of the day. The sun remains the same, but each camera captures a different perspective. Another scholar points out that such dialogue is like joining others in carrying parts of the same truth, but in different vessels.[45]

In interfaith dialogue, one comes to learn as well as teach. Each participant comes committed to his or her tradition, but at the same time is aware of both its strengths and its limitations, its failures and mistakes. It should be noted, however, that such criticism should not come from a person in another tradition. (As they say with families: they can be critical of the family among themselves, but do not easily accept criticism from outsiders!)

It might be said that in interfaith dialogue one steps outside of one's "religious bubble," one's comfort zone, to try to explain beliefs that have often been taken for granted and perhaps never examined carefully. This can be difficult because it sometimes brings one to question certain beliefs even wonder if one accepts them. This can be scary and might move us to rethink where we stand regarding our own tradition. This is not to say that interfaith dialogue should move the religious person to lose his or her faith, but it certainly should move one to clarify and question the various meanings and interpretations of one's tradition. For the person who has not accepted any religious tradition, such dialogue can also serve to clarify his or her position in this regard.

Different types of interfaith dialogue have been identified. First, there is **dialogue of the head**. This is more often conducted by professionals, who address academic questions in a scholarly manner. This being said, even in more informal dialogues among non-professionals there needs to be clarity and the presence of people who can serve as reliable resources. There is also **dialogue of the heart**, where religious experiences and feelings are shared, prayers and meditations are participated in, and individual stories are told. There is the **dialogue of life**, where the participants share their joys, sorrows, hopes, frustrations and sufferings. There is the **dialogue of love**, where we form new friendships and walk among others with new understanding and appreciation of who they are. And finally, there is the **dialogue of hands**, where we join people of other faiths in actions to promote peace, justice, compassion for the less-fortunate and ecological responsibility.[46]

In their 1995 Mission Statement, the Jesuits dedicated themselves to interfaith dialogue world-wide. They highlighted four signal aspects of this dialogue: **dialogue of life**, carried on with the awareness that we all live together sharing one world; **dialogue of action**, whereby we share the tasks that have to be done to meet the needs of others; **dialogue of religious experience**, whereby we share in worship, prayer and meditation; and **dialogue of theological exchange**, wherein scholars in various traditions share insights and interpretations.[47]

A leading expert in interfaith dialogue, Paul Knitter, points to four elements that are important for such dialogue. First, this dialogue requires a willingness to face and experience difference in beliefs. Second, interfaith dialogue requires a trust that facing these differences can bring us together rather than divide us. Here one agrees to disagree and is willing to be enriched by new and different perspectives. One grants that in attempting to understand ultimate mystery, all only "see through a glass darkly," (1 Corinthians 13:12) and that each tradition can make its own unique contribution toward comprehending this mystery. The third element is witnessing, or honestly attempting to share with others, the beliefs that one treasures. Here there can be a mutual sense of inspiration. The final element is the willingness to be open to new insights and even change one's religious perspectives.[48]

It is also useful to note what interfaith dialogue is *not*. First, it should not be a debate, where the participants come to argue their positions or to point out where others are wrong in their beliefs. Such adversarial positions make productive dialogue all but impossible and produce alienation rather than unity. Secondly, dialogue should not have as its purpose missionary activity or the conversion of the others. Here Christians have been particularly wary since their religion has always had such a strong mission element. Finally, such dialogue should not be an effort to form one big happy religion where there are no differences or contradictions. Authentic interfaith dialogue must face diversity and discuss it openly and honestly so that the mutuality is open and real rather than naïve or deceptive.

Why Engage in Interfaith Dialogue?

Francis X. Clooney, S.J., an expert in comparative theology, maintains that interfaith dialogue should be an integral part of the Christian tradition. He points out that Christians have always been open to understanding other religious traditions and incorporating them into its own. Coming from the Jewish tradition initially, Christians had to incorporate Judaism into the new insights of Christianity. As Christianity moved into the Gentile world it was influenced by both Roman and Greek thinking. Both Jewish and Greek thinking shaped early Christian beliefs on God, creation and incarnation. Later in the Middle Ages, Greek thinking shaped the theology of Aquinas and other key Christian theologians. Sharing traditions with Islam, Christianity has also had to understand the common ground between these two religions. Jesuit Missionaries into the Orient, such as Francis Xavier (1506-1552) and Matteo Ricci (1552-1610), made great efforts to learn about the Chinese language, culture and religion and accommodate Christianity to the Orient. In our own time, Bede Griffins, a Benedictine monk lived in Hindu ashrams in India, became a noted teacher and discovered much common ground between Christianity and Hinduism.

Clooney suggests achieving religious literacy is an important reason to participate in interfaith dialogue. Such literacy is most certainly important for Christians who hope to be well-educated and prepared to take part in a global society. Religious literacy includes knowing the historical and theological background of different religions and also knowing how to compare the various belief systems. Clooney does not think that achieving such literacy should be threatening to Christians. He says, "I do not see how a commitment to Jesus of Nazareth could possibly serve as an excuse for interreligious illiteracy, ignorance about the religiously diverse world in which we live. Interreligious literacy, not ignorance of our neighbors, is a Christian virtue."[49] Clooney adds that such literacy can be the basis for getting involved with disciples of other religions involved in projects for peace and social justice. In addition, such dialogue is a way of creating solidarity among religious communities in a secularized world. He writes that "In a seemingly secularized world, we need to create possibilities which bring us together for religious learning, conversing, arguing, stating and defending the religious truths people live and die for. Interreligious literacy requires a community and does its share to help create one."[50]

Besides religious literary, there are other reasons for participating in interfaith dialogue. Such dialogue can be a time for self-exploration—a time to help us sort out our own beliefs and values. In college, many students discover they have been relying on the beliefs given to them by their parents and teachers. They are often faced with the challenge of making these beliefs their own, or even of deciding whether or not to set some of these beliefs aside. Often college students undergo a "religious leave of absence" in order to decide whether they want to attend church services for their own reasons, and to assess their religious beliefs. Discussion of religion with those from other traditions can help students to express what they do or do not believe, to clarify their beliefs freely and on their own.

At the same time, such dialogue can help them understand the religious search of others and how they are also trying to come to a mature understanding their own tradition. Therefore such dialogue should go far beyond the facts of another religion and should include a careful listening to how others "wrestle" with their beliefs. These are opportunities to compare notes with how others search of a purpose in life, their own individual callings, their deepest questions and their doubts.

Another reason for engaging interfaith dialogue might be to prepare to participate in a future that is becoming increasingly more global. The world seems to become smaller as the means of travel and communication improve. In a matter of hours, one can be in an entirely different culture, with languages, customs and religions quite different from our own. Business, education or just pleasure travel challenges us to be more knowledgeable and comfortable with the ways and beliefs of other people. Closer to home, one has to just look around in our cities, classrooms, offices and factories to see how diverse we are becoming.

In addition, technology and social networks open up unlimited possibilities for contacting diverse cultures and religions. We can talk to, text and email people in many different countries and share their insights and beliefs. Students and even whole classrooms in China, Africa or Russia can converse with each other, sharing their and beliefs. It become increasingly more difficult today for people to remain in their own little cultural and religion "bubble," unaware of the struggles and the concerns of others.

Finally, sharing the ideals and values of others can perhaps lead us to action on behalf of the needy. Students of differing faiths are now teaming up to build houses for the poor and serve others, whether that be in Appalachia, Africa or India. Working together and praying together, large numbers of young people are becoming a force in the world.

How To Conduct Interfaith Dialogue

Raimon Panikkar (1918-2010), a well-respected expert in interfaith dialogue, discusses some of the attitudes that should be brought to the table. First of all, he cautions that one should not approach such dialogue with an air of superiority. Even though one may hold for truths that are "best" for the self, it does not mean that they are the "best." Absolutism in belief can lead to intolerance and even contempt for others—hardly the posture needed for unity.

Another attitude to avoid, according to Panikkar, is the one that thinks no matter what truth there is in other religions, the same exists in a higher version in one's own. No matter how good the other's path to salvation, yours is the better. Another version of this is "parallelism," which maintains that whatever is good in another religion, there is a parallel in your own. This position does not acknowledge that there can be beliefs in other religions that are unique and that not replicated in one's own. Again, such a position can easily lead to an air of superiority.

Keeping a balance in all this is no easy matter. One has to come to the conclusion that "our neighbor's religion not only challenges but may even enrich our own."[51] On can see that a great deal of tolerance, humility and broadmindedness is called for when participating in such dialogue.

Many of the traditional models for conducting such dialogue are limited. One can have the attitude that there are many paths to the same summit, but what if there are in fact different summits and possibly dead end paths? One can approach the endeavor with the image that different religions are like the many colors of the rainbow, but then how does one handle when one "color" blends into another, as in the case of Hinduism and Buddhism, or Judaism, Christianity and Islam. How does one explain that one religion might have less light than another, or may even be in darkness? Or, if we explain religions as having their origins in revelations to humans, what role is played by different cultures and languages? Is diversity on the part of the divine or is it on the part of the different receivers?[52]

Wayne Teasdale points to key elements of productive interfaith dialogue: 1. intention, where each person comes with a sincere desire for mutual understanding. 2. A specific focus, that is, some specific topic and not just a general, vague agenda (e.g. views on ritual, morality, salvation). 3. A specific method that is well-organized and mutually agree upon (e.g. large group with a leader; small groups with a specific agenda; panel discussion with questions afterward). 4. Specific goals and expectations (e.g. better unity among congregations, mutual understanding on specific topics, planning for some joint action) After each dialogue, the results should be noted and summarized (e.g. new friendships, new insights and attitudes, clearing up of stereotypes).[53]

It is possible to set down some rules for interfaith dialogue. First, the dialogue must be free, so that no one is being pressured to give up their beliefs or be converted. There are no wrong or right views here, just a sharing of each others' beliefs with no pressures or tensions. Secondly, the dialogue must recognize the complexities in each religion. There is no such thing as one Christian tradition, one Hindu tradition, or one Jewish tradition. Each of these traditions has many divisions and many differing sets of beliefs within their own traditions. All the differences should be taken into account and honored if the dialogue is to be enlightened. Moreover, individuals within each tradition have their own unique ways of practicing that religion. These individual approaches must be accepted and respected. Thirdly, the discussion should not simply be academic, geared to impress the other with one's knowledge of the tradition. Accent should be on the personal beliefs and practices. Good dialogue should not be a symposium and debate, but an honest and sincere sharing of view. This should not a confrontation between official churches or religions, but a candid sharing of personal perspectives. Finally, such dialogue should be a personal encounter among individuals, who share their faith, their hopes and their love.[54]

The partner in interfaith dialogue is always the Thou: honored, respected, held in esteem. The person "begs" to differ instead of being confrontational or argumentative. We expose our personal history according to our comfort zones. We share our search, our questions, the challenges that our faith presents, the questions with which we wrestle. We build trusting relationships and ultimately friendships. We try to get to the point where we can comfortable pray together, share each others' religious services and work together on projects or service.

Interfaith dialogue involves what some refer to as a "crossing over." This implies a willingness to move into another's world of symbol, story, belief, devotion and ritual. We put ourselves in someone else's place, try on their moccasins and walk their path. Some compare it to going to a foreign country where one has to step out of the familiar, learn another language and adjust to another culture and lifestyle. Here, the best results come from letting go, not holding back, reaching out beyond the familiar. Such "crossing over" requires flexibility, courage and adaptation; but in the long run, it is the only way to grow and expand our horizons.

Summary

It is clear that religion phenomenon is characterized by diversity. We have shown some of the distinct differences among religions in just a few areas: the God question, ritual and afterlife. Such differences can be a source of division and conflict or they can be integral to a process of enrichment. To bring about the latter, it is necessary that these differences be faced, properly understood and discussed with mutual respect.

Theologians of religion have suggested that there are three models whereby religious differences are addressed. The first is exclusivism, which approaches religious differences from a position of superiority and even judgment. The second is inclusivism, where one religion sees the others only from its own perspective. Here the truth and salvation elements are relative and partial and find their validity only through the one true religion. Pluralism, on the other hand, advocates that all religions come to the table as equals, even if that means giving up some of the beliefs that are core to their tradition. Some pluralists urge Christians to give up their beliefs about incarnation and resurrection so that they come to discussion on equal grounds.

Some today urge that pluralism has its own limitations, especially in its demands that religions forfeit key beliefs for the sake of a more fair discussion. They propose a model wherein religions hold on to their central beliefs and try to explain them in an atmosphere of mutual respect and humility.

Interfaith dialogue holds more and more importance today as we move toward a globalized society. Such dialogue is necessary for clarification of one's own beliefs; a clearer understanding of the religious beliefs of those we study, work or live with; as an means for avoiding conflict and violence; and a way to join with those of other faiths in actions for peace and justice. In order to help others more effectively engage in interfaith dialogue we have extensively explored the What, Why and How of the dialogue.

◼▶ VIDEOS ONLINE

Hubble Images and God
> https://www.youtube.com/watch?v=tJ-aFOTb-Zw

Hillsong: "Yahweh" Worship and Praise Song featuring David Ware
> https://www.youtube.com/watch?v=9tZ1fWz4fAE

Martin Sheen's official 'Beyond Religion' interview
> https://www.youtube.com/watch?v=SYHlTihh5RY

H.H. Dalai Lama, Is there only one true religion?
> https://www.youtube.com/watch?v=eQrUWmzshsI

Inter-religious meeting in Assisi: Cardinal Roger Etchegaray
> https://www.youtube.com/watch?v=ej3GGZvJXvI
> https://www.youtube.com/watch?v=gObnwmpPbwM

John Hick's Theodicy
> https://www.youtube.com/watch?v=-OPhiLD7J3g

Paul Knitter on John Hick
> https://www.youtube.com/watch?v=FXE7jmUYoQg

Fresh Light on the Jewish-Christian-Muslim Dialogue
> https://www.youtube.com/watch?v=17FNZT0IZY0

Raimon Pannikar
> https://www.youtube.com/watch?v=1eoSg3hMups

Raimon Panikkar, The Window
> https://www.youtube.com/watch?v=Kvsov6OuTWs

▨◼ NOTES

1.   Karen Armstrong, *The case for God* (New York: Anchor Books, 2010, c2009), 9.

2.   Ibid., 12.

3.   Laurie Patton, "Hinduism" in *God*, ed. Jacob Neusner (Cleveland: The Pilgrim Press, 1997), 320.

4.   Thomas Berry, *Religions of India* (Beverly Hills, CA: Benzinger, 1971), 27-31.

5.   Neusner, *God*, 570.

6.   Stephen Prothero, *God is Not One* (New York: HarperOne, 2010), 189.

7. P.C. Nahar and K.C. Ghosh, eds., *An Encyclopedia of Jainism* (Delhi: Sri Satgura Publications, 1988), 264.

8. Mark S. Smith, *The Early History of God* (Grand Rapids, MI: Wm. B. Eerdmans Publishing, Co., 2002), 43ff.

9. Jacob Neusner, "Judaism" in *God*, ed. Jacob Neusner (Cleveland: Pilgrim Press, 1997), 7.

10. Rodney Stark, *Discovering God* (New York: HarperOne, 2008), 186ff.

11. http://quod.lib.umich.edu/k/koran/browse.htm,Sura, 36:77-83.

12. Karen Armstrong, *Muhammad* (New York: HarperSanFrancisco, 1992), 109ff.

13. Ibid., 52.

14. Jonathan Brockopp, "Islam," in *God*, ed. Jacob Neusner, 89ff.

15. http://quod.lib.umich.edu/k/koran/browse.htm The Table, 5, 5-10.

16. Rodney Stark, *Discovering God* (New York: HarperCollins, 2007), 23.

17. Ibid., 34.

18. Ibid., 58.

19. H. Byron Earhart, ed., *Religion in the Japanese Experience* (Encino, CA: Dickenson Publishing Co., Inc., 1984), 11.

20. Lao-Tzu, *Te Tao Ching* (New York: Ballantine Books, 1989), 20.

21. Beth Gruber, *National Geographic Investigates: Ancient Inca* (Washington DC: National Geographic, 2007), 45ff.

22. *The Upanishads*, Part 1, verse 1

23. Jacob Neusner, *The Way of Torah* (Belmont, CA: Wadsworth, 1993), 1340.

24. Francis A. Sullivan, SJ, *Salvation Outside the Church?* (New York: Paulist Press, 1992), 5ff.

25. Leonard Feeney, *Bread of Life* (Cambridge, MA: 1952), 146.

26. Sullivan, 137ff.

27. Ibid., 145.

28. *Lumen Gentium*, 16.

29. Sullivan, 167.

30. See Karl Rahner, SJ, "Anonymous Christians," in *Theological Investigations* Vol. 6 (New York: Crossroad, 1982), 390-398.

31. Sullivan, 189.

32. Pope John Paul II, "Dominum et Vivificantem/On the Holy Spirit in the Life of the Church and the World," in *Origins* No. 53, 16/4 (June 12, 1986).

33. Pope John Paul II, *Redemptoris missio*, No. 8, 15; No. 5, 10 .

34. Congregation for the Doctrine of the Faith, *Dominus Iesus*, http://www.vatican.va/roman_curia/congregations/cfaith/documents/rc_con_cfaith_doc_20000806_dominus-iesus_en.html.

35. "Dominus Iesus" in *Sic et Non: Encountering Dominus Iesus*, eds. Stephen J. Pope and Charles Hefling (Maryknoll, NY: Orbis Books, 2002), 3-23.

36. Jacques Dupuis, *Jesus Christ at the Encounter with World Religions* (Maryknoll, NY: Orbis

Books, 1991), 46ff.

37.   Paul Knitter, *Jesus and the Other Names* (Maryknoll, NY: Orbis Books, 1996), 68-69.

38.   John Hick, *God and the Universe of Faith* (London: Macmillan, 1973), 148-179; Paul Knitter, *No Other Name?* (Maryknoll, NY: Orbis Books, 1985), 182-86.

39.   See S. Mark Heim, *Salvations: Truth and Difference in Religion* (Maryknoll, NY: Orbis Books, 1995).

40.   *Dominus Iesus*, 4.

41.   Wolfhart Pannenberg, "Religious Pluralism and Conflicting Truth Claims," in *Christian Uniqueness Reconsidered*, ed. Gavin D'Costa (Maryknoll, NY: Orbis Books, 1990), 97.

42.   Keith Ward, "Pluralism Revisited," in *Religious Pluralism and the Modern World*, ed. Sharada Sugirtharajah (New York: PalgraveMacmillan, 2012), 67.

43.   See Paul Sorrentino, *Religious Pluralism: What do College Students Think?* (Saarbrucken: VDM Verlag, 2009); "Spirituality in Higher Education: A National Study of College Students' Search for Meaning and Purpose," (UCLA Higher Education Researchx Institute, 2004).

44.   Hans Kung, *Global Responsibility*, (New York: Crossroad, 1991), xv.

45.   M. Darrol Bryant and Frank Flinn, eds., *Interreligious Dialogue* (New York: Paragon Press, 1989), 11-16.

46.   Teasdale, 28ff.

47.   Rodney L. Peterson and Nancy M. Rourke, eds., *Theological Literacy for the Twenty-First Century* (Grand Rapids, MI: Wm. B. Eerdmans Publishing Co., 2002), 252.

48.   See Brennan Hill, Paul Knitter and Wm. Madges, *Faith, Religion and Theology* (Mystic, CT: Twenty-Third Publications, 1997), 198ff.

49.   Francis X. Clooney, S.J., "Reading the World Religiously: Literate Christianity in a World of Many Religions," in *Theological Literacy for the Twenty-First Century*, eds. Rodney L. Peterson and Nancy M. Rourke (Grand Rapids, MI: Wm. B. Eerdmans Publishing Company, 2002), 250.

50.   Ibid., 256.

51.   Raimon Panikkar, *The Intrareligious Dialogue* (New York: Paulist Press, 1999).

52.   See Pannikar, 11ff.

53.   Wayne Teasdale, *Catholicism in Dialogue*, (New York: Rowman and Littlefield Pub., 2004), 34ff.

54.   See Pannikar, 62ff.

10

Social Issues and Religion

I call him religious who understands the suffering of others.
— Mahatma Gandhi

In keeping silent about evil, in burying it so deep within us that no sign of it appears on the surface, we are implanting it, and it will rise up a thousand fold in the future. When we neither punish nor reproach evildoers, we are not simply protecting their trivial old age, we are thereby ripping the foundations of justice from beneath new generations.
— Aleksandr Solzhenitsyn

In this final chapter we are going to look at how religions relate to social issues, specifically poverty, women's rights and peace. Quite often religions have not done well in these areas—religious leaders have often identified with the rich classes, denigrated women and fought wars over religious beliefs—but this is not our focus here. We are going to look at how religions today are often working diligently to serve the poor, recognize the equality of women and seriously engage in efforts for peace.

Poverty

The global economic picture is one of extreme contrasts. On one hand, there are the extremely wealthy, who seem to be rapidly gaining ground these days. On the other hand, billions of people live in extreme poverty. The World Bank estimates that 2.8 billion people, nearly ½ the world's population, lives on just $2 a day. Most of these impoverished people live the so-called developing countries. The worst poverty exists in South Asia and in the Sub-Saharan African countries, 40-50% of the population lives in extreme poverty. It should be noted that that over the last 25 years there has been notable improvement with regard to poverty. The United Nations Millennium Development has estimated that between 1990 and 2015, the proportion of people living in extreme poverty has been cut in half. Great advances have been made in food production and in making clean water available.[1]

In the United States, about 48.5 million people or 15.9% of the U.S. population had income below their respective poverty level. (An income below $14,200 for family of 3 is considered below the poverty level. That is increasing each year with the highest levels of poverty existing in Southern States, especially Mississippi (22%) and New Mexico (21%). Blacks and Hispanics are disproportionately poor in this country.[2]

Of course, poverty is much more than lack of income. Poverty is also hunger. About 17% (2 billion people) of the world's population suffer from chronic hunger and severe malnutrition. Poverty is also poor health and early death. Poverty is lack of heath care. It is estimated that 30,000 children die each day from preventable causes. In some African countries, the babies are not named until they are a month old because so many do not make it to that age. In Sub-Saharan African countries the average life-span is 46 years and even that number is plunging due to the spread of AIDS.[3] Poverty is also the loss of one's childhood. Worldwide, 180 million children under 14 work in conditions that endanger their health and their lives. 8.4 million children are trapped in slavery, trafficking, prostitution and pornography.

Poverty is the denial of education. One billion people in the world are illiterate. In Sub-Saharan Africa, the average time at school is four years, and many children never see the inside of a classroom. This prevents many from acquiring the skills needed for employment. Poverty is about being subject to extreme weather events that wipe out your housing, your farmland, and your way of making a living. It is about losing your parents to AIDS or having your animals or your land taken away by developers. Poverty is crime that arises out of desperation. Poverty is powerlessness: not having access to free markets, having to pay bribes, being constantly in debt to moneylenders, and being subject to greedy landowners or corrupt government officials.

Listen to some of the voices of the poor around the world:

"In Malawi half the population misses meals for many days, especially in the hungry months of January and February." "In the evenings, eat sweet potatoes, sleep. In the mornings, eat sweet potatoes, work. At lunch, go without" (Farmer in Vietnam). "If you don't have money today, your disease will take you to your grave" (An old woman in Ghana). "Being poor is being always tired" (A Kenyan). "Our mud home is in very bad condition. It leaks and looks like it is falling but we cannot afford to maintain it. This has made our lives more miserable." (A Malawan). "Rich people are now catching all the fish near the coast with trawlers and large fishing nets. They leave nothing for the poor fishermen" (Fisherman in Indonesia). "When one is poor, she has no say in public, she feels inferior. She has no food, so there is famine in her house; no clothing, and no progress in her family." (A woman in Uganda).[4]

Causes of Poverty

Most studies reveal that the two most common causes of poverty are poverty are lack of education and lack of employment. The two, of course, are linked. Without education, a person is not able to gain the literacy or skills needed to get a job. Obviously, without work there is no income and the family descends further into poverty. The children are often made to do the menial tasks around the house or are put out to work and do not have the opportunity to gain an education. The cycle continues from generation to generation.

Lack of land is another cause of poverty. If a family owns a small tract of land, poverty prevents them from proper care of this land and soon it becomes infertile. Drought, insects, and failed crops from lack of fertilizer can cause the family to sink even further into debt. Lack of proper nutrition and poor health can also take away their energy to work the farm. If they rent the land from a landowner, failed crops can put them further in debt and render them incapable of paying off their debt. The remoteness of their land can also prevent them from bringing their crops to market in order to earn an income.

Global Markets

Many believe that globalization has contributed to world poverty. A lot of money has been made by large international corporations, often at the expense of the local farmer or craftsperson. In developing countries, when the farmers take their goods to the market they find that their goods are competing with cheaper products from other countries. In addition, they are often at the mercy of unscrupulous middlemen who take much of their profits. If they have skills to make things like clothes, shoes, furniture and jewelry, they often find that their products are passed over for cheaply manufactured items sent from the global markets. Being poor, they have no means to lobby or even protest. In India, one sees highly skilled families working around the clock on looms in their apartments for a pittance while their magnificent woven products are collected and sent to Europe and the United States and sold for high profits. Or one sees young women spending long days weaving fine rugs for small wages, while these rugs are sold abroad for high prices. In Costa Rica, the bananas are harvested on the backs of migrant Nicaraguan workers who make a few dollars a day. These bananas are then exported by large corporations to supermarkets around the world. The executives of the corporations involved are rewarded with millions of dollars in salaries and bonuses. The old adage is confirmed: "The rich get richer and the poor get poorer."

Corrupt Governments

Corrupt governments have also been a cause of poverty. During the colonial periods the peoples in such areas as Africa, Asia and Central and South America lost power over their lands. Many of their resources were stripped from their countries and shipped abroad. The indigenous people often found that they were little more than slaves, while the colonials took the best land and the profits. Only in recent times has the yoke of colonialism been thrown off in many nations around the world and freedom given to the native peoples.[5]

Unfortunately, some of the native leaders who came to power after colonialism were equally corrupt and betrayed their own people by amassing great wealth and oppressing their countrymen. We saw this in the extreme with leaders in Africa like Idi Amin (d. 2003), the brutal leader of Uganda in the 1970s, Charles Taylor, former president of Liberia who was convicted of war crimes in 2012, and Muammar Gaddafi (1942-2011), the savage dictator of Libya. Corrupt leadership from one military coup to another has prevented the money from oil-rich Nigeria to get to the masses.[6] Throughout most of Africa, many hard-working people are impoverished because the enormous resources have been used to enrich the elite.[7]

Other Causes of Poverty

There are numerous other causes of poverty. Violence and war takes millions of productive lives, destroys economies and displaces millions of refugees. We have seen this in the unspeakable slaughter of nearly one million people in 100 days in 1994, when the Hutus slaughtered the Tutsies in Rwanda. In the Darfur region of Sudan, ongoing conflicts have taken hundreds of thousands of lives and driven millions into no-man's-lands, where they are vulnerable to roaming gangs of militants. The violence and chaos in Somalia have driven hundreds of thousands to seek refugee camps in Kenya.

Corrupt leaders in Asia have also oppressed and impoverished their people. For example, the infamous Pol Pot (1925-1998) led Cambodia in the mid 70s and killed millions of his own people through forced labor and executions. More recently Kim Jong-il (1941-2011), the former North Korean dictator, lived a life of extreme luxury and spared no expense for this military, while millions of his citizens suffered extreme poverty, died of starvation or languished in concentration camps because of their political views.

Greed and reckless decision-making on the part of U.S. banks and financial institutions brought our economy to the brink of collapse in 2008. Many Americans lost their homes, their jobs, and much of their life savings. Natural disasters like Katrina (2005), which devastated parts of Louisiana, and Sandy (2012) killed 253 and brought devastation to 6 countries. In the United States these storms destroyed homes, lands, and businesses and plunged many Americans into poverty. The earthquake in Haiti (2010) killed over 300,000 people and left over one million homeless. The tsunami in Japan (2011) killed over 20,000 people, left many more unaccounted for and caused a nuclear crisis. These, as well as so many other recent natural disasters, such as drought, mudslides, floods, and forest fires have impoverished millions and have provided dire warnings about what can be expected from global warming and climate change.

Ways to Alleviate Poverty

There are many ways to alleviate poverty which are important to keep in mind during our later discussion about how religions are assisting in this effort.

Quality healthcare is a key asset for avoiding poverty. Without good health, it is difficult to manage a household, care for children or hold down a job. It is important that all people, but especially those that live in developing countries, receive adequate health care as well as the medications they need. The poor often experience anxiety or depression and also need assistance with mental health. Figuring out how all this can be done will continue to present a major challenge to governments, world organizations and religions.

Proper nutrition is another essential to keep people out of poverty. Without proper nutrition, people lack the strength and energy to properly carry out their responsibilities and will eventually see their health affected. The U.S. Agency for International Development defines food security as "a state when all people at all times have both the physical and economic access to sufficient food to meet their dietary needs for a productive and healthy life."[8] This should include knowledge of a proper diet as well as access to it and also access to safe water and sanitation. At present there does not seem to be a shortage of food in the world, so much as it is difficult to ship food to the places where people are hungry and live in remote areas. Those who wish to help also receive resistance from local suppliers who do not want to see their prices affected.

Most concerned parties agree that **basic education** can lift many families out of poverty. In many developing countries, the people speak indigenous or tribal languages and cannot become literature until they learn their country's official language or a universal language such as English. To do this they must start from scratch and learn to speak, read and write another language. No easy challenge this! Basic reading and writing skills are needed so that people can read signs, count out their money at the market, apply for jobs, and apply for credit or any other service. At the same time, skills need be taught so that the poor can obtain jobs that will give them necessary income. Providing schools, teachers and learning materials to those in developing countries will be a daunting task for local, national and international agencies.

The **availability of credit** is important for the poor so that they can purchase what they need. Rural people need funds for machinery, livestock, seed, fertilizer, etc. Others need money to purchase cloth and materials for sewing, or funds to purchase inventory to be sold in the city. The recent expansion of microfinance institutions either from within developing countries or from developed countries have been most helpful in this regard. In 2006 Muhammad Yunus won the Novel Prize for decades of managing the Grameen bank in Bangladesh, which is credited with helping millions of poor people with micro loans.

Access to utilities and technology, especially electricity, cell phones and internet use is very important for the poor today. Many non-governmental agencies and religious organizations have helped provide these. Lighting provides the opportunity to study and work; cell phones assist greatly in communication for business and emergencies, and the internet can provide access to broader markets, needed information and provide further education.

Christian Views on Poverty

Churches have varied on their views toward wealth and poverty. On the one hand, church leaders throughout history have often identified with the "royals" and the rich. Until recently, many Catholic bishops lived in mansions and were chauffeured in limousines. Some Christians see wealth to be a blessing from God. Oral Roberts once prayed with his televised audience, "Lord give us lots of money!" On another, occasion he told his followers that he was to raise $8 million dollars or "he would be called home."[9] So-called "prosperity preachers" secure wealth for themselves by praying with their congregations for the "blessings" of acquiring large sums of money. When Joel Osteen, a popular prosperity preacher who reportedly lives in a $12 million home and is worth $40 million, was asked by Piers Morgan whether he felt guilty about amassing great wealth as a preacher, he said "I don't ever feel guilty because it comes from – it's God's blessings on my life. And for me to apologize for God's gifts – how God has blessed you, it's almost an insult to our God."[10]

Others argue that Jesus is the model for Christians and that he lived a simple and detached life, with "nowhere to lay his head," sacrificed his time and even his life for others, and declared "blessed are the poor" (Luke 6:20). They believe that the Christian ideal is one of simplicity and sharing. Jesus told the rich young man that if you "sell your possessions and give to the poor, and you will have treasure in heaven. Then come, follow me" (Matthew 19:21). At the same time, many believe that from this position of detachment and simplicity (where the basic needs of shelter and food are met), Christians are called to serve the destitute, the starving and needy. A number of Catholic religious orders for men, especially the Franciscans and Jesuits, and most congregations of religious women were founded to include a vow of poverty (simplicity and detachment) along with a mission to serve the poor.

The World Council of Churches has been a leader in studying the needs of the poor world-wide. They have studied 19 countries, especially those in the southern hemisphere, and have asked the poor to give voice to their concerns and their needs. Their studies found that excessive wealth often leads to greed, selfishness and hard-heartedness. The wealthy are often quite materialistic and individualistic. One Methodist minister serving in Brazil said, "The poorest the church, more solidarity one finds. The richest the church, less solidarity is found. I am a preacher in a rich community, but what I really have is a bunch of individuals. I don't have a community."[11]

Other studies find that the wealthy often seek power and want to use this power to protect their possessions and maintain the 'status quo' in their government if it works to their advantage. The wealthy often have a "spiritual poverty," in that they are bored from overconsumption and lack of challenge, and are caught in an endless search for entertainment. They found that the poor often perceive church leaders to be rich and enjoying luxurious living. Some see the Pope as the monarch of a Vatican worth billions, who lives in a palace with 11,000 rooms, wears expensive silk robes, a jeweled miter, and rides in a Mercedes popemobile.[12]

There is no clear theology of wealth and poverty in Christianity, and most preachers seem to avoid the topic. Some Christians see poverty as the "will of God," The poor are encouraged to be subject to this will and long-suffering in their poverty. Those who are better off often try to ignore those in poverty as "beneath them," and they promote a form of Christianity full of comfortable hymn singing which supports the status quo and carefully avoids issues of justice and social change."[13] They might quote Jesus' saying that "the poor you will always have with you" (Matthew 26:11) and perhaps view poverty as a necessary evil about which little can be done. For many of the poor, this can turn into a fatalism—a helpless giving in to poverty as "God's will."

Christians dedicated to serving the poor are inspired by Jesus' identifying himself with the prophetic statement that he read aloud in the synagogue: "The Spirit of the Lord is upon me, because he anointed me to preach the gospel to the poor. He has sent me to proclaim release to the captives, and recovery of sight to the blind, to set free those who are oppressed" (Luke

4: 18). Others find direction in Jesus' mission to teach, heal and forgive the "little ones." Still others treasure the story of the Judgment when the kingdom is given to those who responded to the needs of others, "For I was hungry, and you gave Me something to eat; I was thirsty, and you gave Me something to drink; I was a stranger, and you invited Me in; naked, and you clothed Me; I was sick, and you visited Me; I was in prison, and you came to Me.' And when the King was asked how this can be he responded: 'Truly I say to you, to the extent that you did it to one of these brothers of Mine, even the least of them, you did it to Me" (Matthew 25:35-45).

Liberation Theology

The image of Jesus as liberator of the poor has emerged out of Central and South America, where the poor have been deprived, oppressed and killed since the time of the conquistadores four hundred years ago. After Vatican II, the bishops of these areas met several times and committed themselves to be in solidarity with their poor. Sometime later this position was formulated into a theology of liberation by Gustavo Gutierrez and was followed by an avalanche of books and strong movements toward liberation of the poor in Latin America from oppressive dictatorships and military group. This was a "theology from below," and its followers stood in dangerous solidarity with the oppressed. This mission produced many martyrs, including Archbishop Romero, priests including the six Jesuit professors in El Salvador (along with their housekeepers), and the well-known three American nuns and a lay woman who were also murdered in El Salvador.

Catholic Social Teaching

The Catholic Church has a body of teaching on social justice that dates back to the 19th century with Pope Leo XIII and developed through the teachings of subsequent Popes, Vatican II, a Synod and various Bishops' Conferences. The 1986 document, "Economic Justice for All" by the National Conference of Catholic Bishops is a powerful contemporary statement on the responsibilities that all have toward the poor. It was produced after years of consultation with experts in many areas, such as theology, politics, economics, and sociology.

These documents take the position that God speaks through scripture, reason, human experience and the work of the Spirit in human history. These documents "begin with a basic commitment to the equal dignity of all men and women as creatures of God; to the notion that human flourishing must be worked out in the community; and to the proposition that all God's gifts are to be used for the good of all humanity."[14] These documents express a special concern for the poor and the oppressed. They are concerned with human rights, the right to private property, participation in governance, labor unions and governmental monitoring of markets to protect small merchants and the poor. These documents span over a century of national and international events and changes, so they are not all consistent with modern thinking. At the same time, they provide a strong foundation for Catholic thinking and action with regard to social justice. Throughout these documents there is a commitment to human dignity, freedom, the common good, inclusion, and participation of all. The most recent stress of the "preferential option for the poor" has become fundamental to Catholic thinking, a position that the poor should be given first consideration in all policy making. The gospel values of love, compassion, inclusivity, non-judgment, forgiveness and service of others resonate throughout this treasured tradition.

Christian Relief Services

There are many Christian organizations dedicated to helping the poor. We will merely mention several international and American examples.

International

Christian Relief Service. Its mission is to work through partnerships and in collaboration with grassroots charitable groups, churches and human service agencies throughout the world in order to help those in need in their own local communities and to enable people to help themselves.

The Salvation Army. This is a Christian international movement whose ministry is motivated by the love of God. Its mission is to preach the gospel of Jesus Christ and to meet human needs in His name without discrimination. It was started in 1852 by William Booth and came to the U.S. in 1879.

Catholic Relief Services carries out the commitment of the Bishops of the United States to assist the poor and vulnerable overseas. They are motivated by the Gospel of Jesus Christ to cherish, preserve and uphold the sacredness and dignity of all human life, foster charity and justice, and embody Catholic social and moral teaching. They promote human development by responding to major emergencies, and fighting disease and poverty. For 60 years their mission has focused on the poor overseas, using the gospel of Jesus Christ as their mandate. They continually seek to help those most in need, providing assistance on the basis of need without regard to race, creed, or nationality.

U.S.A

St Vincent de Paul Mission hopes to carry on Jesus' mission to foster hope by providing spiritual, emotional and material assistance on a person-to-person basis to the poor, lonely and forgotten in their community.

Catholic Charities USA (CCUSA) provides strong leadership and supports the work of local agencies in their efforts to reduce poverty, support families, and empower communities. Throughout its 100 year history, CCUSA's local agencies have helped create hope for over one billion people, regardless of faith or socioeconomic status.

Poverty and World Religions

Other world religions also are concerned with the problem of poverty. Here we will give an overview of how other religions relate to poverty in Hinduism, Buddhism, Judaism and Islam.

Hinduism

Hinduism finds it source in India, a country which saw much prosperity in previous centuries. In modern times, it is attempting to recover from two centuries of Britain's colonial domination. Though there is overwhelming poverty in India at present, India is poised to be an international giant.

Hindus distinguish between voluntary and involuntary poverty. Voluntary poverty is taken on for religious reasons to purify the self and pursue spiritual goals. The poverty of the great Gandhi is an example of this. Involuntary poverty is a situation where one is poor and has no choice in the matter. This latter poverty is not desired because Hindus prize economic success and even have a goddess of prosperity called Laksmi who is cherished.[15]

Hinduism also distinguished between poverty and destitution, where food, shelter and clothing are not available. This kind of poverty is considered to be dehumanizing and from early on rulers were expected to alleviate such wont. There are many people in India who live austere lives but still maintain their dignity. At the same time, there are countless Indians who live in squalor and starvation and sleep on the pavements or on railway platforms.[16]

In Hinduism there are certain groups that have a high risk of living in poverty. Those from lower castes often experience discrimination and find it difficult to find good jobs. Even though "untouchability" has been outlawed, the Dalits are still often given the low-paying jobs that no one else wants to do. Women, who are usually dependent on men, are also subject to poverty when deserted or widowed. Farmers, who are dependent on weather for their crops, are also vulnerable to be thrown into poverty. Visiting parts of India, with its huge population and chaotic social structure, one can witness squalor that is indeed startling!

The Hindu notion of *karma*, where one's actions affects one's rebirth, also can influence attitudes toward poverty. Poverty can be viewed as a result of some former life, which can give a sense of inevitability to one's status. At the same time, Hindus believe one's good deeds in this life can result in a better future life and this can be a source of hope.

The Hindu belief in the interconnectedness of all things leads to a sense of justice, where all should have their needs met. The *dharma*, or law of Hinduism, states that all persons are my brother or sister and that I must therefore do all I can to alleviate poverty. In addition, the belief in *moksha* or liberation, calls Hindus to free themselves and others from the bonds of destitution. Moreover, by helping to free others, one's self also becomes more liberated. In addition, charity, which is one of the chief virtues of Hinduism, calls both the State and its citizens to reach out to the needy.[17]

Buddhism

Christians, Jews and Muslims often see poverty in the context of the struggle between good and evil, a result of greed and injustice. Buddhists on the other hand, see the primary struggle as being between ignorance and wisdom. From this perspective, poverty is bad because it causes *dukkha*, or suffering. *Dukkha* is a central notion in Buddhism and is multifaceted. *Dukkha* is sickness, old age, death, and the transitory aspect of reality. Buddhist wisdom teaches that everything is impermanent, transitory and that actually all that we think to be real is in fact an illusion. Suffering or anxiety comes from clinging to people or things as though they were permanent. Peacefulness therefore comes from "letting go"—freeing ourselves from all attachments. For the Buddhist, such letting go brings "moksha" or freedom. Such liberation can only be achieved from regular meditation and holistic righteous living.

In this context, attachment either for the rich or the poor causes suffering. The monks and nuns, Bhikkhus and Bhikinis, live in voluntary poverty in order to avoid attachments and be free to follow the pursuit of enlightenment. The laity, both rich and poor, are urged to live simple and unattached lives All are called to alleviate destitution through love and compassion because such a state hinders one from living the spiritual life and participating in healthy meditation. The Buddha himself taught that one must feed the hungry before preaching to them. He said of a student: "If he were feeling very hungry, the pangs of hunger might have prevented him from taking in the Dharma [teaching] fully."[18]

Buddhism arose in the Brahman society in India as it moved toward egalitarianism, with the elimination of the caste system and recognition of the dignity of women. The goal of Buddhist spirituality is to live a life of humility, love and compassion; a life that reaches out to the needy. *Karma* and past lives are still recognized by Buddhism, but not as a reason to be resigned to poverty or to feel deserving of one's wealth. Both the poor and the wealthy are called to detachment and the wealthy are asked to use their wealthy to benefit the destitute. All are taught to work to achieve the "no self," to set aside the false self that is cut off from others and insensitive to their suffering. Dukkha, or suffering and unhappiness, comes from greed, ill will and delusion. As David Loy, a well-known expert on Buddhism comments, "For better karma, these must be transformed into their wholesome counterparts: greed into generosity, ill will into loving kindness, and delusion of separate self into the wisdom that realizes our interdependence with others."[19]

Today there is a movement in Buddhism called "Engaged Buddhism" led by the well-known Bhikku, Thich Nhat Hanh. This movement encourages today's Buddhists to live simply, share their goods with others and avoid all harm to humans, other species and the earth itself.

Judaism

The modern Hebrew word 'oni' means poverty or social phenomenon in which people are trapped. In the Hebrew Bible, the word had a broader meaning of "misery" or "suffering," which could be brought on by indigence, childlessness or oppression. The Hebrew Bible expresses God's concern for justice for the poor: "You shall not abuse the poor and destitute laborer, whether a fellow countryman or a stranger... You must pay him his wages on the same day, before the sun sets for his is poor and urgently depends on it; else he will cry to the Lord against you and you will incur guilt" (Deuteronomy 24:14-15). The Bible implies that poverty is a result of evil oppression and that the poor can expect divine support.

The poor were usually those who had no land, women thrown out of the home through divorce, the sick and the handicapped. (As we see in the gospels some thought the latter to be receiving punishment by God.) Poverty is associated with virtue, whereas wealth can cause hubris and result in pride and haughtiness. The poor on the other hand can be humble and meek and are called to "inherit the land" (Psalms 37:11). This seems to be the background for the beatitudes: "Blessed are the poor in spirit; for there is the kingdom of heaven...Blessed are the meek, for they shall inherit the earth" (Matthew 5:3-5).[20] The Hebrew did not usually see poverty as a punishment, although laziness was condemned. The question of poverty is explored thoroughly in the Book of Job, but in the end remains unresolved.

The alleviation of poverty is a moral imperative in the Jewish tradition. The human needs for shelter, food and clothing must be supplied by the community. This is strongly emphasized in the prophetic tradition. The right to private property is defended and there has not been a strong tradition of sharing goods. The modern communal kibbutz model in Israel is an exception. Taxation, agencies for distribution, and private donations have been the most common means of helping the poor. Often the highest level of helping is preventing individuals and families from falling into poverty by enabling them to have land and jobs. Another Jewish principle with regard to helping others is to start with those closest to you, your family and neighbors (both Jews and non-Jews). The motto here seems to be: "Charity begins at home."

Islam

Dealing with poverty has been central in the Islamic tradition, beginning with the early revelations to Muhammad. Hundreds of verses in the Qur'an and Hadith are concerned with the claims of the poor and the moral obligations of the rich to assist the poor. Two of the five pillars of faith are related to poverty; one requires that *zakat* or alms be given to the poor and another requires fasting during the month of Ramadan, which in part can remind Muslims to think of the hunger of the destitute. Unfortunately today the *zakat* has not been an effective way to alleviate poverty. Policies with regard to assessment are vague, some evade paying it, and there is inefficiency and even corruption in distributing it.[21]

Islamic societies guided by "sharia law" shy away from both capitalism and communism. Unfortunately, in countries like Tunisia, Syria, Egypt, Sudan, Libya, and Yemen the governments have been led by dictators. The "Arab Spring" in 2010 and subsequent revolutions in the Arab world saw many young Muslims rebelling against these governments. Many of the Islamic economies in the world are stagnant with a great deal of unemployment, and unfair distribution of wealth and poverty. In fact, Muslims, most of whom are not Arabs, constitute the largest number of the world's poor.

The central theology of the Qur'an says the Allah the Creator has dominion (ownership) over the heavens and earth and that humans possess only a contingent right to ownership as servants of God. There must always be a balance between individual ownership and the claims of the community (*umma*). Individuals have a right to own property and the resulting social inequalities are God's will and part of the test to which humans are subjected. Allah gives endowments and talents and individuals are born into certain families, places and circumstances. At the same time, human choices help determine the lot that people are given. No one is to envy the way "God has made some of you excel over others." From this perspective, poverty and wealth are neutral. What matters is how one lives in their allotted position. As for the poor, they will enter paradise before the rich, because the later are inclined to be selfish and miserly. The only hope of the rich is to be purified through acts of charity. The ideal, of course, is to be somewhere in the middle, not too rich to become corrupt and not too destitute to be able to grow spiritually.

In the ideal, all Muslims are called to charity to their brothers and sisters, for it is through charity that people come closer to God.

Women's Rights

On November 6, 2012 a long presidential campaign ended in the United States with the reelection of President Obama. Nine men and one woman had been candidates and in the final election four men ran for the offices of President and Vice-President. On November 15, 2012 the 18th National Congress of China introduced their new leadership and seven men walked onstage. Two weeks later Pope Benedict XVI appointed six new Cardinals— all men.

After all the talk of gender equality, the many advances that women have made in business, the military, education, government and religions, one is still tempted to say: "the more things change, the more they remain the same."

In many areas there are still blatant examples of the oppression of women. It is estimated that 32 million girls around the world are deprived of a primary education. Hundreds of thousands of American girls are the victims of sex-trafficking. Global victims of sex-trafficking run in the millions. U.S. National studies estimate that 1 in 5 young women will be raped during their college years. 1 in 4 will experience domestic violence in their lifetime. The horrific earthquake in Haiti left many women vulnerable to gang rape, especially in the tent cities. In the Congo, 12% of women have been raped at least once in their lifetime. The situation is similar in countries like Sudan and Somalia, where roaming militia rape at will. In China, the one-child rule and the preference for boys caused many parents to abort girl fetuses. Similar practices occur in India, where boy babies are preferred. In 2012 a Pakistani teen girl was shot by a Taliban gunman for advocating for the education of girls.

Male dominance has a long history. Some cultural historians maintain that it began to gain strength about 3,000 BCE. With the development of warfare, males were usually stronger and more inclined toward violence. After victories where the males were killed, the women were taken off as slaves and concubines. Males were also thought of as the primary source of life in that a small person was contained in their sperm and women served only as an area for preparation of the birth. (It was only in the 18th century that that central role of the woman's ovum in reproduction was discovered.)

Although there were some cultures in early Europe and the Near East where women played more dominant roles and where goddesses were central in worship, most cultures have been male-dominated.[22] The Greek culture, which has been most influential on European as well as Christian culture, often took a dim view of women. Aristotle described females as "misformed males," a description that was picked up by Thomas Aquinas in the medieval period and was carried on for centuries.

Quite commonly women were also thought to be unclean because of their menstruation and giving birth. It was also common to think that women were more given to emotion and were intellectually inferior, so they were not fit for education. Some thought learning might even weaken them further and prevent them from having healthy babies. Being weak and fragile, women were thus not fit for warfare or for the rough and tumble of politics. (Women were not allowed to vote in the United States until 1920.) There's a story about Sojourner Truth (1797-1883), a Black advocate for the abolition of slavery and the right for women to vote. In 1858 she was giving a rousing speech at a convention and someone, disbelieving that a woman could speak so powerfully about political matters, shouted out that Sojourner was a man. She calmly unbuttoned her blouse and exposed her breasts to assure the heckler that she was indeed a woman! In another famous speech she commented on the notion that women were weak and fragile. She proclaimed, "Look at me! Look at my arm! I have ploughed and planted, and gathered into barns, and no man could head me! And ain't I a woman? I could work as much and eat as much as a man - when I could get it - and bear the lash as well! And ain't I a woman? I have borne thirteen children, and seen most all sold off to slavery, and when I cried out with my mother's grief, none but Jesus heard me. And ain't I a woman?"[23]

Women's Rights During Religious Beginnings

Many religions seem to have begun by viewing women more positively than the traditions they evolved into. The Vedic tradition that preceded Hinduism in India honored the rights of women and was open to their education and religious participation. It was only with the rise of Hinduism with its concerns for caste, racial and linear purity that men were moved to control women's sexuality and who and when they married.

Judaism produced the Genesis story where both women and men were created from the same material and in the image and likeness of God. Adam and Eve were "one" and partners in their life decisions. Only later was the story interpreted to show that Eve was weak in the face of evil and inclined to be a temptress who would lead her man into evil. This notion became very prominent in later attitudes toward women.

Christians began as disciples of Jesus who was very comfortable with women, ignored the taboos about their impurity, chose them for his disciples and allowed them to be the first witnesses to his resurrection. The early communities as portrayed in Acts and the letters of Paul note many outstanding women who act as apostles, teachers and leaders. It did not take long before the patriarchal cultures of Judaism and then Rome influenced the fledgling Christian communities. An all male hierarchy and priesthood was established and women were gradually excluded from official positions in the Church. A woman's diaconate did manage to prevail for several hundred years before it was terminated.

Islam began at a time when Arab women had few rights in their culture. Muhammad and his revelations improved the lot for women, which in the tribal culture was quite bleak. They were offered more independence in marriage and the right of inheritance. The Prophet's treatment of women in Medina was much more progressive than how women were treated in the Arab tribal areas. Unfortunately, many of these advances for women were lost as cultural forces and extremists prevailed.

Major Religions Look At Women's Issues

In the following section, we will review how the major religions are addressing the rights of women and look at the actions of some leading women in each religion. Commonly, religions have viewed women as inferior and have often tolerated abuse of them. Today, women still struggle for equality within their own religions, and cultures often use their religious traditions to justify patriarchal structures and the oppression of women.

Women in Hinduism

As mentioned earlier, Hindu women eventually lost what they had gained in the early years of Vedic Hinduism. In 800 BCE, the Brahmans began to dominate Indian society and religion. Women lost their roles in public rituals and were relegated to domestic rituals, where they still preside at home altars today.

Once the Laws of Manu were formulated in Hinduism, women were classified with slaves and outcasts and would henceforth be servants of their husbands. Women were considered to be unclean because of their menstruation, as well as seductive through their powers of sexual attraction. As a result, strong rules were developed to control women, sequester them in their homes, marry them off as children to assure their virginity, arrange their marriages and even dispose of girl infants. Large bridal dowries had to be given for a daughter and her "Sati" became a custom, where the widow would throw herself on the flames that were cremating her husband because effectively her life was now over. Women lost their right to be educated, seek divorce or to inherit. Even though scriptures like the Gita proclaimed equality: "I am the same in all beings, and my love is ever the same," this did not seem to apply to women.[24]

Things improved for Hindu women in the 5th century BCE, when the scriptural Puranas became popular and pointed out the women could be spiritually liberated over and above their roles as wives and mothers. In the domestic and temple rituals, goddesses were given a more central position and became role models for many who felt called to be leaders, warriors or rebels. Heroines like Sita, who acted out of love for her husband rather than obedience, was honored by many women. Women were able to become great poets and saints. As we will see later, the way was open for some women to become "Mothers," or spiritual leaders or gurus.

Indian women gained many rights when the post-colonial Constitution was established in 1948. Child marriages and Sati were no longer legal. Women were given access to education and jobs. Today, 95% of girls are enrolled in primary school, although many do not finish because they are required to work to support their families. In the urban areas many young women are receiving higher education and aspiring to the professions, even to be in the military. Many marriages are still arranged in the context of caste, but generally with consultation and agreement on the part of the couple. Divorce can be sought by either husbands or wives.

On the dark side, honor killings, where women are killed for dishonoring their families, prostitution and sex-trafficking are practiced in India, and the legal system seems either unable or unwilling to address these issues.

On the whole, the ancient Hindu teachings still stand as the Sanatana Dharma," the eternal way, for its followers. As in any religion, there are traditionalists who follow these teachings as laws about religion, marriage, the roles of men and women, chastity and other aspects of life. Many others view these truths as ideals, values and guidelines, but may not follow them strictly in contemporary society. In the following section we will look at some of these truths that are helping women gain equality and freedom in Hindu society.

The Divine Feminine in Hinduism

Many women in the other major religions struggle to find feminine images of the divine. The Hindu religion has had such images in abundance for thousands of years. Brahman, whom Hindus view as the very ground of being, is held to be beyond either materiality or gender. Brahman is manifested in countless ways as both female and male, as goddesses and gods. These manifestations, which are usually presented with images and statues, present the infinite variety of images within God and creation. A wide variety of stories and allegories tell of the human struggle to recognize the connectedness and oneness of all reality.

Given the widespread oppression of women in India, one has to wonder whether belief in this pantheon of goddesses has been effective in liberating women. Defenders of the goddess tradition point out that such images would be much more effective for women were they not interpreted by males. They point out that even with its limitations, the goddess tradition has for thousands of years helped women affirm their dignity in the midst of abusive situations and strive to overcome obstacles. Many young women have been helped to be successful in careers by the energetic Laksmi, the consort of Vishnu. Many women have been inspired to stand up for their rights by Durga, who is portrayed as a ferocious woman riding a lion and is fully armed to defeat the buffalo-demon. Many wives, including Kastubai, the wife of Gandhi, have been given the courage to be true partners with their husbands by the beautiful Sita, the consort of Ram. Even the blood-thirsty and terrifying Kali, who symbolizes the dark side of life, has inspired many women to fight for the lives of their children and deal with the grief of losing them through disease or hunger.[25]

The Dignity of Women in Hinduism

The Hindu tradition presents both good and bad attitudes toward women. Female scholars have set their minds to recover the positive teachings and promote them. Vedic poetry describes a woman as "the seed of the tree of life," and the laws of Manu often place women on a divine pedestal and calls for them to be honored. In the agricultural communities, women were looked on as symbols of fertility and nurturing. Popular devotions to Krishna, which emphasize the heart, have inspired many women to lead the spiritual life in their homes with their families.[26]

The Divine Mother

In the Hindu tradition, motherhood, the source of life, has been held in high esteem. Where nature was valued, the feminine was identified with it and was given titles of Mother Nature and Mother Earth. (The domination and abuse of nature conversely negatively affected the treatment of women.) Women today want to reclaim the more positive traditions.

A popular name for goddess is *mata* or *amma*, which means mother. Many female Hindu saints and gurus have been given this title and mothers traditionally are held in honor in Hindu families. *Devi*, the Mother Goddess, is worshipped throughout India with her many avatars or incarnations. She is the life force, the liberator. She is Mother Earth, especially for those active in ecology. She is Mother Ganges for those who go on pilgrimage to the sacred river. She was Mother India for those who struggled for liberation from British colonialism, and is now Mother Universe for those who want to see a bright future for modern Indian.

Notable Female Hindus

Today the mother goddess is embodied in powerful women like Mata Amritanandamayi (b. 1953). She is popularly known as Amma and has brought peace and inspiration to millions. People wait in long lines to talk with her, receive her hugs and be blessed by her. Her foundation, Amma.org, has built hundreds of thousands hospitals, schools, shelters and homes for the poor around the world and she and her organizations have sent millions to disasters like the 2004 tsunami, the 2005 Hurricane Katrina, and the 2010 earthquake in Haiti.

Another outstanding Hindu woman is Anuradha Koirala, who fights to rescue and rehabilitate thousands of young girls caught up in Nepal's sex trafficking. Her organization courageously raids brothels and patrols the India-Nepal border to rescue as many victims as they can. They have helped over 12,000 Nepali women and girls. In 2010 Koirala was awarded the CNN Hero of the Year Award.

Women in Buddhism

Many of the 3 million Buddhist women are on the move for freedom and equality. After having first been refused ordination to become nuns, many woman are now ordained. They have established Buddhist universities where young nuns and lay women can receive good educations. They have established primary and secondary schools, orphanages, hospices and retirement homes. They have founded organizations for ecology, peace, and for fighting domestic violence and sex trafficking.

After his enlightenment, Buddha made a break from the caste system, which was very advantageous for the many women from lower castes. He also rejected the strong patriarchal structures of his culture and taught that male and female karmas were equal. For Buddha, the mind, which was his focus for enlightenment, had no intrinsic gender so women were therefore also capable of enlightenment.[27] He was eventually talked into ordaining Buddhist nuns. Soon after Buddha's death, the Indian patriarchal culture began to take its toll on Buddhism. As the religion moved to other cultures in South Asia, China and Japan, many of the gains that had been achieved by women were lost. Although Buddha had been persuaded to ordain nuns, that practice was eventually suppressed.

Buddhist Values Treasure Women

Modern Buddhist women seeking equality point to the teachings of Buddha himself. One of his central teaching as that people can be the architects of their own consciousness and for him, consciousness was gender-free. Buddhist meditation, which is designed to free one of all that causes suffering, and Buddhist asceticism both aim to produce the loving compassionate person. Both women and men are called to achieve these goals. The four noble truths of Buddha, which describe the universal prevalence of suffering and teach how to heal suffering, are open to both men and women; and the eightfold path of righteous living is a path that can be taken by either sex. And, of course, the ultimate goal of enlightenment is open to all people.

Many women today, including a significant number of Western women, are attracted to progressive forms of Buddhism because there is no male-dominated hierarchy with which to contend, no rituals from which they are excluded and no forms of service that are closed are to them.

Many Buddhist women are inspired by Quan Yin, who is revered at The Lady Buddha. They point to Pajapati, Buddha's aunt who raised him after his mother died and who was able to persuade the Buddha to allow women to enter the Sangha (community) and live as ordained nuns. They revere Sanghamitra, the daughter of the great Indian Emperor, Ashoka, and a great promoter of Buddhism. She, along with 16 nuns, brought Buddism to Sri Lanka, where it still flourishes.

Buddhist women realize that they still have a long way to go toward equality. Although there are now ordained nuns in Vietnam, Taiwan, Tibet, India, China, the United States and Canada, many of them don't have access to the donations that the monks have and therefore have little to subsist on or to allow them to gain education.

Women and "The Liberation of All"

Buddha's goal was "to liberate all sentient beings," which was a goal treasured by Buddhist women. They too hope to be liberated from the oppression and discrimination to which women in so many cultures are subjected. Their religion offers them the confidence, dignity, love and compassion needed to deal with their day-to-day struggles.[28]

Buddhist women have to give a careful look at the Buddhist teaching that one must liberate the self and achieve the "no self." So often the "'no self'" for them has meant to be self-effacing servants to men. Many Buddhist women today reject that interpretation and view the "no self" as the "true self," the unselfish person open to serve others while still maintaining self-dignity.

Buddha taught his followers to "be a light unto yourself." This has helped many women move away from subservience and dependence. Buddhism has taught them how to see themselves as equal, independent persons of dignity. Whether they bend down in the rice paddies of China, work in the factories of Vietnam or teach children in Japan, many Buddhist women are gaining a new sense of self that is free, equal and independent.

Notable Female Buddhists

In recent times many outstanding Buddhist women have done amazing work. **Karma Lekshe Tsomo** founded Sakyadhita (Daughters of the Buddha), an organization of thousands of Buddhist women who gather yearly in some Asian city to present papers, network, offer support to each other and meditate. **Khunying Kanitha Wichiencharoen** (d. 2002) was a Buddhist nun who worked tirelessly to save young women in Thailand from prostitution and sex–trafficking. She was a lawyer who gained many rights for women in Thailand and founded an AIDS hospice, an orphanage, a clinic for homeless pregnant women and their infants and a youth center.

Women in Judaism

The Jewish Torah offers both positive and negative views on women. The two creation stories point to a certain equality in that both are created at the same time in the image of their creator (Genesis 1) and are made from the same material (Genesis 2). The covenant with God is made with both men and women, although only men receive its mark in circumcision.

In the biblical world, women had few rights in marriage, where they were "purchased," had no divorce rights, and spent their days serving their husbands and raising children. They had no right to study Torah and had to stay in their own area to the Temple, where they were forbidden to preside. They could not be religious leaders. Men taught their trades to their sons and in their morning prayers thanked God that they had not been born as a woman.

In the rabbinic period that followed the destruction of Jerusalem and saw major changes in Judaism, women were given more rights. They were no longer purchased for marriage and their consent was required. Women were given marriage contracts which gave them rights to funds and possessions if their husbands divorced them or died. They were also given rights to participate in business and to have medical care, and rights after divorce were given to them. They were also allowed to assume leadership in home ceremonies such as the Sabbath service.[29]

At the same time, women were still considered to be unclean by virtue of their menstruation and the process of giving birth, as well as having dangerous seductive powers. For the most part, they were to stay in their roles of wives, mothers and homemakers. The men were to be the providers and hold positions of leadership.

In the last fifty years, Jewish women have gained many new rights in society. They have pointed out that Torah, Talmud and other religious texts were all written by men and lack the feminine perspective, which women scholars now can offer. (The Talmud seldom even mentions women.) They point out that God has been portrayed as a man, a warrior or judge, neglecting the treasured feminine image of the divine in the scriptures. Changes have come gradually, especially in the Reform and Conservation congregations, both of which allow women rabbis and cantors. The Orthodox congregations have changed more slowly; they now have rabbinic assistants and women have been given more opportunities to study Torah and commentaries. There are a number of Jewish beliefs that are put forth by women to achieve equality in Judaism. Here we will consider several of them.

Beyond a Male God

Though the male pronoun is used in Torah, the God of the Israelites was nameless and transcending gender and imaging. God describes self to Moses as "I am who am." When it comes to later imaging of God, feminine images are also used. In Isaiah, God is described as a mother (Isaiah 49:15-16; 66, 12, 13). Hosea also refers to the Mother-God (Hosea 11:1-4). In the Book of Wisdom, there is the magnificent image of Lady Wisdom, who partners with God in creation. In their prayer groups, some Jewish women find peace and inspiration in Shechinah, the gentle and loving presence of the divine feminine.[30]

A More Feminine Torah

Since Torah and the other key texts of Judaism were written by men, many Jewish women want to see a feminine perspective given to these writings. In their studies, women look for elements of hierarchy and patriarchy that are more cultural than they are revealed and therefore are subject to change. At the same time, they look for beliefs about liberation and stories of outstanding Jewish women that have been neglected. In addition, Jewish women want to recognize the voices of many Jewish women in the past and in recent times from all over the world, voices that can offer new insights into the Jewish tradition.

Notable Female Jews

Several prominent Jewish women should be mentioned here. Susannah Heschel is the daughter of the Rabbi Heschel and a expert on the Jewish tradition in her own right. She is a professor at Dartmouth and has written extensively on biblical topics, gender issues, and anti-Semitism. Her book *On Being a Jewish Feminist* has had a profound influence on many Jewish women. Ruth Bader Ginsburg serves as an Associate Justice on the United States Supreme Court. For many years she has been a strong advocate for women who wish to enter the field of law and has been an influential promoter of women's rights in the United States.

Women in Christianity

Christianity sees its beginnings with followers of Jesus of Nazareth, a Jewish reformer. The gospels show Jesus opposing the Jewish divorce laws which favored men, ignoring the taboos against talking with or healing women in public, instructing women in Torah in public and in their homes, dining with them and even selecting them as his disciples. The latter was unheard of in his time. Women were clearly present in the crucifixion stories and are featured as the first witnesses of his resurrection. Mary of Magdala is portrayed as a key disciple who actually funded his mission and was the first to witness his resurrection. The gospels show a great reverence for Mary, Jesus' mother, and give her a central place in the birth stories, Jesus' first miracle at Cana, and at the foot of the cross.

Paul, the apostle to the Gentiles, at times follows cultural custom in requiring women to cover their heads and not speak out in church, but generally shares Jesus' inclusive view of women. A number of women are his closest associates in ministry: Priscilla, who worked side by side with him in Rome, Corinth and Ephesus and served as a prominent leader; Lydia who helped establish the church at Phillippi, and Junia, who is called "an apostle." In Paul's epistle to the Romans, he closes by citing ten women who were leaders in house churches.

The early churches were served by virgins, widows, deaconesses, along with women who acted as prophets, teachers and apostles.[31] Tragically, much to this influence waned under the influence of Greek and Roman culture. Under the influence of Augustine, Jerome and other church fathers, women were characterized as weak, inferior, and not fit for ministry. As an all male ministry evolved, women were to be considered "dangerous and tempting."

In later centuries, some women were able to gain prominence, such as Hildegard of Bingen, one of the most powerful Abbesses in Europe, Catherine of Siena, who was an advisor to Popes, and Teresa of Avila, a mystic and reformer of convents. Mary the Mother of Jesus was held in high esteem and many devotions developed around her, but her image was often so cosmic and majestic that it was out of reach as an example for the average women.[32]

Unfortunately, during the Middle Ages, many women mystics and healers were declared to be witches and were either imprisoned or burned at the stake. (It is estimated the over 100,000 women were executed as witches.)

Neither the Protestant or Catholic reformations restored women to any prominent roles in the church. In both movements the leadership was given over to men. In the 17th century, radical movements like the Quakers gave prominence to women, who were allowed to teach and lead services. In some cases, these women were punished or imprisoned—one was hung.

In the modern era, things began to change. In 1890, the famous suffragette, Elisabeth Cody Stanton put out the Woman's Bible, which attempted to locate and eliminate sexism in the Bible. There was some talk of ordaining women, and some women became famous on the preaching circuit.

Today there is a strong movement among women in Christianity. There are many leading women theologians, biblical scholars and religious leaders. Nearly all the Protestant churches ordain women to ministry, even to the level of bishop. The Roman Catholic and Orthodox churches refuse to allow women to be ordained, Women who receive ordination as Roman Catholic priests are excommunicated from the church. Regardless, there are over 100 such women priests and a number of bishops, and the number is growing each year.

Gaining Gender Equality in Christianity

There are many Christian beliefs which can assist women in gaining equality in the churches. Here are two:

The Discipleship of Women

We have seen that Jesus himself opposed the oppression of women and reached out to offer them healing and compassion. His selection of women disciples is unprecedented. Obviously the early church carried on Jesus' tradition until culture and patriarchal leaders all but eliminated it. Many women scholars, missionaries and those working in ministry want to return to these original practices and gain equality for women on all levels. Many Catholic women are alarmed by the recent investigation of the nuns, the suppression of female theologians, and the excommunication of some involved in ordination. They view these moves as antithetical to the gospels and the way of the early church.

The Equality of Women

We have seen that both the Hebrew and Christian scriptures are concerned with the dignity and equality of women. Feminine images of God, Jesus' reverence for women and descriptions of life in the early church point to this value. Culture, which in the past helped annul the Church's openness of women, has now in many ways moved ahead of the churches. Women are gaining equality in the military, government, corporate life, and the courts. At the same time, some churches are lagging behind, even to the point of ignoring the openness to women in their own scriptures and tradition.

Notable Female Christians

There are many prominent Christian women involved in ministry today. We have space to mention only a few. **Joan Chittister** (b. 1936) is a Benedictine nun with a Ph.D. from Penn State; in her extensive writing and brilliant speaking, she has been a force in the Christian women's movement. **Bishop Barbara Harris** (b. 1930) has a business background and was president of a firm before she the first Episcopal bishop. Besides her church leadership, she consults with corporations on ethics and is dedicated to prison ministry and questions of social justice. **Bishop Patricia Fresen** (b. 1940) spent over 40 years in a Dominican convent and served as a teacher. She received her doctorate in theology in South Africa and took a position teaching in the Catholic seminary and in the University of Johannesburg. She was ordained a Roman Catholic priest in 2003 and then ordained a bishop. She was forced to withdraw from the Dominicans and the University, and was excommunicated from the church. She now lives simply in Germany and soldiers on as the founder of the Roman Catholic Women Priest movement.

Women in Islam

Most of the Muslim women throughout the world are illiterate and poor. Many live in horrible conditions in refugee camps with their children, fleeing from violence and wars in Darfur, Palestine, Lebanon, Pakistan, Afghanistan and Ethiopia. A good number are migrant workers throughout Europe, or victims of drought or AIDS in Africa. Theirs are the basic issues of food, water, shelter, education and health. Many Muslim women in the Arab world struggle with issues of inequality in marriage, in the courts and in education. In countries where sharia law (Islamic law) is enforced, their lives are controlled by extremist clerics. In the United States, Muslim women are stereotyped as being male-dominated or even as terrorists. Although many Muslim women in the United States are lawyers, physicians, executives, professors, and serve in the armed forces, even as fighter pilots, they are pictured as subservient and sequestered.

Today there is a strong feminist movement among Muslim woman (sometimes referred to as a gender jihad). Many women scholars call for new interpretations of the Koran that are more in line with the contemporary experience. Others call for a reclaiming of the radical teachings by Muhammad himself with regard to women—beliefs that have been lost among the tradition laws of conservative clerics.

Gender Equality in Islam

There are a number of Muslim beliefs that support the dignity of women. First of all, Muslim women today point out that the equality of these sexes is strong in the Koran. With regards to their creation and final reward, both genders are treated the same. Both are equally watched over by the same merciful and benevolent Allah. Often the Koran refers to humankind and does not make a distinction between male and female. There is no "Adam's rib" story and any account of a "fall" in the original Koran so there are no grounds for blaming Eve for the human condition. Muhammad treated women with great respect, consulted them and selected them to be spiritual guides. He helped with chores, prayed side-by-side with women and honored them in ways which were radically different from his times. Muslim women point to all this equality as good reason for no longer tolerating abuse and injustice toward women in Islam.[33]

Justice for women in Islam

Muslim women today assert that Muhummad had a unique sense of justice with regard to women. They point to the facts that the Prophet treated women fairly and outlawed the killing of infant females. They make the point that so many of the practices against women today such as requiring them to cover their entire bodies in public and secluding women at home, requiring them to be servants, separating them at prayers, stoning women for adultery, preventing them from having education, not allowing them to drive, requiring that they marry only Muslims, and so-called honor killings are not Islamic at all and must be eliminated from Muslim life. Muslim scholars point out that the laws allowing polygamy, the superiority of men, and the requirement of women to be obedient to their husbands, even though they are in the Koran, come from an earlier Arabic culture and are no longer relevant today.[34]

Notable Female Muslims

We should note several prominent Muslim women who champion their gender. In 2012 **Razia Jan** was one of the CNN Heroes of the year. She founded Razia's Ray of Hope Foundation and established a school where 350 Afghan girls receive a free education. Surrounded by the dangers of the Taliban who violently oppose feminine education, Razia soldiers on amidst threats and dangers. She has provided tens of thousands of shoes to Afghan children and has financially supported many rug weavers and their families. **Amina Wadud**, Ph.D. is a scholar of the Koran. She advocates for equal participation of men and women at Friday services in the mosque and has held controversial all-women services. Her two books, Koran and Women and Inside the Gender Jihad have been extremely influential on Muslim women world-wide. Amina has been disowned by many conservative Imams and has received death threats.

Peace and Religion

As is the case with gender equality, where the reality of a religion often does not live up to its original beliefs, most religions have had a complex relationship with peace and violence.

While all religions value peace, there are many examples where they have turned to violence. The Christians conducted the Crusades against Muslims in the Palestine, as well as inquisitions against heretics. Muslims conquered most of the known world and established an Islamic Empire. Millions of Protestants and Catholics were killed during the Thirty-Years War following the Reformation. Western nations, often in the name of religion, destroyed whole "heathen" cultures in Central, South and North America and Africa. The slaughter has continued in modern times. During the Nazi regime in Germany (1933-45), a largely Christian country, millions of Jews were killed for being considered to be racially inferior and were labeled "Christ-killers." In 1947 over a million Hindus and Muslims were slaughtered as the two groups fought over the partition of India from Pakistan. In 1984, there was a clash between Hindus and Sikhs where nearly 1,000 were killed.

We have also seen violence within the religions themselves: Sunnis against Shia in the Muslim world, Catholics against Protestants in Northern Ireland, the Taliban against more moderate Muslims in Afghanistan and the racially charged slaughter of black Africans by the Muslim Janjaweed in Darfur.

At the same time, many heroic religious leaders have been at the forefront of peace movements and have been strong advocates for non-violence. The Hindu Gandhi led his people in a non-violent resistance to the Western colonialists in both South Africa and India. Anglican Archbishop Tutu (b. 1931), Bishop Huddleston (1913-1998) and Catholic Archbishop Hurley (1915-2004) led non-violent movements against Apartheid in South Africa. Tibetan Buddhist leaders, the Dalai Lama and the Vietnam Buddhist monk, Thich Nhat Hanh have been strong international advocates for peace and non-violence. In the United States, Dorothy Day, Trappist Thomas Merton, and Catholic priests Daniel and Philip Berrigan and John Dear have been strong advocates for non-violence. Rev. Martin Luther King, Jr. led a non-violent movement for civil rights for Blacks and Cesar Chavez won labor rights for migrant workers through non-violent marches and protests. Archbishop Oscar Romero was a champion of non-violence as he condemned the violence that his El Salvadoran government used upon his people.

In the following section we will give an overview of peace insights in the major religions and provide more details on some of the important peace advocates.

Hinduism

Hinduism has its own traditions with regard to violence. The Vedas describe creation as coming from the dismemberment of a cosmic person and the Hindu epics describe violent battles where the gods act as warlike figures. The Gita is told in the context of a war, which ultimately is sanctioned as a duty. The caste system has resulted in oppression and violence, especially against the Dalits, the so-called untouchables. Their reaction has been largely non-violent and many have converted to Buddhism and Christianity to avoid discrimination.[35]

Hinduism also has a strong tradition of the sacredness of all things, which serves as a basis for non-violence. God, or Brahman, is viewed as the source of all creation, dwells in all and thus renders all reality sacred. The divine is the source, sustainer and goal of all creation, and thus all reality is interconnected by the divine presence. Krishna teaches that "God dwells in the heart of all being" and that everything reflects the glory and the power of the divine.[36]

Ahimsa (do no harm to anything) is a Hindu virtue that flows from the awareness that the divine is in all reality. To hurt oneself and others is to offend the divine that is within all. The Gita says, "And when a person sees that the God that is in himself is the same God that is in all that is, he hurts not himself hurting others."[37] Ahimsa becomes a force that is stronger than violence and which no force can wipe out. The Hindu greeting to another consists of putting the two hands together, bowing and saying *Namaste*. For the devout Hindu, this means: "The divine in me bows to the divine in you."

Mahatma Gandhi studied and practiced *ahimsa*, and transformed it from a virtue practiced by ascetics into a force that could be used by all to resist injustice and violence. His mission is said to have begun when he was thrown off a train because he had purchased and used a first class ticket on a train, a practice forbidden to "colored people." Sitting all night on the cold deck of the station he suddenly realized what it meant to be an outcast. He decided to non-violently take up the cause of his oppressed fellow Indians in South Africa and then took his mission to India. He believed fervently that the divine was a life force within all, both oppressors and oppressed and that he would be given the power to stand up to beatings, being jailed, humiliated and mocked, but would never be deserted by his God. It was his conviction that non-violence was the Truth and that ultimately God was Truth. He demonstrated that ahimsa was not passivity, but rather an indomitable power that took bravery and courage and which enabled one to face suffering and even death for peace and justice. It pitted the power of love for one's enemy and forgiveness against the demonic forces of hatred and anger, with the firm conviction that the former would ultimately win out.[38]

Buddhism

In spite of Buddha's teachings on righteous living, love and compassion, Buddhists have sometimes turned to violence. Over the centuries, the Buddhists have been at war with the Tamils (mostly Hindus) and only recently has there been a peaceful resolution. Japanese Buddhists had their "warrior monks" and Shogun fighters in the middle ages. In the modern era, most Japanese Buddhists supported Japanese nationalism and their country's involvement in World War II. It was Zen Buddhism that developed the martial arts for fighting. Many Buddhists turned to violence against their Communist enemies in Cambodia, Vietnam, Thailand and Myanmar. For a half century Tibetans have struggled against outside occupiers. Currently the Dalai Lama has his hands full trying to dissuade his young people from turning to violence against their Chinese occupiers and their efforts to obliterate Tibetan culture.

Buddhism over the centuries has been predominantly a peaceful religion. The Buddhist path abjures anger, hatred, and greed because they cause suffering and violence. Buddha taught that hatred has never stopped hatred and that if we can stop greed we can stop suffering. Killing is plainly and simply against the first Buddhist precept, which is: do not kill.

Buddha taught that peace begins with peace of mind and then can be spread to others through example and teaching. Buddha teaches that we are the architects of our own consciousness, lights unto ourselves and that the enlightened way to build a peaceful consciousness that is constantly mindful to the dignity of self and others. The holy person renounces all violence toward all living things. The Buddhist path is one of harmony and non-violence. It seeks through meditation to root out ignorance, one of the first causes of violence. Ignorance involves false notions about reality, individuality based on illusions, and a self-centered based on a disordered love of self.

Buddhism is about personal transformation which calls for renunciation of all that is toxic in our psyche; bitterness, self-pity, desire for revenge, all of which drive us toward violence. Buddhism calls for self-liberation. It calls one to reach out to others with self-sacrifice, compassion and generosity.

The Dalai Lama is the leader of Tibetan Buddhism and has spent the last fifty years leading his people who are in exile in Dharamsala, India in the ways of peace. In addition, he has been constantly on road teaching non-violent ways toward peace and justice. He firmly believes that love of peace, justice and freedom will always ultimately triumph over cruelty, oppression and war. In 1998 the Dalai Lama was awarded the Nobel Peace Prize.

Aung San Suu Kyi has now become known world-wide, especially since she was released from many years of house arrest and was visited by then Secretary of State Hillary Clinton and President Obama. In 1990, she was elected Prime Minister of Myanmar (Burma), only to be deposed, imprisoned and then put under house arrest, separated from her husband and two children. Her crimes: being an advocate for non-violence and opposing the violence of her government. Now that she has been released she has been elected to Parliament and has become an international hero.

Judaism

Judaism has seen its share of violence. The Hebrew people are described as conquering their neighbor, taking over the Land of Canaan by violence and warring with neighboring nations. More often Jews have been on the losing end of violence. They were conquered by the Assyrians, the Babylonians, the Romans and the Syrians. Areas where they lived were conquered by Muslims. They have experienced discrimination, persecution, pogroms, and alienation from their homeland. Six million of their men, women and children were gassed and their bodies cremated in ovens in the Nazi camps. They fought the British and the Arabs to secure their homeland in Israel and are now a militant world power with nuclear capabilities.

The Hebrew greeting, *Shalom*, means peace. The Hebrew Scriptures hold up peace as an ideal. The Hebrew prophets often cry out for the end of violence and the coming of peace. Isaiah gives his vision of Israel about peace: "He shall judge between the nations, and shall decide for many peoples; and they shall beat their swords into plowshares, and their spears into pruning hooks; nation shall not lift up sword against nation, neither shall they learn war any more" (Isaiah 2:4).

Judaism sees peace as the highest good. Peace is to be with God, self and others (the basis of the Commandments). Generally, revenge is condemned along with unprovoked aggression. Given their history, it is easy to see where self-preservation would always be a high priority.[39]

The Genesis stories tell of all creation and life as coming from the hand of the Creator. Humans are created in the image and likeness of God. Humans stand in a sacred covenant with God, who liberates them and protects them. All of this argues for the sacredness of human life and leads to the commandment: Thou shalt not kill.

One of the best known Jewish advocates for peace is Elie Wiesel (b. 1928). When Elie was fifteen he and his family were sent to the death camp, Auschwitz. He and his two older sisters survived the camps and after the war he became a writer. His *Night* became a best-seller and he began his career as a writer and tireless advocate for war refugees around the world and for world peace. In 1986, Wiesel was awarded the Nobel Peace Prize.

Christianity

Christians have not always followed Jesus' injunctions to love your enemy, pray for those who persecute you and turn your cheek when struck. As mentioned earlier, the historical record for waging persecutions and wars is extensive.

Since the time of Augustine, Christians have tried to follow his just war theory, which he borrowed from the Romans (who were not an especially peaceful people as they militarily dominated an extensive empire for 1000 years). The just war stipulates that war is only justified if it follows a just cause (such as saving lives), a right intention (such as the restoration of order), is done with legitimate authority, and proportionate means are used. Obviously such general norms are open to all variety of interpretations. Often the warring parties both consider their participation in a war "just."

Parallel with the just war theory, there is a strong tradition for non-violence in Christianity. One of Jesus' beatitudes is "Blessed are the peacemakers." In his own life he was a non-violent person. He dealt with people with humility, love, forgiveness and healing. At the same time, he was a strong advocate for justice and took vehement positions against hypocrisy, oppression, abuse of office. When it came time for his arrest, Jesus counseled his followers to put aside their swords. When Peter cut off an ear of one of the arresting party, Jesus healed the injury. When Jesus returned to his disciples after his resurrection he greeting to them was "Peace be with you." No incrimination for their desertion, cowardice, or in the case of Peter, outright denial. Just "Peace be with you."

Christians follow the Jewish tradition that all life comes from God the Creator. Christians add dimensions to that teaching in that they consider human life to be holy and sacred and that all are called to share in grace, which is God's own life. Christians are called to faithfully follow Jesus' example to treat all with respect, love and service. Christians also give "the least of the brethren" special consideration for their protection and nourishment.

Islam

The followers of Muhammad were so fervently committed to the revelation from Allah received through the Prophet that they soon began to spread their political and religious influence. They conquered all of Arabia, where Islam began and then continued their conquests until their Empire conquered the weakened Persian Empire to the East, Central Asia and China, South Asia, North Africa and the Horn of Africa, the Middle East, the Byzantine Empire, and areas in East and West Africa, Spain and Portugal, areas of Eastern Europe and Russian, and even areas in Western Europe. In 732, the slashing Arabian cavalry was stopped at Tours, France by stalwart infantry led by Charles Martel.

Islamic scholars as well as the majority of the 1.3 billion Muslims (25% of the world's population) today will tell you that that Islam is in fact a peaceful religion. The word Islam is derived from the *salaam*, which means "peace." In today's world, Muslims are having a difficult time convincing others of this view since 9/11. Since that fateful day, the images of the destruction of the World Trade Center, the wars in Iraq and Afghanistan, as well as the many images on television of bearded Arab terrorists have convinced many Americans that Muslims are dangerous. Little do they realize that violent Jihadists are only a tiny segment of Islam. Nor do people realize that the vast majority of Muslim are not even Arabs: they are Africans, African Americans, Indonesians, Pakistani, Russians, Persians, even Chinese. Hopefully, now that the infamous Bin Laden is gone, his image will be replaced by all the hardworking Muslims who are raising their families and being good neighbors and sending carefree Muslim children to school.

Ironically, belief in Jihad can help Muslims support peace. Jihad has come to mean violence, terror, suicide bombing, but that is not its meaning in the Koran. Jihad appears in the Koran 35 times, but only a few of these times does it refer to war, and here the notion is similar to the traditional just war theory. These later quotations have been wrongly interpreted by extremists to mean terrorism. Jihad literally means "struggle" and generally refers to the human struggle against greed, violence and hatred. It refers to the struggle for a more peaceful and just society, the struggle to build a better world. We have seen Jihad in the Arab Spring, where many young people are struggling to gain freedom, education, jobs where they can be paid enough to raise their families. They are engaged in the same human struggle that we all experience.

The Koran also honors the sacredness of human life. It teaches that humans are the most dignified of all creatures in that they come from God and are to return to God. In the revelation, God says: "We created humans of the finest possibilities." They were created equal and to be in solidarity with each other. The diversity of gender, tribe and nation is so that they may recognize each other as brothers, sisters and friends (Koran 7:129, 95:4, 49:13).

There are many outstanding Muslim leaders today and it is unfortunate that they do not get publicity instead of the terrorists. Tawakkul Karman won the Nobel Peace Prize in 2011. She is a young mother of three in Yemen, who has been a human rights activist in the country. During the uprising there she organized peaceful student rallies in the capital of Sanaa, for which she was arrested. When she was arrested, she returned to the rallies. She is a member of Parliament and a vigorous advocate for freedom of press and speech. She has courageously stood up to the tribal leaders who steal land from their people and has stood up to oppressive government leaders. When she received her Nobel Peace Prize, Tawakkul said: "I give the prize to the youth of revolution in Yemen and to the Yemen people."

Summary

Religions of today face many challenges with regard to a multitude of social issues. We have chosen only three: poverty, women's rights and peace. Billions are locked in poverty world-wide. Poverty brings with it hunger, poor health, illiteracy and powerlessness. We looked at the many causes of poverty and discussed several ways to alleviate it. We gave an overview of Christian views on poverty and examined the Catholic tradition on social justice as well as liberation theology. We also examined how Hinduism Buddhism, Judaism and Islam deal with poverty.

Religions seem to go through cycles in their approach to women. Often religions begin with progressive views, but these are lost over time. We have discussed how the major religions have dealt with women's rights throughout their history and how their beliefs have begun to be used to offer women more equality.

Violence and peace have been of concern for all the world's religions, and their histories include the experience of both. Here we have focused on the how the major religions have connected their beliefs with peacemaking.

▢◀ VIDEOS ONLINE

Poor Kids BBC Part 1, 2011
> https://www.youtube.com/watch?v=8BN7ml6b-e4

Hunger and Poverty in America Documentary
> https://www.youtube.com/watch?v=7yL8oJJAEDs

BBC World Debate Why Poverty?
> https://www.youtube.com/watch?v=KNIEb3injpc

Bill Moyers and Peter Edelman, *Fighting Poverty*
> https://www.youtube.com/watch?v=5Af_m4FIfO8

Nuns on the Bus, *Des Moines Kick-off*
> https://www.youtube.com/watch?v=Xd7W4rN-aXs

Sister Simone Campbell, *Hardball with Chris Matthews*
> https://www.youtube.com/watch?v=xQR2sVC7EZs

Mobilizing Faith, Fighting Poverty (Marshall)
> https://www.youtube.com/watch?v=1bXS_CEch4I

Living Liberation Theology Part 1 of 2
> https://www.youtube.com/watch?v=cmzTqTXT1t0

A Personal Reflection on Extraordinary Lives
> https://www.youtube.com/watch?v=VvJyl8V8Z_g

Living below the poverty line: Concern's work in India
    https://www.youtube.com/watch?v=NK_XC_IYX6Y

Human Trafficking Movie Part 1
    https://www.youtube.com/watch?v=A4bLeY2xwtg

Human Trafficking Documentary
    https://www.youtube.com/watch?v=b09qBldQwgo

Karma to Nirvana: Amma's Kitchen
    https://www.youtube.com/watch?v=PFHQQlwNDKs

Anuradka Koirala
    https://www.youtube.com/watch?v=EpMX1eSVWpY

Ven Karma Lekshe Tsomo, *Women in Buddhism*
    https://www.youtube.com/watch?v=GbAijRlg0-E

Susanna Heschel
    https://www.youtube.com/watch?v=tq8J7lsT3xE

Sister Joan Chittister, *The Divine Feminine*
    https://www.youtube.com/watch?v=0vArr4vZmb

Afghanistan - Razia's Ray of Hope
    https://www.youtube.com/watch?v=3arZ5BNeR-E

Archbishop Tutu, *Forgiveness*
    https://www.youtube.com/watch?v=raG6eIL-LM0

His Holiness the XIV Dalai Lama, *Peace Through Compassion*
    https://www.youtube.com/watch?v=fHJG41Q2Vj

Elie Wiesel, *Don't Sleep Well When People Suffer*
    https://www.youtube.com/watch?v=_lJ-8wx-MBo

Tawakkul Karman, *The Arab People Have Woken Up*
    https://www.youtube.com/watch?v=3fuGp8OUk6E

◼️ NOTES

1.   See Sudhir Anand, Paul Segal, and Joseph E. Stiglitz, eds., *Debates on the Measurement of Global Poverty* (Oxford: Oxford University Press), 2011, 26; also see statistics and data at http://iresearch.worldbank.org.

2.   See Alemayehu Bishaw, ed., *Poverty: 2010 and 2011: American Community Survey Briefs* at U.S. Department of Commerce, Economics and Statistics Administration, U.S. Census Bureau, http://www.census.gov/prod/2012pubs/acsbr11-01.pdf.

3.   Steven C. Smith, *Ending Global Poverty* (New York: Pelgrave, 2005), 2ff.

4.   Ibid., 20ff.

5.   Michael Taylor, *Christianity, Poverty and Wealth* (London: WCC Publications, 2003),12ff.

6.   Greg Mills, *Why Africa is Poor* (New York: Penguin Books, 2010), 2.

7.   Ibid., 11.

8.   Smith, 32.

9.   See from the Associated Press, "Oral Roberts' son, his wife face scandal at university," *Los Angeles Times* (October 6, 2007), http://articles.latimes.com/2007/oct/06/nation/na-roberts6.

10.   See Steve Krakauer, "Joel Osteen: Apologizing for wealth is "almost an insult to our God," *CNN Piers Morgan Tonight blog* (January 26, 2011), http://piersmorgan.blogs.cnn.com/2011/01/26/joel-osteen-apologizing-for-wealth-is-almost-an-insult-to-our-god/.

11.   Taylor, 8.

12.   See Google Answers, *Q: Net Worth of the Roman Catholic Church*, (August 14, 2002), http://answers.google.com/answers/threadview?id=54617.

13.   Taylor, 28.

14.   See Mary Jo Bane and Lawrence M. Mead, *Lifting up the Poor* (Washington, D.C.: Brookings Institute Press, 2003), 15.

15.   Arvind Sharma, "Hinduism and Poverty," in *Poverty and Morality*, eds. William A. Galston and Peter Hoffenbert (New York: Cambridge University Press, 2010), 165.

16.   Ashis Nandy, *Talking India* (New Delhi: Oxford University Press, 2006), 134.

17.   Patrick Olivelle, *The Law Code of Manu* (New York: Oxford University Press, 2004), 18.

18.   David Loy, "The Karma of Poverty: A Buddhist Perspective," in *Poverty and Morality*, 47.

19.   Ibid., 53.

20.   See Noam Zohar, "Jewish Perspectives on Poverty," in *Poverty and Morality*, 207.

21.   See Sohail H. Hashmi, "The Problem of Poverty in Islamic Ethics," in *Poverty and Morality*, 202-203.

22.   For findings on early cultures where women played more prominent roles, see Maria Gumbutas, *The Language of the Goddess* (New York: Thames and Hudson, 2001); For the development of patriarchy see Gerda Lerner, *The Creation of Patriarchy* (New York: Oxford University Press, 1987).

23.   See Fordham University Web site: Sojourner Truth, "Modern History Sourcebook: *Ain't I A Woman?*" Delivered 1851, Women's Convention, Akron, Ohio, http://www.

fordham.edu/halsall/mod/sojtruth-woman.asp.

24. *Bhagavad Gita*, 9:29.

25. Jeaneane Fowler, *Hinduism* (Portland: Sussex Academic Press, 1997), 36ff.

26. See Katherine Young, "Women and Hinduism," in *Women in Indian Religions*, ed. Arvind Sharma (New York: Oxford University Press, 2002), 19ff.

27. Rita M. Gross, *A Garland of Feminine Reflections* (Berkeley: University of California Press, 2009), 7ff.

28. Barbara Crandall, *Gender and Religion* (New York; Continuum, 2012), 48ff.

29. Jeremy Rosen, *Understanding Judaism* (Edinburgh: Dunedin Academy Press, 2003), 78 ff.

30. Rabbi Malka Drucker, ed., *Women and Judaism* (Westport, CT: Praeger, 2009), 190ff.

31. See Elizabeth Schussler Fiorenza, *In Memory of Her* (New York: Crossroad, 1984), 186ff.

32. Hans Kung, *Christianity* (New York: Continuum, 1995), 453ff.

33. Reza Aslan, *No God but God* (New York: Random House, 2006), 71ff.

34. Crandall, 185ff.

35. Sathianathan Clarke, "Dalits Overcoming Violation and Violence," in *The Ecumenical Review* 54, no. 3 (2002): 278.

36. *Bhagavad Gita*, 10:32; 18:120 at http://www.bhagavad-gita.us/

37. Ibid., 9:29

38. See Thomas Merton, *Gandhi and Non-Violence* (New York: New Directions, 1965), 8, 32ff.

39. Lawrence Schiffman and Joel B. Wolowelsky, *War and Peace in the Jewish Tradition* (New York: Yeshiva University Press, 2007), 517.